The Weight of a World of Feeling

The Weight of a World of Feeling

reviews and essays by Elizabeth Bowen

Edited and with an introduction by Allan Hepburn

NORTHWESTERN UNIVERSITY PRESS | EVANSTON, ILLINOIS

Northwestern University Press
www.nupress.northwestern.edu

Printed in the United States of America

10   9   8   7   6   5   4   3   2   1

Library of Congress Cataloging-in-Publication Data

Names: Bowen, Elizabeth, 1899–1973, author. | Hepburn, Allan, editor, writer of added commentary.
Title: The weight of a world of feeling : reviews and essays / by Elizabeth Bowen ; edited and with an introduction by Allan Hepburn.
Description: Evanston, Illinois : Northwestern University Press, 2017. | Includes bibliographical references and index.
Identifiers: LCCN 2016017430| ISBN 9780810131569 (pbk. : alk. paper) | ISBN 9780810131545 (cloth : alk. paper)
Subjects: LCSH: Literature—History and criticism.
Classification: LCC PR6003.O6757 A6 2017 | DDC 824/.912—dc23
LC record available at https://lccn.loc.gov/2016017430

CONTENTS

BOOKS AND OCCASIONS

AUTOBIOGRAPHIES

LAST REVIEWS: 1948 TO 1971

ACKNOWLEDGMENTS

First and foremost, I wish to thank Phyllis Lassner. A champion of Bowen's work when no one else was even paying attention to it, she has been an equally strong champion of this volume. She brings an astonishing wealth of information to bear on all matters related to Bowen, and I am grateful for her advice about literature of the Second World War and mid-century culture generally. Librarians and archivists have been invaluable in helping me find lost materials. In particular, I relied upon the expertise of staff at the University of Cambridge Library, the British Library, the BBC Written Archives Centre, the Huntington Library, the Harry Ransom Humanities Research Center, the Firestone Library at Princeton University, and the Lamont Library at Harvard University. At the McLennan Library at McGill University, Lonnie Weatherby searched databases that I did not even know existed. Kevin Droz, my peerless research assistant, helped at every stage of preparing this book: transcribing, proofing, fact-checking, finessing. Bevis Clarke, proprietor of Clearwater Books in London, drew my attention to Bowen's "Advice to a Young Writer." Bowen was the "shadowy third" in my conversation with Claude Deshaies, who listened patiently to my tales of discovery. A Standard Research Grant from the Social Sciences and Humanities Research Council of Canada permitted travel to archives. The Fonds du Québec pour la Recherche en Sciences et Culture funded research assistance. I thank the Woodberry Poetry Room at Harvard University for sending audio files of "The Technique of Fiction." The estate of Elizabeth Bowen has kindly granted me permission to publish these reviews and essays. I am especially grateful to Anna Davis at the Curtis Brown Group in London for her assistance in making this volume come to fruition. Lastly, I thank Henry Carrigan at Northwestern University Press for his astute guidance and two peer reviewers who made helpful suggestions for improving this book.

Elizabeth Bowen lived in and through books. A constant reader, she had a magisterial knowledge of British, European, and American literature. She only began reviewing books, however, in August 1935. By that time, she had four short story collections and four novels to her credit. Her fifth novel, *The House in Paris*, was published on August 26, 1935, just nine days after her first book review appeared in *The New Statesman*. She reviewed regularly for that journal, known for its leftist politics, until 1943. During the same period, she accepted requests to review for *Purpose*, *The Spectator*, *The Listener*, *The Bell*, *The Observer*, and other publications. From 1941 until 1950, and again from 1954 until 1958, she filed weekly columns for *The Tatler and Bystander*. Especially after she began to travel to the United States in the 1950s, Bowen was solicited for reviews by the *New York Times Book Review* and the *New York Herald Tribune*. Her reviews are filled with first impressions of novels, autobiographies, memoirs, illustrated books, biographies of politicians and artists, short story collections, and literary criticism. In a manner of speaking, Bowen's reviews form a reader's diary that stretches from the 1930s to the 1970s. That diary includes entries about *Finnegans Wake* and *Bonjour Tristesse*, alongside commentary on George Orwell, Jean-Paul Sartre, Ian Fleming, Agatha Christie, Joyce Cary, L. P. Hartley, Somerset Maugham, Kate O'Brien, Elizabeth Jenkins, Ngaio Marsh, Thomas Mann, Rumer Godden, Upton Sinclair, Richard Wright, and dozens of other writers. Taken together, these documents intimate a poetics of fiction worked out through a vast corpus of classic and contemporary examples.

As a literary activity, book reviewing is hard to classify. Reviewers direct readers to worthwhile books and, by doing so, enliven public debate about style, form, and content. For some writers, reviewing energizes their thinking; reviewing, as an activity that involves judgment, nourishes creative work. For other writers, reviewing, as a form of journalism, consumes time that could more profitably be spent bringing short stories or novels into being. Notwithstanding the quibbles of creative writers, distinctions among different kinds of writing tend not to be hard-and-fast. In Anthony Powell's *The Kindly Ones*, Nick Jenkins, the protagonist, cannot adequately describe what it means to be a writer: "I tried to give some account, at once brief and intelligible, of the literary profession: writing; editing; reviewing; the miscellaneous odd jobs to which I was subject, never, for some reason, very easy to define to persons not themselves in the world" (169). Those who belong within the world of writing understand how piecemeal the literary profession can be; those outside do not see the connections, however tenuous or abstract, among diverse kinds of writing.

Reviewing provides a public service. By triaging new books, reviewers save time for other readers. A review sets a value on a book, even if preliminary and fleeting. Virginia Woolf, trying to encourage good habits among common readers, counsels that reading should be invigorating and pleasurable: "to read a book as it should be read calls for the rarest qualities of imagination, insight, and judgment" (*Second Common Reader*, 269). The reviewer can draw attention to qualities that less insightful readers might miss. In this regard, reviewing is a first incursion into canon formation. Some books are saved and others damned. There is no necessary correlation between the quality of a book and its fate with the reading public at any given time. Critics may roundly pan a book that subsequent readers find worthy—a neglected classic. At the time of its publication, a good book may be judged severely, while a lesser book garners accolades, or a bad book may climb to the top of bestseller lists despite reviewers' harsh verdicts.

Certain modernists—T. S. Eliot reigns supreme in this regard—could make or break the reputation of a new writer by offering a blurb or preface that explained the hidden virtues of a book. Similarly, a book review from someone perceived as an eminent critic could launch a book or cause it to sputter out and disappear. Bowen notes that "Arnold Bennett, book-critic, was the kingmaker; the bestseller lists waited upon his pen" ("A Man and His Legend," 778). Yet such authority is transitory: it does not outlive its own day. Bowen did not aspire to be a "kingmaker," though she offered shrewd assessments of contemporary writing. She liked books of all sorts. Driven by curiosity, she educated herself by reading Henry

Reed's *The Novel since 1939*, Ben Jonson's plays, biographies of Byron, and whatever else came her way. Indeed, she thought of herself as a reviewer rather than a critic. In practice, the line between a reviewer and a critic remains hazy. The reviewer perceives trends and summarizes plot, whereas the critic adjudicates literariness. The reviewer formulates opinions and passes verdicts, whereas the critic provides context to widen understanding. All that being said, both critic and reviewer function as arbiters of taste within the parameters of their respective tasks: the assessment of publications past and present.

Even though many modernist British writers were tireless reviewers—H. G. Wells, E. M. Forster, L. P. Hartley, among others—scholars have devoted very little attention to the role of the reviewing in writers' careers. In the early twentieth century, unsigned reviews in the *Times Literary Supplement* and other venues led to cowardly attacks and abuses of anonymity. "The law gives book reviewers a very wide licence in the legitimate exercise of their calling," wrote E. J. MacGillivray in 1941 ("Legal Cases," 42). In the summer 1943 issue of *The Author, Playwright and Composer*—the official organ for the guild of creative artists—nine distinguished authors expressed their opinions on the topic, "Reviewing Reviewed." H. G. Wells deplored unsigned reviews, his own among them: "In my early journalist days I wrote unsigned reviews and I am bitterly ashamed of most of them" ("Reviewing Reviewed," 73). Young writers might accept reviews as a way to establish credibility with their peers; they abuse the authority conferred by publication in order to fortify their own reputation. E. M. Forster forgives young reviewers for lashing out at their seniors or peers: "unless there is plain and even angry speaking on the part of young 'irresponsible' reviewers the academic corridors will never get aired, and literature will be stifled" ("Reviewing Reviewed," 68). Storm Jameson laments reviewers' tendencies to advance their own careers: "Most English reviewers look on a book as a springboard for displaying their ideas, their cleverness in having ideas, or their feelings, which the book has either excited or outraged" ("Reviewing Reviewed," 68–69). As a rule of thumb, the book review should not be about the reviewer. In such a misguided model, the book mirrors the reviewer's tastes, instead of challenging or edifying the reader's taste.

A book review should accomplish several tasks. A good review describes what a book is about, in terms of genre, intentions, style, and audience. A good review establishes a context in which to understand the book at hand and whether the book is worthwhile with regard to that context. On the one hand, the reviewer should assess whether the book is successful on its own terms. An author cannot be held responsible for not doing something that he never intended to accomplish: if the author is not aiming at a particular target, there is no fault in missing it. On the other hand, Phyllis Bentley, discussing the obligations of the reviewer, declares that "some novelists' intentions are barely worth fulfilling . . . and the reviewer has the right to say so. The reviewer has no right to impugn the author's sincerity without indisputable evidence — indeed he has no right to attack any feature of the book without adducing evidence" ("Reviewing Reviewed," 65). A book reviewer has to be held to the high standards of fairness and honesty. The onus rests on the reviewer to produce proof to support an opinion. Synopsis, when used to make a point, lies within the rules of fairness. Invective falls outside the mandate of the reviewer, as do parody, meanness, and out-and-out ridicule.

In their brief essays, the contributors to "Reviewing Reviewed" worry about making public pronouncements on their friends' books. When they do so, reviewers become partisans rather than impartial evaluators. Without some objective assessment, literature devolves into coterie productions. Writers speak to minuscule audiences; presses cater to narrow agendas. One correction for such narrowness is a knowledge of foreign languages and literary traditions. Harold Nicolson claims that a reviewer who aspires to be a critic must have a broad education: "He must be an educated man with an acute sense of literary value, and he must possess, not only a sound knowledge of our own literature, but a sound knowledge of the literature of at least one other country. He must be a man of widely recognized integrity and must possess sufficient objectivity to assess fairly the motives and methods of a writer whose work happens to be uncongenial" ("Reviewing Reviewed," 71). His gender bias aside, Nicolson pinpoints the difficulty of preserving objectivity. That challenge increases when the book under review displeases the reviewer.

Unwilling to leave the question of reviewing alone, *The Author, Playwright and Composer* featured a symposium on "Rates for Reviewing" in the summer 1947 number. Some authors expressed their unhappiness at the low rates of pay for reviews, while acknowledging that reviewing was not their principal activity. "I think reviewing should continue to be a side-line," claims Rayner Heppenstall: "Only writers practised in other fields are likely to have critical opinions worth reading" ("Rates for Reviewing," 65). John Betjeman grumbles about low fees and the taxes to be paid on revenues. William Plomer concludes that remuneration and standards have no correlation: "It seems doubtful whether the standard of reviewing has much to do with the fees paid for it. The standard of reviewing can only be raised by the cultivation of the reviewers' understandings, and some of the best reviewing is done by persons with disinterested intellectual curiosity, expert knowledge of a subject, and adequate incomes, to whom the fees must be of small moment" ("Rates for Reviewing," 66). C. V. Wedgwood, the popular historian, calls hack reviewing "the blight of our time" ("Rates for Reviewing," 68). According to Wedgwood, uniform rates would do nothing to improve standards. Sometimes reviews written for no fee at all are the most valuable. Wedgwood notes that "the most expert reviewing is done in the learned periodicals by men and women of the highest intellectual distinction for very small fees and frequently for nothing" ("Rates for Reviewing," 68). Like many other writers of her generation, Elizabeth Bowen could not afford to review for free. In fact, she derived a substantial proportion of her income from reviewing. In the 1946–47 tax year, she earned £2,164, of which £525 came from *Tatler* reviews (Elizabeth Bowen Collection, Harry Ransom Center 12.5–6).

While earning a living from reviews, Bowen sharpened her opinions about literature. She sometimes wrote about a single book; more usually she was assigned a batch of books that she reviewed together. As her reviews prove, she was utterly immersed in the literature of her time, as well as classic novels. When given the chance, she reported on *Adolphe, War and Peace, Wuthering Heights, Bel-Ami*, or *La Princesse de Clèves*. She had a fondness for contemporary French fiction and seized opportunities to review new works by Colette, Albert Camus, Simone de Beauvoir, Henry de Montherlant, and François Mauriac. Her tastes were refreshingly wide-ranging. In the latter phases of the Second World War and through the postwar years, she read memoirs and autobiographies by Resistance fighters, prisoners of war, fighter pilots, and Civil Defence volunteers. She perused American literature with deepening knowledge. She exercised her passion for thrillers and mysteries by reviewing new releases in those genres. Above all, she admired "tensity" in plots, as she called the effects of suspense; the tautness of construction and the eventfulness of the thriller, she thought, should be present in all stories and plots.

Bowen's most sustained critical enterprise by far was her weekly column in *The Tatler and Bystander*, which she kept up, on and off, for thirteen years. The magazine was aimed at the horse-and-hounds set, with enchanting photo-spreads of debutantes and country demesnes. On October 1, 1941, Bowen took over the role of in-house book critic from Richard King, who had occupied the post for nearly thirty years. Bowen inherited King's format for the book pages: a long lead review followed by brief notices, ending with a plug for an amusing release—perhaps a children's book, a *Britain in Pictures* installment, or a detective novel. Bowen did not adopt King's amateur approach to literature along with his format for the column. Whereas King wrote about books in gossipy terms, Bowen offered the insights of a professional novelist and short story writer, without sacrificing her charm or her willingness to encourage writers. She took her job seriously. She seldom took holidays. (Margery Allingham, the mystery writer, replaced Bowen for three weeks in 1948.) Bowen usually submitted copy in advance of publication to cover her obligations while she was abroad or busy with other commitments. With some fanfare, Bowen quit *The Tatler* in October 1950. The magazine gave her a heartfelt send-off and a full-page photo. The departure turned into a hiatus: Bowen resumed the weekly column in 1954 and stayed the course for another four years. She definitively gave up the job in 1958.

British book reviewing was a clubby affair in mid-century Britain. Authors praised their friends' books and awaited praise in return. Bowen, despite her professional stature, is no exception to this rule. She reviewed her friends' books with dutiful enthusiasm. C. V. Wedgwood, Lord David Cecil, L. P. Hartley, May Sarton, Evelyn Waugh, William Plomer, Maurice Bowra, Elizabeth Taylor, Ivy Compton-Burnett, and others figured among Bowen's circle of friends and also featured in her reviews. She understood that literary London was a craggy world where favors were expected and reciprocated. On October 8, 1947, just before leaving for Ireland, Bowen wrote to her friend, John Lehmann: "I shall be calling in at the 'Tatler' before I go for more review books, and shall make a point of taking out the three new titles you have sent there for me" (John Lehmann Collection, Harry Ransom Center). In the same letter, she anticipates other titles to come from Lehmann: "If any other of your books that you would like me to see are to appear within the next four weeks, would you post them to me in Ireland direct?" Whatever those books may be, Bowen implies that she will give them a nudge in her column.

The Tatler gave Bowen free rein over the books that she reviewed. On September 22, 1954, she lavished praise on L. P. Hartley's The White Wand. It is not entirely clear that Hartley had seen this review by the time Bowen posted him a congratulatory note on September 19, 1954: "I have loved The White Wand, which last week I tried to write about, however inadequately, for the Tatler: What a Venice story! And as for The Go-Between, I nearly wrote to you but hardly knew what to say: you must know, as the rest of the world knows, what a triumph it is—absolutely satisfying on every page" (Papers of L. P. Hartley, John Rylands Library, University of Manchester Box 1/2). Having complimented Hartley, she adds a paragraph about her own forthcoming book, A World of Love: "I long to know about your next book. I've finished mine—which J. Cape peevishly complain is rather short. But myself I like it." Bowen and Hartley were long-standing friends and intermittent correspondents. He had reviewed Encounters, her first book, in 1923. She and he made a habit of reviewing each other's books over the years. In the event, Hartley, having been given advance warning by Bowen, reviewed A World of Love for The Spectator in March 1955.

Bowen's correspondence with writers strikes a balance between professional appreciation and friendship. People whose books she had publicly reviewed thanked her personally. Those whom she did not already know she quickly came to know. After reviewing From the Life by Phyllis Bottome, Bowen received a note from the author, to which she responded on October 2, 1944. The private letter supplements the public review:

Dear Miss Bottome,
It was extremely nice of you to write to me about my review of your "From the Life." I felt the review was inadequate, as my reading of the book raised a great many questions in my own mind which were difficult to put into words. I think you show ruthlessness—though I know this ruthlessness to be proper in an artist, at any rate with regard to his or her own work—when you speak of the book as a failure; but if you felt that it did not make

sufficiently clear what you wished to make clear, I can see that it would not satisfy you.

To have used anonymous friends or imaginery [*sic*] characters I think would have been a soft option, and I can see how you did not do so. What you say makes me look forward particularly to your own Memoirs (are you working on these now?) in which you propose to deal with your own life-pattern, and the actual education, in the sense that Adler has made you see education, of a human being. What you said about Adler in your short study of him added to my wish to read your longer Adler book. I feel sure that he must be the first of the psychologists from the point of view of an artist.

I was so tremendously struck by that novel of yours, "Within the Cup," in which you gave that view of the English and their state of mind prior to and during the war, as seen through the eye of a young Adlerian psycho-analyst. I must try to read the book you mention—Claud Mullins' "Crime and Psychology." I do hope that understanding on a fairly high psychological level may enter into our rebuilding (or as I think of it rather, curing) of the world.

I hope we may meet some day. Thank you again for writing. (Letter to Phyllis Bottome, British Library 78835 f. 231, 1–2)

Bowen's charm masks differences of opinion. For the most part, she decries psychology and psychoanalysis as so much bunkum. In *To the North*, for instance, Bowen mocks Adlerian psychology. Nevertheless, she does not allow her personal opinions to preempt a friendly exchange with Bottome. As in her reviews, she takes a generous view of writers; she understands that writing, whether it is done well or badly, exacts its penalty of time and effort. She subsequently reviewed Bottome's *The Lifeline* and *Eldorado Jane*, both with kind words.

Although Bowen took her duties as a reviewer seriously, she did have occasional lapses. The weekly deadlines were arduous. On July 2, 1946, she wrote to William Plomer that she had been working on her novel and having guests to stay at Bowen's Court: "Henry Reed & his friend Michael and a friend of mine from Dublin, Josephine MacNeill, were there for some time. They were all very good & left me alone all day, so I got on solidly with my novel and am now deep in it. Henry even did some of my *Tatler* reviews for me, which left me more time for the novel: a friendly act" (William Plomer Archive, Durham University MSS 19/7). Bowen suggests, if obliquely, that her *Tatler* reviews can be done to measure. Yet having someone else write her *Tatler* column was the exception rather than the norm. Under normal circumstances, she did not farm out her obligations. Moreover, Bowen kept up a jokey relationship with Plomer. She may have mentioned this "friendly act" because it was unusual, even funny, if slightly discomfiting. Aside from this letter, no evidence suggests that she shirked her duty by filing columns penned by her friends.

According to Victoria Glendinning, Bowen was a "notoriously kind reviewer of novels" (*Elizabeth Bowen: A Biography*, 146). In truth, she pulls no punches when she detects charlatanism or vacuous style. She had clear likes and dislikes. She could never find much to say about George Orwell's books, regardless of his notoriety. She dutifully read all of Evelyn Waugh's novels—the two novelists were close in the early 1930s and remained friendly over the years—but she treated Waugh's novels with reservation rather than exuberance. Elizabeth Taylor's and Ivy Compton-Burnett's novels elicit strong, positive reactions. Writers with "gusto," a word of strong approval in her lexicon, draw Bowen's special admiration. James Joyce had gusto. So did Arnold Bennett. By contrast, she dislikes writers who want only to advance their ideas, as Mark Van Doren does in *The Transients*: "He writes English almost too well, and his novel, in which the more personal side of his imagination escapes, perhaps, for the first time, has the essayist's leisurely, introspective pace" ("New Novels," 225). Putting too much emphasis on the metaphysical crushes novelistic purpose. Concentrating on ideas at the expense of action results in preachiness. No novel, she feels, should have the "introspective pace" of an essay.

Whenever Bowen suspected a writer of exercising style at the expense of story, she objected. "*At Swim-Two-Birds* could be better—which is saying a good deal," she writes about Flann O'Brien's novel ("Fiction," 180). She judges O'Brien unduly influenced by Joyce's masterpiece, *Ulysses*. An exact style, one fitted to its subject and the author's guiding idea, is essential to good fiction. Faced with Hugh Walpole's *The Inquisitor*, she seethes: "Almost every incident in this novel suffers from being written up and inflated; all would be more telling were Mr. Walpole's writing more precise and cold" ("New Novels," 284). She deplores Walpole's impact on contemporary writing: "One does wish he would not keep encouraging other authors to do the wrong thing. At a literary dinner the other night he stated that it was the function of the novelist to create character. Why? This fallacy, coupled with a more recent yearning to be poetic, has sidetracked the English novel for too long. Characters in a novel are important only in what they generate (which is the stuff of the book), in their activity, and in their underlying generalness" ("New Novels," 284). In all instances, Bowen prefers action to character, or action to ideas. A novel is nothing if it does not, first and foremost, tell a good story.

Throughout her reviews, Bowen articulates general principles of fictional technique. She spells out the inner workings of fiction incidentally, as she understands them, while providing an opinion about the book at hand. Taken together, Bowen's reviews outline her comprehensive yet limber thinking about fiction. Despite the number of books that she reviewed, she remained alert to the design, style, machinery, experimentation, commitments, successes, and shortcomings in an author's work. Whatever else novels achieve, they have "to respect the human pattern, a pattern largely made of attachments," as she claims in a review of Desmond Hawkins's *Lighter Than Day* ("Fiction," 147). Novels cannot but take up the dilemmas of human interaction in all their diversity. Novels reveal the complexity of human relations, not as a transcription of contemporary life but as an artistic pattern. In Bowen's estimation, novels do not displace reality: they add something to reality. A novel is not, after all, a documentary. A successful novel aggrandizes life without falsely exaggerating characters or situations.

In all her pronouncements about novelistic technique, Bowen insists that plot precedes characters, not the other way around. She speaks against fiction in which a character performs an action in order to demonstrate a character trait. In the case of *Follow the Furies*, one of the first novels she reviewed for *The New Statesman*, Bowen likes the freedom that characters have from theory or predetermined plot: "There is no guying of characters, no wink between author and readers at anybody's expense" ("New Novels," 225). Characters should not behave like marionettes pulled this way and that. In Bowen's opinion, characters stand or fall by their entry into action. Personalities materialize through plot. She therefore insists on the value of the novel as a social force: the interaction among characters brings them into being. They do not exist prior to action. The novel, as Bowen claims on many occasions, should focus on exchange, not individual consciousness. The human pattern becomes visible through attachments that characters have to each other, whether in peace or war, love or despair.

After the Second World War, Bowen expressed impatience with the high modernist novel of consciousness and called for more examples of "the social drama novel" (*People, Places, Things*, 323). "Since 1930," she observes, "religious and political sentiments have contributed equally to make the English novel dynamic and to rescue it from the psychological cramp that threatened to overtake it towards the end of the preceding decade" (*Listening In*, 142). As a way of easing the cramp brought on by a strict concentration on inner states of being, Bowen ranks conflict, isolation, and survival high on the list of experiences that the novel could possibly take up. At the same time, she notices that journalistic reportage has stolen a march on novelistic discourse. Nonfiction appeals to readers because of its truth-telling, its closer relation to reality than fiction. Bowen therefore called for a return to the social novel, in which action, not introspection, is inevitable. Her landmark essay, "Notes on Writing a Novel," published in 1945, breaks novelistic discourse into component parts—plot, character, scene, and dialogue—as well as three less expected elements: angle, advance, and relevance. She uses military metaphors of advance and clearance to convey the necessity of an offensive direction in plot: "Characters most of all promote, by showing, the advance of the plot. How? By the advances, from act to act, in their action" (*Collected Impressions*, 260). Narrative has to move forward. Action determines the tempo of a plot.

Bowen likes directness in fiction. She despises "the twistings and turnings, the blurs, the fogs, the halts, the tedious mystifications and ill-concealed uncertainties that impair the narrative interest of so much modern fiction. Ideally, I think, the *story* of any novel ought to be absolutely direct and clear: all the effect should come from an inside force" ("Book Reviews," March 19, 1947, 346). The writer strips away unnecessary complications. This paring back applies to plot as well as to language. "I see little point in adjectives that do not imply judgment: if one wishes to abstain from judgment one should abstain from them," she wrote in a *Tatler* review on November 26, 1941 (308). She thought a great deal about style and its relation to language. Style is intrinsic to a given situation: a writer cannot apply style to prose like paint to a wall. Style acts as the medium for language. Drawing upon Flaubert's concept that vision already implies a style, Bowen understands style as an a priori way of seeing. Nonetheless, style should not interfere with vision; it should not become an obstacle to or intrusion on what is seen. Style should be, as Bowen claims in "The Technique of the Novel," as transparent as glass.

In her analysis of fiction, Bowen distinguishes between plot and situation, although she sometimes rolls the two concepts into one ball: "There is the plot: that is, the author's intention. And inside that plot (or, situation) and in it only can the characters operate" (*Listening In*, 184). "Situation" means a concept or image of what the novel is about—a point of origin that exceeds materialization in language, which is plot as an author contrives it. For Bowen, the situation has an element of the visual and the poetic about it. It motivates narrative without being reducible to synopsis. It precedes the temporal unfolding of plot. The situation is the irreducible kernel of the story. In *The House in Paris*, for example, the situation is elementary: two children, crossing Paris, meet in a house owned by a sinister and ailing woman. The plot, by contrast, is the sequence of events that explain that situation. As Bowen clarifies in "The Technique of the Novel," "the situation is what the novel is about. It is also the incentive and inspiration of the writer who writes the novel. And when the situation has been conceived or found—or I should more generally say has found itself for the writer—then it is something which both the plot and the characters equally exist to serve, to serve, that is to say, by expanding and making more concrete and more real" ("Technique of the Novel," n.p.).

The writer must first envision the situation in order to make it palpable through character and plot. Vision means not just neutral recording of details and events. It extends to a perception of pattern or design within events. Fiction makes that design apparent, whether the events are invented or historical. "History in the making is not pleasant," Bowen wrote in her *Tatler* column on April 29, 1942, just after her house in Regent's Park was shattered by bombs: "Nor can it be said to be interesting—for interest implies some degree of detachment, and some hope of getting the general plan of the thing" ("With Silent Friends," 150). The writer's vision establishes the density—the implications and shadings—within a situation. Perception enlarges the range of meanings latent in the situation. Nonetheless, the author cannot conceal the situation from the reader. The boundaries of the situation, as against the plot, ought to be present from the first pages of the novel. Reviewing Walter Allen's *Rogue Elephant* on September 18, 1946, Bowen lays down a principle about authorial integrity with regard to the author's showing the stakes of a novel from the outset: "It would seem to me a moral-technical rule that a novel (as apart from a detective story) should be above-board; that all the cards in the pack should be face up before we begin to watch" ("Book Reviews," 374). Information cannot be intentionally withheld from the reader. Furthermore, Bowen implies that novel-writing is something of a card game in which tricks can be performed, but during which the reader must not be deliberately deceived. The game can be expected to have some legerdemain in it, but if the novel only traffics in tricks, the result is vulgar, not novelistic.

Like many authors in her generation, Bowen found resources for narrative technique in cinema. Like a filmmaker, an author can work with frames, shots, scale, shadow, lighting, and movement to materialize narrative. On many occasions in her reviews, Bowen evokes "camera-work" to describe a narrator's detachment and point of view. She notices the "camera-passages" in Inez Holden's *There's No Story There* ("With Silent Friends," 150). Another author, exploiting "the technique of the movie camera, gives us a series of close-ups of character after character" ("Book Reviews," October 8, 1947, 55). William Sansom, who assisted in making film documentaries, focuses "his camera on reality," as Bowen claims in her review of *Something Terrible, Something Lovely*: "For, it goes without saying, any artist *is* a walking camera—sometimes consciously, sometimes not, he is forever making exposures, then developing, in his internals, the results" ("Book Reviews," April 28, 1948, 119). Like Christopher Isherwood in *The Berlin Diaries*, Bowen means that the artist takes in impressions that may or may not develop into photographs in the darkroom of the imagination. Moreover, narrative can spotlight certain features, faces, or gestures to throw a situation into relief, to give it point and density. In good prose, she seeks "cinema-like vividness" ("Book Reviews," January 29, 1947, 169). In cinema as in fiction, style and vision merge.

Although Bowen champions neutrality of vision, she understands fiction, especially the novel, to be the embodiment of feeling. Her own novels — *To the North*, *The Death of the Heart*, *Eva Trout* — center on feelings produced through human interaction: bewilderment, cruelty, anguish, shame, ravishment, joy. For Bowen, the novel lays bare feelings first for characters, then for readers. Regardless of what characters say or think, another realm of experience lies behind their words and thoughts. A character may be "confused by joy or by surprise, or, in the most ordinary case, rendered speechless by love or emotion," as Bowen puts it in "The Technique of the Novel" (n.p.). A novel that fails to tap into a wellspring of feeling falls short of its mission. The novel spells out what characters may feel but cannot themselves say, let alone enact. A character may be speechless, but the author and the narrator cannot run that risk. By the same token, the narrator cannot be too articulate in relation to a dumbfounded character. Too many words can intrude upon the character's inarticulate feeling. The narrator may know more than a character, but it would be wrong to lord that knowledge over a character who cannot find the words for his or her emotion.

According to Bowen, if a novel does not, in the first instance, exhilarate, it cannot succeed: "I cannot feel that it is the business of novels to be 'improving' — but, on the other hand, they can and should exhilarate. They should give one the feeling that human existence is a fascinating (if maddening) iridescent, quivering, mysterious, and, above all, exciting affair" ("Book Reviews," September 24, 1947, 406–7). Bowen's essays and reviews give a sense of what writers must do to catch hold of the fascination and mystery in human existence. These pieces also convey the degree to which she was implicated in the Irish, British, American, and European traditions of fiction, and the degree to which her own novels and short stories, in pursuit of the "iridescent, quivering" affair called human existence, respond to contemporary developments in fictional technique.

Editorial Principles

To locate the materials in this volume, I first consulted J'nan M. Sellery and William O. Harris's *Elizabeth Bowen: A Bibliography*. Certain pieces, however, escaped their notice, such as the review of Richard Aldington's book about D. H. Lawrence in the *New York Times Book Review* and the tapes of "The Technique of the Novel" at Harvard University.

By tracing hints and clues in Bowen's correspondence, I was able to locate other materials as well: "Advice to a Young Writer," "English and American Writing," "Paris Bookshops," "I Love Driving at Night," and "Old America." The Sellery and Harris bibliography suggests that *The Tatler* reviews began on October 3, 1945, and ended on November 23, 1949. In fact, Bowen contributed to the magazine from October 1, 1941, to March 28, 1950, and then again from January 20, 1954, until April 30, 1958.

In *Collected Impressions*, Bowen compiled book reviews published before 1950. In *Afterthought*, she included reviews of four works: Virginia Woolf's *A Writer's Diary*, Eudora Welty's *The Golden Apples*, Rosamond Lehmann's *The Echoing Grove*, and E. M. Forster's *Alexandria*. The selection of reviews in these two miscellanies is not at all representative of the quantity of Bowen's output in the genre. In *Collected Impressions* and *Afterthought*, she did not trouble with any of her *Tatler* reviews, despite their many flashes of brilliance and insight.

Three principles governed the selection of pieces for the present volume. First, if the reviews appeared in either *Collected Impressions* or *Afterthought*, I omitted them on the grounds that they are fairly easy to access. For the sake of completion, I included reviews that were previously collected by Hermione Lee in *The Mulberry Tree*. Secondly, in the sections devoted to reviews from 1935 to 1942 and from 1948 to 1971, I have included all the reviews that Bowen left uncollected in her nonfiction collections in order to make them accessible. Thirdly, from the vast amount of material published in *The Tatler*, I have selected a small number of reviews. In doing so, I have favored literature over history, and fiction over critical or biographical works. As the *Tatler* reviews demonstrate, Bowen read extensively in wartime reportage, as well as in detective and thriller fiction. She liked reviewing classics—Thomas Love Peacock's *Nightmare Abbey* and Gogol's *The Government Inspector*—when they were released in contemporary editions.

Bowen's *Tatler* columns ran to 2,500 words on average. Because she reviewed multiple titles each week, I have chosen commentaries that have general interest or provocative content. More often than not, the lead review gave rise to extensive analysis. The last book received a couple of sentences, usually synoptic, rarely critical. Within each column, breaks are distinctive. Seldom does Bowen compare books with each other. As a result, it is easy to excise one section from the whole column, as I have done in the majority of cases. When I choose reviews that ran side by side in the same *Tatler* column, these are printed continuously. If the two were separated by a review of another book, asterisks separate the selections. For years, Bowen's column in *The Tatler* was called "With Silent Friends." Later, each column was given a headline. I have chosen not to use any titles in *The Tatler* reviews because they are repetitive and because they do not address all the material in a column; in short, the headlines, assigned by an editor, are not useful in navigating the column. I have kept titles from *The Spectator*, *The Listener*, and so forth, because they usually home in on a specific aspect in the review itself.

I excluded several salient reviews due to a lack of space. I regret not being able to reprint, for example, Bowen's review of *B.B.C. War Report: 6 June 1944 to 5 May 1945*, in which she discusses the impact of radio broadcasting on perceptions of the Second World War. Likewise, I have omitted the review of Francis Steegmuller's *Flaubert and Madame Bovary*, which affords Bowen the opportunity to speculate on the public identity of the writer. Flaubert, she writes, "cannot be called 'a typical writer'—if, indeed, such a thing exists? He was rather a sort of magnificent exaggeration, or personification, of an element in every writer of note. In everything he did or was he was outsize" (*Tatler*, September 10, 1947, 343). Certain writers, Flaubert chief among them, magnetize her thinking about fiction. A review of Saki's complete short stories reveals Bowen's fondness for that writer's Edwardian masterpieces. Her summary of Lord David Cecil's *Lord M., or the Later Life of Lord Melbourne* dwells on "that most mysterious and contradictory of creatures, an entire man" ("The Civilised Lord M.," 294). Such passing comments spark speculation about "a typical writer" or "an entire man" in a mid-century milieu where the nature of writing and the notion of the hero or antihero were subject to intense scrutiny. Due to lack of space, reviews of Steegmuller's, Saki's, Cecil's, and others' books could not be accommodated in this selection.

As far as possible, I have edited this volume for consistency and readability. Because the majority of these reviews and essays appeared in print, they have few or no variants. To my knowledge, no typescripts exist for these reviews. Editorial interventions are therefore few. For the short autobiographical statements and essays, archival sources are all that exist; where appropriate, these have been annotated to indicate variants and ambiguities in the source text. Either through Bowen's inadvertence or through a copy editor's error, punctuation is occasionally wrong. Minor errors—a missing comma or a comma that should be a semicolon—have been silently corrected. Bowen had a fondness for commas; she uses them more than contemporary usage dictates. Nonetheless, she did not always insert Oxford (or serial) commas in lists; for the sake of consistency, I have added Oxford commas as needed. Where Bowen uses ellipses in her own prose, I have kept three dots; where an ellipsis also ends a sentence, there are four dots. When she excises text that ends a sentence in a quotation, four dots—the ellipses plus the period—have been used. Bowen sometimes forgets to observe rules of parallelism; she omits a correlative conjunction or a word required to complete a parallel structure. Such errors have also been silently amended. As is common among British speakers of English, Bowen does not always distinguish between "that" and "which" as relative pronouns. Following her lead, I have not used "that" for essential clauses or "which" for inessential clauses.

Quite apart from her sharp-angled syntax, Bowen has several grammatical habits that form her style. She has a fondness for appositives. In an assessment of Desmond MacCarthy's *Drama*, Bowen allows an appositive to grow out of the preceding clause: "This present halt in the life of the theater, the unnatural dark damaged silence of Shaftesbury Avenue, invites us to look back, look forward, and take stock" ("The Perfect Theatergoer," 18). The "present halt" stands in apposition to "the unnatural dark" as the singular verb clarifies. Sometimes appositives blur into multiple subjects, one overlapping with the other. In a review of a novel by May Sarton, Bowen writes: "This scene, and Sprig Wyeth's reactions, is one of the many in which Miss Sarton has sharply pointed, and brings home, the moral of *The Birth of a Grandfather* . . . ." The sentence implies that "Sprig Wyeth's reactions" stands in apposition to the "scene," which is unlikely. The syntax would have been clearer in a slightly different clausal construction: "This scene, as well as Sprig Wyeth's reactions to it, is . . . ." In Bowen's sentence, the singular verb, "is," agrees with scene, yet the "scene" and "reactions," different from each other, dictate a plural verb for the sake of agreement unless the clauses are read as appositives. Where Bowen's intentions are not clear, as in this case, I have left the sentence as it is in the published text.

Although Bowen's reviews appeared in both British and American magazines or newspapers, American spellings have been adopted throughout this volume for uniformity. Certain words, such as "Resistance" and "Occupation," vary between upper case and lowercase spelling. Certainly the wartime and postwar milieu heightened the significance of these terms in European minds. Context determines the significance that Bowen accords to "occupation" or "resistance," and she occasionally leaves them lowercase. Especially in *The Tatler* reviews, the name of publishing companies and the price of books are listed parenthetically; this information has been removed, except when Bowen wishes to make a point about the value of a book or when the price is integral to the syntax of a sentence.

Transcription of an oral text—as in the case of the lecture, "The Technique of the Novel," and the radio interview, "We Write Novels"—requires punctuation that captures intonation and intention without too flagrantly violating grammatical sense. In her published essays and fiction, Bowen had a habit of emphasizing small words—prepositions or first-person pronouns—and she does so when speaking as well. These unexpected emphases have been italicized in "The Technique of the Novel" and "We Write Novels." In "The Technique of the Novel" in particular, Bowen speaks in short phrases, as if commas were rife in the syntax. She pauses to weigh her words or to gather her concentration; she does not commit rashly to a phrase. Although many of these pauses have been represented through punctuation in this transcription, punctuation also has to make sense of syntax. Not all pauses, therefore, are marked by a comma, dash, or semicolon. Nor is Bowen's syntax always coherent; it follows the improvisational vectors of oral delivery, in which sudden inspirations dissolve the logic of grammar. Paragraph breaks have been added where they seem most appropriate. Though Bowen often stuttered when speaking, her delivery in "The Technique of the Novel" is relatively smooth, with infrequent lapses and slight hesitations. Some words are pronounced peculiarly. "Traits," for instance, is pronounced "trays," in a pseudo-French fashion. Other words, sometimes unintelligible, may be mispronounced; these instances are flagged in notes.

To vary the pace of this volume, I have included short autobiographical pieces and essays. Bowen's views on fictional technique guide the selection of materials. Sections are loosely structured around prewar, wartime, and postwar writings. As a record of engaged reading, the essays and book reviews in this volume create a picture of Bowen as a key contributor to modern and mid-century conceptions of fiction. Spanning the years from 1935 to 1971, these pieces register the turns that fiction takes through the Second World War, the welfare state, and the emergence of a late modern aesthetic.

THE WEIGHT OF A WORLD OF FEELING

TECHNIQUES OF THE NOVEL

Advice to a Young Writer

I am very much impressed and interested by this collection of work. There is something arresting about it both in expression and in content. I gather that the stories and other pieces are arranged in chronological order, which I like, as it is a guide to the way the writer's mind (or creative faculty) has been moving.

Opening this book of manuscripts at random, one's eye—which means, of course, one's imagination—is immediately caught by any sentence it strikes, and cannot but read on. This, I think, is one test of writing being really a *writer's* writing.

The first stories, with the sharp brutal twist to the plot in the final paragraph of each, have—using the word in the[1] high professional sense, not the derogatory sense—an extraordinary efficiency. "Breakfast Is a Happy Meal in Heaven" I like less; it doesn't quite "take" with me personally. As against which, "The Intruders" is vivid and admirably built.

It is difficult to criticize so personal a talent; and one already so far formed. (I detest the word "talent" but can think of no other: I would not wonder if there were constituents of genius here; but it is a genius that will still have to integrate itself, find itself.) I do not want to counsel you, Miss Williams, to do anything that would mean forcing your imagination out of its natural course. I think the increasing *fullness* in the pieces towards the end of this collection is encouraging; even though sometimes it has cost you some loss of the sharp, taut effectiveness of the earlier stories.

I like best of all the first chapter of the novel. I don't think this at all necessarily means you should be a novelist rather than a short storyist; but somehow in this chapter as a bit of writing, what I meant by the "fullness" of which you *are* capable comes out.

I like least the play—not because of any particular faults in it as *theater*, as to which my own ideas are still very hit-and-miss, but because it is so abstract. That, of course, is my own taste; but one's own taste can't quite be cleared out of any attempt at judgment, however dispassionate one may be trying to be.

So you must allow for my taste (which could easily be a weakening element) in any criticisms I make.

I think your writing still too disembodied. One feels the poetic significance of persons or objects you write about, but not nearly enough their physical reality. Consequently, there too often is an effect of thinness. Concentrate your *vision* on any material thing you introduce, whether it be a chair, a plate, or a person. No inanimate object *is* inanimate; everything has something else sheathed in it. I remember a line I read in some modern poem about "the passionate inner existence of objects."[2]

Have you read Flaubert's novels? If not, do—I think then you'll see what I mean. He was really a poet-mystic, but he schooled himself to an extraordinarily plain (outwardly, it could have seemed banal) objectivity. Don't just use a chair, for instance, as a "property" for the action of a story, *or* as a four-legged thing seen through subjective distortions—no, every time you write the word "chair" force yourself to break off and contemplate the chair-ness of a chair.

I should like you to attempt what may seem most against the grain for you—some realistic-naturalistic pieces of work. These may not be in themselves successful, but I think the attempt would be good for you; it would correct some quality that at present you have in excess. Keep, if you can, quite away from fantasy. At present the characters in your stories tend to run to one or the other of two extremes: either they are grotesques or they are too much etherealized.

When I said, at the beginning, that your talent was personal, I did not mean that your mode of expression was. You are absolutely clear and pure of the vulgarities of autobiographical writing. You retreat from yourself, from the circumstances of your life, if anything too much. In too many of the first-person stories the "I" is a boy or a man. At the same time, because you either do not bother to or do not know how to build up an impression of masculinity, of the masculine nature (a thing there certainly *is*), the effect is unconvincingness, shadowiness, at the very worst, though this is rare, a slightly "literary" atmosphere in the story.

You have enough power to be able to write as the young woman you are: I do not think there is any fear you would ever be trivial or trite or squalid.

Beware, I say again and again, of abstractness. Also, because you are Welsh (which I think I should have guessed even if I had not known), curb your metaphysicalness. Curb it, that is to say, till you have got an absolutely firm hold, to be felt in your writing, of concrete reality.

Allow *pleasure* as much place as you can. The sensuous joy one does feel in things and moments; the pleasure in the thing-for-its-own-sake. I don't think the Welsh and Irish feel this kind of pleasure as naturally, as constitutionally, as do the French and English. I suppose that comes from what's inevitably referred to as the "dark" streak in Celts.

The Russians, such as Turgenev and Tolstoy, seem to me the ideal writers in a particular and important sense: they feel and give pure sensuous pleasure, and at the same time the soul is never absent—they never for a moment try to deny the darkness.

I have a great feeling for and belief in your writing. I think that with every year you are going to realize your powers, and order them, and balance them against each other.

English and American Writing

Impressions of American writing, in this country, are to be gathered at one remove. American books are rumors before they reach us; some never reach us at all. The preceding rumor makes independent, sometimes fantastic, growth, and on the whole does the book disservice—one has formed preconceptions before an actual copy comes to hand. A book is harder to focus when it does not come too fresh; it already carries an overload of opinion (a fact recognized by American publishers, who, on receiving the new manuscript of an English author already contracted to them, always press for "simultaneous publication." Today, that exaction from the American side is not necessary: conditions maintaining here make it likely that the appearance of an English book in America may be months in advance of its appearance at home. American critics and readers thus have the first rake-off; and the book makes its bow, belatedly, in its own country under the same disadvantage as indigenous American work.)

American authors of standing have, one imagines, their standing contracts, just as they have their safe reputations here. For the introduction of the younger, newer, and possibly more advanced, we are dependent upon the enterprise and acumen of our publishers, and on the whole we are not at all badly served. If our publishers are not encouraged to act still more boldly and promptly in the matter of imports, that may be charged to our own dubious hospitality. Reviewers, whether out of inertia or unconscious protectionism, too often fail to give the necessary lead. The American book, particularly the "advanced" novel—crime fiction is more alertly received, and belles lettres and biography get their share of notice—tends to travel only a short way, then fall flat. For any sight of new trans-Atlantic work in poetry or the short story we are indebted to one or two of our magazines, such as *Horizon*. It is, I believe, to the editor of *Horizon* that at least one of the charges of dullness against present-day English writing is to be traced: he is glad of the trans-Atlantic pipeline.

New American writing does, in the main, insulate itself upon arrival here. Its prestige remains in pockets, among the cognoscenti, except insofar as *Horizon, New Writing*, and others serve as outgoing channels. There appears an immutable difficulty in (in the radio sense) reception: this *is* foreign stuff, of a foreignness which would be less difficult to assimilate were it not submerged. "The trouble between us," said one American friend, "is our speaking nominally the same language: we misunderstand one another below a certain depth." The psychological alphabet is different.

If the American writer working at any depth below superficiality is a foreigner in our country, what is he in his own? Apparently, a foreigner there also. We have been given, lately, glimpses of the avant-garde American literary scene—for instance, "The State of American Writing: 1948," a symposium, in the August *Partisan Review* of that year, and Stephen Spender's "The Situation of the American Writer," in the *Horizon* of March 1st. The inside statement and the visitor's impression correlate:

both emphasize the wide gulf in the United States—gulf both as to outlook and in prospects—between the unaccommodating artist and the steady royalty-earning middlebrow who has toed the line. Almost all contributors to the *Partisan* symposium show the writer (that is, of their own kind) as in a state of resistance to a directive the major publishing houses and magazine interests attempt to impose. Not only Hollywood, apparently, grooms for stardom. The writer may not envisage astronomic sales; he can but wish a livelihood and his own fair-sized public; and to that, even, the bridge can be engineered at a price, a cost to integrity, he must refuse to pay. Success—or so, at least, suggests Stephen Spender—has therefore come to have sinister connotations; and as to the demarcation of failure there are no hazy lines. The American writer, we are to infer, who will not allow himself to be edited into acceptability cannot look to his writing to support him. A resort, not solution, is university teaching. As to the number of universities scattered about the States we have some idea; what we may find harder to grasp is the immensity of the distances between them: the teacher-writer can but feel himself enislanded—far from fellow artists speaking his own language, and, *as* an artist, bled by the drawing-off of his psychic energies for teaching. Alternative, the big city, stimuli, and a greater hope of congenials—against that must be counted the wear-and-tear, and the nagging fear of submergence for those not economically secure.

Stephen Spender stresses what had occurred to me after reading the *Partisan* symposium—the factor of "creative loneliness." The creative American writer is enislanded not only geographically but socially. With the mass of his fellow Americans he feels out of contact; further, the massiveness of the mass, and its impermeability, oppress[1] him. Yet that very oppression is his subject—or is it not? He is up against an *unconcentrated* problem. The meaningless perpetual motion of a middle-class society, which he sees as factitious, exasperates him; he confronts bulky chaos and the complacency of a synthetic culture. All the same he is not, like the generation before him, an ex-patriot, either in fact or in wish. The last ten years (or so one gets the impression) have shattered the European illusion; he has no dream Parnassus, no ideal milieu. To find his own roots, he must find the roots of his race, and the search is complicated by the network of cosmopolitanism under America's Anglo-Saxon surface.

His own Americanism may date back for not more than a generation or two: it is remarkable what a number of young American writers have non-Anglo-Saxon names.

Isolation, and the sense of being displaced (or inherently placeless) persons, may account for the tendency of minority American writers to group, to align where possible, to reach out to one another for vital contacts, to seek a *foyer* or forum. (The *foyer* found, most often, is one or another of the admirable "little magazines," e.g., *Partisan*. These, indeed, strike one as being not only meeting places but strongholds.) In America the intellectual wears no mask of nonchalance—one can see why the "well-bredness" of his British equivalent irritates him. His impassioned seriousness rebukes flippancy; what may shock *us* is his overweening intellectual class consciousness. This last has, in fact, created one kind of regional literature of its own; the intelligentsia makes itself, often, its own subject.

"But I think," says John Crowe Ransom, in the *Partisan* symposium,

> we must honor also those American writers who as a matter of course fulfill themselves and proceed to some positive and formally complete art. We have them, and though they are generically little ones they sometimes are distinguished. Probably they live in the 'regions,' the parts of the vast continental area of these United States (like the politically 'backward' South), where a normal and successful life goes on after the local fashion, and there is no compulsive consciousness that these times are only an interim, in which one enlists in some revolution in order that happiness may be possible again. They would scarcely be the natives and residents of New York City where life is lived grimly, at least by the literary colony, in the sight of ruined Europe. These artists may be considered, as they would consider themselves, to be in their duty too. Otherwise I am puzzled about the populations of the vast continental area where a normal life goes on, etc. A great many people are there, and evidently they mean to work out a stable living and to have an art for the complement and affirmation of the life. Who is going to reject them? Theirs will be the artists, if we are to have any at all, who will take the places left empty by James, Forster, and Fitzgerald, and will make the revivals less peremptory.

"What is the meaning of the literary revivals (James, Forster, Fitzgerald) that have taken place of late?" had been one of the questions posed to the participants in the symposium. A question frequently asked, and not yet so far as I know finally answered, here. John Crowe Ransom, in the foregoing paragraph, seems to have pinpointed the average non-average writing American's position. Has the "compulsive consciousness that these times are only an interim" set up some cramp or hitch in creative power? The artist need not, I suppose, love life as it is, as he sees it round him, but should he not at least be enough fascinated, enough imposed on, by it to hate it fruitfully, as did Flaubert? One must have a certain *body* in work; for that, it would seem essential to take life not as a structure, to be analyzed, but as a fabric on which to try nerves and senses out, an atmosphere in which, however rebelliously, to be saturated. Minority American consciousness—finer, more anguished, possibly more spiritual than our own—sometimes seems to have overshot itself, to have devoured its ration, to have exhausted its air. The French intellectual, at his most tormented, in the most atom-splitting of his moods, is happier: there is behind him, around him, in him, the preposterous unignorable richness of *la vie normale*—classic, hypnotic, richer for its absorption of decay. However involuntarily, French writing is still "a complement and an affirmation" of life.

I see the demand that art should be a complement and an affirmation as, on the part of the living, not only inevitable but natural—must it be written off as in the vile sense popular, or middlebrow? Can art find no life it *can* complement and affirm? For the regional writer, embedded and receptive, the question solves itself. The American Southerner, rooted in rich compost, still apparently has it: the position of Faulkner seems to be unshaken; to him has been added Eudora Welty and Capote.

Regionalists are leading. Is the same true here?

In Britain, less psychic tensity is to be felt in work. The artist, from general evidence, seems less rattled. Revolution pursues its practical, unsensational course, leaving the revolutionary to feel discarded. In us, the events of the last years have acted too, as depth-charge,[2] but at a less great depth. We are affiliated to, though not at the heart of, the European tragedy: possibly we are too near to it to see it. Compared to the Americans we are less rather than more shocked; and, on the whole, the effect of the war here has been to bring the artist nearer to people—he is less conscious than he was of being off at a tangent; his position is in consequence less extreme. Our own awareness of world crisis is possibly less potent than the American in the sense of having been less sudden — there, the break with Isolationism seems to have torn out something with it, leaving a sort of wound-hole, with nerves exposed . . . For whatever reason, the younger English writer seems more hardy, resilient, less suffering than his American brother.

Here, for the writer, however advanced, however "difficult," the smallness of the country operates favorably: one is less likely not to be heard if one speaks in a small room. Machinery for the promotion of the middle-brow either acts less exclusively or is less forbidding; and the very factor (which one has to admit) of national boredom and claustrophobia makes for a quicker attention to new voices. It cannot be said that the economic difficulty — already aired, though not yet perhaps sufficiently — is less acute here, or that its semi-solutions are either more easy or less distasteful: our literature faces the same loss through sidetracked energies. What does seem less pressing is the aesthetic difficulty — for this reason: "normal life . . . after the local fashion" is no longer despicable or suspect. On the contrary, its survival — or revival, according to how you see it — does in itself offer subject for art. We have no longer any security to despise; the man in the street is in his own way no less buffeted than the artist. The war and postwar shifting of the struggle on to the foreground, material plane seems to have cleared a hinterland for imagination; and community of experience, of the *terre à terre*[3] kind, has widened language; that is, widened its meaning. An entire territory — domestic, social — from which the artist formerly had decamped now offers itself to be re-explored.

I suggest that our coming novelists are domestic, because the "ordinary" reveals to them an extraordinary face. Joyce Cary, a senior, first gave us this apocalyptic view. P. H. Newby, Elizabeth Taylor, John Mortimer all show a swinging-round of the needle to a magnet the elder aesthete might least expect. In this phase of reconstitution nothing *is*, really, ordinary: Philip Toynbee founds a psychological anagram on a tea party. Does this preoccupation make, in the artist-writer, for loss of height? And, does this at any rate temporary suspension of the divorce between art and life connote dullness? (One must return to the charge.) Certainly this new romantic avidity for the banal affects style, or has made a style of its own; and this lacks the tang, the particular sublimation given by dislocation and discontent. One flavor may be missing—the exotic. Another factor in judgment must be, these writers have little to show up to magazines; they are continuity-seekers, therefore book-writers, wanting pace and space of their own. They are separatists, indifferent to the forum; regionalists, seekers if not inhabitants of a "South." The metropolitan illusion (like the European illusion for America) seems to have collapsed.

Psychologically, the Atlantic has seldom been wider; contemporary English and American writing can seldom have been more difficult to compare.

On Writing *The Heat of the Day*

The idea of a novel to be called *The Heat of the Day* formed gradually: I began actually to write it at the time in which I have set the book's first chapter—September 1942. I believe that in the imagination of most writers a book accumulates slowly, and that what is last of all known is how the book should *begin*. Then, with a click, some scene or incident suggests itself as an opening. In my case, I happened to drop in to an open-air concert in Regent's Park, and suddenly I realized, as I sat listening to the music, that *here* was where my novel began.

The title contains, for me, a triple idea of noon—the noon of our century, the glaring ordeal of that mid-war period, and the fact that the principal characters are undergoing the test of their middle years. Relentless midday seems to seek out and demand truth. The characters at once dread and desire truth in each other. In the case of the lovers, Robert and Stella, this creates an ordeal. *Is* love blind: is, perhaps, the most beloved person the most difficult to know? Does one want truth if it would destroy happiness? Stella, haunted by this question, finds it impossible ever quite to dismiss Harrison's terrible suggestions from her mind.

The Heat of the Day, however, is to me more than a novel about a situation; I have attempted to paint a picture of a time, and of a place inside that time—the London of the war. To me, this, just as much as the predicament of the characters, is the subject of the novel: the time and the predicament indeed are, for me, inextricably linked . . . *The Heat of the Day*, which was not finished till April 1948, was not written straight ahead: I laid it aside at intervals to write short stories (those which have appeared in my collection *The Demon Lover*). It now seems to me that several of those stories were unconscious sketches for *The Heat of the Day*: though the writing of them interrupted the writing of the novel, they somehow helped me to crystallize the idea of it.

I was in London, living in our Regent's Park house, throughout the war, and another interruption to the novel was a practical one: we were repeatedly and heavily blasted by V1s, which shattered not only the inside part of the house but my writing routine. In a way, however, I was glad not to come to the writing of the last chapters until the war was over: I wanted to be able to look back and see the war as a whole. I wanted to place those years at any rate a little bit in perspective.

I do not know whether *The Heat of the Day* is "better" than my other novels; but I am conscious that something new has emerged in it. I had, it is true, lived ten years more of my own life since the writing of *The Death of the Heart*; but I think what I see most in *The Heat of the Day* is some reflection, however small, of awe-inspiring exterior things.

Note for *The Broadsheet* on *The Heat of the Day*

The Heat of the Day took me longer to write than any other of my novels; partly because it was a good deal interrupted by what is in the main its subject, the war, and partly because so many psychological as well as technical difficulties kept cropping up in the course of it. In spite or because of this I enjoyed my work on every page intensely. I imagine no writer really either expects or desires writing to be easy—any too prolonged flow of facility begins to make one suspicious of oneself. I'd always wanted to write what might be called a *present-day* historical novel; I think I had, so far, come nearest to that with *The Last September* (Ireland during "the bad times") though that, now, dates back to more than twenty years ago.

I think that, perhaps, for a novelist it is a relief to turn to exterior rather than interior crisis. These days one feels rather a revulsion against psychological intricacies for their own sakes. It's fatal to one's feeling for one's own characters (as it is, indeed, in my case, to feeling for the characters in any novel I read) if one at any moment feels tempted to say to them what used to be said to oneself during adolescence—"For heaven's sake stop fussing over yourself and try and get on with something more important!" . . . I have always enjoyed the kind of story which is most visual, least analytical; and that, I suppose, is the kind I prefer to write.

I have had on the whole quite a varied life, to and fro between Ireland and England and terms of time abroad. Fortunately I have a passion for first impressions—arriving in new places, meeting new people. As an Irishwoman, I never take England quite for granted: the country and its inhabitants for me continue to have the fascination of slight strangeness. Even if I could be anything like such a good writer as Jane Austen, I could never get stimulus, as she did, from a small, fixed world and an ultra-familiar scene. For my short stories, but also I think for my novels, I depend on sudden, vivid, significant, therefore haunting glimpses of things. As against that, my actual *writing* can only be done under routine conditions, in a surround of monotony—I cannot settle to anything if I am moving about. I like fixed hours, and a familiar table—in fact, rather a rigid schoolroom or workshop atmosphere. At my home in Ireland, deep in the country, or in London, if I don't answer the telephone, this *can* be contrived.

The best let-up after writing, I find, is either to drive a car or go to a cinema. It's so difficult sometimes to switch right off and talk to people, as one feels both preoccupied and drained out. After a rest and a bath, however, nothing is nicer than going to a party—if it is a gay and amusing one. Still, I often wonder if many authors are as genuinely sociable as they have to appear. I often wonder, also, how it is that so many make such good parents as they do: this is not my problem, as I have no children.

I am, now, just at the end of writing the history of a famous Dublin hotel, the Shelbourne. After Easter I shall be starting another novel, which is already rolling round in my mind. I must say that I could also do with a holiday—but then, so could we all.

Publisher's Blurb for *The Heat of the Day*

This is a story set, outwardly, in a particular phase of the Second World War, but is not a war novel, being perennial in subject. The scene is embattled London, though the experience, memories, and desires of the characters open, also, on other places and times — the past, the future, Ireland, the coast of Kent. There are three main characters: inevitably, a triangle[1] situation. Of two men, between whom there exists an unequal rivalry, one is the hunter, one the hunted: they never meet.

The third of the characters, a woman, is asked to face the impossible — a charge, of the blackest, brought against the person she values most. We are to live in the theater of her state of mind. How far dare we know each other; how far is the heightened vision of love compatible with a willing blindness; how far might not an enormity be one form of honor? Henceforward in the relation between the lovers the triple question is to be kept in play.

The accuser, the listener, and the accused have one thing in common: the noon of their lives coincides with the glare of the noon of their century. Hence the title. For each of them, the war is the exteriorization of an internal conflict — such wars do not finish, only shift their ground. Upon these three — Harrison, Stella, Robert — rests the pressure of their time: whether they are their time's creatures or its factors they do not know . . . At the periphery of the story are other, younger or older, people, at a further remove from what is happening — a boy in the army, an elderly lady who has adopted madness, the feckless Kentish wife of a soldier. Roderick, Cousin Nettie, and Louie do not advance the plot; they reflect the plot . . . In the London foreground of *The Heat of the Day* stands a series of bright-lit rooms encased in darkness; in the background is a house in another country.

The possibility of there being no present, nothing more than a grinding-together of past and future, enters, at a point in the story, a woman's thought. Against that, there is the actuality of moments, and the power of a moment to protract itself and contain the world. All through *The Heat of the Day*, what might be drama runs into little pockets: this is a domestic novel. Within view of the reader there is no violent act. Persons hesitate or calculate; and at the same time are inseparable from history.

The Technique of the Novel

As to the technique of the novel, there are, as we know, no absolute laws. The novel is, above all things, a free form. It was *as* that that it was called into existence, when the need was felt, in the century of realization and reason, two hundred years ago, for an expression of human experience, or a means of the discovery of man by man, which should be less rigid than then was the drama, and less continuously exalted than poetry. The freeness of this form is at once stimulating and sometimes rather disconcerting. It seems that, for all that, the novel is particularly apposite to our tentative age. This very stimulus works, I think, in a peculiar way, and in a variety of ways, on the creative writer. Each writer must make his own experiments and, through those experiments, arrive at the discoveries which may be, indeed, which must be, uniquely his or her own.

All the same, there are a few general questions which may be asked, and which are asked, as to the technique of the novel. When I give you an example of some of these, when indeed I speak to the heading of some of these, you may feel that they are almost too naive, and that they are questions which will be asked by people who did not know anything about the writing process at all. But they are questions which recur, which are asked in very good faith, and which are to a certain extent disturbing when one tries to answer them, because the answers can only be suggested, not ever quite, finally, established or found. And you will realize that, though I am the one who stands up here and speaks, I do not speak didactically; I speak as someone still in this process of experimentation. And though I shall not, like the lawyer in court—they truly say, "I suggest"—I suggest, you will realize that a certain element of suggestion, a certain element of being something merely offered by me to you, is there.

One question which is of the first importance in the novel: the plot or the characters, the personages or the story. To that, my answer would be that the two are really inseparable, and that the only danger is in the developing of either one at the expense of the other. All of you will know what I have in mind when I think of the two extremes of over-development, how over-development of character, as it were in a vacuum, leads to the very static, so-called "psychological novel," which finds it difficult to progress, and which, while it may probe down into interesting and important depths in psychology, somehow fails—or so we feel now—to present mankind in the state in which he is really important, the state, defined by Aristotle for the *Grammar*,[1] of man in action. The other extreme, the development of plot at the expense of character, is of course our very estimable friend, the mystery or thriller, the suspense story, which though it does, while we read, establish a complete grip on even, I think, the most sophisticated or intellectual of us, tends to fade out of the mind directly the book has been closed. It is remarkable, in speaking of the mystery story, that its greatly increased and deserved prestige comes from its extension into the area of character. So that the finest of the mysteries or detective stories are really drawing into themselves a good many of the most respectable, and also the most haunting, elements to be found in the novel.

The thing that really comes first, the thing at the core of the novel, is the situation. And I speak of this situation because I mean by that a particular and very important fusion between the idea, which is intellectual and brain-conceived on the one hand, and the image, which is imaginative, visual, and sometimes in nature poetic, on the other. The situation is what the novel is about. It is also the incentive and inspiration of the writer who writes the novel. And when the situation has been conceived or found—or I should more generally say has found itself for the writer—then it is something which both the plot and the characters equally exist to serve, to serve, that is to say, by expanding and making more concrete and more real.

I think that the situation gives birth to the story, a little perhaps before it gives life to the characters. If I were asked which came first in the sense of time—I do not say in the sense of importance—the plot or the characters, I would reply, "the plot." The plot is thought of, or the plot builds out from, the situation, at first in a very simple and abstract form. And the characters, in the first place, come into existence: they too at the start are rather simplified or abstract in order to play the parts which the plot demands, and in order, together with the plot, to bear out the situation or internal idea.

If one can go back to the first, almost childish, process, that early stage in the conception of the novel, I would say that one thought of the characters almost as persons in a morality play. There must be a proud man. There must be one fearless but rather dangerous person. There must be one person perhaps inclined to be destructive, most of all to themselves. There must be one character apparently simple and undeveloped, but liable to show unexpected magnitude and unexpected power. That sounds like a formula. And as you can all feel, no real creation of character can be done to formula. But the formula gives place so quickly to this rush of imaginative life that the characters fill themselves out. They acquire not only the characteristics which they were first meant to have, but also those complementary characteristics, those alternatives, those apparently contradictory traits without which no person can be rounded off or complete. They acquire physical characteristics.

I once said, in writing about the novel, that at the outset of the story, my characters were rather like persons seated opposite to me in a railway carriage. I conceived the English railway carriage in which, rather embarrassingly, but sometimes in a hostile way, four or five travelers sit at each side, in rows, gazing across at each other. And I envisaged such a carriage or compartment as it used to be, during after-dark travel in the war, when the whole thing was darkened down to a single small blue lamp up in the ceiling.[2] So that when one first entered the carriage and sat down, one saw only opposite one four or five veiled forms, without features, without characteristics. And only as these people moved or expressed themselves, and partly as one's eyes naturally became accustomed to the half dark, did the features and the personality that goes with the features begin to emerge.

That is, at least, what happens to me in the case of my characters. But here is an excellent example of the danger of generalization, or the danger of apparent law as to novel creation or construction, because I have talked with friends who tell me that their characters enter the scene into the consciousness of the writer with a completeness and with a suddenness which made them like a new personality simply opening a door and walking into a room. You must think for yourselves, those of you who are engaged on, or interested in, that part of the writing of a novel, which way the character addresses himself to you.

These characters, as they become less abstract and more concrete, as they lose their original simplicity, and develop all those wonderful and almost confusing traits of complete, real life, are almost certain — and this may be a commonplace — to give trouble to the author of the book. I do not say that they give trouble to their creator, because I think few writers have the sense of having created or invented their own characters. A certain amount of ingenuity goes to the first phase. But quite soon, the sense of the character being contained in the author's first idea is gone. And these people, as they become three-dimensional, develop sometimes a volition of their own. And that very interesting conflict, which produces one of the major crises in the writing of the novel, begins: a sort of discordance between the characters as they have grown to be and the parts they were intended to play in the frame and under the influence of the idea of the story. This conflict has to be solved, sometimes by a throwing out of a character which becomes too rebellious, in which case he may have been misconceived at the start. Or occasionally by an adaptation—a perfectly honest adaptation—of certain details or, it may be, proportions of the plot to suit the exigencies, the rather striking demands, from one or two characters who may be concerned, because there may exist such an inherent reality in these people that the author will tend to trust them instinctively to the extent of sacrificing what may begin to seem to him a rigid, arbitrary, or brain-spun idea.

Another question about the novel on its technical side: how great is the importance of the dialogue? That this question should be asked, and increasingly, does show that a potential importance, and a *new* sense of the importance, may be there. Dialogue always—onward, that is, from the nineteenth century at the start—has been used, and used effectively. It creates for the reader a feeling of immediacy. It breaks up what may be the rather intimidating look of the long, solid chunks of print, or the paragraphs, on a page. Children always go, I'm told—I did—for books which, with the pages flicked over, show that they contain plenty of conversation. And I believe that I have been present in a lending library when I have seen a good many people choosing their weekend reading, making a selection, on much the same terms. Here is a feeling of something liable to be light, amusing, and dramatic—something which will not make too great a demand on the concentration, something which is bound to be effectively done.

The Victorian novelists used dialogue, though, I think, rather sadly, they were on the retreat from the high peak of excellence in which, in immediately pre-Victorian days, it was used by Jane Austen. And there is, in our time, in the last one or two decades of our century—in fact, I would say ever since the close of World War I, and the sort of *risorgimento* with regard to the novel and story which came with that—there has been a very great revival in, interest in, and sense of importance of, the dialogue. And we do, I think, expect now that it should do something more than illustrate character, or be used for extreme drama, or comicality and absurdity, or as a sort of a diversion, an interim, a resting place in the plot.

Dialogue now, when we use it, is expected, isn't it, to really be a very structural part of the plot itself. Dialogue is not merely a little pet ball to and fro between characters, or group of characters. It is really action. It is something happening. Indeed, in the nonviolent novel, which aims to imitate everyday life, dialogue is the nearest thing to drama and the emergence of passion and feeling which we have. We are assuming a novel which excludes murders or chases or train robberies or people falling over a cliff. We are assuming the novel which claims our attention through its resemblance to life. And yet, in writing the novel, we are feeling inward for what in life is most dynamic, and trying to suggest, if not to expose, the very strong forces, often unconscious, which move in the heart and mind, or soul, of the so-called ordinary, human person. This used, at one time, to be done by the thoughtful novelist, generally through a rather lengthy analysis or by what might be called inward description. Just now, are we not in a state of a certain revolt against the possible tediousness and the staticness of long analysis? And do we not wish to show people by a very sensitive recording or registration of the rhythm of their speech, and still more by the pressure behind that speech, of what they do actually think or feel?

The interesting thing in the use of dialogue is that it may be written, in a way, on two planes. One can have what the person intends *to* say, the impression they mean to create, the little bit of harmless show or showing-off, which some of us do put on when we talk. After all, it's our only indulgence. We can do the dialogue as it would appear, as it is intended to be heard by the one who speaks. And we may also, without injustice to that character, show what is betrayed by the speaker, show what may be present in his mind, or in his unconscious, molding the form of the sentence, dictating the choice of the noun or the adjective. So that, in writing dialogue, we have in mind, first, the old, accredited aim of illustrating character, of suggesting the type of person, the extraction, the nationality, the age, the class or income group, the region from which they come. All that will come out in their choice of words, in the formation of their speech. We show, then, what they claim to be or hope to be seen or heard as. And if we can, we also suggest the pressure, somewhere within the speaker, of an unconscious force[3] or maybe a pleasurable force. It may not always be something dark or distressing or evil. It may be that the person is confused by joy or by surprise, or, in the most ordinary case, rendered speechless by love or emotion. But the fact is that what people say only to an extent represents them. And that we care most now to deal realistically with dialogue in the sense of not making persons more articulate than they would be in real life, and yet allowing something—what is behind their speech—to come through.

I hope I have not made to sound too complicated what is really the unconscious aim of the writer in these days when he sits down to do a passage of the dialogue. It's always a little deceptive to shred up the impulses and the urges and the self-made rules under which one works, because the great virtue of imaginative writing—and we think now of imaginative writing—is that it is not done entirely under the direction of the brain or under the control of the judgment. But I only know now that, in reading back over the passages of the dialogue I write, and finding as I often do that I need to recast those passages several times, I ask myself what the purpose is, what I am narrowing down to, why I want to eliminate certain things, why I want to give more force to others. And I feel that I have that triple purpose in view: illustration, representation by the character, and the involuntary showing through speech by the character of what they really are.

At the same time, the entire purpose, I think we may say, in the writing of dialogue now, is to give an effect of very great spontaneity and naturalism. It is really death to a dialogue to give any hard formation to the sentences. We want the spontaneous and impulsive appearance. And so the writing of dialogue may be the most extreme case in the novel of art having to conceal art. We want the dialogue to do a lot more than it appears *to* do. We wish it to appear to be totally spontaneous and naturalistic without actually being so, because, if we were to take down through a recording machine or through a concealed stenographer a passage of conversation between two people or a group, which might in real life sound totally quick, spontaneous, and economic, and try to put that dialogue into a story as it stood, we should find almost certainly that it straggled, it was unduly prolific, it was not totally keeping to the point we wanted to express. It's quite amazing to contrast spoken dialogue lifted from real life and the precise, shapely dialogue which we have to find to play the part needed in the novel.

A third, and I think probably a last question, again, often asked: how much should the writer be bound by ideas of style and form without fear of overcoming or seeming to be too rigid or artificial? In fact, are style and form a good thing or not? This has been exceedingly often asked me, particularly by young people, who have, and one may honor them for it, a very great dread of anything in art which might seem unspontaneous or too constricting. They say, "surely life is a free and in the main an impulsive process. Are we forced to, or would it not in fact be wrong to try and squeeze and deform our picture of persons, our representation of action, our idea in fact of the process of life into a set, methodical style? Would it not be said to sacrifice much that could be said, much that might fill out, or enliven the picture? Must that be sacrificed to a preconceived idea of what gives a shapely and correct form?" I don't know how much you either share in or have come across this revolution or, at any rate, instinctive revolt against form and style as something that threatens to be deadening, over-intellectual, or arbitrary. And I have always thought that that[4] particular question was a very good thing for me as a writer who has been practicing for a long time to be asked. It's a good thing to be shaken up a bit in one's ideas. And because I respect the question — it's occasionally asked simply by somebody who wants to be a little superior — but on the whole I think it's asked by people who are deeply concerned with the future of the novel and the short story, and who feel a fear that all forms of imaginative prose fiction may be left behind as inappropriate to the times in which we live. And there is some idea that if we can have a break with form and style, it may give a new lease of life, or a new form of appeal, to the novel and the short story.

If one goes further in talk with the asker of such question, as to his idea of what style is, I think one may quite often find that he has, what at any rate I should call, a slight or indeed a grave misconception as to what style is, and that he is tending to think of style as a sort of overlaid, artificial surface to the material of the writing, rather like a veneer of walnut or mahogany laid on what should be a plain, strong table or chair, and that this surface is applied for the sake of being a little easy, a little pleasing, and for reasons which are perhaps a little low. And he thinks of style as something not really integrated with the expression or the idea, but something perhaps laid on when the book is complete. He sees that the author may reread his manuscript and think, "My heavens, I have forgot all about style!" and go back and start at the first chapter and apply style almost out of a tube or with a paintbrush. And in that case our young person feels that he is doing a very bad thing to the manuscript. And of course in that case I should entirely agree. But what I would like to put to him would be the idea of style as what Flaubert said it was: an actual way of seeing things. And that style is not just a matter of sentence formation, of pleasing sounds or effective words, but that it really arises in the first place from the whole sight, view, and conception of which the author has of his subject and of his scenes. And he's trying . . . And that the search for style — style in each case being unique to the author himself — is really a search for the words which will best serve the purpose, and the words which go most directly to the imagination of the reader, and are less obtrusive on their own account.

In fact, style is an attempt to dissolve language, to a certain extent. It's trying to give language the transparency of glass. Style is also capable — it is so much a matter of sound too, of the sound instinctively heard in the mind as we read.[5] And because it's a matter of sound, its variations — the slow and the fast, the abrupt or the smooth — are very, very important. And these variations should accord with the actual variations in the story. In fact, style is really inseparable from the way the story is told. It is the ideal telling of the story, at which I think we all aim. I don't say that we want to obliterate language altogether. We don't want to find for language merely an inconspicuous sort of perfection.

There may be moments when we want to hammer the words we have in mind from their very strangeness and discordance onto the consciousness of the reader. We are trying to convey something disturbing or harsh. And we will, in that case, use harsh, discordant words. We will turn our sentences upside down. We will take, if we think the heat of the occasion and the pressure of the story demands[6] it, we will deliberately break up every conception of style and produce something — what is for the time being — convulsive or over-loud. It's not a sleek, tame thing, a style, at all. One thinks of it as a nervous animal, a nervous horse. Something responsive. Something which can be controlled, held back, or urged forward. It is in fact a language and the way the language[7] can be seized upon and fused into the imagination of the writer, and it is also the play made by the writer on the visual power, on the reception of the reader. It is an atmosphere.

If style can be comprehended first of all as something which should, ideally, keep to the remains of the classic rules, but which is essentially to be molded, and used, and developed, and given texture and feeling and heat and light by the person who uses it—if I could convey that idea to my young revolutionary against style, or rather break down the misconception of style he had, I think he would probably find that he, with all his feeling for spontaneity, would come, possibly, at his age, and in his freshness, into a style more true and more alive than I have so far found.

The same thing applies to form. I believe form, or shape, to be implicit in the conception of the story. It comes with the idea, with the situation. And above all, it is not a restricting thing. I don't think it is merely that the form is like one of those little tin—I imagine you have them here— stamp things with which one stamps down with pastry if a pie is being made and then pulls away from around where the stamp has fallen everything else. I don't think that form clamps down and involves a kind of ruthless sacrifice of material or of imaginative reality, which might be there. Because if the form is conceived of in the first place, the reality will grow up inside that. When I mean form I mean quite straightforward, structural things that I believe one should know: more or less what the length of the story will be; what the plan will be; what the time and place; the number of characters to be involved. Perhaps one might call that "plan" rather than "form." But it should, I'm sure, be fairly clear at the outset. It can be altered; it can be adapted. But that should only be very deliberately done. And in that case, form, rather than being restrictive, will make for strength. It will make for the concentration, which is the absolute secret of any force of language, or feeling, or expression in creative writing.

Compression, not over-compression, but that thing which is gained, just as I probably find it easier to speak to you inside these four walls than I might be doing if we were all seated charmingly about on an enormous green hill: it would be cooler, it would be more suitable to the day. But I think just as people gain by being in a room in some energy, just as things gain by being placed in relation to each other, just as a city gains by a plan, I am sure that the impulse is directed and helped, and the material is held together and the real creative purpose is intensified by this really proper feeling for and creative use of form.

In talking about the technique of the novel, there is a danger of making it sound, even as one talks, to be a technical, a structural thing, a method[8] of contrivance and ingenuity. What we must not ever forget is that the novel is, first and last, a work of the imagination. As such, it will continue to be written. And, as such, I feel certain, it will not ever lose its hold on us.

We Write Novels: An Interview with Walter Allen

Allen: It seems to me, Elizabeth Bowen, that your novels possess a combination of qualities that are rarely found together. First of all, there's the element of social comedy. Then there is your tragic sense, which comes out particularly, I suppose, in *The Death of the Heart*. There's your intense awareness of atmosphere: the very feel of time and place or of place at one particular time and in one particular weather. The beginning of *The Death of the Heart*, that scene in Regent's Park, or the sense of wartime London in *The Heat of the Day*. In one hundred years' time if anyone wants to know what living in London in 1941 was like, there they have it perfectly recorded for them. And one finds it in your latest novel, *A World of Love*, with your wonderful evocation of a hot summer day[1] in Ireland. I'd like you to tell us something about your extraordinary sensitivity to the mood of place and time. Is it with you the whole time? Is it with you when you're not writing novels?

Bowen: I think it is. Really to be in a place, a new place or a place that affects me strongly, is an event. It's something of tremendous importance to me. The mixture of time and place, being in a place in the autumn, or in a shower of spring rain, or a particular time of the sunset—it does affect me extremely strongly. I think more so, often, than my personal relations with other people. It's always in the background and at the same time in the foreground with me.

Allen: I wonder how it arises. I suppose we are all aware of the mood of time and place in some degree, but in your case it's obviously abnormal compared with the rest of us. Is it possibly the influence of Ireland: Irish light, the Irish climate, the Irish scene?

Bowen: Yes, it easily could be because Ireland certainly is conditioned—well, that's a dull word—but it changes quite dramatically and dynamically the whole time. I've often wondered in myself why my mood suddenly went sad, then seen it was the perfectly practical thing. A heavy cloud had passed over the sun, and there was a sort of transformation of everything; spirits go down. There probably is, I should think, no country, as you suggest, in which the weather is at once so stimulating and depressing and fluid the whole time, and creating a sort of drama on its own account.

Allen: I can understand that. When I first went to Ireland I immediately realized that there was some meaning in "Celtic twilight." Do you consider yourself, Elizabeth Bowen, an Irish novelist or an English novelist?

Bowen: Well, I belong to that race inside a race called the Anglo-Irish. Most of the Anglo-Irish I could quote are a great deal more distinguished than I am, but their heredity[2] I'm very proud to have. Bishop Berkeley, and . . . and W. B. Yeats—they've been the giants of the Anglo-Irish.[3] Those splendid social comedians and, I think, great novelists, Somerville and Ross, who I don't think sometimes are appreciated on their dramatic side—they were Anglo-Irish. And it may be that belonging to, to be Anglo-Irish, I think you must have your main roots and heredity in Ireland, and I have.

Allen: I immediately think of another Anglo-Irishman: Shaw. Or Wilde. It seems to me that you, all of you, have a common quality, which is the quality of detachment.

Bowen: Yes, I can see what you mean about detachment. I mean I can see it in the others, and I suppose it exists in me too.

Allen: I think that your keen sense of social comedy, the comedy of manners comes from that. I mean because it is one of the Anglo-Irish things, isn't it?

Bowen: It is tremendously. It's a mixture of observation and satire, and sometimes quite affectionate satire. But keen awareness, I suppose, partly because in a small country we're near to each other. I see that social comedy coming out in the Irish Irish. I mean in Joyce and Frank O'Connor and Seán O'Faoláin. But the Anglo-Irish have it perhaps in a more acute form even.

Allen: Of course what's important to us is that they are detached from us, from England, and can see us from the outside, as I suspect you do.

Bowen: I do. I've lived, I suppose, almost more years in my life in England, but I can remember well when I first came to England as a child. I remember thinking, "This is England and these are the English." Although the scene of almost all my novels, except two, and a few short stories has been in England, I sometimes see how the novelists who haven't been English—to quote a great name, Henry James—how you get a particular angle on a country that you love and are absorbed in up to a point, but don't quite entirely belong to.[4]

Allen: I'm sure that this quality of detachment is one of the most valuable qualities a novelist can possess. But let's go[5] back, if you don't mind, to this question of atmosphere and of the mood of place and time, because it makes me want to ask you this question: How do you write your novels? What's your starting-off point? Is it character or situation, or is it the mood of a place and a time?

Bowen: It's the situation first of all. But even when I think of the situation it implies some kind of a mood. When I had the idea for[6] *The Death of the Heart*—of a young girl, almost a child, stranded with new people in a new place—I also saw the scene: where it would be, the time of year in which it would begin, the cold of winter, and the kind of house in which it happened. In[7] *The House in Paris*, which is one of my novels that[8] I am most fond of, I saw these two children by accident arriving in the same house and shut up together for a day. I saw that kind of cold, wax-floored, French house on a February day[9] and the rather dim light coming in through the windows. I think I begin most of my novels with a visual picture. The situation or the idea is something I see pictorially, and it is always surrounded by some sort of atmosphere or time of day or season of the year, even though the story may move to and fro.

Allen: Wasn't your first impulse to be a painter?

Bowen: It was. I always thought all the years I was a child, and in fact right up to the time I was twenty years old—I cured myself of hoping to be a painter. I was working seriously for two years, for two terms at a school of art, and found that I hadn't got what it took. But that habit of mind or habit of imagination, I should say, which a painter has, has remained in me tremendously. I do write, I think, from the eye. I always see things.

Allen: You write intensely visually. Most of us who are not painters, I'm afraid, are not visual. In other words, that is why painting is so very valuable to us, I suppose. But, Miss Bowen, what's your aim as a novelist? What do you think is the novelist's job? In a long article you wrote some years ago, you described a novel as the non-poetic statement of a poetic truth, which is an excellent epigram that's haunted me ever since.

While I can see that that is true of your novels, I don't see that it's true of all novels.

Bowen: No, I suppose a novelist, however much they try and be objective, if they generalize about the novel, they can only think in their own terms up to a point. I would say that it is true of the novels of Graham Greene for one.[10] I mean that he takes a moral or spiritual or strongly emotional situation and ties it down in a beautifully concrete clear-cut story of action. I think I'm moving more towards action and less towards analysis in the novels I write. I think you must have action and a story, and a plot, but that the aim is to present what happens in the light of imagination. To illuminate it and give it a meaning, you isolate some small story, because all stories are small really and have the character of a short story. It sounds rather pompous to talk about universality, but I think that a story is only interesting to me and worth it if it contains something which is universally true, of which the truth and the importance extend beyond the story itself. One might say that a novel illustrates something; directly one says that it sounds pretentious too. But I think few stories are worth telling entirely for their own sakes, just that they begin and end. You haven't had any imaginative experience or enlargement if you read them.

Allen: I agree entirely and I meant to ask you this question: who are your favorite novelists, your favorite novelists of the past?

Bowen: Well, other than in the English language, Flaubert. I think *Madame Bovary* was the first novel I read when I first grew up which gave me an idea of what a novel could be. How much could hang on a small story.

Allen: And in English?

Bowen: And Proust in French; I think he's a very dangerous influence. In English, Emily Brontë, Henry Fielding,[11] Dickens, Jane Austen, Henry James, although I think he again is easily too much of an influence. And among the novelists who are alive, E. M. Forster and Virginia Woolf—who is, I think, of most value as a novelist because she can't be pinned down inside the frame of a novel.[12]

Allen: That's an extremely fascinating list. I thought that you'd mention Henry James because it does seem to me that your work as a novelist over the last twenty years or so has been a development from perhaps social comedy to the evocation of mood in terms of character, which has gone side by side, I think, with an increasing complexity in your style.

And I find now that some critics are rather reacting to your prose style, in the same way that they react to the prose of the later James novels. What do you think of that? What's your reply?

Bowen: Well, I suppose it is that with each novel I try to use fewer words and make the words do more. The very desire—though it might not seem a desire to simplification—I do want to obliterate words. I want to give the full possibility of sensation and visual power in words so that the sensation I have in mind when I write should go straight to the reader. Of course, if I so use words that the words tangle up the reader and obstruct him, I have misused them, and I know that I do occasionally do that. My last novel was extremely short, and it was reduced considerably because I took out a great deal; it seemed to me that if I could find one word of one syllable which would do the work of a long paragraph filled with words, that that was the ideal thing to do. Sometimes when I get my sentences in inverted order, which has often been pointed out, sometimes with very severe criticism, which is entirely justified, it's because I try to put the words in a sentence in the way that they would have struck the beholding[13] eye. I remember in *A World of Love* I had a sentence about a young girl coming into a drawing room, the day after the party, and I said, "but pyramidal the flowers were on the piano." I deliberately put "pyramidal" first, because in that rather odd, strung-up mood the girl was in, I thought, first she would dimly see what appeared to be a pyramid, and then flowers. And then realize the thing was on the piano. Really many of my inversions come from that.

Allen: In other words, they are, in a way, an attempt to render the visual image as a painter would render it.

Bowen: Yes, they are.

Allen: That's extremely interesting. Well, there is one last question I should like to ask you. That is, do you think there are any particular advantages or disadvantages in being a woman novelist? What part does sex itself play in writing novels, do you think?

Bowen: I would say that in the experience sense it was a disadvantage, because in spite of all the immense changes in the last fifty years, women, I think, tend to lead rather circumscribed lives. You can't generalize but the average woman isn't less free as a rule, either through marriage or children. I have no children but one is more tied and therefore one has much less experience in terms of actual happenings. You couldn't be an engine driver. It's absurd to think you'd write a better novel if you'd shot a tiger, but there isn't anything to stop me shooting a tiger, except that I've a lot of other things to do in other places. I think what Jane Austen said — and I think that to me she's one of the finest novelists in the English language, because of that thing that's been so often pointed out. She used her limitations and disabilities to produce a very keen and exact and penetrating sense of the small world in which she lived, and I see that, you might say, concentration in the work of most of the women novelists whom I admire most. Colette even seemed to be an example of it, with her cats and her gardens and her children. Of course, there are considerable dangers, because women tend — I think we tend — in our own lives and in our art, to be on the subjective side. It's been said, hasn't it, that art is often trying to make a pearl round the grain of sand in the oyster. It's trying to overcome some disadvantage. I think that women often write most happily if they — well, perhaps it sounds strange to say — if they work on a small canvas, but they bring into the thing the generic qualities which women tend to have of observation, of interest, and of that thing which you say I have, that awareness of time and place, which I think I've noticed in a lot of my friends, women friends, old or young. I think it's possibly rather a feminine trait. Not ultra-feminine, it can happen too in men, but I think that imaginative awareness of surroundings and also practical preoccupation with surroundings. I've often heard it said that a woman can hardly go into a room without wanting to push the furniture around, or do something about a room. There's no doubt that we are, I think, not only practically but imaginatively and sometimes almost emotionally concentrated on things and places. And that appears in the work — I don't think of Emily Brontë, she was almost purely poetic — but it can appear admirably, I think, in the work of women who write. Or it can appear badly if it gets pedestrian or if it gets self-indulgent or if it gets too, one might say, purely domesticated. I think it needs effort for a woman to shake off her surroundings completely, and possibly part of the effort results in a work of art. You're trying to sever the shackles of your existence.

Allen: It seems to me, Elizabeth Bowen, that the works of the women novelists you've named, Jane Austen, Colette, and your own work, prove that there are no disadvantages at all.

Reviews: 1935 to 1942

New Novels

Eleanor Carroll Chilton, *Follow the Furies*; Mark Van Doren, *The Transients*; George Albee, *Not in a Day or Seven. New Statesman*, August 17, 1935.

All three of these novels come from America. *Follow the Furies* is by a long way the best. Its theme, which would in a headline blacken into "The Right to Kill," might lend itself to sensational treatment, but Miss Eleanor Carroll Chilton has built round it a calm, measured, unabstract, and strangely attractive book, making no attempt to mobilize hectic sympathy. Her manner is, I think, for a book of this kind, ideal. *Follow the Furies* has the solidity of a Mrs. Wharton novel, an equally sober and unobtrusive excellence of style: its social scene is set with the same sureness and grace. Miss Chilton knows how to render the charm of a house and household, how both to assume security and to convey its appeal. She gives value to pleasant, unsuspicious relations between people, and can command the idiom of easy, intimate, funny talk. Though the interplay of her plot is between two generations, these are not forced into the conflict novels have made stale. There is no guying of characters, no wink between author and readers at anybody's expense. The atmosphere, like that of a good house, is at once natural and dignified.

That this is in no sense a dreadful book adds force to the tragedy. The Lintons' pleasant stone house is not a stage set for drama, or for the decision that confronts Barbara Linton when she comes home from college, having graduated Phi Beta Kappa. She has a sympathetic, didactic, successful-novelist father, Hugh Linton; and a brilliant mother, his wife, Grace. But Grace Linton has just been struck down by an appalling form of sclerosis—whose last phases are too bad to contemplate—deformation, idiocy. Barbara decides that her mother ought to be spared living longer. If one may distinguish between theme and subject, the subject of this novel is the inflammation of a young, self-regarding, sensitive, passionate person by ideas received, or forced in, from outside and not ready, yet, to be brought to bear on life. Barbara, like the hero of M. Bourget's *Le Disciple*, is the victim of ideas: there is, in spite of its placid, faultless modernity, a ninetyish atmosphere in this book. After her fatal act, Barbara's sense of doom and black isolation take the form of a persecution mania in which she envisages a hostile God. To handle a theme like this without melodrama or fuss, in a low-pitched way, is an achievement. Miss Chilton has not written a merely "painful" book. Her technique has no tricky brilliance; it is staid, traditional: the novel is a monument to its effectiveness. Her characterization and dialogue are very good.

After a book that absorbs you till you do not know you are reading, *The Transients* is rather literary. Mr. Van Doren is a well-known and formidable American critic. He writes English almost too well, and his novel, in which the more personal side of his imagination escapes, perhaps, for the first time, has the essayist's leisurely, introspective pace. New England is its setting, and a New England earnestness and metaphysical uneasiness pervades the story, which, chiefly about the love of two not quite human beings, doomed to live on this earth for a span of time, is a little vague. Though the publisher says, "No reader will miss its significance," I, for one, have; but possibly that is my fault. Appreciation is limited by one's experience, and the adventures of John Bole and Margaret Shade correspond to nothing in mine. I should be sorry to irritate Mr. Van Doren with misapplied criticism. Is it a tribute to say that the book gets on one's nerves in much the same way as *The Immortal Hour*[1] did? In the earlier chapters, when John is in jail behind the village blacksmith's house, it looks as though this might be yet another *The Passing of the Third Floor Back*:[2] John sees through doors, and "was smiling now as though the sunlight had crept around his lips and eyes." But that clears off: the hero has pointed ears and is, though innocently, amorous. When he is let out, Madge, the blacksmith's daughter, hopefully follows him. But when John and Margaret, at once his doom and his complement, reunite, they shake off Madge and have a good many rather high-hat discussions about "mortals." They have a honeymoon in a deserted house among autumn woods, and talk for a week, at the end of which John has his expected apotheosis and disappears. He disappears dissatisfied, for he has not talked enough yet. Margaret perceives this, the last day of the honeymoon. "That was it. He was uncomfortable not for the reason that she was; he had no scruples; he was not changing his mind. It was merely that he still found something on his mind that needed to be said. He was still not done explaining himself. She would not say justifying himself. No, because he really had never wavered, in spite of all he had confessed yesterday about the difficulty of the week. It was exactly as it had always been: he wanted to make her understand everything more fully than he had feared she did. He was suffering because he would not talk." No doubt a good many honeymoons are like that. But there seems to be little point in threshing everything out if you are going shortly to disappear. There must be more to Mr. Van Doren's book than this, and I would not wish to discourage anybody from reading it. Wistful, semi-ascetic novels of less merit than this get a good press in England. *The Transients* written by an Englishman might have been infinitely more embarrassing.

Not in a Day or Seven is a rattling good story about an American woman who slides her way into business and makes a big success. Claudine Whitter is described on the wrapper as a female juggernaut of business. She is one of those solid, nerveless, single-minded women with an octopoid personality. The first chapter, childhood and early days, led me to think that the novel would be picturesque: Claudine, child of the marriage of a Kentucky colonel who is also a Jew, called Sam Cohen, and a Russian ex-vestal virgin of easy ways, is whisked over to Europe on each occasion of her mother's elopements. However, Claudine gets going, gets into her stride, sends herself to an exclusive finishing school and achieves, during one vacation, her first objective: marriage into the conventional world. She seduces the pretty, virginal Jeremy Whitter, son of the Whitters of Whitterville, who make razors, then whisks him to the altar with rapid propriety. She has learnt that to succeed one must be *très femme*, and her earliest triumphs are domestic and social. Her bridal ambitions—modest enough in view of ensuing successes—to make over the Whitter house—one of those charming crazy extensive wooden structures overlooking the Hudson across a wide lawn—into a Roman villa, she, oddly enough, does not realize for thirty-seven years. But meanwhile she accomplishes almost everything else. She patents a safety razor, coaxed from the eccentric Whitter uncle, who had invented it, raises her own factory, and reduces the family firm to comparative non-entity. On the strength of this her Wall Street triumphs are fabulous. This is, refreshingly, *not* a book about the heart of a business woman: Claudine does not reel or quaver before the stroke of passion: she has no heart, marriage canalizes her sensuality, and her respectability is ponderous. In no form does Nemesis appear. This light-hearted, grim, efficient, and slightly vulgar book is to be recommended for holiday reading, in trains, on hotel terraces, or by the sea. Mr. George Albee tells a story admirably.

New Novels

Hugh Walpole, *The Inquisitor*; H. L. Davis, *Honey in the Horn*; Helen Beauclerk, *The Mountain and the Tree*; Rosalind Wade, *A Fawn in a Field. New Statesman*, August 31, 1935.

The Inquisitor is another of Mr. Walpole's novels about Polchester. It is in patches nicely cozy and satirical, as a novel about cathedral town society should be, but it is very long: the subject is diluted in much writing. Polchester stays unsubstantial, like one of those railway-poster cities—dipped in violet shadows, with spires a supernaturally placid orange, and viridian lawns—that, though you might buy a ticket, you would never arrive at. Though actually, in *The Inquisitor*, poor Polchester is anything but placid: it is disturbed by psychic rumblings from the dead inside the cathedral and political rumblings from the unemployed in the downtown quarter. In fact, there is stage thunder, culminating in a riot and several messy deaths. A town character, Stephen Furze, a usurer, disappears; town and cathedral societies get the jitters; a cosmic uneasiness hangs over everything. The clergy here, from the bishop down, are introspective, psychic, and highly articulate. The cynical Canon Ponder reads middlebrow novels . . . There is nothing Mr. Walpole does not know about self-dramatization and a particular kind of queasiness: his masculine characters are a prey to both. The two young women, Penny and Elizabeth, are nobler.

This novel, so far as I can see, aims at being at once a thriller and a spiritual experience. As the former it much more nearly comes off. Mr. Walpole uses the traditional and honorable machinery for working up excitement: the "he little knew" manner, and "the first of a sequence of events which . . ." These hints of worse to come encourage one through. Of its second aspect, or aim, I can only say that the word "beauty" circulates with a rapidity that makes one shy: one cannot explain why. Also, ominousness and ambiguity are overworked. On p. 297 Mr. Walpole describes a garden as "darkling," and this seems to me the adjective for the style he adopts. I say adopts, because Mr. Walpole's manner must be by now well under his own command.

Mr. Walpole commands also grimness and, sometimes, humor. His pathos is not good; it seems facile; I believe it to be synthetic. Almost every incident in this novel suffers from being written up and inflated; all would be more telling were Mr. Walpole's writing more precise and cold . . . Mr. Walpole has standing, and should be allowed, by this time, to write how he likes; he deserves better than slighting and cynicism. But one does wish he would not keep encouraging other authors to do the wrong thing. At a literary dinner the other night he stated that it was the function of the novelist to create character. Why? This fallacy, coupled with a more recent yearning to be poetic, has sidetracked the English novel for too long. Characters in a novel are important only in what they generate (which is the stuff of the book), in their activity, and in their underlying generalness. The forbears that Mr. Walpole, admittedly, derives from occupied themselves with the particular—quirks, tricks, affectations, regrets, funny noses, lovable little ways. Is this what he means by creating character? Mrs. Proudie, Becky Sharp, Micawber generate nothing. Trollope is admirable because he was unpoetic; Thackeray was as hard as nails; Dickens was not a gentleman and did not have to regret that he did not really like Proust. Their own bouncing vitality blows their inactive characters across on hearty gusts. But Emma Bovary, Bloom, Charlus are memorable for their activity.

The publishers of *Honey in the Horn* put one off by describing the book as "pure poetry." I should like to clear Mr. H. L. Davis of this at once. *Honey in the Horn* is a nice, airy, picaresque book about settlers in

Oregon, 1906–1908, nearly as enjoyable as *Sard Harker*,[3] like it but not, I think, deriving from it. There is no nonsense about this book—it is at times sentimental, so are settlers, probably—and the writing is serviceable and good, though here again there is too much of it. Movement through Oregon country calls for camera work (it is possible that Mr. Davis is conscious of this and is visualizing a *Covered Wagon*[4] made by a Russian). It is hard luck on a novelist that pages of prose should be only a substitute for a few good shots. Mr. Davis has a feeling for big stretches of country, and for lighting (which is perhaps what his publisher means by "poetry").

> They were overtaking the settlers' train at last. Below them was Looking Glass Valley, all open grassland among old orchards and caved-in houses and blackened remnants of haystacks. They could see the road clear across it and the settlers' wagons making long pale-blue shadows on the grass as they wheeled out of the road to camp . . . . The wild grass of that valley had the power of reflecting light exactly like a body of water . . . . Close to the water (the Deschutes River) it was beautiful . . . the mock-orange and wild cherry flowering over the swift black water. Over it stood tall straight-up-and-down bluffs where hawks nested to catch fish in the rapids, and one with a two-foot salmon still wriggling in his claws flew so close over Clay's head that he stood up in the wagon and tried to kill it with the lash of his whip.

This wants the camera . . . *Honey in the Horn* deserves the success it has had in America, and is to be recommended to anyone feeling townbound and stuffy.

Miss Helen Beauclerk's *The Mountain and the Tree* is not, strictly, a novel and ought not to be reviewed here. Her information on the subject of early cults, mysteries, erotic symbolism, rites, orgies, and sacred misapprehensions about the facts of life is immense, and its sources are unexceptionable. From the purely fictional point of view so much learning and atmosphere rather clog the narrative. Her four stories, linked by a theme that I cannot quite discover, are spread through time, from the prehistoric Stone Age in Crete to Asia Minor in the third century A.D. Their plots are ambiguous in a high-class way, and Miss Beauclerk's artificially mystic and singsong style had a soporific effect on me. Inevitably, and unhappily for Miss Beauclerk, the stories—especially the second and third—court comparison with *Marius* and *The Imaginary Portraits*.[5] Beside these their style is flaccid, the emotion behind it unaustere. This book seems to me affected and pretentious, which is a pity when it must have been so much trouble to write.

Miss Rosalind Wade writes about the sorrows of her generation. She does not write well, but probably does not want to. She has a great deal to say. One of the most depressing things about the agonies of youth is that they are conventional and almost always follow the same course, which must be why middle-aged people like to read about them so much. When you are no longer young and still not middle-aged, they simply make dreary reading. Miss Wade has heaps of conviction and vitality. That *A Fawn in a Field* seems to have been written several times before is no reason why it should not be written several times again. It is a story about two young people, with mothers living in Chelsea, who have Bohemian friends, get engaged, sleep together, but finally do not marry. They are exceedingly youth-conscious.

Three of the novels on this list cost 8s. 6d. Are modern novels to be sold by the ounce? If so, my favorites would cost about 4s. 6d.

New Novels

> Humphry Cobb, *Paths of Glory*; Lennox Kerr, *Woman of Glen-shiels*; Margery Sharp, *Four Gardens*; Francis Stuart, *In Search of Love*; Arthur Behrend, *The House of the Spaniard*. *New Statesman*, September 14, 1935.

Paths of Glory appeared a fortnight ago, and has drawn a machine-gun fire of adjectives. It is clearly not a book that you can feel calmly about; it is difficult to appraise and not possible to dismiss. Its accuracy as a war document is, apparently, open to question, but I cannot feel that the book stands or falls by this. *Paths of Glory* is less a novel "about" the French front line during the last European war than a study of pressure, distortion, and the confused, abject indignation men in the mass feel: it is a novel about war. Mr. Cobb narrows his war down to the execution of three men to save a general's face. He is certain enough in his moral touch, and writes well enough—not simply in the sense of literary facility or persuasiveness, but in operating on the reader's imagination with a deadly effectiveness—to be allowed an artist's prerogatives. It is possible that these executions did not happen. But it is equally possible that they might. Mr. Cobb pursues war to its meanest and last implications, as the French pursue love or Americans drink. Had Mr. Cobb, given an equal seriousness of purpose, chosen to place this incident on the Ruritanian front, it would have been immaterial: its gravity stays the same. It could not have occurred in the British army; the British are not so thorough.

Paths of Glory has been compared to *All Quiet on the Western Front.* It entirely lacks, however, the Teutonic mawkishness, and it is not gratuitously revolting—physically, at least. Its horrors are on a different plane, and more frightening because they have a more general relation to life. Mr. Cobb makes war not so much a specific malady, occupying in space an area, in time a term of years, as a mobilization of every human faculty to suffer and to deteriorate. He outrages, deliberately and, I think myself, magnificently, reticences and decencies which we English still agree to observe—I cannot myself see why. By hinging the plot of the book on an incident that may, arguably, be preposterous, he turns what I take to be an indifferent flank to attack by people who will dislike this book for subconscious reasons connected with family portraits, "the little grey church across the park," or from a sense that, war or no war, one must be decent in order to live at all . . . It is hard for an adult person to examine authority. The exercise of an authority that reason cannot support puts men in a wretched position and makes crooks of them. With things as Mr. Cobb sees them, there is much to be said, humanly, even for General Assolant . . . I should like to quote from this book, but quotations would have to be too long. It certainly should be read.

Woman of Glenshiels and *Four Gardens* are both books about women—or, rather, a woman. Both follow their central figures, Mary and Caroline, from girlhood to late maturity. Mr. Kerr's is the more serious, Miss Sharp's the more charming book. At the outset, Mary, the worker of Glenshiels, looks like being one of these "strong" characters—the whole book, at the first glance, appears forbidding, with pages in dialect and a smoky setting. Actually, Mr. Kerr has written not only an excellent but a very likeable book: its stuff is grim and its implications are serious, but his manner stays undramatic—lively but calm. Mary has faults; she is a born *bourgeoise*, attaching herself passionately to objects—the green coat-and-skirt of her girlhood, the furniture of "the Room" in her married home—passionate in her opposition to ideas. "Her business in life was to live." Her feeling for order is almost poetic. Imagination and theory being her enemies, her relations with Donald, her first lover, are a tussle. The war helps her break him; after a white-feather incident in her presence his pacifism collapses; he joins up; her smiles reward him and he is killed. With Dan, her husband, superficially a plain man, her troubles are not at an end: Dan does not drink but he reads, and after his loss of work she sees him as an escapist . . . Mary's visit to the County Court—where Dan stands in the dock for a breach of the relief laws (for which his wife is responsible)—is very good. She has always stood by the law; now it is her enemy. "She shivered and stared submissively at the empty benches . . . . Their feet rang on the uncovered wooden flooring and they dared not walk far."

Caroline of *Four Gardens* is a much milder person. She does not live deliberately; her gentle, apologetic imagination centers round four gardens. This is a *vie rêvée* novel, written in terms of common sense, with surprises and consternations very skillfully chronicled. Miss Sharp's style is accomplished, at once composed and alert. Her book is excellently concrete; I cannot remember one abstract noun in it. I think it is a book principally for mothers, but no one could fail to like it, or read it with any displeasure; everyone in it is either nice or funny and everything turns out well. If you have behaved well and gently your whole life, and been genuinely fond of people, you cannot fail to be happy, even as a widow with six tulips in a roof-garden, a teapot, and a cake.

In Search of Love is disappointing. I had looked forward to knowing Mr. Francis Stuart's work, and do still hope to know the rest of it, for his qualities as a writer appear even here. But I feel it must be a pity he wasted them on this book, which, straining after topicality, only achieves out-of-dateness. Margaret Hubbard, the chauffeur's widow with a bosom suggesting repose to everyone, is a dear thing: no wonder they starred her as Everybody's Mummy. But Coral, the British film star, is not a success; her get-ups reek of the 1920s; she would never get an offer from Hollywood. Mr. Stuart too clearly expects her to dazzle. Her adventures read like an early Paul Morand story retold in Dublin. The whole virtue of a smile is that it should be involuntary: again and again in this book one finds oneself wishing to smile.

The House of the Spaniard is a very good thriller, in the John Buchan manner, but all the better for that. Mr. Behrend has a feeling for country and quickly moving events. I enjoyed it, and recommend it with confidence to anybody wanting to read a thriller. It gives you that welcome "rather he than I" feeling, suspends your own anxieties, and increases the comfort of an armchair.

New Novels

> Arthur Calder-Marshall, *Dead Centre*; Louis Marlow, *Fool's Quarter Day*; Phyllis Bentley, *The Whole of the Story*; Barbara Goolden, *Victory to the Vanquished*; Elizabeth Madox Roberts, *He Sent Forth a Raven*; Donald McPherson, *Go Home Unicorn*. *New Statesman*, September 28, 1935.

Dead Centre, a novel about a school, is a picture of a concentration camp. At large in adult society the adolescent may be a misery to himself, an embarrassment to other people; corralled, as it becomes convenient that he should be (cutting out the dope about formative influences), he becomes "a case": his confusion gets pathological. Coffin-like lack of space inside a system, obstructed energy, and a steady deforming pressure to which masters and boys are alike subject, and that seems to originate nowhere, are the matter of Mr. Calder-Marshall's very brilliant book. It needs no villain: apathy spins the plot. Actually, there is little or no plot; the effect is static; action in it is more or less simultaneous; you read crossways rather than read on. *Dead Centre* is constructed from a number of monologues, overlapping like tiles, each three or four pages long, in which boys, masters, and school servants speak. A few of the sections are narrative, furthering what plot there is; most are soliloquies. Each opens incisively, with the gusto of egotism. Legitimately, for Mr. Calder-Marshall's purpose, each speaker is, on his own plane and inside a likely idiom, pretty articulate.

Miss Canaan opens: "As a matron of a large school, I've lots of girls under me, but I'm used to command. I saw two years' service as an officer in the WAACs . . . ." Mr. Borroughs (25 years): "This life is hell. I live at secondhand. I'm wasting my youth teaching others how to use theirs . . . ." Mr. Small (34 years): "Though I know many would say I am a hopeless idealist . . . ." Podmore (15 years, 2 months): "I hate this school. It is wicked and immoral . . . ." Green (14 years, 3 months): "I did a good thing the other day . . . ." Hanley (17 years, 6 months): "I'm too old for school. My fingers itch for a job . . . ." Rose (13 years, 3 months): "When the food comes, they help themselves, taking all the butter and two or three slices of bread . . . ." And so on. The placing of every section, to get its own fullest significance as well as its psychological overlap with the next, is, clearly, very important. The most unlikely proximities have to be telling. If it did not come off, Mr. Calder-Marshall's construction would be no more than ingenious, and would obtrude. But it does come off: the sections articulate; he gets his full effect of crowded isolations. In no other book of his that I have read does Mr. Calder-Marshall's ability as a writer appear so plainly, though I think *About Levy* is a better book— more progressive than *Dead Centre* and bending back less rigidly on ex-perience. Mr. Calder-Marshall commands the speed and concreteness of good American writing, without the explosive idioms.

Insofar as the book is a study of arrestedness and paralysis, one or two of the special cases and one or two bits of drama—notably the seduction of the maid Ada—seem to me out of place. Insofar as it is a tract, or an attack, I feel that its application should be more general—there is a good deal here that could relate only to one or two particular public schools. The book would have more force if it gave more sense of alternatives; few of the boys portrayed, or self-portraying, appear to have it in them to do better anywhere else. The assumption that experience is crippling, that one cannot hope to slough it off, seems to me wrong. Is one to take it that they are born stunted—sired, mostly, by old Richburians? Richbury seems to have, like most schools, that frightening accepted quality—that you never truly leave it; age cannot deliver you . . . Only the Pro and Mr. Jarrold give you any impression that there *is* anywhere else . . . Still, *Dead Centre* remains a book it would be a pity to miss; at once detached and frantic, with enough purpose to save it from virtuosity.

Fool's Quarter Day is another study of claustrophobia—this time in a love affair. There is little that Mr. Marlow does not know about mental squalor or the ignoble undersides of feelings. His inert hero has a kind cousin, Angela, who as a mistress mothers him too much: he longs to sleep alone in a hotel, but cannot move out of her over-cozy flat. The heroic and strange young girl, Leo, offers him love and asks for a child by him, but his relations with Angela, and her oppressive pregnancy, have got him into a sort of slough: he muddles things with Leo, then misses her all his life. The book contains two more disagreeable female portraits . . . The difficulty about cutting morals out of a book is that it leaves no point of departure for anybody's behavior. Passages in this book are very good indeed; the whole has an immense vitality and not a line is negligible. One cannot overlook Mr. Marlow's novels, though I, personally, cannot like them.

Miss Phyllis Bentley loves life; she says or implies she does at the beginning of almost every story in this collection, and really it is refreshing: to read her after Mr. Marlow is like going on the water wagon for days, then sitting down to a good north-country tea. At the opening of one of the stories someone talks about Freud, but this is not really her line of country at all, nor does she for a minute pretend it is. She is good-natured, natural, and full of pity; she is not mawkish and she has a command of words. Her collection, *The Whole of the Story*, really does give the whole of every story: nothing is left in midair. Her short plots are very good; neither Hardy nor Maupassant would have sneezed at them. If you dislike so-called modern short stories, read these, which are not.

Victory to the Vanquished is a novel to read when you want, above all things, to sit down and read a novel *qua* novel. It would be good in the spare room if you wanted a visitor not to appear before lunch. It is the *idées reçues* novel at its best; apparently dragging things up but leaving you back where you were, without what is called a nasty taste in your mouth. Iris, a divorced wife, a gallant girl with a touch of desperation about her, utterly on her own again now that the lover she had married is dead, gets in touch by chance with her five-year-old daughter Cherry, a child starving for beauty and full of her mother's temperament, who has been left behind with Iris's ex-husband Duncan and his second wife Elsa, a smug pair who live in Knightsbridge. Elsa's sister Flavia is married to a brilliant barrister, Mervyn, an *âme damnée*[6] person who, unhappily, drinks. He regrets having married Flavia because he loves her innocence and feels she is getting a poor deal. Emil Hecht, the lonely German publisher, also loves Flavia's "oddly bald forehead, round blue eyes with childishly dilated pupils, the comically stern mouth, the tiny neck . . . ." But she only loves Mervyn, and her big dog. At the end there is a development about Mervyn and Iris, who both feel pretty rotten. Another Iris once drove her car into a tree, and I think this book is not unlike *The Green Hat*[7]—though its manner is quite different: curter, more wary, and very much less exotic. There is the same sort of gallant desperation, which is a little wearing if you are not in the mood. It is very well done indeed: the writing is easy, vivid, and quick with its own kind of feeling; not overly sentimental. The dialogue is natural and good; the situations are not forced. One has to respect Miss Goolden's command of her powers; she has written, clearly, exactly the book she meant to write. Do not allow the column inside the wrapper to put you off.

Miss Elizabeth Madox Roberts has an inexorably mystical, loud stop, quasi-biblical style, which I cannot bear, though I understand that there are people who like it. Her style booms so loudly that it is impossible to make out what is going on in the book, or why, or what it is going to lead to. This is a pity, because the setting is good: an isolated Kentucky homestead. The time is the last war. Wolflick farm represents the Ark, I think, and there is the same congestion in its inside. The carpenter writes a book about the cosmos; the heroine, Jocelle, is raped by her cousin Walter on his way to the war, and her aunt Martha takes a darkling, exalted view of the occurrence. Normally, I like reading about Kentucky: without what its publishers call "its prophetic music," *He Sent Forth a Raven* might have been a nice book.

Go Home Unicorn is an excellent thriller, in which biology and the occult mix. I found it too frightening to finish late at night. The scene when a disembodied female head of unutterable malignancy, followed by a wisp of ectoplasm, trails down an upper-class Montreal dinner table between the candles is particularly good. And I got very fond of the unicorn, who embarrassed the intellectual débutante so much. Unless you are too nervous, certainly read this book.

New Novels

Edward Anderson, *Hungry Men*; James Steele, *Conveyor*: John Peale Bishop, *Act of Darkness*; André Malraux, *The Royal Way*,

translated by Stuart Gilbert; R. H. Mottram, *Flower Pot End*;
Philip Henderson, *Events in the Early Life of Anthony Price*. Reviewed in *New Statesman*, October 12, 1935.

America goes on exporting readable novels. Many of them have any
amount of faults—it is a matter of temperament whether these put you
off or not—they are boisterous, unripe inside, slick in manner, or senti-
mentally naive. But they are about *something*; they get you somewhere;
they move. The camera work is so often excellent. They may irritate
but they seldom bore. It is true that the American literary novel—wads
of prose about high-class people's feelings—is often very dreary indeed:
emasculate, consciously rarefied. *Act of Darkness*, the third novel on this
list, at its worst comes dangerously near this, but it saves itself: there are
excellent passages; its author's gusto outweighs his love of distinction.
The first two are better: they have no cooked-up emotion. They ignore
personality, with its inside hangovers. People getting about so fast, in order to live, that they have no time to annotate regrets or keep on tapping
emotions to see if they ring true are a relief to be with sometimes. Century consciousness stamps these American books: this is an American
century, why balk at it? These people are assimilating what happens.
They have learned to maintain themselves, by a quick constant action of
the nerves, in what we still find an unfriendly element. American novels
are hardly ever nostalgic (for nostalgia see Mr. Mottram, below). What
they regret they exploit: the Old Kentucky Home has made Broadway.

Hungry Men is a picaresque novel about tramps—bums, hoboes. The
hunger in it is hunger, nothing to do with the soul; not a character knows,
throughout, where he will eat next. The men are not born vagrants but
that shifting workless mass, dislodged by the slump and with no future,
ranging the States in freight trucks or hitchhiking on state roads from
city to city, picking up what they can. The book, which is not pathetic, is
excellently written. Acel Stecker, the hero, began in a band and wants to
get back into one, but is willing to try anything. Things he successively
wants and has not got—a meal, a girl, cigarettes, a razor blade, his own
length to stretch on on any floor—assume a large importance, magnified
by desire. What he does get—the new suit, bought with his pay as a stew-
ard's mate on a ferry, Corinne, the black-and-white Oxfords—sees him
a long way. Largely, I think, because of its matter-of-factness and gusto,

this book is hard to discuss at all relevantly, and I have not room to quote here. It should certainly be read. It has no philosophy.

Conveyor is called a proletarian novel. It is an angry book: a picture of a speed-up in a leading Detroit motor works. The conditions shown are quite ghastly, like the beginning of a Russian film; but, oddly, the book has no political bias. The people in it have no time to be characters; they either enjoy or suffer. Jim Brogan starts with a pretty bungalow near the edge of the city, a desirable young wife, and a satisfactory child. The three are on very good terms. "The roses round the door make me love mother more"—there is no doubt that the amenities promote the affections. The Brogans end in a tenement, on squalid terms with each other, mutually hostile and suspicious. The book is not about personal relations—most of what happens happens inside a factory or in the all-night queues of workless men—but in a general picture of defeat and deterioration the family life of the Brogans plays its part. Jim Brogan would hate Moscow. His outlook is quite bourgeois: he loves possessions and only wants a fair deal. The disintegration of his pride in himself is frightening. *Conveyor* is not enjoyable, but it should not be missed.

Act of Darkness has a Virginian setting. The combination of lust and rotting colonial elegance is Faulkneresque, though Mr. Peale Bishop adds ideas of his own. The fifteen-year-old narrator's uncle Charlie is tried for rape on the accusation of the daughter of another county family, who would rather see him hang than admit that she was seduced. His trial, at which the nephew is, most unsuitably, present, takes up too great a part of the book: I think myself, aesthetically speaking, that some of the evidence might have been summarized. Personally, I can never resist the charm of a Virginian background, though we are given so much of it: red woods, shady sidewalks, cold eighteenth-century churches, tarnished drawing rooms, county family feeling—which seems still crazier here than it does anywhere else. Grandfather, the old Southern gentleman, never drinks before nine at night, then he drinks. "Whisky makes life supportable, even if it doesn't make it intelligible. Where's that nigger?" The doomed uncle, Charlie, his wife Caroline, and their house, which is her house, are very good, too. Ardista, the poor white girl, is Little Emily to the young narrator's David, but Charlie, on his way to the major catastrophe, does for Ardista too: his last victim, and his undoer, is an intellectual spinster friend of his wife's whom he has always disliked, so he does not know what came over him. Rape in Virginia, even if you are white, is apparently a capital offense, which heightens the interest. The early part of the book is overwritten and heavy, but the story speeds up as it goes along.

The Royal Way has been excellently translated by Mr. Stuart Gilbert, but should be read in French: a haze of oddness hangs over English words in their Malraux contexts. Two men, Vannec and Perkin, follow the overgrown "royal way" through the Siamese jungle to discover temples, hoping to bring back carvings. This is the plot: the subjects are, chiefly, death and eroticism. Parts of the book are like a Conrad novel written by Dostoevsky. The descriptions are magnificent and terrible. This is the only important book on the list today: it stands halfway down because it cannot be classified. Why should it take a Frenchman to be adult?

The two English books that follow are very thin. I cannot see why Mr. Mottram wrote *Flower Pot End*, a nostalgic novel about an unselfish clergyman in a rectory overlooking a quaint slum, his renegade brother, his faithful-hearted housekeeper Rose, who loves the renegade brother, and her niece Patsy, a fresh girl. There is not even much documentary interest, though slum clearance does come in. I suppose the town must be Norwich. This is one of those reputable novels that pad publishers' lists. But surely Mr. Mottram should have done better?

And surely Mr. Henderson should have restrained himself from publishing *Events in the Early Life of Anthony Price*? I can see that he may have felt it needed writing; it may even have done him good to write—in which case, of course, he was justified in doing so. But surely he should have kept it to show to friends? The writing is good enough to make one feel he may write a much better book, in which case he will regret this one. Of the reality of the experience in it there is no doubt, but experience, to have any value outside of oneself, needs to be related to something more than a personal sense of grievance. Let Mr. Henderson read *A Portrait of the Artist as a Young Man* again: it seems quite clear that he has read it once.

New Novels

Mikhail Sholokhov, *Virgin Soil Upturned*; Howard Spring, *Rachel Rosing*; John Brophy, *I Let Him Go*; Mrs. St. Loe Strachey,

The Frozen Heart; Simon Jesty, River Niger; Trygve Gulbrans-
sen, Beyond Sing the Woods. Reviewed in New Statesman, October 26, 1935.

Virgin Soil Upturned is a novel without a hero—or, rather, the hero is an
idea: collectivization—embodied, as the story continues, in the Gremyachy Village Stalin Collective Farm. From the characters, any vestige of
the romantic, a bourgeois tradition, has been entirely stripped. It is true
that Davidov, "a metal worker Communist, one of the 25,000 workers
mobilized by the Soviet Communist Party to organize collective farming," is, at times, gigantic in his persistence. For the people of Gremyachy,
a Don village, do not take to collective farming gladly. There is an under-
current of White intrigue. Evicted kulaks hang about the village, spreading disaffection and making for no good. Individualism and property
sense are still rampant—peasants who had voted for the collective farm
slaughter their livestock sooner than see them go there. The elected farm
manager turns out to be a snake, with White sympathies. The women
are, as ever, wayward and intractable: collectivization of fowl does not
appeal to them; later, news that Gremyachy grain is being deported for
use at a collective farm in another village precipitates a female riot, in
which Razmiotov, chairman of the Village Soviet, is debagged, and Davidov beaten up. Nagulov, a zealot, secretary of the Gremyachy Village
Communist Party, who has laid out a lukewarm supporter with the butt
of a pistol and gone too far in the matter of collectivizing the fowl, is
reproved at headquarters and expelled from the Party. Razmiotov has
led off badly by trading the blood bull imported for stock for a motor
bicycle—purpose unspecified. There is a hangover from religion about
the village, and sex is giving the same trouble as ever. Desire cannot be
socialized. Nagulov's pretty wife insists on wearing suspenders, carries on
with a kulak, and makes a dead set at Davidov when she has left home.
Razmiotov's mistress, a tiger woman, removes her goods from the collective farm by force, and starts going to church again . . . In the face of all
this, slowly but gathering momentum, the collective farm proceeds, like
a tractor toppling stickily over the brow of a hill.

Fanaticism, introspection, and persecution mania ravage this cast of
minor characters; there are shapeless quarrels and endless monologues.
The more you are ground down into the community, the more need you,

apparently, have to find yourself interesting. So that this remains a novel in the grand Russian tradition. The great light landscape, as ever, dominates everything—nights snapping with frost (and loud, round about Gremyachy, with the bellows of covertly slaughtered beasts), the burning of cold stars, anonymous plains. The book opens upon that everlasting romantic, the solitary horseman. The scenic writing is great with exhilaration and beauty. The break between Sholokhov's people and Turgenev's people stays exterior, political, arbitrary—no will can dictate what we are to feel or be. Signs of the times most appear in the prevalence of bullying—an authorized, high-class bullying of everyone in the name of everyone else. Two evictions of kulaks that occur in the book would aliment the worst dreams of a *Daily Mail* lady reader as to what may happen when the Reds get their way—people marching into the house and taking her fur coat, taking everything. As would, also, the aspirations of Nagulov, a simple soul, wife-deserted, learning English at nights in order to be with us when the Revolution is here.

> "So you've drunk the blood of your English working-classes, of the Indians and other oppressed nations? So you've exploited other men's labor? Stand up against the wall, you bloody reptile." That's all the conversation I shall have with them. They'll be the first words I shall learn. So that I can get them out without hesitating.

There is robust humor. A kulak's wife, in the course of being evicted, tries to make a getaway with a live goose, up to now her own, and a setting of goose eggs. Diemka, a collective worker, seizes the bird's head:

> Dribbling with spittle, her feet firmly planted against the step, the disheveled woman pulled the bird towards her. The goose had at first given voice to a stupid cry, but now it was silent, and evidently Diemka was choking it. But it flapped its wings madly, and white down and feathers whirled like snowflakes about the porch. It seemed that in another minute Diemka must be victorious and tear the half-dead goose from the woman's knotted hands. But at that moment the bird's feeble neck quietly cracked at the joints and came apart from the body. The woman's skirt flew over her head, and she tumbled thundering down from the porch,

her body bumping heavily on each step. Groaning with surprise, Diemka, holding only the goose's head, fell into the basket on the floor just behind him, and crushed the half-hatched eggs. A tremendous outburst of laughter shook the icicles from the roof.

The cossack's farewell to his ox, bound for the collective farm, is, on the other hand, very moving. On the whole, however, I cannot recommend *Virgin Soil Upturned* to lovers of animals. Nor, for the matter of that, to an at all nervous bourgeoisie. But the vitality and largeness of the book overcame my own apathy about collective farming. And there is more than vitality—Sholokhov's approach to his subject has a high bland quality, almost like amusement, that I suppose is art. If you are not squeamish, if you are reasonably disengaged from belongings, read *Virgin Soil Upturned*. And be thankful you do not *have* to—I note that: "By a Soviet order every supervisor of a Collective Farm is forced to read this book. Over 1,500,000 copies have been sold in Russia." One way to best sell.

Mr. Howard Spring takes us back to the bloody reptiles; to long sleek cars, rich rooms, hot hotels, mirrors, and Persian cats. And—one book being read hard on the top of the other—an almost equally odd world it seems. *Rachel Rosing* is one of those success novels with a sting in the tail, about someone making a series of objectives, then coming down finally over some minor error. It is not unlike a Bennett success novel, only more uneasy and less concrete. Rachel Rosing, the beautiful Manchester Jewess, starts down and out at Blackpool, but her good head and cold heart do brilliantly for her. Then, in her rich husband's house in Portman Square, she is, repeatedly, rude to an imperial orange Persian cat: also, she is offhand with her lover's sister. These two antagonisms combine, in one accident, to wreck her. She comes to a hideous end—virtually, it is an end. This unmodern moral tale, written with an Edwardian sophistication, is to be recommended for reading after dinner.

I Let Him Go is the history of a conscience. Mr. Brophy writes better than he tells a story. Several chapters read too much like essays; much of their excellence is irrelevant to the plot. The scene is Liverpool, London, Cairo. Should one hand one's young wife's murderer over to justice? Mr. Brophy's hero, for reasons shown, does not. The book is serious enough, both in its claims and in its qualities, to merit a fuller review, but I have not space here.

Mrs. Strachey's naively noble, mid-nineteenth-century heroine visits Paris and loses her heart to Lamartine during the 1848 Revolution. Their heroic mutual feeling for one another comes nearest expression in a talk over a fire in which he has burnt some papers. Margaret returns to England, cold with sorrow, and marries a patient lover. The settings are good; the book is well documented and written with dignity. It deserves, and no doubt has found already, many readers.

River Niger is hysterical and explosive. It is about voodoo and black blood, has a Cornish setting and, were it intelligible, need not have been dull. T. E. Lawrence wrote a generous letter about it, which is printed as preface to the book. "Its verbal ping-pong was too clever for me. I saw I was only a retired colonel." He detects Faulkner, Firbank, Meredith, and "some Priestleyness." To this I can only add, query, James Branch Cabell.[8] He adds: "It is almost wanton in its merit." Lawrence read to the end with admirable patience. I stuck like a fly in the style halfway through. At the beginning of each part there is a quotation from Faulkner, who, I think, has it, in the long run, though I thought I smelt Powys, too.[9] But there must be a Mr. Jesty somewhere. Much depends on how you feel about voodoo. "A Tartarean night that fouled the very will. A scream from Judy split this dome of hell."

After this, *Beyond Sing the Woods*. This Scandinavian novel is clean and cumbrous. If you are easily bored, or if you do not like your emotions about nature dragged up and inflated, preferring to have them left quiet and even cryptic, you may not like this book. But I take it to be a good Scandinavian novel. It covers two generations. The men are men of the woods, virile but not impulsive. A certain amount happens: a bear troubles the neighborhood, ice breaks under a sledge-load of people, a crag topples into a valley, crushing the body of a son of the house who has already been stabbed on his way back from a ball. "Summer came, and autumn and winter; spring again and summer . . . . the years passed." The windows of Bjorndal manor are often dim with ice, and quite often a funeral winds away. The women are melancholy, but less dull than the men; the woods continue to surround everything; the atmosphere is timeless. All the same, this novel is honest and not a fake. German critics praise it highly, and I can see why. To those who read Scandinavian novels with pleasure I recommend this one, very good of its kind.

New Novels

Rebecca West, *The Thinking Reed*; Catharine Whitcomb, *I'll Mourn You Later*; Hans Duffy, *Lucasta's Wedding*; Martin Hare, *A Mirror for Skylarks*; P. G. Wodehouse, *Young Men in Spats*. Reviewed in *New Statesman*, April 11, 1936.

This week's batch of four novels, with Mr. Wodehouse as an annex, should make good Easter reading: there is still time to get them on Saturday. They are not all light but they are exhilarating; their trend is grim but, like detective stories, they give one a cozy feeling of immunity: in one, the characters are unthinkably unfortunate in a way one likes to believe peculiar to the French, while the three others are about the sorrows of the rich—not simply those general sorrows against which even money cannot defend one, but the fatigues, the frustrations, the fear of not giving oneself as good a time as one ought—inherent, apparently, in the possession of money. Their implicit morality gins one up; the modestly spent Easter will be enjoyed with a touch of smugness; rich readers, if any, will find companions in misery. There seems no doubt that wealth does produce a mentality subject to special ills; if it is not one's own these remain agreeably foreign. An Easter novel should be a day out. Unshared capitalist pleasures keep a good deal of glamor; myself, I like to read about subtly gorgeous interiors, ballrooms, baccarat tables, pink southern mountains seen across private bays, and people having what *I* should regard as a good time—though that they do not enjoy it may be consoling.

Miss Rebecca West's *The Thinking Reed* is a big book, both in bulk and in subject; there is a good deal more matter than the afflictions of wealth here. Her writing covers a really immense field with an air of athletic ease: intellectual writing, in the exact sense, but at the same time flexible, vivid, and never cold. *The Thinking Reed* seems to me to be the classic novel, such as is not often written today: imagination (or vision) and sheer top-form professional ability now seldom go together; it is hard to find a mean between satire and good faith. The settings have depth, they are not only painted; they are not abstract, or there to illustrate moods. The characters expand, they behave inevitably; you almost feel a quiver when they collide, and hear, if they are women, their dresses rustle. The book as a book appears to me to have almost no imperfections; it rounds itself off, it is impossible to think beyond it. (I do not know whether this is a criticism or not.)

Isabelle Sallafranque is a proper heroine—young, beautiful, gifted, and very wealthy, an American with French blood, living in Paris. Her first husband has been the victim of his own wild flying; her reigning lover, André, makes her the victim of irrational scenes. Herself, she is determined to be rational, to "live according to her own soul, to describe her course through life as her intellect might have been able to plan it." But she and the Marc Sallafranque whom, having escaped from André, she marries, are, both being immensely rich, moved relentlessly as the hands of a wound clock around a dial of vicissitudes and pleasures. Their married life is "made as difficult by Marc's wealth and position as if his work had compelled them to live in an unhealthy climate." The unhealthiness never dissipates; when the Sallafranques do ever leave Paris something between subservience and fatalism compels them to visit either St. Moritz or Le Touquet. Their friends are horrible, and are always there. So they go their doubtful way, shadowed by the implacable lyrical hatred of M. Campofiore, an official who, on behalf of the government which subsidized Marc's factory in the Pas de Calais after the war, is always on their tracks. The time of the book is pre-slump: in the Sallafranques' set expense is no object with anyone.

Life treats Isabelle ironically. Violence is shocking to her, but twice it becomes impossible to tear herself free of the tissue of the minor but dreadful fate without it. So that twice she is forced into staging a violent scene: the first loses her a suitor she would have preferred to Marc, a Virginian with whom she hoped to be rationally happy, the second, her unborn child, around whom she had come to center her hopes of sanity . . . Between Marc—grotesque, dynamic, with "indiarubbery sides" and tough springy hair like a dog's—and Isabelle there exists the strong tie of unlikeness, often of opposition. "Hardly ever did he move in the sphere of logic and analysis which was her natural home; and she looked at him with infatuation, recognizing that in this long lighted room of well-made and glittering men and women he alone had the dark bloom of romantic and passionate things." She had married him, when the shocked Virginian failed her, to escape the artificial violences of André. There is certainly nothing artificial about Marc: he sweats, he drinks, he shows off out of sheer good faith; once he kicks a waiter on the behind. Marc is as sympathetic as Isabelle is ponderous: Miss West's irony is so fine as to be (no doubt intentionally) baffling.

Wealth is not the motif of *I'll Mourn You Later*: all the same, moneyed leisure, with its fretting alternatives, provides the springboard from which the chief women characters take their nervous jumps. The book, an American first novel, exceedingly well-written, is tense, brilliant, and nervy, like an almost too fine summer's day in a new place. From the suavest Boston of facials and sheer stockings come the widowed Elizabeth, a gentle club-woman, her spirited married daughter Henrietta, and Henrietta's husband Bill, to reopen for a few days, for Elizabeth's mother's funeral, the old family home in a New England village. The scene is set here, and is idyllic—white houses standing back on their lawns, flickering shady sidewalks, a June hush. But the atmosphere is electric: ancient family feeling comes out like a smell the instant the house is opened; moreover, the neighborhood is riddled with insanity. Two old family friends have toppled over the edge of that classic New England eccentricity into mania; a friend of Elizabeth's girlhood is back from Virginia with her once beautiful face kicked off by a horse. Official lunacy has its headquarters next door: in the asylum a lunatic boy howls punctually till he dies of an accident at Elizabeth's feet. Elizabeth's ne'er-do-well brother and his bedraggled wife are staying over the funeral; in the course of their visit a horrible suicide and later on a seduction take place in the faded, elegant, family home. Much happens in ten days. But the past has let in on Elizabeth such a rush of disturbing sensation that events stay exterior. A little troubled, in uncrushable white linen, she dreams, regrets, and ponders. Henrietta, the practical ecstasies of young American marriage (see *Appointment in Samarra*)[10] having been interrupted by Bill's return to Boston, is less fortunate. It is hard to give the character of this odd, distinguished book. Against the background of horror and summer sweetness the two women stand out—articulate, elegant, sensuous, almost too civilized.

Lucasta's Wedding is a funny, pungent, apparently artless book, done with a high degree of accomplishment. It is set in a world in which young ladies cannot go shopping without a maid. Lucasta does not enjoy being an heiress much: having read early a history of the popes, her days are darkened by an awful delusion about her uncle. From the Sunday when Mr. Nanson picks his way through the Gloucestershire buttercups to lunch with the Monallys, his niece's destiny is inextricably entangled with that unscrupulous, high-spirited family's. Blonde, sweet-natured, stubborn, and fatalistic, Lucasta is very nice. There are pictures of Anglo-Florence, of a pink dripping castle in Ireland, of London. Hans Duffy has done the whole thing brilliantly.

A Mirror for Skylarks is a French novel by an Irishwoman, in English. Mme. de Montlevé, incompetent and angelically good, struggles to run a pension in a Parisian suburb. Her pensionnaires are a human zoo; their frightfulness almost exceeds the bounds of art. To the pension, with its shadow of debt and human squalor, returns from school Irène, the Montlevé daughter, childish without illusions, cool-headed, sensual, to be surprised by a passion for a nice English boy there. Their views of love conflict and the end is tragic. I feel a good many people may not like this book, and recommend it, therefore, with a touch of defiance. Recommend it I do.

Young Men in Spats is a Drones Club book. Eggs, Beans, and Crumpets tell each other the tales. There is an upsetting one about cats, and one about Tennyson. Freddie Widgeon has no luck. (See comment on page 126.) There are three Mr. Mulliners at the end.

The Weather in the Streets

Rosamond Lehmann, *The Weather in the Streets*. *New Statesman*, July 11, 1936.

Miss Lehmann belongs to a generation that, for the most part, finds maturity difficult. Its emotion—congested, one cannot know how synthetic— is, though not pleasant to suffer, easier to suffer than to express: there has come to be perfected, for dealing with emotion, a frigid kind of bravado, irony with a current of mawkishness, in which the public school spirit has an unhappy counterpart. Many good novels show a muffled dismay. *One* sort of emotional novel is not, unhappily, rare: it is, as a rule, so shocking as to leave one with the impression that only second-rate people are uninhibited now. There is a masochistic frankness, but almost no spontaneity.

Miss Lehmann is an exception to all this. The most remarkable, the most natural of her qualities is the power to give emotion its full value and play, to transcribe into prose emotion that is grown up and spontaneous, fatalistic but not abject, sublime without being high-pitched, infusing life but knowing its own isolation. She attempts to make no relation — necessarily a false relation — between emotion, with its colossal, unmoving subjective landscape, and outside life with its flickering continuity of action and fact. She writes, in fact, to underline the disparity, which is the subject of *The Weather in the Streets* — its plot being the story of a love affair.

> Beyond the glass casing I was in was the weather, were the winter streets in rain, wind, fog, in the fine frosty days and nights, the mild damp grey ones. Pictures of London weather the other side of the glass — not reaching the body . . . . In this time there was no sequence, no development. Each time was new, was different, existing without relation to before and after; all the times were one and the same. [And later.] Now I see what an odd duality it gave to life; being in love with Rollo was all-important, the times with him were the only reality; yet in another way they had no existence in reality. It must have been the same with him.

Circumstances increase this natural isolation of love. Olivia, sensitive, wary, tentative, and a touch defiant, discouraged, and in her own view declassed by a futile marriage, now over, becomes the mistress of Rollo Spencer — assured, charming, easy, and essentially fortunate. The defensive husk she has acquired irks her a little and does not quite fit. Like most solitary people playing their own hand, she is absorbed, if not always fortified, by an intensive inner life. In any world — with her family, on the night she dines with the Spencers, with her London friends, so gentle, bleak, asexual, intimate — Olivia is alien, uncertain, nostalgic. She is like someone sitting a long way from the fire, but near a mirror reflecting the firelight. Whereas Rollo is more than an inmate of *his* world, his world is part of his nature; she sees in him the strong and happy flowering of it. From this world, now their love affair has begun, she is bound to know him apart; she is conscious that, in being with her, he is dissociated, however happily, from the major part of himself. Their love has for him the exhilaration of island life, whereas for her it is a continent.

The figure of Rollo Spencer, sometimes no more than a big, fatal silhouette, sometimes seen in strong light—with his "upper class charm," his intensities of purpose, his confusion of motive—is magnificently put in. Olivia's awareness of her lover never exceeds the bounds of love or art; she apprehends him rather than observes him; in thought, in the narrative of her consciousness, the idiom of love is never departed from—which, pitching the book so perfectly that there is never a drop in it, is in itself very fine art. The changes of person—from the third to the first in part 2 (giving the effect of blurred, too close-up, climactic, subjective vision), then back to the third again in part 3, for sadder detachment, a sense of brutal collision with the outside world—are very telling. Apart from this, there is not a single intrusion of "technique," though technically there are few flaws in the book. As a writer, Miss Lehmann's competence is so great that she has been able to sink her competence in her subject. There is no showing off—which is too rare. Her style has a sensuous, vital simplicity, to which her brain gives edge.

No one can write better than Miss Lehmann about the aesthetics, the intimate charm—much more than charm—of luxury, the unwary civility of the old world, privilege, ease, grace. She has always been able to place, and to evaluate, glamor. She has also a great command of contrast—between groups of people, settings, seasons of the year, moods, different idioms in talk. Olivia's solitary though gregarious life in London, her visits home, her times with Rollo Spencer make a strong triangle in the structure of the book. The Curtis family life, with its dialogue, is delicious. There are few "minor" characters in *The Weather in the Streets*: Kate, now a cool young matron, Kate's children, Mrs. Curtis, Lady Spencer, Marigold, Etty, and Anna are more than a mere supporting cast; they have an opposing reality of their own, and play a positive part in the plot. Miss Lehmann has accomplished a remarkably different thing; she has added, palpably, ten years of age to her characters since their first appearance in *Invitation to the Waltz*. Some features have hardened and others blurred; that first lyrical freshness has left Olivia and Kate.

Everything that went to make Miss Lehmann's three other novels is present in *The Weather in the Streets*, and still more has been added, which is as it should be. This book, which has lovely qualities that are inimitably its writer's, is outstanding as a sheer piece of good work.

This Freedom

Eleanor F. Rathbone, Erna Reiss, Ray Strachey, Alison Nielans, and Mary Agnes Hamilton, *Our Freedom and Its Results*, edited by Ray Strachey. *New Statesman*, October 31, 1936.

The woman's freedom movement was a revolution in miniature: its implications were, and remain, immense. It struck that giant bourgeois, the English nineteenth century, in the midriff, at the point where convenience and sentiment were most closely allied. The pioneers were not only indomitable, but well-armed: "exposures" were still shocking; truths could still, at that time, be powerfully distasteful: now they are bromides which slip off the tired moral sense. The decencies were at a premium; the chain store had not yet succeeded the private shopkeeper, and the Christian ethic, avowed with a good deal of bustle if not practiced, offered a weak flank. With the growth of the middle class and of the dominance of the moneymaker, the oppressed woman had multiplied like rabbits in Australia: she was the fruit of a graceless society. The suffering of the poor woman had been generic; the upper-class woman, in a structure of manners, had been able to play her own hand adroitly or not. The middle-class woman, secure technically, fed, boarded, and clothed, with some leisure and literate, looked round to discover herself disregarded personally and economically, as well as socially in any broad sense. Revolt seldom starts in the ranks of *manqué* people: it is positive people who turn on an order they overtop, and it was with positive and exceptional women that the woman's movement began. Their attack on property in its most sacred and muddled sense, their comment on exploitation before the word had been uttered, was so outrageously timed as to be telling. Prejudice shuddered, shifted, retreated—though still muttering. A man-made war gave impatient women their opening, and no ally came out of the peace better. A good deal remains to be righted (as these five essayists show), but, broadly, the woman's movement has accomplished itself. Though the upheaval already seems exceedingly distant, our freedom, to quote Mrs. Strachey, is in fact less than a generation old. Our sex, because it is *the* sex, is still on its promotion: it has news value, and is subject to constant comment.

But interest has shifted to a more deadly struggle. The women leaders bent a system their way: the time had not come yet to strike at its roots. Solidarity was of the first importance to them; it would have been fatal to split over an issue.

Our Freedom and Its Results is a survey and an assessment. These five essays on change, on a revolution that was at once swift and gradual, complement one another ably without overlapping: inevitably, the same points have to be stressed, and inevitably the same conclusions drawn. Experts have been recruited by Mrs. Strachey: their outlook is disengaged, their writing lucid. Miss Erna Reiss has condensed a volume into her "Changes in Law," which, with its marginal dates, is impressive and clear. Mrs. Strachey, dealing with "Changes in Employment," commands a cool-headed rhetoric. Miss Rathbone's "Changes in Public Life" and Miss Alison Nielans's "Changes in Sex Morality" summarize the two best-known advances in the movement, and flag out the ground held. Mrs. Hamilton has, in "Changes in Social Life," to cover ground trodden faceless by popular journalism: her subject, less concrete than the four others, has been the prey of opinion for many years. This makes the excellence of Mrs. Hamilton's essay—informed, humane, dispassionate—all the more appear. Placed, rightly, last in the book, it gives the foregoing essays relation to one another and to itself. Morals, with their inevitable expediency, are the outcome of any order, and change with it: manners are morals in pleasing or unpleasing flower. Manners now, in a world so much affected by women—the aesthetics of manners, their implication—are, broadly, the theme of Mrs. Hamilton's essay.

And what now? So much has been consolidated: the necessary excitement has subsided, but, with anticlimax allowed for, women are still, apparently, staying the course. They are free to do what they ought, what they can, what they have it in them to do: they have no excuse for not doing it. They face a clean, drab road, denuded of sentiment, and ought to be feeling a wind from the horizon blowing about their brows. They are, in fact, untrammeled. But there is a negativity in the feminine nature that does not so much check ambition as dissolve it. An innate passivity, more than biological, makes one more glad, and apter, to reflect life than to affect it. Professions a woman may practice with any success without disengaging herself from this cloudy side of her nature are few. The home, with that subtle communication with objects and people, is the tempting if no longer the natural sphere.

Unrestriction has brought with it the burden of flat identity, and inhibiting free choice. Who has not seen that look of distaste and apathy in the eye of a young girl being asked about her career? The few occupations or practices that women really enjoy as much as they enjoy enjoying themselves are those in which it is intolerable to be second-rate, and in which second-rateness is patent immediately. They face up to routine work with the same thoughtless philosophy with which they approached housework and the care of futile relatives. Their incentive and enemy is transferred emotion. The content of Mrs. Strachey's book is dismaying: we are like the children of a self-made man, aware with chagrin and pride of the early struggles, arraigned by an inheritance we cannot use fully, our own incapacity all the time bearing us down. The war that got us freedom knocked out our aspirations. As for the relations between the sexes, in which our newfound calmness and liability were to achieve so much, they are more articulate perhaps, yes, but as muddled as they ever were and considerably more dowdy.

Little, however, has been claimed for the future of women by these five sensible writers, and one must be grateful to them for showing as little impatience with the present as they do. A valid incentive, an emotion even, is now lacking: one can no longer desire what one has. The two great escapes remain for both sexes: art and love. But historically, apart from its other excellences, Mrs. Strachey's book is full of value, and should be honorably received. Abuses corrected are too quickly forgotten. For the grim work of the women pioneers, for their voluntary gracelessness, we are dumbly grateful, but we are overpowered by it, and intolerably shown up. We enjoy an integrity, a safety, a leisure whose lack we cannot envisage, because we have never lacked them. The repercussions of a moral idea, of a disinterested indignation on public opinion, are fascinating to hear of: the opposition's façade, even, makes one nostalgic: that was a fine fort of folly, worthy of powder and shot.

Short Stories

Stella Benson, *Collected Short Stories*; Edward O'Brien, editor, *The Best Short Stories of 1936: English and American*. New *Statesman*, December 5, 1936.

Stella Benson's death has left a gap in writing: that there cannot be another novel of hers this year, next year, or ever breeds more than melancholy, an irritated feeling of deprivation—of interruption, almost as though the wire on which she had been speaking were senselessly cut. Her silence still seems accidental. She was unself-consciously odd; her quick, personal writing came like spurts of confidence from a naturally abstracted person, between long silent journeys of curiosity across continents or in her own mind. The world she ranged was fantastic, but she saw it objectively, with geographical features, craters, and ridges able to be mapped out. She presented her maps of fantasy matter-of-factly: she was not an escapist; she lived in her own element, dealt with her own facts. Human queerness seemed to her rational, and she gave it its place in what rational life there is: her creatures are curious only in being unnervingly likely: they have the universal sub-mentality—they are ostentatious, shy, hopeful, frustrated, anxious to boast, unable to communicate, a race of ex-gods or unhappy fairies, in ignominious bodies. Desire, its power of enlarging the person who feels it and of making its object momentous and clear, interested her: she did not measure desire, or rate it by its object, and therefore gave no special place to love. In fact love, as a sentiment, disintegrates at her touch; her Mr. Robinson's feeling for the brood of young mice, his nostalgia for the group of shadowy diners on the hotel terrace have more hopeless dignity than a sexual passion. The beloved is, in her view, no more than the mouse, the pet of prisoned fancy; she pities the self-bound self. Pity, with her, is lively, sapient, penetrating but cold, with a mocking edge to it: a sort of fairy pity. But pity was the deep source of what emotion she had: she suffered the intellectual for his humbling muddles, the successful for their aberrations, the confident for their qualms. She could anatomize vanity without spite or fervor; she was a satirist with no moral stance. She was innocent of archness and whimsicality—those foes of the English fanciful writer—for archness and whimsicality condescend. Her feeling for human beings was incidental: she was a novelist, bound to write about them, so she swung round a sixth sense, a cosmic imagination, to bear on them vaguely, almost fortuitously, but with a fatal exactness. She liked better landscape, dogs, and moving figures when they were like ants. Mass mentality was her major nightmare, and she had many: the American nation, in which she chose to locate this, was an abstract monster to her. She liked private enterprise—in pirates, angels, brigands, inquiring Orientals, indomitable shabby women, dogs.

These connected short stories show Stella Benson's proclivities, her powers, her prejudices. They are valuable, apart from their own merit, as the last writing of hers that we shall get, unless there are letters. She wrote so well—the poetic plainness and vitality of her style cannot be enough praised—that whatever she did was, in different degrees, good. She was not a short storyist: these stories give the effect of style and imagination being applied, with ability, to an unfamiliar form. Clever people can do anything—but she was used to exploring any chosen subject more continuously. There are several fantasies (of which the first, "The Awakening," is the best). The straight short stories seem to be germs of novels: one wants to see them expand. "The Desert Islander," "Hairy Carey's Son," and "The Man Who Missed the Bus" are disturbing and excellent. And there is the satire "Tchotl," hardly a story—one cannot all the time be fair to Americans.

Americans are more than fair to themselves in Mr. O'Brien's *Best Stories of 1936: English and American*. In gusto and verbosity they overpower the English. A sort of neutral dullness—mistakenly called highbrow— too often settles on the English writer when he attempts, as he now often does, this form. The stories in this collection are examples of the short story written for its own sake (as opposed to the stories of Stella Benson, written for fun, or to order). Proper revulsion against decorated, ingenious writing has brought in, over here, a flat, clattering style in which one hears the typewriter. If anonymity in style be the objective, this has been achieved—it would be difficult, opening the English half of the book at random, to tell one writer's work from half a dozen others'—but achieved at a loss of the color, tempo, and temper that are a great part of style. There is, also, monotony of subject: sex-troubles of inarticulate young people recur and recur. The noncommercial—or art-for-art's-sake—short story would not have so few commercial openings in England if it were not so often academic in feeling and complacently dull. We look elsewhere for moral exercises: no one wants short stories that are a labor to read. The best stories in this half—Arthur Calder-Marshall's "Straw Hat," T. O. Beechcroft's "May-Day Celebrations," H. E. Bates's "The Mill," G. F. Green's "A Death in the Family"—are differentiated and vigorous. Leslie Halward has written better stories than "The

Mother." Christopher Isherwood shows a brief, able sketch. None of the other short stories ought to be damned, but they do not collect well: there is too much of the same thing.

American story writers certainly have a start here: their idiom is striking, their subjects have foreign charm. Several American stories in this volume do suffer, also, from literary blight, or are self-consciously high-class—"Annunciation" is a bad case of this. But on the whole their half has variation and speed. The two manners in American writing—the staccato, the prosy—are well exhibited here: the best of the stories commit themselves to neither. Dorothy McCleary's "The Shroud" has a gruesome vivacity. Tess Slessinger, who cannot have written a dull page, is fairly, if not handsomely, represented by "A Life in the Day of a Writer": she is young, but she has her dangers ahead. Almost all the stories are adequate; some err on the homely, chatty side. William Faulkner is, inevitably, there.

An Unknown Society

Conrad M. Arensberg, *The Irish Countryman: An Anthropological Study. The Listener*, April 28, 1937.

At the outset of his agreeable book—based on six lectures he delivered at Harvard—Dr. Arensberg disposes of the popular misconception of anthropology, then makes clear its actual nature, intentions, scope. "We are prone," he says, "to think of the anthropologist as a collector of strange facts about savages, and, at best, semi-civilized peoples." This error, which met him in County Clare, had been my own: I am relieved to find it taken as pretty general. That view of the science of man as esoteric, forbidding, has, Dr. Arensberg says, been made obsolete by changes, by a widening, in the nature of the science itself. Anthropology has come into closer touch, interacts and advances with the younger sciences on promotion now: what it may have lost in height it has (I gather) gained in accessibility. Dr. Arensberg's argument is deep, though clear; it is to this effect: there is no exaltation of the primitive for its own sake, and there is no isolation of phenomena; primitive society is, simply, society in which the primitive elements present in all societies appear plainly and are not yet deformed.

Dr. Arensberg took, for his survey, a region just inland from the Clare coast, and the community living there. The region is inaccessible ("unspoilt," in tourists' terms) and almost untouched by change—which anywhere in Ireland works slowly enough. The people, courtly and unsuspicious, showed their ways to the stranger without comment. Here the life of that little landowner, the Irish small farmer, continues in unbroken tradition, in, for observation, its purest form. The pattern, on a poetic and somber ground, is open, ordered, repetitive: one can inhabit Ireland and only half see it; to the traveler seeing Ireland as a picture it may never make its existence felt. The County Clare small farmer, like others throughout the country, works his land with his family, hires no labor, consumes what he produces, and has little over to trade. Markets (the "strong" farmer's disaster) thus hardly affect him; he is his own master; his land is his world—a world single in interest, often remote in space. On the hedge-crossed green plains and up the harsh sides of mountains, these white cottage farms are dotted across Ireland: they are more than numerous, they *are* the country itself. Standing each in its own few acres of tillage and meadow, they are approached by long boireens that fray off from the byroads: each is a state in itself, patriarchally governed. Here the rule of the man of the house is absolute: his consort has her own dignity; having brought in her fortune, she maintains by endless and self-directed work her place. The children work on the land; while they still attend school they are the news-bringers; their subjection to the family interest is entire. The closeness of the family corporation is broken only when the son chosen to marry (not always the eldest son) marries, and brings his contracted-for bride home, with *her* fortune. Then the old couple retire in honor, to the West Room; the brothers and sisters disperse; a new reign begins.

Brothers and sisters disperse—emigrate, go to England, go to the towns. But the family tie stays unbroken; it strengthens when it must stretch; it is deep down, below surface emotion, and plays a big part in the practical structure of life. The farmer does not stand alone; he has behind him—and by him at any crisis—a great system of relatives, his own and his wife's. The comparative slightness and brittleness of the family tie in

England leads many Irish to find the English nature shallow; they have often, also, an inherent contempt for landless people.

Catholicism, with its imposed mystical order, is, Dr. Arensberg shows, the keystone of this unquestioning, ordered, and, in its own way, ceremonial life of remote farms. The supernatural is always present, like moisture, in the air of the West. Outside religion, and in a sort of neutral relation to it, are "the other people," the fairies; and the dead never depart, they congest family life. The past is, there, the most powerful part of the present. And, having their share in the past, the old men are dominating.

Dr. Arensberg notes the protraction, in Irish people, of a strange, negative youth. The unmarried man stays "a boy" into the seventies—listless, placid, with a blank, kind, blue eye. The boy only graduates when he marries, and marriages are made late; they wait on the father's will. Celibacy is common, and not thought a disaster. Sexual love plays little part in life: natures are oriented another way. The young men (some in their forties), negligible but carefree, gather, at nights or on holy days, at the bridges and crossroads; the decent unmarried girls keep company with one another. The majestic old men sit by fires and talk.

A delightful chapter of *The Irish Countryman* is devoted to Shops, Pubs, and Fairs—the interrelation of country with country town. Dr. Arensberg brings to his subject, besides a first-rate equipment for reasoning observation, the best kind of newcomer's open-mindedness. His style is excellent—though he does use some hideous, I suppose unavoidable, words. *The Irish Countryman: An Anthropological Study* is an absorbing, and never obscure, book. Let no plain reader be frightened off by the subtitle (as I nearly was myself) and let no one consider that enough about Ireland has been written already: this is a quite new contribution, not to be missed.

Ben Jonson

C. H. Herford and Percy Simpson, editors, *Ben Jonson: Volume V. Volpone, or The Fox. Epicoene, or The Silent Woman. The Alchemist. Catiline*; L. C. Knights, *Drama and Society in the Age of Ben Jonson. New Statesman*, May 8, 1937.

There has been, in regard to Ben Jonson, just the slightest campaign of intimidation; taste seemed to have formed round him a pretty close borough. Intellect (in its most knotty, male, and forbidding sense) has been stressed in the plays, by the critics in exaltation, at the expense of nearer, sensuous qualities. His lovers like so well to find him recondite that his plays have been set apart, for the common reader, as special, abstruse, and cold, the cognoscenti's pleasure. The plays have not, by reputation, that enlarging, heroic extravagance to which, in Tourneur, Ford, Webster, the common fancy turns, these days, for release—they have been made to sound like the first note of fancy's knell. As compensation-literature they promise little. Other Elizabethans' godlike infantilism makes them rank high for comfort; their violent world corresponds to that of most private fantasy, which the emotions, with their *espagnolisme*,[11] govern, in which the fanatic is supreme. To the child's-eye view, brought more and more to poetry, Jonson shows disconcertingly adult, at once recondite and *terre à terre*. His morality (an austere note) is constantly emphasized.

Morality is a strong form of perception: as such, at its strongest, it blunts or bends on the muddle nowadays. It has come, in practical life, to stand for little more than an ineffective comment. Art, however, still needs to use it; it may be implicit but it has to be strong. By the plumb-straightness of lines and trueness of angles any work of mind is, ultimately, judged: fancy may diverge from the upright, but there must be an upright. There must be, in literature, the mind's disengaged comment on engaged emotion—this *is* the work's morality. In this sense, morality is more than inherent in, it is the very nature of, the Ben Jonson plays' superb competence. What has been, possibly, overlooked in the plays is how much the moral intellect has been given to feed on—or, in other terms, through what depths it drops a plumb line.

The sensuous element is immense. This is Renaissance theater: in those days one had a world at the fingertips, and the fingertips had not thickened. Immediacy of sensation comes through the language—concrete, and with an exact touch. The boom was at its height; wealth came in at every port. Magnetic new precious objects were on the market; each brought a world with it; luxury meant sublimation, not just dull expenditure. Learning, with its range of subtle experience, Latin elegance, outlandish mystery all struck the English shore. The world was not yet mapped; experience had no limits; a new mistress was an America. Intellect quickened love. The table soared into art, above the levels of subsistence or gluttony.

> . . . we will eat our mullets,
> Sous'd in high-countrey wines, sup phesants egges,
> And haue our cockles, boild in siluer shells,
> Our shrimps to swim againe, as when they liu'd
> In a rare butter, made of dolphins milke,
> Whose creame do's look like opalls.

Mammon's "I will haue all my beds, blowne vp; not stuft: Downe is too hard—etc.," Volpone's speech to Celia over the jewels, and a dozen more passages all show a lyrical freshness in greed itself, that first innocent flush of pleasure in the palace hotel—however much the context lowered the dream. Desire of objects, representations of pleasure offered their full bloom to Jonson's scalpel. He cut just deep enough to show the melancholy, the corruption beneath.

The force and speed of intellect going through these four plays—three major comedies and the tragedy *Catiline*—generate their first quality: dramatic excitement. The tension of the language, its oppositions, the play of concrete images make every page theater. *Volpone* is, apart from everything else, social comedy at its cruelest height, and *The Alchemist*, with its crookish hilarity, its double crossings, its showdowns, is readymade, the first-rate scenario. *Catiline*, for all its menacing longueurs, comes back and back to the close-up: it never fatally soars off into a wordy void. Each play, spherical, revolves fast and steadily on the axis of its idea. Plot spins the passion.

These four plays have one subject: the obsessed person, the person of one idea. From the vantage point that obsession gives, he perceives in others the greeds, delusions, and vanities that are exploitable, that are to serve his ends. The megalomaniac is curiously empowered. One dominating and single view or purpose gives each of these plays unity. They are areas mapped in the specialist's own terms. Morose, in *The Silent Woman*, is an exception: his desire is negative, so he is a negative figure, outwitted before he enters—the comedy, embroidering his defeat, is accordingly more complex, less centralized than the others. But

Volpone, Subtle, Catiline are positive and effective; they work with tools they despise — tools, sub-passions, whose very shoddiness makes them splinter and cut the user's hand. The divagations of greed — avarice, lust, snobbishness — are pressed flat, like horrid ferns, between every page of the plays. Was Jonson really anti-acquisitive, or was he magnetized to the instinct by what it offered his art?

Here are fine, fertile, extroverted crooks, not wasting a moment, not eating themselves like Bosola. They have no metaphysical worries; even ghosts are imperious: "Do'st thou not know me, Rome?" Hilarious complicity, the confederate spirit, never got better play. There is the grand alliance of Dol and Face:

> DOL: Yes, say lord *Generall*, how fares our campe?
> FACE: As, with the few, that had entrench'd themselues
> Safe, by their discipline against a world, Dol:
> And laugh'd, within those trenches, and grew fat
> With thinking on the booties, Dol, brought in
> Daily, by their small parties. This dear houre,
> A doughtie *Don* is taken, with my Dol;
> And thou maist make his ransome, what thou wilt,
> My *Dousabell*: He shall be brought here, fetter'd
> With thy faire lookes, before he sees thee; and throwne
> In a downe-bed, as darke as any dungeon;
> Where thou shalt keepe him waking, with thy drum;
> Thy drum, my Dol; thy drum.

There are stampedes, but no demoralization; the master crook deserves well, like a good whip.

Mr. Knights's study, which should be read, relates the age that made food for these plays to our own age in terms of social and economic ideas. He discusses the sixteenth-century boom, with the unrest and flood of greed it let in, the breakup of the simpler order, the thrust up of the rentier class, upheaving the values that kept it down, the complexity, vitality, and uneasiness the upthrust gave society, the distress below, the abuse of nobility. He dates back the connection between hard money and subtle sense, and shows how gold from America fostered the humanities. He shows the seedling, then, of the modern evil, now grown to its height. His work fills in the plays' background, gives further point to illusions, lights up the texture.

For the Herford and Simpson editorship of this Volume V of Ben Jonson, the accessibility and pertinence of the notes, the excellence of the type, we have once more to be grateful.

Agreeable Reading

Lady Carbery, *The Farm by Lough Gur*; Reardon Conner, *A Plain Tale from the Bogs. New Statesman*, October 9, 1937.

Happily, taste in books about Ireland, or books coming from Ireland, differs as widely as taste about everything else. Irish output increases and is extensive; the English public, whatever its predilections—gunmen, the Little People, slums, islands, post-Joyce adolescences, or upper-class nostalgias ("God be with the old days!")—has been brought to see there is no norm. It is unlikely that *The Farm by Lough Gur* and *A Plain Tale from the Bogs*, for all their similarity of format and title, will find themselves on the same drawing-room table for long. They *are* both, in their own way, drawing-room table books. They stand for two views of life which are incompatible. But happily, as I say, there are drawing-room tables enough. Into the fierce, leisureless household with no drawing room, neither, I feel, should properly find its way.

Lady Carbery's book is the transcript of a Mrs. Mary Fogarty's memories of her childhood and youth on a County Limerick farm. The transcription, on its own merits, seems to me almost faultless—unaffected, lucid, just colloquial enough. Mrs. Fogarty's past is given memory value— that is to say, the style encloses the past in the glassy light one sees in a south of Ireland sunset, in which there appears the landscape of an island of saints, a scene set for exaltations and tenderness, into which tragedy enters, but never squalor. The tale is framed in sentiment, but in sentiment of a high order. Life in Ireland floats almost wholly submerged in fantasy, like an iceberg with just its tip exposed to the unkind air. In most Irish lifetimes, the period of actuality is painful, but is also miraculously brief. Childhood protracts itself, and second childhood starts early. The old relive their youth with lyrical energy.

Mrs. Fogarty was born Cissie O'Brien, daughter of a "strong farmer" of Drumlaigh, by Lough Gur—a small, beautiful, haunted lake. O'Brien family life followed the patriarchal pattern, employees and children sharing the life of home. Inside a ring of communal joys, sorrows, and interests, the children lived with their parents and with each other, a close-knit life of amazing moral intensity—lit by religion, shadowed by superstition, widened by literature and by rumors of traveled friends. The parents are remembered as parents should be remembered—the father just and gentle, the mother sweet. The day's work done, the O'Briens sat down by the lamp in "the little room" and read aloud the classics— everybody from Shakespeare to Louisa Alcott. Art does certainly help to make a mold for memory: here, I think, the determining influence was Miss Alcott. I detect as close a resemblance as difference of scene allows between the March girls, with Marmee, and the O'Briens. But possibly all idyllic homes are alike.

Apart from nostalgic charm, the sentiment, and the story, *The Farm by Lough Gur* has substantial documentary interest. It is full of portraits, generalized enough to be important, particularized enough to be interesting. It offers a detailed picture of that rare thing—untroubled, contented life in nineteenth-century Ireland, without politics, ambition, or family bitterness. Observances, legends, and superstitions are recorded without comment. A social structure appears under the sweetness. And the sweetness ought not to put anyone off: it is endemic, not artificial.

There is no sweetness about *A Plain Tale from the Bogs*. Mr. Conner has had a really horrible time and, no doubt rightly, feels that everybody should know it. Thus, his manner is aggressive; his use of the present tense makes one feel one is being constantly, angrily buttonholed. Here are no landscapes or idyllic interiors: Mr. Conner's youth was passed in unresigned urban misery. His autobiography opens among the flying bullets and shocking street scenes of 1916 Dublin: he at that time so nearly came to a bad end that we are lucky to have this autobiography. His father's being an employee of the British got him a bad time with little patriots in the streets and at school. Adolescent hours of frustration and introspection went by in the empty top rooms of his rat-ridden home: here his dreams were intruded on by a sadistic father and a housekeeper whose husband had been hanged. His experiences in Cork, where he was sent to finish his education, were hardly happier. He came in for the horrors of the Black and Tan regime and subsequent brutalities of the Civil War. In fact, Mr. Conner's seems to be one of those unfortunate natures that are magnets to horror and squalors of every kind: if anything nasty is going it never fails to come his way. (Just as there are people who never fail to catch 'flu.)

England did not give him a better deal. He had hoped to find a future across the water, but encountered severe privations, reverses, snubs. Severe bouts of manual labor nearly killed him; from his experiences as a door-to-door salesman he has gathered dreary tales of the nymphomania of housewives and of the seamy insides of simple homes. As a jobbing gardener he witnessed goings-on of all sorts. At ugly intervals, he plumbed the depths of being a down-and-out . . . Mr. Conner has certainly no reason not to dislike humanity. But his narrative would be very much more moving if it were not saturated with self-pity. It should be said that the bogs do not figure in this story, except that the author's forbears in happier days cut turf there. I am glad to say that we leave him feeling a little better, successfully married, a successful author, sternly attending parties he feels bound to denounce—when he has done with them he denounces our age all round. He is fortunate in being highly articulate.

I call A *Plain Tale from the Bogs* a book for the drawing-room table because it is just the thing that well-to-do people like. The reading of frightful books by unhappy people may seem to the middle classes to be some sort of oblation. Suffering is very popular with the library public, who undoubtedly get a kick, a sort of oblique kick, from reading about how it feels to be down and out. Hence the present flood of down-and-out literature. These books get lapped up with a sort of piety, with a sort of morbid pleasure in profiting from an injustice that one cannot, or does not wish to, correct. While this boom in abjection lasts, I predict a lively future for Mr. Conner. He could be still more disconcerting if he were a trifle tougher—or should I say, drier? At present, he is a little *wet*.

Two Ways to Travel

Elinor Mordaunt, *Sinbada*; Sheila Kaye-Smith, *Three Ways Home. The Listener*, October 13, 1937.

Here are two autobiographies—women writers'—both respect-worthy pieces of work, not frisky, coy, or aggressive. Mrs. Mordaunt and Miss Kaye-Smith have not much, except their profession, in common: Mrs. Mordaunt is an extrovert, who has traveled the world with the maximum of discomfort and energy; Miss Kaye-Smith's adventures have been largely interior. She was invited to write her autobiography with a religious bias, whereas Mrs. Mordaunt was given a free hand. It is true that both were tomboys in youth. In this they conform to what is, for remarkable women, almost a regulation. Miss Alcott, with her Jo March in *Little Women*, created a prototype of the future authoress—or, at least, Jo has set the pace. I know almost no authoress, at all events of at all mature years, who must not confess that she was a tomboy in youth, indifferent to frivolity, seeking manly exercise, full of adventure fantasies, set on forswearing marriage. Even some decades ago this had come to such a pitch that there was a boom in tomboys: during my own childhood they were all over fiction. They were then exceedingly *bien vues* by grown-up people. To the naturally affected, indoor, and dressy child the tomboy, held up as a model of spontaneity and love of outdoor life, soon became a nightmare. Victims of this new snobbery, dozens of little girls must have forced themselves to climb high trees, ride ponies bareback, and be knocked about by their brothers—though all the time in an anxious and academic spirit. Contempt for one's sex became the hallmark of personality . . . There seems no doubt, however, that Mrs. Mordaunt and Miss Kaye-Smith were tomboys born, not made.

Here the resemblance stops. Mrs. Mordaunt must from the first have been one of those—very, I think, attractive—hard-riding personalities with little or no time for the inner life. Also, circumstances allowed her little time for reflection: if she ever did stop to think, her London garden was bombed, a door blew shut on her head, or she fell down and broke yet another bone in her leg. Through the affections alone she took a series of hard knocks, but she rebounded from these without divine aid. Her youth was unrepressed; her family—cheerful, easy-living but virtuous—moved from place to place in England and are last heard of near Cheltenham. She showed few early traces of literary temperament, except that she and a girl cousin were at one time "quite unaffectedly mad about Shakespeare." The death of her fiancé made a blank, from which she fled, after refusing other proposals, to join cousins out in Mauritius. Here, after a very gay time, she finally married a planter. Over the failure and tragedy of her marriage Mrs. Mordaunt, with likeable dignity, draws a veil. In those two-and-a-half years she bore two dead children and published a book called *The Garden of Contentment*. At last her friends prevailed on her to return home. Finding herself very much out of place at Cheltenham, she set out again, almost at once, in a dreadful barque, for Australia—which had the merit of being as far as one could go. She was alone, in wretched health, knew nobody in Australia, and had thirty pounds in her pocket and no more in the world. The voyage was of Defoe-like, primitive horror: immediately upon her arrival in Melbourne she gave birth to her third (and first living) child. In Melbourne she supported herself and her son by arts and crafts—pen-painting mats, stencilling curtains, and embroidering objects for high-class homes. She must have left her mark there. She liked Australia, where the charm and courage one infers from her writing made her, as elsewhere later, an accepted success.

In view of all this, Mrs. Mordaunt stayed longer in Australia than she ever seems to have stayed anywhere since. Tough, fragile, ingenious, and incautious, she has gone on whizzing around the globe. *Sinbada*'s extent and celerity make one blink. Almost all her objectives have been remote. She hates comfortable ships; apart from this, she seems to have dreaded nothing. Except for appalling illnesses and unheard-of accidents, she fell on her feet everywhere. For some weeks she was Queen of the Cannibal Isles.

Miss Kaye-Smith's lot has been cast in quieter places. Her early development took place in Hastings and in the country around. Quite early she was got down by her vocation—a regional novelist's. There has been a quid pro quo about her relations with Sussex—I take it that much of that county's colonization, arising from Sussex consciousness, may be owing to Miss Kaye-Smith, who in turn owes Sussex so much. *Three Ways Home* begins methodically: one is given the history of the family hyphen. Miss Kaye-Smith's life was first bounded by the conventions of Hastings; she sensibly lost no time in waging war against these; she escaped straight off into fantasy. Her first novel was published when she was quite young: on the strength of this she started visits to London, for glimpses of the emancipated life. A first of these was Mrs. Alice Meynell: "I spent one Sunday evening at her flat, and was profoundly shaken by the experience . . . . The talk, the piano playing, the simple yet pleasant meals served in pottery bowls . . . pronounced in me a definite disquiet."

But Miss Kaye-Smith's life has been a journey of the spirit. This she narrates in simple, as it were, lay terms, and the story does not lend itself to ridicule. The authoress makes a connection—her own connection—between religion and art. Her novels keep pace with, or keep just a step behind, her religious experience: they fall into groups under the headings of her successive conversions. Only their scene does not change; her publisher would not stand for this . . . I feel it to be greatly to Miss Kaye-Smith's credit that *Three Ways Home* should be as unembarrassing as *Sinbada*, if not quite so lively.

Then and Now

> Lennox Robinson, Tom Robinson, and Nora Dorman, *Three Homes*; Dorothy Hartley, *Irish Holiday*. *New Statesman*, September 17, 1938.

Nostalgia is one of the strongest elements in imaginative writing—it is lack of regret, the harsh wish to break with the past, or to resent its power, that makes so much anti-nostalgic prose nowadays shallow, labored, and poor. However much one may dislike the past morally, it is futile to refuse to assimilate it: the very attempt inhibits half the faculties and drains much of the nature out of personal life. No doubt one would be freer with no attachments, but one would be free uselessly, free in a vacuum.

As against this, it is dangerous to overwork nostalgias: they do still tend to figure rather too largely in one kind of romantic intimacy; they become odious when they have been given the too purely literary mold, and they may land one in bogs of infantilism. Childhoods, described with sensitive self-solicitude, crop up all over fiction and belles lettres. One ought to write or speak of one's own youth with an amiable dryness, perfectly undramatic; memories of being so charged with emotion, one's treatment of them cannot be too matter-of-fact. *Three Homes*, the work of two brothers and a sister, is a model of how such a book (a record of family life) should be written. Its three authors each write alternate passages; there has been collaboration in the scheme of the book; a certain family likeness underlies style and outlook, but at the same time there is a freshness of feeling, a felt independence rare in collaborations. Mr. Lennox and Mr. Tom Robinson and Mrs. Dorman remain clearly differentiated. There is little or no self-portraiture, and the styles are impersonal, but it is possible, opening the book at any passage ahead, to tell which of the three is writing: the difference is less in style than in the kind of affectibility shown in remembering common experiences. In the complete picture (for *Three Homes* is a very complete picture) oppositions and contrasts are brought out; the very inconsistencies as to fact are telling; one gets the sense of family life as being a complex unity.

Three Homes is not marred by a touch of false sentiment. The three houses—Westgrove, outside Cork, 5 Fisher Street, Kinsale, and Ballymoney Rectory—in which the Robinson family successively lived are evoked with startling completeness, with an admirable absence of reminiscent singsong and no literary fuss. Every phrase goes direct to the reader's imagination—surely this is ideal? The three styles, each with the common quality of being at once imaginative and matter-of-fact, make to the same end—they give objects and incidents the power to re-create the feeling they once inspired. The writers seem to praise without prejudice, to condemn without resentment. In Ireland, what is commonplace in England is always rather more lyrical, more disconcerting, at once more deeply natural and more insecure. There are always more changes and chances to be contended with—uncertainties of fortune, freaks of temperament, plain physical danger, false starts, and enmities. In the middle of all this, the natural genius continues to find outlets that are comfortable and plain—neighborliness, love of places, family life. Genius almost certainly does appear, or has appeared up to now, in the Irish aptitude for family life. Occasionally this genius goes awry, and pathological unhappiness results—for relations so closely affect that they can torture each other. In happier cases, however, life remains lyrical, dignified, pervaded by a sweetness that is perhaps climactic, and at the same time brisked up by an astringent wit. Sociability is a great element—life in the south of Ireland was, and still can be, exceedingly gay. Perhaps at one time the sun really did shine more—picnic parties had seldom to be abandoned, and ladies wore muslins throughout the summer. A little money went a most astonishing way. Life was very stylish, however insecure. Celtic gloom was kept in its place, like smoke under a floor. In the days of the Robinson family's youth, the Ascendancy was still the Ascendancy.

Three Homes presents, among other things, a valuable picture of a society. Protestantism in Ireland is not a political accident; it is a very positive facet of Irish life. The Kinsale part of the book is the most interesting from the purely documentary point of view—the complexities of Irish small town life, with its strata of snobbery, can seldom have been so well presented before. Mrs. Dorman, as a sociable growing girl, and her brother Tom, as a sociable boy, found Kinsale delightful; their brother Lennox, as a difficult child, was oppressed by it . . . *Three Homes* is full of agreeably touched-in portraits—of dashing Cork business people, of genteel Kinsale notabilities, of gardeners and cultured gentry and shady cooks. Even people who now find, with perhaps some excuse, the entire subject of Ireland boring should not fail to enjoy this very civilized book, in which the past of a class that stretched over Europe is seen in its gentle brilliance, with an unmisty eye.

Miss Hartley feels for Ireland, for its seabirds, its lore, its primroses, a mystical enthusiasm into which we Irish find it hard to enter. It is, however, exceedingly gratifying. *Irish Holiday* is an account of her trip, in a car, through parts of Ireland, with Giraldus Cambrensis[12] and a living companion called Leon. Miss Hartley is learned, vivacious, inquisitive; she shows an informed interest in domestic arts and crafts, energy, and a most impressive indifference to discomfort and even danger. Her descriptive passages are nice; the only pity is that she should be whimsical. More and more high-minded English people seem to be coming to Ireland, and no doubt it is for them that this book is written. *Irish Holiday* concludes with some notes, in an appendix, on camp cooking which should be very useful to English people camping in Ireland or traveling in caravans . . . Why is the decay of society in any country always marked by an influx of tourists?

Overtures to Death

C. Day Lewis, *Overtures to Death*. *Now and Then*, Winter 1938.

At any time, the appearance of a new collection of poems by Mr. Day Lewis is an event. But coming in this present unhappy autumn, *Overtures to Death* has an importance outside literary experience. Above the too many confused, urgent, uncertain voices we wait to hear the poet lift his note of authority. Stress, tension have tuned us up to listen: it is essential for us that what *is* essential should now be said. Where, under this constant threat to peace, do we stand—in our relation to the outside world, in our relation to ourselves? We hardly even know what questions to put to our own hearts. And at this moment when we most need vision, the everyday man's vision is cruelly blurred. Art keeps its immutable values, but if we are to draw strength from art (and we do need strength) we must have art that speaks in our own terms, that comprehends our entire experience. Mr. Day Lewis's poems seem most great now because of their double relevance—they have a poetic relevance to all time, and are at the same time relevant to our perplexing day. Their rhythm is the rhythm of our common emotion; they are intelligible in the profound sense.

The poetry we need now must be at once heroic and stripped bare of facile "heroicism." At the same time, it must explore personal feeling to its most shadowy depths. Purely *stern* poetry—discounting our reluctances, our love of the dream, our homesickness for safety, that makes the familiar more beautiful—would sound a metallic, unmeaning note today. The spirit of man cannot but abide more and more closely by what it loves: at the same time, it must stand ready to sacrifice even this. The imperative demands of life seem to make necessary the acceptance of death. It is necessary now to be at our most human, our most living. "Nothing is innocent now but to act for life's sake." Only in their simplicity, in their certainty of what is valuable, do men rise to their full height—like the fishermen of the *Nabara*.

> Simple men who asked of their life no mythical splendour,
> They lived its familiar ways so well that they preferred
> In the rudeness of their hearts to die rather than to
> surrender . . . .

"Overtures to Death," a sequence of seven poems, comes halfway through the collection: the lyrics and the heroic narrative poem, "The *Nabara*," attach themselves to the central sequence in feeling. In spite of their dark name, these poems in the sequence show the poet's power at its midday height. For these seven poems are not poems about Death; they are expressions of the consciousness of living, in different aspects but always at its most intense. Death is faced as the summer-up, the touchstone, finally, of our power to live. What has been our power to live will be the measure of our power to die—or, before dying, to face Death squarely as a factor in Life. We have been too much dwarfed by the fear of Death; we have thought of Him as an unseemly menace, or we have wreathed Him in false emotional fantasies. Mr. Day Lewis sees nothing possible but a clear envisaging and, from that, a resolute attitude.

> O Lord of leisure, since we know
> Your image we shall ne'er outgrow,
> Teach us the value of our stay
> Lest we insult the living clay.

Mr. Day Lewis hates not Death but its power to intimidate life, its power to make people insure themselves by cautiousness.

> I hate this cold and politic self-defence
> Of hardening arteries and nerves
> Grown dull with time-serving. I see that the heart lives
> By self-betrayal, is by circumspection killed.

"The *Nabara*" is stirring, magnificent—a sea incident of the Spanish War. It should be learned by heart by children who may still be learning to patter out "The Revenge."

No poet can be more conscious than Mr. Day Lewis of visual beauty—of its momentousness, its melancholy, its overtone. "Maple and Sumach," "Regency Houses," "The Bells That Signed," "In the Heart of Contemplation," "Behold the Swan" are some of the shorter poems that ring in the senses, that evoke around moments the significance of an eternity. Here, the repose of a scene, of a bird, of a cloud encloses, inside the glassy beauty of the image, the imminent threat. But these are not defeatist poems. Never was there a less defeatist poet than Mr. Day Lewis. Long or short, the poems in *Overtures to Death* express more than a steeling-up of the spirit: they convey resolution not to accept any doom as final; they set up an ultimate and living belief. "When They Have Lost" summarizes the spirit underlying this whole book—

> Then shall the mounting stages of oppression
> Like mazed and makeshift scaffolding torn down

Reveal his unexampled, best creation —
The shape of man's necessity fullgrown.
Built from his bone, I see a power-house stand
To warm men's hearts again and light the land.

New Novels

Franz Kafka, *America*; John Dos Passos, *U.S.A.*; George Buchanan, *Entanglement*; Luigi Pirandello, *A Character in Distress*; James Hanley, *People Are Curious. Purpose*, January–
March 1939.

Kafka, who did not visit America, projected about the continent this
anxiety dream — a dream in its own wild way so circumstantial that it
might be the sum of a lived-through experience. Kafka's *America* is that
first dark taut strip you see ruled across a ship's door in the morning
half-dark as, with nerves keyed up all night by the idea of arrival, you
come upstairs to go on deck: you are rushing towards New York. The
existence of land again, the breath from land, is exciting — actually, this
dark presence is Staten Island, but it is more than land, more than an
island; it is the New World. To meet it is an imaginative act. This momentary fever of apprehension is in real life a moment only; throughout
Kafka's *America* it is continuous. Karl Rossman, Kafka's sixteen-year-old
hero, arrives in America a delinquent, banished from home because of
a grotesque sexual accident. Within an hour of docking he loses his box,
happens on his rich uncle, recovers his box again. His box, containing,
with all his belongings, a photograph of his parents, represents Karl's only
possible continuity. Time in *America* has a dream value, just as New York
contracts into a few façades, the threatening blur of a dream. For two
months Karl lives with his uncle, learning to ride. Then his uncle's friend
Mr. Pollunder sweeps him off one night to stay at his country house, an
unlit house at the end of a rustling avenue. Here Karl is attacked by the
amazonian Miss Clara, Pollunder's daughter. At midnight he receives his
box from his uncle, with a letter saying relations between them are over
because the nephew did wrong in going away.

Then begin the travels with the terrible Delamarche and Robinson, the loss of Karl's parents' photograph, the Occidental Hotel sequence, the dismissal for a third unknowing crime. The domination of Brunelda, Delamarche's mistress (who had only to point with her umbrella in order to make a man enter her house forever), is broken by Karl's enlistment as one of the cast of the Nature Theater of Oklahoma. We leave him traveling west by train with the troupe:

> Broad mountain streams appeared, rolling in great waves down on the foothills and drawing with them a thousand foaming wavelets, plunging underneath the bridges over which the train rushed; and they were so near that the breath of coldness rising from them chilled the skin of one's face.

—But at this the dream breaks off, or is reabsorbed in some unspeaking layer of the consciousness. Throughout, there has been no justice, only, making itself felt, a capricious but unquestionable power. This is the viewpoint of the oppressed child. *America* is not an allegory; it keeps, rather, the fairy tale's authenticity, the fairy tale's parallel with the inner life. It is experience in terms of hyper-consciousness and of complete submission. It is also a superb picaresque comedy. Scratch America's surface of modern comfort and you find this terror-world underneath—a world of which the European stays conscious, to which his nerves, persistently on the stretch, never become acclimatized. It took Kafka, who did not visit America, to capture the continent's unbearable quality.

Even through Mr. Dos Passos's adult and balanced writing the unbearable constantly seethes up. *U.S.A.* comes oddly after *America*. This trilogy is documentary, not an affair of the nerves. The structure is so complex, the movement so extended and endless, each character carries such a vast dossier that the effect is, wrongly, to stun the imagination. Time—calendar time, not dream time—is a factor; the characters interweave, collide, vanish at last. They are too lifelike to live. Coupling, their experiences form repetitive patterns, like those thousands of same motifs stamped over a wallpaper. The action shuttles endlessly to and fro across the U.S.A., to and fro across the Atlantic. *1919*, the middle book of the trilogy, is set in immediately postwar Europe: it is *désabusé*, savage, and tiring. *The 42nd Parallel* and *The Big Money* are better; they seem to come nearer what ought to be their mark.

The intention of *U.S.A.* is vast, and as such ought to be saluted, but a sort of profuseness in the execution defeats it. One cannot care for so much. Unpromising childhoods, ambitions, frustrations, passive travel, embraces, undesired pregnancies, political disillusion, and a general sense of human indignity mount up into an incoherence that stuns. Indignation and vigor are palpable — but there are too few passages in *U.S.A.* when a single spirit ever shows itself likely to stand at its full height. Mac, Eleonor, Charlie Anderson, all the others are shown as being born circumscribed. The circumstances under which they suffer seem to be the aggregate of their own incapacity. The Dos Passos command of detail, his from-moment-to-moment circumstantiality, are superb. But he evokes too little because he tells too much.

Mr. George Buchanan's *Entanglement* bears a certain likeness, in method, to *U.S.A.* But *Entanglement* is a better-lit photograph. There is much less of this last novel, its pattern is clearer; its intention can more fully emerge. Here there are about forty characters, effectively touched in, differentiated completely: the characters, for their purpose, cannot be complex — in fact, though faultlessly motivated, they are a little flat. The time (dated from day to day) is the recent past: spring 1937 to the spring of this year. Present at public functions, at plays one oneself attended, subject to the stresses felt by one's own nerves, these characters are thus driven in among one's own memories — so many foreign bodies, irritants. They all have a harsh probability; they are oppressed by life (the scene is London), by getting from place to place, by failures in their relationships with each other, by economic wrongness, and by the threat of war. Only two of the characters have been given depth; there are[13] two men who are battlegrounds — Charles Manwick, managing director of an engineering firm (boxed in, as a private being, with a cold wife in an expensive, correct flat, prey to restless doubts and anxieties, playing with yoga), and Kevin Rede, the young electrician, who comes into Manwick's orbit for a short time, is keen-minded, moves coldly from love to love. These two change and progress; the rest are immobilized, two-dimensional only, rooted in circumstance.

Nothing runs to waste in this book, which has the clearness and quickness of an excellent film. Complexity, uselessness are recorded in it simply and usefully. (Mr. Buchanan *can* write with terrific drive, though he has also passages which are threadbare or lame.) He sums up this story which has no ending in his last paragraph:

> Whatever way it goes, the entangled human life remains, shining and dark, unfitted to geometry, with contradiction and paradox. Its essence is always more inventive than any man's imagination that it contains.

Pirandello's short stories ought to be better known. They are, apparently, about 400 in number, of which A *Character in Distress* can only include nineteen. Of these, some show the germs of plays; some are weighted with more metaphysics than a story can carry. But four or five are short stories *purs et simples*, and as such could not be better. These have the Latin hardness and briefness: "The Husband's Revenge," "A Widow's Dilemma," "His Medals," and "Tortoises for Luck" show a command that is worthy of Maupassant, and that has a stranger imagination behind it. Apart from their interest as stories by Pirandello, these are first-rate as stories about Italy. Why are there not more Italian short stories? There were two or three memorable genre Italian films. What scenes form the short story—those glaring flats and villas outside towns, the palm-planted modern avenue, those cemeteries with stiff-creped figures, the hill town resort, the café, that inscrutable privacy of domestic life, enclosed, with family passions running high. Modern Italy jumps to the senses immediately, at the same time keeping a puzzling element. The novelist might not find much to pursue here, but should not the short storyist make this vivid, theatrical, discontinuous country his own? . . . "My Last Journey" was written a few weeks only before Pirandello's death: it has a Kafka-ish quality about it—the agony of not knowing where one is.

People Are Curious, a collection of stories, contains some of Mr. Hanley's most important work. His anti-poetic style, with its relentless repetitions, is put to superb use here—in the title story especially. In the other long story, "Seven Men," he precipitates confusion deliberately. But the shorter tales, such as "From Five till Six" and "The Lamb," impose on him their inherent economy. One outstanding quality of this writer is his power to render, in deliberately "flat" terms, a particular scene, and, at the same time, to make felt the general implications behind it. In feeling he stays on a level with his characters, though in vision he is above them. He does not so much render as transmit the subhuman, the low-leveling moods—complete fatigue, apathy, inanition, the sudden intolerableness of some quite small thing, the stupefying dominance of the idée fixe. His characters—with the exception of one obsessed Irish lady—are all workers dulled by strain or tensed up to ready exasperation. Mr. Hanley has, also, to keep emotion to scale: his world is so much his own (at least in writing) that he must be the scrupulous judge of what is *true*. Overstatement is fatal to such stories as his—its effect is felt in these stories once or twice, though it is hard to put one's thumb on the fault.

His language makes for a sort of foggy evenness, from which he can make faces, figures emerge at the whole height of human expression. He can explore the territory of the dream behind lives whose harshness lets fancy play little part. His writing is never photographic; it is arbitrary, selective, more persuasive than its bluntness allows it to appear. His strength lies in never giving too much: he appears to be able to measure human consciousness and to know exactly how much it can contain—at a given moment, under a given mood. He can trace the effect of the thing seen on the apparently unseeing character . . . "People Are Curious" is the story of a man and woman, down and out, pushing their child in a perambulator from one town to another, towards possible help: they arrive to find help muddled away. "A Changed Man" is about an accident in a tunnel. "The Lamb" is brief and ghastly; "The Dead" shows people immobilized. An impassive pity stands over it all.

Gusto

Lionel Stevenson, *Dr. Quicksilver: The Life of Charles Lever.*
New Statesman, February 25, 1939.

Charles Lever, wholly Irish in temperament, was half Irish by birth. His father, a Lancashire Englishman, came to Dublin, set up as a building contractor, married a Miss Julia Candler from County Kilkenny, and prospered; his undertakings included Maynooth College, two or three churches, the General Post Office. He remodeled the Parliament Building to house the Bank of Ireland. The James Levers seem to have swum the Dublin waters like a couple of ducks; they had, too, that particular flair for family life that seems to belong to the period. In North Dublin, then out at Moatfield, the Clontarf villa, the interior was cozy, rosy, and gay. Charles Lever's boyhood, at home or with his Kilkenny cousins, was idyllic—too idyllic: it lasted a long time. He grew up dashing—the typical jolly fellow, set on a sort of full-blooded extravagance, detesting, denying the melancholy element, with darkness only in the pit of his mind. The melancholy that threatened him was the cureless melancholy of the volatile man.

Love of the grand manner obsessed him, as it does obsess the Irish. The Ireland he loved, and was to perpetuate, was the Ireland of his original view—the garrison swagger, the grandiose coastline, the castle with its noisy society. When he came back to live near Dublin as an editor, this canvas gradually tore across: he had only one more glimpse of happiness in the country, when he returned there as a fêted old man—and even then he was come on bowed and silent, his head leaning heavily on his hand. From such a youth as Lever's, it is only possible that life should be a steady decline. The pleasure he got from writing was the pleasure of a pretty steady recourse to the hardier part of his temperament, and of recourse to his lasting fantasies. Reality got at him through money troubles and ill-health; these two detestable menaces were upon him almost the whole time. He stood up to these best in the heart of his family—which, increasing, moved with him round the Continent, continuing the idyllic Lever tradition—and in society, where he stood at his full height. He liked Continental society—the small court, pillared and sunny resorts full of smiling expatriates. Himself, he was a born expatriate—with his temperament, he could hardly be otherwise. Dublin, after the Templeogue[14] years, unpleasantly haunted him; London he detested (or so he said). His resolution to live like a gentleman made him shun literary society—but even at a distance he caught its phobias: he grew disheartened, suspicious, saw enemies everywhere. His relations with his publishers were one long anxious unhappy muddle. He had a thousand projects, a thousand abandonments.

From Mr. Stevenson's careful biography, Lever's portrait emerges clearly enough. The man is not important, but he is striking and touching. The life he lived with such energy, the troubles he circumvented or overbore might have been summarized: Mr. Stevenson has been overconscientious, given us too much. The boyhood, the Ulster practice, the years in Brussels make the best reading—as they must have been, also, the best years to live. If the life were given less fully, the significant passages— the editorship of the *Dublin University Magazine*, the Templeogue house, the aspirations, the political antipathies—could have been gone into more fully, which would have been repaying. English Italy, at the height of its nineteenth-century bloom, is too familiar already from other lives: that atmosphere pickled Lever in its pleasantness, blurred him a little with its amenities, but did nothing that was important to him. Those years, the man's spirit ran underground: he was face to face with himself at detestable Trieste, where he died.

His writing—he would not have called it his art—was forced by circumstances: he showed the tragedy of exuberance that becomes mechanical. But he stays admirable, and most of all now, when the novel of sheer gusto is unknown. *Charles O'Malley* and *Harry Lorrequer*[15] are high points in gusto literature.

Fiction

Lawrence Durrell, *The Black Book*.; Desmond Hawkins, *Hawk among the Sparrows*; John Steinbeck, *The Long Valley*; John Pudney, *Uncle Arthur. Purpose*, April–June 1939.

Impediments in the way of free English prose writing, in this country, increase our vital debt to the Obelisk Press. Unhappily, the book published abroad continues to suffer in two ways from its exile: it is less read, and it tends to have, for the public, a scandalous piquancy. Prose in this country suffers from its avoidances, from the narrowness of the channel permitted it—the writer is inhibited from the start. No new mode is possible in the grip of a whole set of adverse decencies; the important creative mind perishes if it cannot make for itself a new mode. Bourgeois literature today (or call it conforming literature) is going septic under its tight bands. The corruptible public, guarded from printed plain speech, continues to corrupt itself in an oblique way, steadily drawing poison from the sweet-stuff of novels: almost every bestseller (other than thriller or the pure "funny") has a pathological bias; it is a discreet pattern of symbols and fantasies, the death wish, the back-to-the-womb desire. Our new age is the prey of an old ill-health; before there can be new health, there must be a new decency.

For the present, the writer who makes a new mode must be published abroad. Mr. Durrell has chosen this freedom, and this obscurity. The emergence of his consciousness is impressive; the power and the validity of *The Black Book* appear on each of its pages. Were the book accessible generally, there would be an anxious effort to get the writer taped, and *The Black Book* would get called "another *Ulysses*." It is, in fact, not another of anything. Joyce and Eliot have been digested (not vomited up untimely, as they so often are) and go to enrich the bloodstream. This is not verbal anarchy, or the flaccid chaos of "stream of consciousness" writing; in this writing is to be felt the application of a deeply realized law. The pattern and purpose integrate. Mr. Durrell says: "The question has been decided. Art must no longer exist to depict man, but to invoke God." One cannot invoke God through the constricted sensation, the partial experience. So, by the writing, the sensation is struck clear, the experience given its connotation of dread.

The frame of the book is the room overlooking the Adriatic, the long central scene the South London residential hotel. "Death" Gregory's journal is interleaved with the direct narration of the "I." Monstrous and probable, Tarquin, Lobo, Clare the gigolo, Miss Smith the negress, Morgan the porter, Chamberlain from the neighboring flat inhabit or visit this scene of dusty palms and statues, near the Crystal Palace, subfusc, a timeless hotel whose rooms, all single, are torture cells. There is Hilda, there is (set back in time) Gregory's Gracie, there is the "you" who loves in the snow among the cattle in the fields south of London. There is the school, with the dwarf Marney, the girls and the blocked drain. The prose, sensuous, *accidenté*, but taut with its invocation, holds these figures like flies in a web.

Yes, obstructions in the course of the novel exist. Mr. Durrell, were it not for the Obelisk Press, would have ridden head-on into them, and been forced into silence. Mr. Desmond Hawkins, in *Hawk among the Sparrows*, has found a direct line at a level above obstructions—that direct line only possible through the air. He has sustained his novel, from beginning to end, at a really superb level. There are no concessions or quibbles; the actuality of Mr. and Mrs. Sparge, in their raw, frowsty villa on the moor side of a village, does not have to be softened or limited. The book is a triumph of "treatment"—and treatment, in the great sense, is much more than an affair of skill or discretion; it is a continuous act of penetration—penetration of the matter of the book. *Hawk among the Sparrows* is not that "book about nothing" that Flaubert envisaged and wanted to write. But it does, very much in the manner Flaubert envisaged, "sustain itself by the inner force of its style." That inarticulate trio, the two Sparges and Ellen, those three lives submerged, almost, at the proportion of icebergs in appetitiveness, daydream, or lethargy, are the ideal *subjects*. They have weight, they give off energy; ignorant and dynamic, they generate realness into the book. Uplands, their exposed square villa, is charged, palpably, with the Sparges' physical smell: they are opaque and rooted; the young girl, the adopted Ellen, is transparent and fluctuating. The coming of Mr. Kipter—with his black beard, his shut personality, his preoccupation with birds—to lodge and eat in the Sparges' empty room precipitates the three occupants of Uplands into an existence of desire, resentment, fear. Mrs. Sparge has pursey erotic fancies; Ellen, open to beauty, dreams and glorifies; Mr. Sparge watches, snorting—the bull man. Ellen's love affair with the accessible Harry is at once dwarfed and ruled by the Kipter myth. Indifferent, she lets Harry help himself to her body, and later, in the throes of a miscarriage, has the consummation of attributing to Kipter what would have been Harry's child.

The fantastic size, and the potency, of the shadow that can be cast by one quite small, unmoved man is the theme of *Hawk among the Sparrows*. Or should one say that the theme is strangeness—strangeness around a figure, strangeness that exasperates the senses and tantalizes the heart? Kipter's actual figure is inked in with a sure flatness: the crux of the comedy, the deflation, is done with a compassionate cruelty.

Comedies are rarely beautiful: this is a beautiful comedy. The village, the dissolving stretch of moor, the new houses, the market town, the two young girls, Milly and Ellen, walking, the social pleasures (the deck chairs in the garden, tea with Milly's family) float in a luminous element: Mr. Hawkins's vision. His style descends on the *terre à terre* passages like a slant of light: he can depict the pleasures of frowsty coziness (the cup of tea, the stale bedroom, the planchette) without one superior flicker. At the same time, he can chart aspirations, as one now charts the air. This is a book to reread: even once read it continues to expand and bloom in the mind.

The Long Valley, short stories by John Steinbeck, will disappoint no one who liked *Of Mice and Men* and *Tortilla Flat*. Mr. Steinbeck is now hard on the heels of Hemingway and Faulkner: one or two stories in this collection, notably and above all *The Red Pony* sequence, are as good as anything an American has written—and that is, surely, saying a good deal. "The White Quail," as an exercise in detestation of the high-class woman, is as destructive as any story in *The Woman Who Rode Away*. Mr. Steinbeck ought to guard against obvious ironies. His forte is his smoothness—and, after that, width of scope. He can set a scene fault-lessly, and there seems no fear of his ever settling down to a formula, for he commands a diversity of characters, an acute sense of the forces behind men.

Uncle Arthur is another collection of stories: here the formula *does* show, though the style, unobvious, pointed, vivid, keeps one on the alert. There is a touch of Saki—stripped of the *Tatler* chic. "Uncle Arthur" (the title story) is a nice piece of work; "Edna's Fruit Hat" opens brilliantly but has a creaking end; "Ethel's Engine" is to be recommended to little girls and train-lovers of all ages. Mr. Pudney wrings what must be the final drop of batty melancholy out of suburbia and the English countryside. Humanly speaking, his chef d'oeuvre, here, is "The Maids."

Fiction

James Joyce, *Finnegans Wake*; John O'Hara, *Hope of Heaven*; Flann O'Brien, *At Swim-Two-Birds*. *Purpose*, July–September 1939.

Finnegans Wake is not a book to "review." It should be read in a year, not in a month. Its magnitude, its closeness, its density reprove the quick-running eye; the whole book is within the compass of one single mind only—Joyce's own. Its obscure, but unbreakable, continuity demands analysis possible only over a length of time: this book secreted itself during sixteen years; it formed from a steady drip, like a stalactite. From the preliminary reading of *Finnegans Wake* one gets a succession of reflexes: to be honest, one must not attempt to put these in an arbitrary pattern.

The first reading *is* a preliminary; one is no more than at the beginning of an experience. Thus the "review," with its claim to authority and finality, has no way of dealing with *Finnegans Wake*. The most honest course is to offer a few notes.

A cross-section through almost any paragraph of *Finnegans Wake* shows several different strata of intelligibility. The writing, in fact, is intelligible (or one should say, rather, capable of being intelligible) on different planes. Myself, for instance, I am compensated for my ignorance of Icelandic by a fairly thorough knowledge of Dublin topography. The Dublin or Liffeyside place-names ring bells that echo down passages of half-memory and early fantasies. A Dublin childhood is one possible outfit for approaching the comprehensibility of Joyce. Another is an ordinary knowledge (just up, perhaps, to School Certificate standard) of English, and Anglo-Irish, literature. Beyond this, an outline history of Dublin, Danish Dublin, the city at the ford, and an outline of the Irish mythology. Then, there are the song-sequences, and the pub argot: knowledge of these should make one another solid point for attack. Beyond and behind this is the Catholic experience, then the prodigious learning: here (but I think here only) the ordinary reader must stand down; some of the fun is for special intellects. But the first and the sole necessity for this reading is the free mind. Joyce is the foe of the cultured preconception. His sense is in the senses. His anti-literariness is formidable.

> Behove this sound of Irish sense. Really? Here English might be seen. Royally? One sovereign punned to petery pence. Regally? The Silence speaks the scene. Fake!

Not fake. The writing is inevitable. It is the hilarity, hilarity arising from some, however obscure, self-torture, *not* the virtuosity, that bears one down. The sheer force and drive of the fun is a gale to stand up against. The language has two violent intimacies: the child-talk (the talk to the self in the half-dark) and the lover-jargon, a terrifyingly urgent melting, slurring, and dislocation of words. All nonsense is erotic-infantile, with a pathic source. This tactile intimacy of language disturbs the chastity of the mind. Joyce, *not* conscious of nothing, is conscious of the language affinities:

"Lewd's carol." "And there many have paused before that exposure of him by old Tom Quad, a flashback in which he sits sated, gowndabout, in clericalease habit, watching bland sol slithe dodgsomeley into the nevermore, a globule of maugdleness about to corrigitate his mild dewed cheek and the tata of a tiny victorienne, Alys, pressed to his limper looser."

While the Dean: *"perquestellates his vanessas from flore to flore."*

"As Great Shakespeare punned it . . . ." The velocity of the packed punning, the inter-punning, the allusive distortion, is Shakespearean, with the Dublin nagging note. Some of the puns and distortions need Dublin knowledge — *"the Dullkey, Downlairy and Bleakrooky tramaline,"* *"the hercourt strayed railway"* — but the inexhaustible play on the name of Guinness is clearer: *"The Guinnghis Khan,"* *"the flight of wild guineese,"* etc. Chapel Izod and Lucan (up Liffey) make watery variations; the former sets up the Isolde motif. There is the song-punning: *"Will it bright upon us, Nightle, and we plunging to our plight? Well, it might now, mircle, so it light,"* and the philosophic: *"Nevertheless, Madam's Toshowus waxes largely more lifeliked (entrance one kudos, exits free) and our notional gullery is now completely complacent, an exegious monument, aerily perennious,"* and the literary: *"Sweetsome auburn, cometh up as a selfreizing flower . . . . Distorted mirage, aloofiest of the plain,"* and the contempt-punning: *"we grisly old Sykos who have done our unsmiling bit on 'alices when they were yung and easily freudened,"* and *"their dolightful Sexsex home, Somehow-at-Sea."*

How topical is this book? It has its place in Joyce-time. Insofar as Joyce-time is not an absolute, but only so far, it has its place in our own. It was described vaguely (before its appearance) as being "about the death of civilization." Insofar as the friction of so-called civilization disturbs Joyce, it is about the death of civilization. But it is a book a man wrote largely about himself—and can a man write more?

"Life, he himself said once . . . is a wake, livit or krikit, and on the bunk of our breadwinning lies the cropse of our seed-father, a phrase which the establisher of the world by law might pretinately write across the chestfront of all manorwombanborn."

The book has themes Joyce must find self-explanatory, and which might explain themselves after more readings. It is strung on the Liffey and the old Dane. It is at once nostalgic and claustrophobic, and ends with a plain return to the womb:

> My great blue bedroom, the air so quiet, scarce a cloud. In peace and silence. I could have stayed up there for always only. It's something fails us. First we feel. Then we fall. And let her rain now if she likes. Gently or strongly as she likes. Anyway, let her rain for my time is come. I done my best when I was let. Thinking always if I go all goes. A hundred cares, a tithe of troubles, and is there one who understands me? One in a thousand years of the nights? All me life I have been lived among them, but now they are becoming lothed to me. And I am lothing their little warm tricks. And lothing their mean, cosy turns. And all the greedy gushes out through their small souls. And all the lazy leaks down over their brash bodies. How small it's all. And me letting on to myself always.

The letting-on to the self of sixteen years (the child-monologue in the dark) narrow-deepens into a black opaque, or deploys more shallowly, smilingly, like the river. The accidents of beauty are immense. *Finnegans Wake* is the inevitable movement on from *Ulysses*; in feeling it is a later *A Portrait of the Artist*, and shreds of the *conte*, of *Dubliners*, float up and dissolve again in the prose . . . These are notes on a first reading. With the second reading, the more mature reading, *Finnegans Wake*, in any real sense, starts.

Hope of Heaven is a collection of good O'Hara short-short stories, mostly from the *New Yorker*. The long title story—novelette-length—in the middle shows O'Hara at his best, in spite of a few longueurs. He is one of the ablest Americans writing now; his feeling for tragic irony never cheapens, and almost no one can beat him at dialogue. His Roman Catholic background leaves him that sense of guilt without which emotional writing is soundless, arid, and thin.

At Swim-Two-Birds could be better—which is saying a good deal. If Mr. Flann O'Brien is derivative, he is derivative originally. He has a sense of the comic, but helped out. His language is vivid, his observations subtle, in a way of its own. Dublin does breed nightmare, and fantastic escapes. And there was Dublin, as Mr. O'Brien knows it, before there was Joyce; the trouble is to know which is which, *now*. On the whole, though, Joyce has done as much good as harm.

Fiction

Cecil Day Lewis, *Child of Misfortune*; George Orwell, *Coming Up for Air*; Katherine Anne Porter, *Pale Horse, Pale Rider*; James Hadley Chase, *No Orchids for Miss Blandish. Purpose*, October– December 1939.

The first two novels on this list—*Child of Misfortune* and *Coming Up for Air*—invite contrast, for they pursue the same question: How is a man to live, with integrity? Both are romantic novels—Mr. Orwell's being the more romantic in being anti-romantic avowedly. Both show that naïveté inseparable from very good work: only the second-rate writer ever sophisticates. Both are memory novels—Mr. Day Lewis makes felt that continuous, insistent, poetic association between scene and scene, act and act, that gives every feeling man's life its one unique, arbitrary form; Mr. Orwell's memory (or his hero's memory), like Proust's, exists in its vital relation to the sense: it is a sort of sensuous accident. The contrast, given a rough sameness of theme, is in the accepted values, and the approach. Arthur and Oliver Green are the victims of the fine—not necessarily the over-fine—conscience. George Bowling's conscience is ad hoc and flexible: *he* is the victim of a synthetic world.

 Child of Misfortune opens vividly, and with authority—two little boys at the seaside with their mother and aunt. The group, the arbor, the local photographer, the young Arthur's feeling that the camera is eternalizing the trivial, irrelevant moment, making the moment relevant to all time— all these have a lyric force. The rest of the novel absorbs and extends that moment, and to an extent dilutes it. As a novelist, Mr. Day Lewis shows the poet's great fruitful fault—he cannot reconcile intensity with extension, intuitions with the false and *sauve qui peut* rationalizations of day-to-day living. (Poetry would not ever be emitted if life could be lived at an even rate.) Thus, *Child of Misfortune* is framed on a succession of moments, of intuitions, which diminish a little in force and clearness as the characters move into adult life. Heaven may not lie about us in our infancy, but unmixed sensation certainly does. The brothers in this book, Arthur and Oliver Green, recede from the reader as they *feel* (directly) less and begin to judge more — or rather, as their feeling gets tinged by judgment. It is Arthur who keeps closer to intuition. There is a felt break between the experiences imposed on them and the experiences they seek. As a novelist, Mr. Day Lewis restrains too much his innate feeling for violence: he keeps this too much for another field. There is one, remaining, purely intuitive character — the Anglo-Irish Aunt Joyce: she is memorable, and at the same time fatal, for she diminishes the other characters. With the others, passion is lodged in the inner life; they do not bring enough passion into their interactions to spin the necessary plot. They suffer from their creator's over-fairness, for his distaste for the conventions of "character." The young woman, Letty, for instance, should be more of a trollop — she is flattened by her creator's over-fairness to her . . . The distinction, exactness, and austerity of the writing do not once lapse. To read *Child of Misfortune* is an experience — it is a puzzling and an unnerving one.

In *Coming Up for Air* George Bowling speaks, throughout. George is forty-five, a fatty, an insurance commission agent; he and his wife, "old Hilda" (who used to look like a hare), live a jerry-built life in one of those raw new roads in a building estate at the edge of West Bletchley, a London suburb. There are two children. George's inner revolt starts the day he gets his new set of teeth. He revolts — in a breathless but pointed monologue, from which the reader's interest cannot for one instant detach itself — against the general threat to life today, against the frustration of living. He is a positive man, formed by nature for something that no longer exists: he can no longer function. Behind the threatened war he sees the threat of a future more terrible. Round him he sees nothing but negativeness, mass production, and fear, and the system of joyless escapes — from aspirin to the cinema. His own person, his home, the suburb, the city, the milk bar, where the foul synthetic hamburger bursts in his mouth, all come under desperate review. His wife has decayed since marriage; because he is fat, with false teeth, he expects no more women to love him, except for pay. Against all this atrophy, indignity, and saturating fear George feels a racial anger. Then a sheer sense-connection

(King Zog's name on a placard in the Strand) pitches him back into the past, to the scene of his childhood and adolescence, his fishing and his first physical love—Lower Binfield, a small south Oxfordshire country town. Towards Lower Binfield, not seen for twenty-three years and, till now, gone from the cerebral memory, he now feels a cleansing emotion of the senses: he is drawn to revisit it by acute need. He could regain himself there. In George there is not a trace of sentimental nostalgia: he simply feels that, in order to stand up and face what is coming—the war and its worse sequel—he must refuel himself. So he contrives a week's leave and to Lower Binfield he goes. The rest should not be told here— enough to say that at Lower Binfield the church clock does *not* still stand at ten to three . . . The story of George's coming up for air to find there *is* no air is only not the story of a catastrophe because it is told in a mood of resilience, toughness, and anti-sentiment. George is not a born down- and-out. This is a book to read now.

Miss Katherine Anne Porter, in her three American short novels (or long short stories), transports us to a less trying scene—less trying only because it is not our own. The last (and title) story is the best—a study of doomed love through a veil of fever, the 1918 'flu. In Miss Porter's work profound, weighed, and rather masculine feeling balances virtuos- ity. "Pale Horse, Pale Rider" is, however, in my opinion, the only story of these three that does not to some extent suffer from its length. "Noon Wine," a Poor White story, and "Old Mortality" both strike me as being short stories very slightly inflated: would they not gain force by greater brevity? In "Old Mortality," glamor—the dangerous glamor of an old Louisiana family memory—is gradually flaked off, as a little girl grows up, from a sordid enough family tale. Miranda, at eighteen, finds the shining tide right out, grotesqueries sticking up in the mud. The de- bunking of the Old Southern atmosphere is done with a fatal sureness, touch after touch . . . The quality of Miss Porter's writing, the integrity of the imagination behind it, has been praised, and can still, I feel, not be praised highly enough. Her very longueurs have a deliberation; not a passage sags; they are an affair of art.

No Orchids for Miss Blandish is the last, the last possible word in the brutality novel. It is about gangs, and a kidnapping. The narrator jibs at nothing; everything happens. The only parallel I can think of is the minor and very bloody Elizabethan play, in which innocence suffers infinitely and every passion is let rip. This is a concise, unmawkish piece of dirty work, which strikes what I feel must be the final chord in gangster literature. In its own genre it is superb. It *could* be a parody. To enjoy *Miss Blandish*—and Slim, Eddie, and Ma—may be pathological, but I still recommend the book to those who feel they can take it.

Fiction

> John Steinbeck, *The Grapes of Wrath*; Randal Swingler, *To Town*; Rayner Heppenstall, *The Blaze of Noon*; Jan Struther, *Mrs. Miniver*. *Purpose*, January–March 1940.

The Grapes of Wrath is a torrential book. It is the story of an exodus, and probably not since the Exodus in the Old Testament has a story with such palpable movement been told. But in the Steinbeck epic, the tribes are leaving their race, their land, and the hopes of their land behind them, and being impelled forward into a void. This is mass tragedy. Its climax is at the end, when the mirage, instead of dissolving, has, more cruelly, allowed the people to enter—closed hostile California, with its mirage-burnish of sunshine, its heartless white houses, its peach and orange farms, is seen through black glass, by famished eyes.

Failure of small-farm crops, the foreclosure of the bank mortgages have displaced thousands of families from the middle States. Even before their desperate move to the West, the people have seen the great companies' tractors, driven by the companies' robots, cutting for miles across the flesh of the land, and, like tanks, knocking the homes down. Is it better to face, immediately, the implications of final despair, or to prolong life a little by false hope? The dispossessed families gum their hopes to enticing leaflets from California, leaflets promising work on the fruit farms, high wages, a quick new security, new homes, a future again. The few who distrust the promise dare not make themselves heard. For hope's sake, they lend themselves to the trick. So the teams and implements from the seized small farms are sold at a loss, vile cars and trucks from the junk yards are bought at inflation price, and the families take ship down the state roads, all converging on the one great road across the desert to the West. The few saved belongings go, too. The children live in a daze of excitement and malnutrition; the old (to whom the land left behind has been their very bowels) die by the way; the mindless or inconsistent default at the stopping places and are not seen again. The car-ships are captained by the fathers and grown-up sons; the strain of the cars' un-roadworthiness, the check in the faulty engines is felt by the men in every muscle and nerve. For the trek is a race with time—California has got to be made (and its promise tested) before the small fund of dollars quite gives out. To be stranded means to perish.

With *The Grapes of Wrath* John Steinbeck has come into his full pow-ers as a writer. His imagination is noble, his style direct and in the highest sense serviceable: with him, style is an implement, never (rightly) an end. His method is cinematographic—in the Russian sense. Alternate passages balance the general and the particular alternately; one is sus-pended above the movement, seeing the desperate flux down the state roads, and, then, one is in one of the movement's thousand hearts or nerve centers—the Joad family's truck. The broad implication and the minutiae are thus equally felt; superb montage makes use of the stream-ing, the semi-abstract crowd shot, in which the faces are generalized, *then* of the close-up—the Joads' packing and cooking, hopes, fears, and family dialogue. The characters in the Joad family stand out, distinct but simplified.

Morally, this book is a flail. It is an indictment of what is terrible in America—like that film *Fury* was. It cannot leave the English conscience happy, for we are traveling the American way. There is a deadly ill in this century, with all its indignities of dispossession, with its moral misuse of property, in its movement from the natural to the synthetic, from the instinctive to the imposed. A tin of Californian peaches, with the bawdy picture of fruit on the outside and the glug of syrup inside, is one of the main modern horrors. If *The Grapes of Wrath* did nothing more than rationalize this instinctively felt horror, it would still do much.

To Town is another study of the same ill. Here, the characters are static; a claustrophobic fever hangs over them all. The scene is an un-named North of England industrial city, in which the slums overhang a railway chasm, in which, in the park after dark, there is not enough room on the grass for the placeless lovers to lie, in which children play on waste ground beside the fetid canal, in which death comes grotesquely, affec-tions are meaned and stunted and love means either strain or lust. *Here,* the indictment is poetic; there is none of John Steinbeck's photographic calmness; the scene and the characters take a sort of unearthly light. Randal Swingler is a poet who cannot only perceive, he must add. He has added, not by heightening circumstances to make hard-case writing, but by saturating the characters in poetic imagination—not *their* own (for their sensibility is, rightly, limited), but his own. There are dangers in Mr. Swingler's metaphorical style, but at its best the style is tempered and tautened to meet the stress of a scene. And the narrative has some exigencies—for instance, the two boys drowning, the thrill of the flare-lit market, the joys of the gangster hideout over the railway cutting—that only a poet's style could meet. Inevitably, also, there is the poet's tendency to make the object—for instance, the pile of oranges—or the simple act symbolic—but this is to the good. *To Town* is bare of the grotesque simplifications and labored naiveness of the so-called "proletarian novel." Mr. Swingler perceives the burning spirit, the Elizabethan desperate passionate largeness, inside each of his characters. He has not written "another" of any *kind* of book; *To Town*, with its energy, stands alone, owing nothing to anything but the perceptive impulse that gave it birth.

To *The Blaze of Noon* I can add little that I have not already said in my own preface.[16] The word "original" has been too freely used; "original"[17] ought to be reexamined, plumbed, as a term, cleaned of its false accretions (ingenuity, audacity, freakishness), and used, in *this* context, in its new-minted sense. It is difficult to write underivatively on the subject of love—desire and satisfaction have been so much blurred by our modern infantilism, or by English high-mindedness—but Mr. Heppenstall has already alarmed some of the English public by writing underivatively. Which is to say, by scrapping much emotional junk. Disturbingly (apparently) *The Blaze of Noon* is a *Vita Nuova*[18] of the senses only. By the English rule, the senses must exist only for such calendar objects as gardens, firesides, dogs. Men or women who will implant quite overtly voluptuous kisses on the nape of a small child's neck still prefer to keep adult love as a gawky joke or a yearn.[19] English sensuality, like the contents of a stopped pipe, seeps out in untoward and moldy ways. In France, Rayner Heppenstall, with his useful and pointed style and *originality* (by which I mean no more than a from-scratch and unencumbered approach) could make much the same bid for notice as Henry de Montherlant. (Though he has not yet the whole of de Montherlant's one-sided hardness and palpable *savoir-vivre*.) In England his book has escaped suppression, but a succès de scandale—comfortable to the pocket, but offensive to the literary integrity—threatens it. *The Blaze of Noon* is the story, told in the first person, of a blind masseur's visit to a Cornish house in the course of the practice of his profession, of his realized love affair with his patient's niece, and his unrealized love affair with her blind, deaf-mute cousin. So much for the story; it is the philosophy that is interesting, because it is comprehensive. Mr. Heppenstall (or Louis Dunkel, his hero) has scared the public by his attitude to Love.

Mrs. Miniver is not, strictly, fiction. Her magnetism has been extraordinary—these essays appeared in *The Times*. What the comfortable classes, in England, want is a key to life-consciousness, and *Mrs. Miniver* has supplied this. A little leisure, and self-consciousness, may be a weight and a torment. Intelligence, tolerance, and strong natural feeling—or rather, feeling apposite to its sphere—have fitted *Mrs. Miniver* to live; her own authentic impressions will be seized on and copied and used as a formula. Flaubert spoke of "my Bovary, who weeps in a thousand villages of France." Mrs. Miniver already does not weep in thousands of homes in England. Her style and her humor redeem life from its minutiae. She has been rightly praised.

Fiction

> Graham Greene, *The Power and the Glory*; James Hanley, *Our Time Is Gone*; Dylan Thomas, *Portrait of the Artist as a Young Dog*; Robert Westerby, *Tomorrow Started Yesterday*. Purpose, April–June 1940.

How is war to affect the arts—and among the arts, the novel? All this has been much discussed. There has been a tendency to take up a fragile, prone-to-be-martyred attitude. Brutalization, atrophy, a great wave of philistinism have been foreseen. *Nos beaux jours sont finis*. But are they? People say: "Look at the theater—nothing but leg-shows." Certainly, so far, the war seems to have been death to the "thoughtful" middlebrow play, except those few that show really triumphant virtuosity. Having mooned through a number of thoughtful performances during my six months as a theater critic, I cannot but feel that this is all to the good. It was high time dim English seriousness, full of emotional thinking and *idées reçues*, come to its term. One must be either impassioned or frivolous—this would be a grand time to put on a *Henry V*, full of scarlet and trumpets. And the leg-shows I have seen, and the others that I have heard of, seem to be a hundred percent good.

What has frightened the art-mongers, but need not frighten the artist, is the sudden nonentity of personal life. Individual destiny has to count for nothing; individual sensibility is at a discount. Nothing can justify, nothing can ameliorate war, but the depersonalization it brings about seems to me good. To have to reassess life can do nobody any harm. There is to be no utopia. Nothing will make a little God out of man. We can no longer ignore the persistently monstrous element in human nature, or that tendency in the fate of the world to be magnetized to disaster after disaster. But we need not ignore, either, the divine (or call it the genius) element in man that lies alongside that other, or, either, the power men have, sometimes collectively, sometimes in the fastness of the single spirit, to override disaster and to re-create. The ideas to which we have, most of us, held for the last two decades have now almost all got to be scrapped. But, as Caterina Sforza said when they threatened to kill her children who had been taken as hostages: "I can have others."

The future of writing, and most of all of the novel, seems to me to lie with those writers who can have other ideas or, still more, have had always, inherently, ideas out of accord with, not bred from, what was till lately their time. Such writers have always been recognized; their growth has been watched, perhaps with hostility: now their full day begins. Action and passion will have to rule the novel. For the novel that stays in the trough of individual pettishness for the longueurs of the stream-of-consciousness novel, and, most of all, for the womanish novel (which may be written by persons of either sex) I see no future at all. This is really no time to stew over things. But there must be more than action and passion (the "tough" novel of lately has almost been moronic). Action and passion have to be ruled by feeling. There must be meaning to what is said.

Two magnificent novels, one by Graham Greene, one by James Hanley, head my list for this quarter. *The Power and the Glory* and *Our Time*

Is Gone are both books written for today. *When* they were written is immaterial; they were written *for* today, and today gives them their place.

Mr. Graham Greene has powers that, if his conception of life did not always grow and exceed them, easily could be snares. He is versatile; he has an absolute sureness of pen that could be virtuosity in a smaller man. He covers his ground with the speed, and he shows the exact sense of relevance, of the adept detective-story writer. He deserves to be, and I hope is, a bookstall man, for he has written no novel that is not also a thriller. Dostoevsky novels are thrillers too. The essence of the thrill is tension, disturbance, strife—the cheap word is often useful enough. To appreciate Mr. Graham Greene at anything like his true worth one must begin by breaking down the idea that the great novel must be, to a degree, unacceptable—or, at least, hard to read. *The Power and the Glory* is as easy (in the superficial sense) to read as everything else that its author has written—or rather, as difficult to put down. But it also shows the advance that one always expects of him. Here has been shaken off the last shred of elaboration, the last trace of fanciful feeling for the "queer." The vision, the momentum, and the authority are all greater than in the preceding novels. This is a Catholic book, frightening to the Protestant mind, absolute in its contempt for ad hoc morality. The story is of a priest at once in office and on the run in Mexico, in a State in which religion has been proscribed—a "whiskey priest," a child's father out of a drunken amour, scared, shifty, sordid, and at a loss, ignoble by every ordinary standard, and ultimately a martyr. The Mexican scenes are photographed with the clearness of horror. Every figure stands out, solid and charged with its single significance—the police lieutenant, the dentist, the English child Coral, the poor buffoon Father Joseph, the clean, decent, limited German-Americans. Nothing is underlined; there is no need. This is a thriller about a soul.

Our Time Is Gone is the third of the Fury trilogy. Its length gives Mr. Hanley room to expand his powers. One great element in his writing is *knowledge*—and knowledge in the more than factual sense. The characters are at once gripped at the root and allowed to move freely inside the orbit that each life makes for itself. Mr. Hanley's conception of the different Furys has the sobriety, as well as the sureness, of one who has already traveled with them. Each figure is a little above life-size: at the same time there is no inflation, no sense of strain. Mr. Hanley needs a large canvas; he has been accused of violence and of turgidity; there has been a sort of heroic explosiveness about his short stories and his shorter novels: the fact is that his imagination is gigantic, and his power of feeling so strong that both must have room. Given room, this feeling shows the temperance of its major force. It seems trivial, but it is true, to say that there is less *nonsense* about Mr. Hanley than there is about any novelist living. The Furys, a Liverpool Irish-Catholic family, each maintaining life, acting, expressing passion in his or her own way, could be a subject for nonsense—for sentiment, for grandiosity, for suburban pity—in any other hands. The time is the last war. The scene is, I take it, Liverpool. Denny Fury, the father, is a stoker on a merchant ship commandeered for troops. Fanny Fury, left alone with her best-loved son Peter in prison, goes to scrub troopships and death-ships of their unspeakable muck. The sailor son, Anthony, is the decent one. Desmond, now Captain Fury, the eldest son, is seen as a renegade by his class. Maureen, the daughter, is bound in sin to Mr. Slye. Then Denny is lost at sea; Mrs. Fury goes to the nuns. These are the directions. *Our Time Is Gone* leaves one certain that Mr. Hanley is not only strong, but also on his way to more strength: our today is his, and so are the days to come.

Portrait of the Artist as a Young Dog brings a lately jaded feeling for the short story (at least, on my own part) to its height again. The stuff has that poetic anti-poetic vigor that probably only a poet can command. The scene is Swansea and Gower. To say that Mr. Dylan Thomas has done for Swansea what James Joyce did for Dublin would be absurd: Thomas is Thomas, and Joyce Joyce. In fact, except for the sought analogy of the title, there is no analogy. The Welsh, like the Irish, are truly awful, and it needs vision to see them right through. Mr. Thomas has an eye like a burning-glass: the villas, the docks, the pubs, the parks, the char-a-bancs take on a demented reality. Among the stories, "Extraordinary Little Cough," "Old Garbo," "One Warm Saturday," and "The Fight" stand out in my mind. But they all stand out. I have no room here to quote.

Tomorrow Started Yesterday shows a good conception, but suffers from some defects. Five children drown four of the children's aunt: they do not plan the drowning, but they connive at it. The delay-action of this in their grown-up lives appears. The Wreford children are excellent; they have the secretiveness and apartness and brutishness of their vigorous kind. In the grown-up half there are passages in the trough: it is not easy to tell how much of the Wrefords' malady has been bred by the passive murder, how much is indigenous. As studies of self-centered, intelligent mediocrity, the Wrefords are imperfectly realized. This book shows superstitions and London scenes that belong to yesterday. All the same, it leaves one impressed by Mr. Westerby. Where will he turn now; what will he say next?

Fiction

Henry de Montherlant, *The Lepers*, translated by John Rodker; Desmond Hawkins, *Lighter Than Day*; Stephen Spender, *The Backward Son*; Frank O'Connor, *Dutch Interior*; H. E. Bates, *Country Tales*. *Purpose*, July–December 1940.

"Let me live on my summits," exclaims Montherlant's Costals, in the course of his long revulsion against the girl Solange. "Let me drink myself dotty on the exaltation inspired in me by this full and perfect harmony between what I am and the life I lead. Let me walk on the waters. But no, she burns less than I do, and more slowly. She does not, she never will, belong to this family of the half-mad (both male and female) to which I belong, and which is the only ambience in which I can feel comfortable at all. I was burning; she extinguishes me. I walked on the waters, she puts her arm in mine; I sink."

Not only *The Lepers*, but the three novels after it on my list are written by members of Costals's family of the half-mad—in fact, by desirers of the summit. It may be said to be the handicap of the artist that he cannot evaluate ordinary experience: to him no experience is quite ordinary, he is always translating it to another plane, and he can only perceive the experiences of others through the uncertain accesses of his own pity or in the momentary idealizations of love. The stress laid on Costals's incapacities makes this Montherlant writer-hero a sort of caricature—a flat figure and very incomplete man. Actually, *had* Montherlant been Costals (an interview with the writer on this question is printed at the beginning of *The Lepers*) he could not have written *Pity for Women*—collective name for the series of four novels of which *The Lepers* comprises the two last,

Le Démon du bien and *Les Lepreuses*—for there are characters in these linked novels, notably the three Dandillots—father, mother, daughter—and Andrée Hacquebaut, grotesque and inspired blue-stocking of the provinces, which Costals's imagination would have been too limited to surround. It is Montherlant's vision that makes these four "mediocrities" the surviving figures. Dead or alive, they all tower above Costals, with his little mistresses and his great thoughts. Costals, with his boyish ways (such as rattling sticks along fences), his sentiments, his brutalities, and his quirks (the erotic stimulus got from the plush rabbit), is no more than an isolation of one extreme part of the writer-nature. He cannot be taken to be a product of "characterization" in the popular-novel sense. He is kept inside the canvas of the superb novel by the very irritants—the two female Dandillots and Andrée—of which he complains. And what sort of novelist was he? He enjoyed vast *réclame*, earned big money; his novels, one understands, were in every fashionable home; his lady fans were a constant trial to him. Was he a Charles Morgan or an Aldous Huxley? With a rare mind he must have combined the popular touch.

The translation of the *Pity for Women* series from French into English is not only technically, but morally, difficult. Mr. Rodker is a first-rate translator, and perhaps *because* of his closeness to the Montherlant idiom, all the more do repugnant strangenesses appear. It is regrettable that in this country, and most of all at this time, *The Lepers* should be likely to obtain little more than a *succès de scandale*. Its density, its energy, its austere originality, the underlying fierceness of its morality, ought rightly to give it a very serious place. Montherlant umpires with a scrupulous fairness in the artist-v.-bourgeois conflict even now going on.

In *Lighter Than Day* the sense of the summit also prevails. Mr. Hawkins possesses the power I took to be lacking in Costals, the power to inundate with his imagination the lives of people who would be called "ordinary." In his world, mediocrities do not exist—at the same time, there is no unnatural emergence (no emergence, that is to say, in behavior) of any character from his or her given sphere. In this, his second novel, as in *Hawk among the Sparrows*, Mr. Hawkins shows a very great sureness in the physical, social setting of his scene. His notation of the little society of well-to-do, middle-class people living in big villas, with terraced gardens and tennis courts, on a ridge above a south-country country town, could not be more correct, or correct in a more high sense. To my mind the novelist who is to rise to great heights must have this takeoff from factual ground: not to respect the human pattern, a pattern largely made of attachments, is to deprive exaltation of half its worth. As it is, Mr. Hawkins has given his characters and their setting something greater than verisimilitude; they exist in a reality greater than that of life.

The story of *Lighter Than Day* is simple—it is the story of the love of Clive, second son of the prosperous estate agent and member of an agreeable family, for Benita, visiting niece of Uncle Willie, who, gentleman-aesthete with a head for business, runs and owns the local country-club hotel. The subject is the blinding experience of love. Clive is unformed, and has been docile; Benita remains his senior, if not in years—one has the sense, with Clive, of a nature entering on its inheritance and finding the inheritance intolerable: this is the summit, with unbreathable air. Below it lie the gentle conformities of existence—the home life, the tennis parties, the genial hotel bar, the little birthday dance. Only a poet could span, with justice, without satire or impatience, the distance between the two, or could make the dire stretch of the distance *felt*. Benita goes away; Clive's home burns down as the result of his careless, distracted act. That, as far as the story goes, is all . . . *Lighter Than Day* is an achievement performed so quietly and with such a sure rise of poetic force that it is not at all easy to comment on. There are (I suppose) symbolisms—the catching of the rabbit, the burning of the house. I can only return to what I said at the start—here is inundation, by extraordinary vision, of an "ordinary" world.

To continue Costals's subject of the "half-mad"—*The Backward Son* applies to a boyhood and schooling the test of a dangerous, innocent rationality. In this case a war is rather suffered than waged. The summit here is present only by implication: if it had not been attained by now, since the boyhood of *The Backward Son*, it would not have been possible to have looked back. There have been a hundred novels of maladjustment which have remained nearly plaintive and minor because the writers have not, by the end, detected what was the enemy in the circumstance. Mr. Spender, in maturing into a poet, has by now detected the enemy. The scenes in *The Backward Son*—the Hampstead home, the seaside preparatory school—are as exact and as apparently dispassionate as police photographs of the locations of crimes. This is *not*, in fact, a novel of maladjustment—*The Backward Son* suggests no possibility, for the direct nature—child, lover, or artist—of any adjustment to a world in which what passes as "normal." What is enforced as "normal," is in fact the structure of a neurosis. The boy—at an age when one suffers rather than perceives—is surrounded by relationships, in his family, among schoolboys, into which he cannot enter. He is more than the misfit: he feels penalized. They are, in fact, deformed relationships—or rather, the characters as they are shown (the father and mother, the headmaster, the outstanding schoolboys) are neurotics incapable of relationships, but who have learned to achieve fakes. Outwardly, however, these surrounding characters are four-square, in some cases almost magnetic and surrounded by a powerful atmosphere. It is this rendering of the characters' *face-value* that makes the book as unnerving as it is. The comfortable Hampstead home is better than many, the preparatory school (I imagine) no worse than most. The conversations, the conflicts, could not be so grotesque if it were not for their verisimilitude. Here is a landscape of windmills no sane person would tilt at—but the windmills *are* giants: what is one to do? . . . Incidentally (if this is incidental), Mr. Spender's command of the novel is now complete: *The Backward Son* could hardly be better done.

Dutch Interior shows characters, men and women, in the agonizing constrictions or the illuminations of a series of scenes. Their unnamed setting, and enemy, is Cork—stifling, nerve-wracking city built on a marsh, crisscrossed by water, dazzling with reflections or deadened by rain, overlooked by terraces up the steep hill. From childhood to middle age, these are not fortunate people. Poverty, sameness, conscious provinciality, meanness oppress them: they are too disabused to take the easy escapes. Their intellects are voracious, their wits bitter, their senses quick, and when, even as children, they embrace illusion, they do so exactly knowing its worth. When they stand to their full heights—in talk, on fierce solitary walks about the city, through music, in minutes of love—this is followed by having to stoop again. In the decades the series of pictures cover, these people burn themselves out—the returned American renews his illusion of Cork, then turns bitter and goes away again, brothers quarrel, friendships perish of inanition, a love affair ends with a lie about the paternity of a child. The Catholic curate and the doctor draw their two lines through the talk. *Dutch Interior*—which has been banned in Ireland for reasons more subtle than censorship generally shows—is slowly tragic, but it is never dreary; it is vitalized throughout not only by beauty, but by a sense of sheer spiritual obstinacy: there can be spirits to which a thousand submissions are immaterial. This is a fit book for Ireland to send out to the world now: Mr. O'Connor is more than an Irish writer: he is an important voice in a Europe silenced by war.

Country Tales is a selection made by Mr. H. E. Bates from five volumes of his short stories. The selection has been an excellent one, and I find few omissions that I regret. The short story, I feel, is a peacetime art—freedom, even playfulness of the fancy, seems necessary for it, and our fancies, these days, cannot play over scenes with the old unquestioning pleasure in the thing-in-itself. Will Mr. Bates give us short stories of 1940? If anyone can, no doubt he will, for *Country Tales* shows his high command of his craft.

Come Back to Erin

Seán O'Faoláin, *Come Back to Erin*. The Bell, December 1940.

Come Back to Erin is the ironic title of Mr. O'Faoláin's latest, and greatest, novel. The theme is the interplay, in terms of desire, between the Old World and the New. There is a constant crossing, throughout the pages, of the outgoing and the homing longings in man. The scene passes from Cork and County Cork to New York, then back to Cork again; the protagonists are the brothers (or rather two sets of half-brothers) of the Cork-bred Hannafey family—St. John, the Irish-American, the Cork-bound clerk Michael, lonely and cagey dreamer, Leonard the New York priest, Frankie the revolutionary who has lived for years on the run. It is poor paunchy drink-sodden St. John and arrogant Frankie who tower: the contrast is between them. St. John, after thirty years of hard moneymaking, returns on a visit home: in Ireland he is closed in upon by dreams that set up abhorrences; he disintegrates on his return to New York. Frankie, halted in Ireland and claustrophobic, seeks release in his break for America, to be halted there, again, by his nihilism and sidetracked by an unwilling love affair. Two women who love Frankie—lonely, high-spirited, taciturn Irish Josephine and Bee Hannafey, wistful little pagan, St. John's American wife—make the subsidiary contrast. All these characters flow into the plot, giving it width and depth and a floodlike impetus.

Actually, this novel is too large to come inside the scope of a short review. Its greatness is in the spiritual measure taken of each of the characters—between whom the whole stuff of life seems to stretch. To give the range of humanity, at its highest and lowest, is probably the first task of the novelist: Mr. O'Faoláin has done this. He shows the broken beauty of aspiration in even the meanest conduct of man. And he has regained, here, the magnificent objectivity and the poetic fullness of his first novel, *A Nest of Simple Folk.* The living urgency of the dialogue, the sureness with which each scene is presented cannot be too highly praised. *Come Back to Erin* is a tragedy: it is tragedy pure of every cheap device, purged alike of cynicism and sentiment. To read the book is to suffer, to an extent. But there is a tenderness, a love of man in the writing that leaves a sort of sweetness about the heart.

The Perfect Theatergoer

Desmond MacCarthy, *Drama. Spectator*, January 3, 1941.

A collection of Mr. MacCarthy's essays would be welcome at any time: his *Drama*—dramatic criticisms—could not come at a better moment than this. This present halt in the life of the theater, the unnatural dark damaged silence of Shaftesbury Avenue, invites us to look back, look forward, and take stock. Virtually, we have just now no theater—and how much, how constantly, how intimately, and for what reasons do we feel the loss? The loss, I suppose, can be measured less by our actual satisfactions than by our hopes. There can have been few so blasé that they did not cross a foyer without some slight lift of the heart. The very expensiveness of the evening seemed to guarantee pleasure. And the enthusiasts who for half-days together stood in damp queues for the pit or gallery, and down prison-like passages pressed their way to their seats—did they ever doubt their devotion was warranted? The theater touches the child in us, and the fact that these days we are asked to put away childish things does not make our lack of the exaltation, the outlet, the temporary sense of perfected existence less.

But, on the whole, we have been too childish. It is asked of few of us to be critics; but, on the whole, looking back, we fell short as theater-goers. And it is first of all as the perfect theatergoer that I should like to praise Mr. MacCarthy. It seems clear that he brought to the theater the hope of pleasure, the susceptibility to illusion, the open mind towards the dramatist's concept, the imaginative readiness to meet the producer, the sympathy towards the work of the actor without which, strictly, one has no right to take one's place in the auditorium. But he brought more; he brought the adult power to distinguish between what ought to be and what was. Where response was possible he responded fully; it was after-wards that he analyzed his response. At the same time, he did play and players the honor[20] of not relaxing his demands upon them. His inner touchstone did not, throughout a performance, lose virtue, and to the sense of each scene or passage, to the rightness with which the passage articulated with the whole and to the intonation with which the passage was spoken this touchstone continued to be applied. What is this touch-stone? Aesthetic soundness of judgment coupled with discerning human good sense. The theater has two aspects: in one it is, and should be, sheer artifice; in the other it must not depart from the felt law of human *prob-ability*. Both aspects should be kept in equal regard. To do this uses all of the faculties; one must not only listen, watch, but one must perceive, discern, and in some cases reject. That Mr. MacCarthy used all his facul-ties would be evident in these essays were they no more than notations of so many experiences. Every writer writes, it is said, for his ideal reader: this hypothetical person calls out his best and keeps him up to the mark. If playwrights wrote, producers produced, and actors acted for one ideal member of the audience, Mr. MacCarthy might be said to be that ideal.

Because our theaters are at the moment shut, and I want to accent the present and mark this break, I have written in the past tense of Mr. Mac-Carthy as a theatergoer. The effect of reading these essays is to re-create in one such a strong sense of the theater's possibilities that one finds oneself eager for the doors to open again. On what plays—worked upon by our immense experience and extended by the demands we shall make on them—will Mr. MacCarthy bend his faculties next? This enforced break in the life of the theater may *not* prove wholly a bad thing. It cannot destroy the real tradition, but it should destroy that false continuity by which successes bred imitations or, still worse, mistake engendered mistake. The fresh start will be so marked, so really momentous, that we may hope for great plays to celebrate it. (Our most pressing present loss, to my mind, is Shakespeare as the popular playwright: we really do need Shakespeare to see us through.)

Mr. MacCarthy's dramatic criticisms, in *Drama*, cover twenty-five years. Though the earlier plays or productions might date today, his writing does not; it has a detachment that ties it to no particular time. And the style is evocative: Mr. Granville-Barker's gold fairies of the *Midsummer Night's Dream* of February 1914 appear as present before our eyes. Moscovitch's Shylock, of the Court Theater, 1920, is a close-up for criticism today. The notes on Shakespeare's sense, in various contexts, and on some misinterpretations of it are excellent. There is Maeterlinck 1913, *The Death of Tintagiles*, and a 1913 Galsworthy, *The Fugitive* — Mr. MacCarthy exposes, with a ruthless regret, the desolating conventions of Galsworthy. In 1918 Mr. MacCarthy postmortems D'Annunzio's passion (in the Stage Society's *La Città Morta*) some years before the great man's actual death, and in 1922 he hails Pirandello: the Stage Society gave *Six Characters*. In 1927 *The Father*, then *Miss Julie* caused Mr. MacCarthy to put Strindberg, rather firmly, in what we now recognize as his proper place. We are made to remember the stimulus we got, in 1928, from Capek's *Insect Play*. One is struck again and again, in the earlier criticisms, by Mr. MacCarthy's power of anticipating a reputation.

There are appreciations, generous and perceptive, of Mr. Noel Coward and Mr. Somerset Maugham. And Mr. MacCarthy looks with interest at the success — *The Thirteenth Chair, On the Spot, Dinner at Eight, The Silver Cord*, and others, that moved, thrilled, or scandalized in their day.

Ibsen and Chekov give this critic's powers their fullest scope. Discussing the reception of *John Gabriel Borkman*, Mr. MacCarthy gives a devastating analysis of the postwar mentality, 1921: may that not be ours again. Throughout *Drama* we find critical writing that, while inflexibly high in standard, is friendly, communicative, and clear. Readers will owe Mr. MacCarthy much. And the theater owes him much for his close attention and for his long view.

Advance in Formation

John Lehmann, editor, *New Writing in Europe. Spectator,*
March 14, 1941.

Mr. John Lehmann's *New Writing in Europe* is the examination, explana-
tion, and history of a movement whose full effects have still to be judged.
The book could hardly be clearer or better planned; it was needed, and
Mr. Lehmann, as editor of *New Writing,* is the ideal author for it. We
owe a debt to the Pelican Books for initiating a series that fills wants and
for issuing works of immediate interest at a price that prohibits no one
from buying them. In fact, these publications are one of the most hopeful
signs of the times; they are democratic in the most concrete sense. Up to
lately, high prices made for a time lag between a book's appearance and
its reception by the mass of the people for whom it may have been meant.

The new writing movement of the Thirties was the Romantic Movement of our century. Its start had a major poetic impetus; its direction
was explicitly political, though in most of the writers it had a subjective
source. To call this movement literary would be, in its own view, to mis-
name and even to stigmatize it: it was literary in only a secondary way.
The writers' attitude to language was the inventor-mechanic's; they undertook a de-carbonization of language in the interests of swifter impact
and better use—since the romantic start of the nineteenth century a new
coating of falseness, over diction and feeling, had formed itself. And the
movement, like all revolutions, was a reaction: it reacted against the ana-
lytic, static, and on the whole rather prostrate mood of the Twenties. In
terms of achievement, the movement's greatest value was in attack: the
norm of most writing in England was (and to an extent, sadly, remains)
the norm of middle-class sensibility: art condoled with and flattered, but
largely condoled with, the well-to-do. This traffic the writers of the new
movement abjured completely—though their publications came, by
their own merit, to lie on the drawing-room tables of the inquisitive rich.

In essence, the movement was European: this Mr. Lehmann stresses,
while giving, for English readers, most largely the English facets of it. It
was active in France (with Malraux, Chamson, Giono) and in pre-Nazi
Germany, in Spain with Sender, in Italy with Silone. Also, it was abreast

with left-wing America, and it was towered over by an idea, its idea, of the U.S.S.R. The war in Spain was its crux and rallying point. To the dullest of general minds the war in Spain was a symbol; to the writers it was not only this, it was, in degrees of closeness, the final explanatory experience. So much so that one is left with the impression that after Spain they reacted to nothing more. Mr. Lehmann writes of the Spanish war with a capital W and of the present war with a small one.

Do we owe to the movement our three poets in the purest and strongest English tradition—Auden, Spender, Day Lewis—or do we owe the movement to the three poets? Actually, I doubt whether major poets have much to do with any movement at all. I believe a godlike irresponsibility and infidelity to be generic in the poet's makeup: such people cast off ideas that, long after they have forgotten or even denied them, continue to germinate in slower, dutiful minds. The movement, again, will be remembered for its experiments in poetic drama—the Auden-Isherwood pieces, with their choruses and their power to *épater* (though actually the conventions were narrow, and the satire had a fairly limited range) and Stephen Spender's deeper and more memorable *Trial of a Judge*. Mr. Lehmann gives a chapter to the extension, through the work of the Group and Unity theaters, of the movement's idea . . . It would appear that, at least in England, prose was the medium used by the movement with least effect: the prose writers cut less ice than the poets and poet-dramatists— the exception to this has been Christopher Isherwood, whose prose Mr. Lehmann rightly calls "seductive," and who is, also, funny. Possibly some of the others, like high-minded women of the last generation, too completely ignored or despised the seductive arts. Possibly they assumed that the interest of their subject—the lives of workers—should be self-evident. But should documentation wholly succeed illusion? In stories appears the American influence, but this had been felt, and used, before the movement began. There was also a conscious and desired convergence between reportage and creative narrative art, and while this produced some magnificent reportage—see Mr. Lehmann's quotations from books on the Spanish war—on the storyteller it had a flattening effect. On the whole, the movement's realists are unmoving: the happiest prose-adventures, also the most stylish, have been (as with Edward Upward and Rex Warner) into the realms of Kafka-like fantasy. *New Writing* has been the headquarters of writers whose integrity has been absolute. But to integrity must be added dynamic power—and this has, rather, appeared in the last decade in those other novelists Mr. Lehmann discusses under the well-found heading of "Allies and Independents"—James Hanley, Arthur Calder-Marshall, and Graham Greene.

The movement had two more outstanding characteristics: it was youthful and it was masculine—the eclipse of feminine talent has been marked, and is not, I think, wholly to be deplored. But the obstinate and almost professional youthfulness of the young Englishmen did set certain limitations about their art. Also, one finds in the prose an absence of background, a lack of power either to generalize or to synthesize, that seems to come from the abnegation of social experience. There is a lack of irony, a lack of *méchanceté*. There are no Julien Sorels among the movement, because there is, I suppose, no longer a beau monde. But there will always remain the tendency to idealize some world by which one does not by birth belong, and those of the young men who were of middle-class origin sought an idealized proletariat. Also, they became "intellectuals"—it is notable that Mr. Lehmann identifies intellectuals with writers—and, by grouping, located themselves, whether abroad or in England, inside the intellectuals' world: isolated, special, intensive, charged with personal feeling, and, in the long run, as claustrophobic as any middle-class home. Would it be unfair to say of this group of writers that, though they changed their milieu, they never fully *emerged*, but remained life's delicate children after all?

And *do* movements move? Can writers proceed in groups—that is to say, past a point that is early reached? Whatever the answer be, the New Writing movement will always deserve honor for its altruism, its energy, and the defenseless honesty of its belief in man.

Portrait of the Artist

Herbert Gorman, *James Joyce: A Definitive Biography. Spectator*, March 14, 1941.

James Joyce, European writer owed to Ireland, remained during his lifetime a rather aloof figure. He enveloped himself in no mystery, took up no poses, and had no part in promoting the foolish legends that came to settle about his name. After a protracted poverty and obscurity, due to his refusal to make concessions, he became a person almost everyone talked of and many people were anxious to come and see. He sustained with a simplicity that was disconcerting and that appeared cryptic the prominence into which he had been thrust. He had desired no more—and no less—than the consummation every writer desires: the consummation of his books finding their mark. In his prominent as in his obscure years, he stood clear of those heated intimacies in which so many good writers lose or imperil virtue. He loved his family, liked good company, and was subject to the sort of solitary humor that made him dance by himself in a cloak on a Paris bridge, but the atrocities of human communication were unknown to him: he did not hand himself out to disciples in small change. The circle of people with whom he grew familiar was broken up by this present war. And a winter silence hangs over his death.

In days where there is a bad name for detachment, it is hard to assess the detached man. As to the bare circumstances of Joyce's life there has been, up to now, ignorance: by a number of people he has been vaguely seen as an aesthete piqued with his own country, choosing to live abroad. Actually, the detachment Joyce did achieve, the detachment that made it possible for him to go on writing, was a continuous heroic act of the spirit. Nothing was spared him: extreme poverty, repugnant work for a living, frustrations, humiliations, physical pain, sense of exile were by him felt to the full—but they were surmounted. He was reared and educated in a religion from which a deep nature does not without crisis secede, and from which a lonely nature dreads to detach itself. He was adolescent in a provincial capital, Dublin, that ignored or vituperated his vision, a capital whose intelligentsia devoted itself to, as he saw it, a petty and local myth, a national sentiment. In a Paris indifferent to his eager presence the boy of twenty hanging over his notebooks was excruciated by toothache—he had not a franc for a dentist—that at least did him the service of reconciling him to hunger: he would have been unable to masticate the food he was for days unable to buy. Recalled to Dublin, he for five months watched his mother die in an agony only made supportable by the consolation of a church he knew she knew he had foresworn. Early fatherhood made acute, in a series of foreign cities, that struggle for the very barest subsistence that, apart from art, he accepted as being life.

The vacillations of publishers and the *pudeur* of printers blocked, year after year, the publication of his finished works—in fact, the dealings of Joyce's publishers and putative publishers with him could have opened the gates to dementia. And his writing, with its immense exactions, could only be done at the weary end of a day: when, in Rome, he wore out the seat of his only trousers, this was not on the writer's chair but on the high stool of the bank at which he worked overtime; in Trieste the precise and burning lover of words drummed commercial English into Berlitz pupils at the rate of tenpence an hour. Landlord after landlord threatened evictions from the minute grilling foreign apartments that were the Joyce homes; he saw his wife humiliated; financial quandaries spoilt his relationship with his brother. All his life he was hampered by eye trouble, and just when poverty slackened its extreme grip, blindness was found to be imminent—blindness held off him by operations that were ordeals to his whole frame.

To pile up these facts, from the Gorman biography, might seem to be recruiting for Joyce a pity that he certainly never asked, or felt, for himself. Never was there a less pitiable man. The facts should be known, only, because they make his life history as inspiring as any history of conquest. Also, they invalidate once for all any foolish idea about an Ivory Tower—how many reputed ivory towers would stand the test of an examination of fact? Joyce's equanimity triumphed through everything: it was a combination of an unmoved belief in his art with a Jesuit-instilled rule of self-discipline. Joyce had that kind of hauteur, independent of circumstance, that Stendhal calls *espagnolisme*. He had the Irish qualities shaped and steeled. If his imperturbable manners irritated the bully, they could disarm the bully as well. His gusto for life, his love of round roaring pleasure dictated, during his youth in Dublin, his choice of medical students as his allies: with this pack he ran the city and knew Nighttown.

Mr. Gorman's Joyce biography is exciting. I suppose almost every biography *could* be better done: in this the first forty pages—descriptive—move rather heavily, and a few repetitions and longueurs come later on. Mr. Gorman's writing, however, is admirably impersonal; he is not intrusive and he makes no claims. The Dublin environment and the foreign scenes are well rendered. The book is documented with Joyce's letters—the letter to Ibsen on his seventy-third birthday, written when

Joyce was eighteen, is a superb salutation from youthful to aged genius. There are Joyce poems—everything from the doggerel to the lyric—and excerpts from early essays and, most valuable of all, Joyce's notes on his own aesthetic, departures from Aquinas and Aristotle, worked on through that first Paris winter of toothache. Joyce's father, that grand old unstable stalwart John Stanislaus, civil servant and tenor, stands out excellently. The vicissitudes of the books with the publishers, the Babel and almost Bedlam years in wartime Zurich, the inauguration of the first cinema in Dublin are fascinating matter. Through all, Joyce's love-hate relationship with his own city, Dublin, and the crystallization of Dublin inside his art, appears.

An Invitation to Think

L. Susan Stebbing, *Ideals and Illusions. Spectator*, July 25, 1941.

Professor Stebbing's *Ideals and Illusions* comes with great value to our day. At a time when we desire and need to think, and when our position can only be based on clearness and integrity of the mind, there are dangers that may break the habit of thought. Lethargy does not at present threaten us, but weariness might. The repetition of watchwords, phrases, and slogans, and, still worse, their inflation, tends to lower the currency of ideas. The lay mind, overcast by the inevitable but deceptive emotions of wartime, feels a gulf between itself and the empowered precision of the philosophic mind: in a war in which we believe that we do not underrate the specialist, we may, at the same time, be too ready to relegate the specialist to his own area. (One symptom of this has been, in one part of the public, a barely tolerant disregard for the arts.) As a specialist in thought, a philosopher, Professor Stebbing not only sets out, from her side, to bridge the gulf, but challenges our assent to it. The first merit of her book, from the point of view of the ordinary reader, will be its concreteness—"as a philosopher," she says, "I hate abstractions"—and the matter-of-fact simplicity of its style. She does not write as somebody from an altitude, but as somebody having regard for altitude. Apart from what seems to me to be the value of her position, at once arrived at and made plain in the course of the book by a stage-by-stage elimination of the untrue, there is something tonic about her invitation to us to think for ourselves, and to think again.

It is necessary to take up a position. But it is dangerous, as Professor Stebbing shows, to accept a position that we have not examined. We are today confronted by, and involved in, a conflict of political-spiritual ideals whose nature we may imperfectly understand. Therefore, any attempt to analyze these opposed ideals, to evaluate them, to trace their evolution from political history, to apply them to our own lives, and to predict their effects becomes relevant. Such attempts have been made in the past, when today's crisis of conflict, though foreseen by the thinker, had not yet been reached. Professor Stebbing's book contains a summary of, and her judgment upon, other contributions to this process of thought. She is concerned to expose, and does to my mind expose effectually, the weaknesses inherent in certain declared positions, lacunae in the reason of so-called rationalists, imperfect civilization in the "civilized" approach, either inconsistencies or evasions in the spiritual (or Christian, or Catholic) point of view, and unthorough morality in the moralist. Using throughout an impersonal "I," she identifies herself with the individual reader for whom belief must have some background of reason and in whom belief is put to a new test.

Professor Stebbing, as her book's title implies, is concerned to strip the illusion (or element of self-delusion) from the ideal, and to see the given ideal at its own value, bare. She makes it clear that the existence of an ideal does not imply its moral excellence; the "bad ideal"—as, for instance, present in National Socialism—is her subject as well. She is interested in the unconscious ideal behind the rationalist (or anti-idealist) point of view, and in the rationalism through which the idealist can, only, advance. In examining this and other paradoxes she keeps midway between the public (or political) and the personal attitude, being alive equally to the contacts and conflicts that arise, in sincere people, between these two. Morally, the book may be said to address itself to those who, while resolved to wage and resigned to endure war, have in view that their function is to creative peace, and who see that towards a true, un-negative peace thought *now* must be the creative act. "Ideals and Utopias," "Materialism Is Not Enough," "The Pursuit of Happiness,"

"While Rome Is Burning," "Conflicting Ideals," "The Last Illusion" are some of the chapter titles, and these give some idea of the book's nature and plan. The book admits and clarifies many problems that it makes no rash claim to resolve: it is as much imaginative as it is, in the pure sense, intellectual—in fact, one might call this a helpful book. The human impulse behind it is very real.

Flaubert Translated

Gustave Flaubert, *Sentimental Education*, translated by Anthony Goldsmith. *Spectator*, August 15, 1941.

L'Éducation sentimentale stands in the first six, perhaps in the first three, of the great novels nineteenth-century Europe produced. It has not, I think, been translated, at least in England, before, and the appearance of Mr. Goldsmith's excellent English version is, therefore, important. The reader who has any French at all would still, of course, do better to read the original: the essence of Flaubert's prose commands so much attention that the very slightly greater difficulty of reading another language becomes immaterial. But for those who cannot or will not read French Mr. Goldsmith has lifted a barrier: there is now no reason why anybody's experience should remain incomplete—and not to have read *L'Éducation sentimentale* is, I believe, to be in a state of incomplete human experience. Mr. Goldsmith has so faultlessly kept, in English, the abruptness and suppleness of Flaubert's prose that this work deserves examination by those who, already familiar with *L'Éducation sentimentale*, are interested in translation for its own sake, as an art. The white-heat precision of Flaubert's French and its clearness—he identified style with vision—make translation of it the most exacting test of a man's power to know, and use, his own tongue. Analysis of the shortest sentence is necessary before one is able to render, in English, anything like the equivalent of its content—the very simplicity of each sentence having been achieved by the concentration of Flaubert's entire feeling for art.

And to meet the book, with an English title, in the familiar type and the red covers of the fiction part of the Everyman's Library, is valuable in another way. Flaubert's greatest novel now stands, for the English reader, alongside the classic English and Russian novels with which the Everyman format is associated—and its new position invites a comparison. What makes this latecomer unique—unique even among the other French novels, each in their way outstanding, that are already on the Everyman lists?

Frederic Moreau, whose education in love bears no fruit, for it only finishes when he is capable of no more in life, is a negative, selfish, and aimless figure. He is the completely antiheroic type, not evoking, and not intended to evoke, sympathy. Unlike the heroes of English novels he neither displays prowess nor is endeared to us by humility; unlike the heroes of Russian novels he is magnified by no complexities; unlike the heroes of many French novels he is incapable of exalting any one passion continuously: he is not even consistent in his ambitions. He exists in a series of moments; he does not attempt to synthesize; he reacts nine times for once that he acts. Yet his experience, subject of the novel, is an experience that we behold with awe. The height of the book is the height of the pressure of the emotion through which Frederic moves—and not Frederic alone: there are four women, Mme. Arnoux, for whom he feels that ideal love whose nature is that it cannot be realized; Louise, the gauche little provincial heiress; Mme. Dambreuse, the woman of the world; and Rosanette, the light-hearted courtesan who is too faithful in her relation with him. These four loves, each having not only intensity but in its own way a sort of completeness, cross and recross. And each character, as the book proceeds, comes to carry upon itself the shadows, or one might say the reflections, of the different others. By an art that is consummately Flaubert's own, minutiae and futilities and false starts are used to build up an effect of Fate.

Technically, the novel is on a level that has not been approached again. The plot is elliptic, with scenes moved on and transitions made in a phrase. The method is visual; thought is not analyzed, and no consciousness is examined from the inside. Each scene is made to take its peculiar emotional color from its setting, from the objects surrounding it. From the first page to the last is rendered a beauty that is not to be forgotten—the beauty, immune from feeling, of the thing in itself. Flaubert stands alone as the master of this poetic objectivity. One may say that his characters have been sacrificed to his perception. But it is perception that is the force of the book.

Truths about Ireland

Jim Phelan, *Ireland—Atlantic Gateway. Spectator*, September 5, 1941.

Mr. Phelan's book is, in one sense, topical: it discusses that aspect of the Irish question that is now most immediately in the British mind. But a permanent value is given to the discussion by the way he has placed an immediate problem—that of the future of Eire's Atlantic bases—in its relation to lasting facts. These facts are the outcome of a long-lived but not incurable psychological difficulty between two countries: accepted wrong ideas on the subject of Ireland have, in the long run, made for more trouble than wrong acts. Wrong acts can be canceled, but wrong ideas, if they persist, must continue to generate fresh mistakes. Mr. Phelan makes an important point when he shows that a hangover from unhappy history is *not*, actually, as operative in the present Irish attitude towards England as many English people are resigned to believe. Insofar as the hangover does exist, it operates—or, rather, is able to be exploited—only when some fresh blunder makes a context for it. And blunders arise, on the English side, from an ignorance that, in this writer's view, it is in one faction's interest not to disturb. The ordinary English person's ignorance not only of Irish history but of Irish mentality, hopes, conditions may be said to be natural—there is no reason why the peoples of two very different islands should be presupposed to have true ideas of each other. But now, when every trend of events shows that only understanding can make a possible world, the maintenance of such ignorance, and its exploitation, becomes unnatural and begins to look sinister. Mr. Phelan writes as an Irishman who, both for the sake of his own country and in the general interests of Western peace, desires good understanding between Eire and Britain. He addresses himself, in good faith, to the English reader who is in equally good faith willing to be informed.

Ireland—Atlantic Gateway will, I hope, be read. It is realistic, balanced, informative, and takes the long view. Having declared his position, the author shows no bias in his statement of facts. And the facts are not stated in the esoteric, or *nous autres*, language in which the Irish too often write about Ireland, but in common terms. For instance, the peasant mentality—a phenomenon if you like, but an ancient and very powerful one—may have been understood in relation to France or Russia without being, in relation to Ireland, her past or her present-day policy, either recognized or given its proper place. Again, the semi-imperial relationship of Ireland to Irish-America, although this has so many analogies, has not, to the English mind, ever quite come to light. The Atlantic remains, for Ireland, very much narrower than the Irish Sea—and the psychological geography should be recognized now that the wartime geography puts Ireland so very vitally on its map. "The Irish Empire" chapter is one of the most important in the book. And the chapter on Ulster contains truths that, fairly speaking, English people should know. One may say that the aim of the book is to combat fallacies that Mr. Phelan very rightly considers dangerous to the British conduct of the war. Though in no undue sense an alarmist, he gives alarming accounts of attempts (to which, as an Irish journalist, he has been subjected) on the part of gentlemen, sufficiently influential and beyond this claiming a further august authority, to "inspire" articles with just this fallacious note. As an Irish reader of the English press one has learned, with concern, to know such articles well: the mischief they do is incalculable—they are the remaining blunders towards Ireland of our day.

Indeed—as Mr. Phelan shows in his valuable chapter on Nazi propaganda in and towards Eire—it is, as much as anything, from the British journalistic faux pas that the Nazi propagandist is waiting to take his cue. Beyond this, given the inherent, temperamental anti-Nazism of Ireland, the Nazi propagandist is not on hopeful ground, having committed himself to a number of promises (to specifically different factions) whose inconsistency has already appeared . . .

A final note on *Ireland—Atlantic Gateway*: it is a first-rate analysis of the *nature* of Eire's neutrality. Without suggesting that this should be abandoned, Mr. Phelan does suggest how it not only could, but urgently ought to be, approached.

Life and Letters Today

Osbert Sitwell, *Open the Door* and A *Place of One's Own. Life and Letters To-Day*, January 1942.

How closely are short story and poem allied? Mr. Osbert Sitwell's work in the field of the short story suggests that the—perhaps unconscious—

alliance is close. It seems certain that poetic imagination goes to give his stories their particular force; also, these pieces have elements for which sheer invention could not alone account—for one, what one might call the element of vision. For necessary balance there is a matter-of-factness, or circumstantiality, that is probably (though surprisingly) best achieved by the poet: able to hold a fact—or scene, phrase, or face—at his arm's length, he can re-perceive it and like it for its own sake. With this goes discrimination in the treatment of prose: the medium has been a matter of choice. In good prose the limitations of the adopted medium are at once left and used. *Pseudo-poetic* prose, besides being specious, shows strain—the effort of the non-poet to force his medium into the no-world of his nostalgias and dreams. Mr. Sitwell's prose is not weakened by this attempt: it has a nervous suppleness, it releases vision but it is also concrete, factual, "straight."

To this discriminating exactitude we owe the setting of the scenes of the stories, and the power they have to expand in one's own mind. In *Open the Door* we find, mostly, fantastic plots; at least one character always carries the weight of either crisis or fantasy; one is always on the verge of the supernatural: a door stands ajar or opens, inside some heart or will. At the same time, vision and statement are so combined, or balanced, as to create an imperative sense of reality. There is, also, the fusion of the tragic and comic—I believe that to some readers just this is intimidating, or disconcerting, in Mr. Sitwell's work. One must recognize that it is at the fantastic moment, the moment when tears and laughter seem equally possible, equally extravagantly inexpressive, that the human soul does most often stand at its full height. Such moments these stories epitomize. "Defeat" with its tragedy, "Primavera" with its grotesquerie seem to me the collection's outstanding flowers. There are others that have a deceptive lightness—lightness of manner, never of content. These are war stories in feeling, if not always in subject. At once disinfected and pitiful, they tune in with our sustained underlying mood. They contain truths whose validity might not have been apparent until now.

A Place of One's Own is a long-short ghost story. It is, by implication, a good deal more. Newborough, at the start of this century, provides the vital background and the period setting. As a macabre tragicomedy this is a masterpiece: it is also an honorable reflection on the tenacity of fine-strung human nerves. An innocent, mutually loyal, elderly but well-preserved middle-class couple retire from business and come to settle at Newborough, thus realizing an almost lifelong dream. The imposing Victorian house they buy turns out to be haunted. Their propriety and their reticence are assailed by dreadful manifestations — or worse, by a series of tiny, remorseless flicks from the occult. Horror pervades rooms full of spring sunshine, encompasses even the bridge parties by which the couple mark their social success. And in horror's train comes, always, embarrassment: for months the couple hide their nerves from each other; they combine to hide their nerves from their neighbors; so they have a strong sense of *cela ne se fait pas*.[21] So, in its own way, the stand made here is heroic. And what of the quavering, always well-bred, semi-insane urgency of the ghost? . . . My immediate reaction to this story was that I dare not live in a house with a speaking tube. I am also haunted by Newborough, with its band playing, its summer seasons, its residential blandness, its bath chairs, and this horror, endemic, bred from its very heart.

Dubliner

Sean O'Casey, *Pictures in the Hallway. Spectator*, May 1, 1942.

Dublin would seem to have, as a city, a particular way of imprinting itself in the tender imagination. When to the susceptibility of the child has been added the susceptibility of the still voiceless artist, the results to be shown are remarkable. The emotions of childhood and adolescence are recollected in anything but tranquillity. One may take it that any capital city does something to any child — but, from the evidences of literature, one might equally take it that Paris and Dublin have had up to now a greater power than London to impress, oppress, penetrate, and disturb. London has put out, so far, no Proust, no Joyce; I would say she had found her most tender subject in Dickens. But with Dickens the memory is vested deep in the tale. I know of no London-bred writer who has given to Europe the retrospective monologue as a thing in itself.

James Joyce's *A Portrait of the Artist as a Young Man* is, inevitably, the prototype book about Dublin youth. It is difficult to read Sean O'Casey's *Pictures in the Hallway* without looking for parallels or divergences. Joyce and O'Casey have both placed at a distance their "I" subject by using the third person, not the first: for Joyce's Stephen Dedalus O'Casey has his Johnny Casside. Johnny's feelings and actions are, in the main, to be traced back further than Stephen's—the greater part of *Pictures in the Hallway* deals with a childhood, and we leave Johnny at about seventeen. With the Casside household, as not with the Dedalus, poverty is an ever-active and ever-pressing, tireless, relentless, ingenious foe. There is no father-figure, only two elder brothers; Mrs. Casside is a widow. There is a strong sense of family feeling in the Casside stand made against the world, the conspiracy between Johnny, the youngest child, and his mother in their joint attempt to preserve those illusions by which one lives.

In fact, fierce and tender regard for the life-illusion is a main theme of *Pictures in the Hallway*, as it is of all the O'Casey plays. The temptation to stand aside and brood upon life's bitter mystery gains less ground with young Johnny than with young Stephen—there is the oilcloth, for instance, to be kept unspoiled by the hideous progress through the Casside home of the "dung-chasers" with their carelessly carried loads: only when this is over may one return to contemplation of the flowering hawthorn tree. Mrs. Casside, glad to take in a neighbor's washing for sixpence and a glass of porter, loves to have autumn berries brought back to her from the country, "to brighten up the room a bit," she said, "and make us feel a little less like what we are." Throughout *Pictures in the Hallway*, as throughout *A Portrait of the Artist*, the burning power of the idea, of the image, is to be felt. But in the O'Casey book one feels more sharply the impact of the outside, everyday world. The chapters deal more with different conflicts with circumstance than with interior crises of the mind. With Johnny, desires do not consume themselves; their very force makes him a practical character. He steals the copy of Milton that his unfairly docked wages have made him unable, after all, to buy. While Stephen, alone in the rain on the top of the Howth tram, is crying aloud of women, Johnny is tickling Alice's legs on the ladder of a Dublin Protestant general department store.

The Protestant atmosphere, in contradistinction to the Catholic, stands out sharply, and is very well done. Protestants, in the Casside walk of life, are an active and redoubtable minority. They stand by each other, as a matter of policy, but are not, as Johnny's experience shows, averse from grinding each other's faces down. Snobbishness and hard-fistedness would appear to mark the admirers of King Billy. "Decency"—at least with regard to appearances—is a sine qua non, in the business world, of the creed, and Johnny goes off in a borrowed overcoat, with two well-faked letters of reference, to the interview that leads to his first job. Unwillingly, he makes one of the deputation that present the wedding clock to the loathed Mr. Anthony. And in Johnny's approach to the Gaelic League he confronts the predicaments of the Protestant Nationalist. His is the Dublin of the Lost Leader, Catholic Ireland's great Protestant, the fallen Parnell.

The chapters *are* pictures—and pictures brilliantly done. Dublin at all times, in all weathers. Johnny's day out with his brothers, the visit to Kilmainham jail, the approach to the theater, the days in the store, the ridden-down mass meeting, Mrs. Casside's fight for her son's life, Johnny's dance with the girl in the sunset-bedazzled street, the slaughterhouse alley, the work for Harmsworth's, the embattled election of wardens for the Protestant church—all these, strung on the thread of one inner meaning, are rendered with O'Casey's dramatist's clarity. Some scenes are dreadful enough, but they are redeemed from dreariness by the heroic arrogance of the fight. For Sean O'Casey, revolution—be it only individual revolution—is inherent in the very living of life. For all its detachment, *Pictures in the Hallway* reads like an ultimatum. The human spirit demands its own lebensraum.

Contemporary

V. S. Pritchett, *In My Good Books. Spectator*, May 23, 1942.

"If truth is the first casualty in war, the second is the literature of the period, especially the reflective literature," says Mr. Pritchett, opening his preface to his collected essays, *In My Good Books*. On analysis, the two casualties seem identical—or, at least, the second derives immediately from the first. There is more than war's bringing down "its medical date-stamp heavily" (and fatally) on every contemporary book. There is at present evident, in the reflective writer, not so much of inhibition or dulling of his own feeling as an inability to obtain the focus necessary for art. One cannot reflect, or reflect on, what is not wholly in view. These years rebuff the imagination as much by being fragmentary as by being violent.

It is by dislocations, by recurrent checks to his desire for meaning, that the writer is most thrown out. The imagination cannot simply endure events; for it the passive role is impossible. Where it cannot dominate, it is put out of action.

Time will give our confusion a perceptible character of its own. When today has become yesterday it will have integrated, into however grotesque a form. Until then, the desire for the whole picture must be satisfied by the contemplation of such whole pictures as already exist—in fact, of works of art that came into being either when there was a present that *could* be got into focus or when time had had time to act on what was already past. The subsidence of modern prose writing of any power leaves us, says Mr. Pritchett, alone with the classics. While nothing can stay our wish that these should be added to—for the incompleteness of art is an endless stimulus, second only to life's felt incompleteness without the comment of art—we can readjust to the classics in this temporary pause. This release from our claustrophobia *is* possible—and these essays suggest how great the release can be. If at present we cannot write, and our friends cannot write, we can read. We can add the faculties for one act to the other and, possibly, make better readers than we have been. Any shake-up received by our sets of values may not, in its effects, have been bad. Our susceptibilities may have been heightened; their range has almost certainly increased. The classics have not changed, but we have.

Mr. Pritchett writes as a reader—a reader under conditions his preface shows and I have tried to discuss. The temperament of the last three years has been assimilated into his criticism. In having objectified this temperament and known how to put it to a positive use, he has made an advance on behalf of all of us. He is contemporary in the exacting sense. As a critic he has occupied ground not yet touched by the novelists—of whom he is one. Ranging over (roughly) the last two hundred years, he has succeeded, by a series of implications, in throwing the years we are living into relief. Admittedly, he writes at a period when it is easier to contemplate books than contemplate life, and books are the subjects of his essays. But he goes direct through the form to the living matter. The great novel (he points out) at once attracts and intimidates but above all deludes us with its effect of finality. It may appear to reflect a perfected, synthesized world, of which its author shares the authority. This illusion a closer reading breaks down. The world enclosed in the great French,

English, and Russian novels proves as complex and shifting, as conflict- and conscience-ridden as our own. The writers have used their power to articulate questions to which no one is qualified to reply. Mr. Pritchett, using the interim in which life seems impossible to bring into focus, stud- ies great earlier attempts to focus life. For no artist, as for no insomniac, have the sheep he was trying to count ever stood still. One has to learn, apparently, to count the sheep that keep on jumping about.

Demonstrably, no conditions for writing have ever been really happy. Mr. Pritchett is out to define the weakness of a number of different writ- ers' positions. Fielding, Constant, Turgenev, Thackeray, Zola, Lermon- tov, Gogol, Peacock, Dostoevsky, Synge, and Svevo—to instance a few of the subjects of these essays—each felt equivocally towards his own age. No attempt to create in a book (by means of satire, sentiment, religion, dramatic symbolism, or picaresque simplification) the unity of which life is incapable ever wholly came off. The autobiographer and the diarist were a degree more happy; they could impose the however crazy unity of the "I." For the novelist the task of projection has been at all times, in all countries, differently difficult. Racial or personal makeup, place in society, adverse moral climate or deceptive experience have accounted for those imperfect detachments, those lesions in novelists. On what one might call the English lesions, Mr. Pritchett writes particularly well. Fielding and Thackeray made our only two notable attempts to get a grip on society; otherwise, in that direction we have been weak, as the French and Russians were not. Personal relationships, color-clouded by sex and not placed or framed by any clear sense of economic realities, have been, too much, the English preoccupation. To an extent, the world of the En- glish novel has remained the provincial, if lively, world of the "I."

At the same time—this suggestion runs through the essays—the En- glish have been victims rather than exponents of romanticism. They have been decades behind the rest of Europe in recognizing its inevi- table direction, its political dangerousness, or its economic spring. To life England contributed Lord Byron, but it was to take the art of Stendhal, Lermontov, Turgenev, to show the romantic hero in play. The barricades as much as the tearful boudoir were to be the theater of that tempera- ment; today, the mutilated frontiers of Europe show the outcome of the romantic obsession. From the declamation on the eve of the duel to the Nazi monologue it has not really been such a far cry. It may be said (and Mr. Pritchett has said) that Fielding, before romanticism had got a name, isolated for notice the man of power: there is a new relevance in *Jonathan Wild*.

These essays, singly known to *New Statesman and Nation* readers, gain by being collected. They assume an important relation to one another, and are in such order as to show the development of Mr. Pritchett's critical idea. For its homogeneity as a considered book, *In My Good Books* is not dependent upon its preface—too many prefaces to collections make rather transparent attempts to "bind." Here, the preface does no more than its proper duty in suggesting the lines, the contemporary nature, and the personal object of Mr. Pritchett's approach to books read and reread.

Selected *Tatler* Reviews: 1941 to 1950

Margery Allingham, *The Oaken Heart,* October 1, 1941

Autumn brings round again, this year as ever, her particular pleasures—a tang in the morning sunshine, dahlias, wood smoke, batches of new books. September, in town or country, knows exactly how to console us for the passing of summer. Opposite my window, the Regent's Park dahlias reflect their gorgeousness into the sunny lake—to use the fine old cliché, they make a brave show. And so, I may say, have the London publishers done: they have faced this year's difficult season with quite imposing results. With not only paper shortage but author shortage has the 1941 publisher to contend—many once lively typewriters are now silent, and pens have been laid aside, as the services, the ministries, or the hundred other activities of wartime divert writers' energies into new channels. A great many names are absent from the publishers' lists, and we must wait for peace until we see them again. But happily everyone is not silent: war experiences have already flowered into some quite remarkable books, so that this autumn's lists, though so much curtailed, can make up for their shortness by their good quality. Although the publishing season is still young, there are already new books that one cannot afford to miss.

High among these stands Miss Margery Allingham's *The Oaken Heart.* Miss Allingham has been for some time well known as a detective novelist of the first rank, with a flair for the psychological side of a mystery, a subtle perception of character, and a strong feeling for the atmosphere of a place. For this reason, none of her stories have shown the thin or flat technique of the "shocker." Now, in this first nonfiction book of hers, she puts her gifts to a new and important use. One may say that here again she examines a mystery—but it is the immortal mystery of the English heart. She writes about her own race, which has astonished the world. "You English are an extraordinary people!"—how often has one heard that remark made, and in what a variety of tones. I think, in *The Oaken Heart*, Miss Allingham shows that the apparent English extraordinariness resides in the English genius for staying ordinary under what might be called the most fantastic conditions. (I should like, by the way, to make clear from the very start that this is not one more of the "Britain Can Take It" books.)

Miss Allingham has for her subject an East Anglian village she calls Auburn, that was her birthplace, her childhood's home, and to which she and her husband returned to live. She, therefore, writes as a native. Auburn, despite its nearness to London, keeps unchanged its age-long, inbred, almost tacit traditions, its rare maypole, its slow motion, its ways of speech, and its local family names. Though pretty, it is saved from sentimental idyllicism by one successfully hideous shop. In this Auburn, Miss Allingham shows us a microcosm of that stubborn, serene England that is now at grips with war. Few people in Auburn ever utter that long word "democracy"—yet democracy, a democracy bred of ages, is the very spirit and fiber of that apparently go-easy village life. There is a strength in this that cannot be shaken, and a health that cannot be poisoned by the evils of war. The story of Auburn's reactions—from the summer before Munich up to some months short of the present day—is entrancingly, shrewdly, and matter-of-factly told. Miss Allingham has deep humor, but does not overwork it—myself, I detest village annals that ever verge on the "quaint." Her unsentimentality and her feeling for character are here to be seen at their very best. But she has something more—a dramatic feeling for the grand human spirit appearing in small acts or quite prosaic words.

What is it, though, that gives *The Oaken Heart* its sterlingly *original* quality? You may say that we have already had several books about rural England in wartime, evacuee invasions, A.R.P. crises, bomb stories. Not an English village, however remote, has not known its laughs, its alarums, and its tragedies. (Auburn, in the wartime sense, was far from being remote: it lies direct in the bombers' route to London, and from their dark doorsteps the villagers, speechless, watched London burn. When preparations went up against invasion, Auburn learned she was now in the front line.)

The originality of Miss Allingham's book about Auburn lies, I think, in the length and depth of her view. Though she delights in the humor and variations of character, her eyes are set on something symbolic behind. She respects the laws that these countrified human beings have evolved for themselves, and shows how, through every trial, these instinctive laws continue to hold good. She salutes the sanity of the judgments that, in such a village, draw their life from tradition. Herself an innate villager, she shows herself up against the city-bred, brain-spun, so-called "intellectual" view. She shows how sanely Auburn reacted to many crises — the king of the Belgians' surrender, the fall of France, the invasion threat. One may say that she gives, with equal fairness, examples of the village capriciousness. She is not out to idealize Auburn, nor to, at all explicitly, analyze it. She offers her Auburn as a phenomenon, and invites us to study, in it, what England is.

William Shirer, *Berlin Diary*, October 22, 1941

One of our troubles, in the last two years, has been that while almost everybody is ready to theorize, few people are in the position to make exact statements. With regard to certain facts and affairs, either ignorance affecting to be discretion or discretion disguising itself as ignorance inhibits almost everybody one meets. We have to be content to remain confronted by several unpleasant and sometimes threatening mysteries. Of these, the state of mind of Nazi Germany, since September 3, 1939, has been the most complete. Rumors and shreds of information tend to travel such a dangerously long way; we have been so consistently warned against wishful thinking in any estimations we are tempted to form that, with regard to life (and the daily details of life) in the enemy country, our imaginations may cease to function at all. Now, at last, comes Mr. William L. Shirer's *Berlin Diary*, giving us data for a great deal of thought. Mr. Shirer was a journalist in Europe from 1934 to 1941: during the most crucial of these years he acted as Berlin correspondent of the Columbia Broadcasting System of America. His diary was regularly and imperturbably kept: its publication in America has had a powerful effect on public opinion, and its appearance in England is of the first importance.

Mr. Shirer had, in fact, familiarized himself with (though never acclimatized himself to) the Nazi mentality while its coming dreadful effects on the world were still only to be guessed at. As an onlooker, he watched this horrible plant grow. The Nazi wish to bid for American good opinion, the Nazi hope that America *might* be impressed, led to Mr. Shirer's being allowed, in some cases offered, all sorts of facilities for an inside view. In fact, Germany hoped for a good press, and continued, up to late on in 1940, to desire to get one from Mr. Shirer. He must have maintained his position with some tact—and his reaction against this was the frankness he permitted himself in his diary: a diary, as he says in his foreword, kept for his own "pleasure and peace of mind." We may now reap the fruit of his experiences.

Apart from the vast interest of his matter, Mr. Shirer is the ideal diarist. His sentences are brief and matter-of-fact; the pictures he gives us could not be more vivid. His personal life, with its worries, appears just often enough to give the events round him their truly fantastic scale. He records the German scene from day to day with the exactness and the impartiality of a camera. His impartiality, be it said, works both ways: there are times when we may find his views on England—especially on her non-realism and dilatoriness—on English policy, some English statesman, and English conduct of the war, unpalatable. But frankness is one of the merits of this book, and if we cannot take Mr. Shirer's criticisms, which are fair, informed, and moderate ones, it is high time that we shut up shop.

We find Mr. Shirer repelled, and in the early years almost fascinated, by the Nazi mass-hypnosis at work. To promote this hypnosis, Hitler and his gang certainly did some first-rate theater work: the *Berlin Diary* contains descriptions of pageantry (always centering round the Führer's figure) that for the moment take one's own breath away. Never, in fact, was artistry more ably or more corruptly used. As a result of this hypnosis, the Germans became a diseased race, in whom judgment was suspended, emotion exploited, and will sapped. Mr. Shirer, having a scientific mind, constantly adds to his diagnosis of the disease. One gathers that by the time Germany entered the war the people's emotions had been already so much played upon, overstrained, that no one was capable of feeling much more: quite amazing apathy was the result. Berlin herself was so sluggish that apart from agitation caused by the British air raids, there was never much variation in morale. War, with its worries and deprivations, was from the outset universally loathed. The chief reaction to victories was the hope that these might hurry on peace, and the only spontaneous hatred for England was felt when England refused to come to terms.

With this, however, went callousness—no image of human suffering (on the screen, in talk, in newspapers) ever seemed to worry the German mind. Perhaps callousness and sentimentality always go together— incidents that crop up in the *Berlin Diary* certainly would suggest this. Also, Mr. Shirer is struck by the complete blankness that drops like a shutter over the German face when any at all disconcerting question is asked. One is not, in fact, expected to ask questions to which the answer has not been dictated ahead. The Führer, like the customer, is always right—and it is not for the German to reason why.

Mr. Shirer certainly got about. Having visited the German Fleet at Christmas (1939), each ship twinkling inside with Christmas trees, he comments on the first-rate morale of the Navy and of the democratic camaraderie existing between officers and men. In the German Army, later, he finds the same conditions—in fact, he contests very strongly our too-popular idea that the German soldier is dopey or robot-ish. The German fighters, he shows us, are vital, young in body and spirit—though their youth is being put to a vile use. Entering Paris (an ordeal he dreaded) only a very short time after the German troops, he feels bound to confirm, in almost every detail, the statement that they behaved impeccably. His picture of Paris then—shuttered, deserted, utterly silent in the ironic glory of summer weather—is unforgettable. In a German car he tours the Flemish and French battlefields, and puzzles over the mystery of the collapse—suspicion of a betrayal slowly gaining on him. He is at Compiègne: his account of the day there could not be more dramatic, or more controlled. Not for the first time, Hitler passes quite near him—Mr. Shirer has a great eye for physical mannerisms: not the twitch of an eyelid or the flick of a finger that may reveal (or give away) character seems to escape him, ever. On this occasion he writes:

I observed his face. It was grave, solemn, yet brimming with revenge. There was also in it, as in his springy step, a note of the triumphant conqueror, the defier of the world. There was something else, difficult to describe, in his expression, a sort of scornful inner joy at being present at this great reversal of fate—a reversal he himself had wrought.

After Compiègne, the return to obediently rejoicing (but *not*, apparently, deeply thrilled) Berlin. Soon after this, Mr. Shirer observes with interest the erection of still bigger and better grandstands—for the celebration of the successful invasion of Britain. Not very much later, these, with their large gold eagles, were unostentatiously taken down again. As to why Hitler did not, after all, invade Britain that 1940 summer, Mr. Shirer has theories (backed by some new facts) that are as interesting as anything in the *Berlin Diary*. At the height of that tense time he is allowed an amazing freedom in his tour of the French coast between the "invasion" ports—and forms the impression that here is largely bluff. From Gris Nez he watches the Channel air battles open the Battle of Britain . . . *Berlin Diary* is not easy to summarize; it is still more difficult to do justice to. It is an outstanding book of this autumn—a book that, I take it, no one will want to miss.

Upton Sinclair, *Between Two Worlds*, November 19, 1941

Mr. Upton Sinclair is a prolific writer, and obviously a very impassioned one. On the pink slip loose in the pages of *Between Two Worlds*, he gives an account of his method and frame of mind. "I have," he says, "supported myself by writing fiction since I was sixteen, which means for forty-six years. Now, all I have to do is to turn the spigot and the water flows." It certainly does: this is a torrential novel, in which the flaccid and slightly colorless characters seem to be whirled along. Most of these people, I understand, have already figured in *World's End*: if one has not read *World's End*, their beginnings and backgrounds are bound to be nebulous. To read a sequel-novel of which one has not read the predecessor always gives one a slight feeling of guilt.

Mr. Sinclair has no time for style: his narrative method reminds one of an incoherent person talking in a train. But one must honor his important intention—which is to save the world (even now) by inducing thought and inviting social criticism. He is out to embody history, modern history, in fiction. Living (or recently living) characters appear—not, I think, very impressively—among his fictitious crowd: Mussolini, Isadora Duncan, Hitler, John Sargent, Sir Basil Zaharoff, and others are present. I may say that young Lanny Budd, his mother Beauty, and the members of their cosmopolitan set are not types that invite social criticism. It is hard to enter into their hopes and fears. The story opens in 1919 and closes with the New York crash of 1929. Young Lanny, his French *amie* Marie (who is his mother's age), his mother, and her German lover Kurt (who is Lanny's age) start off as an almost idyllic quartet in the Riviera villa Bienvenu. At intervals, some or all emerge and dash about Europe, from capital to capital. But Kurt has been somber since the German defeat, and Lanny becomes increasingly troubled by world affairs and dabbles, exceedingly mildly, in socialist politics. Papa Budd, the big armament man, continues to supply money from America.

As a picture of pure futility this could be good enough, but Mr. Sinclair lacks or abjures the satiric sense. His people are truly "nice," and pursue, at immense expense, the good and the beautiful. I must admit that I found them pretty fatiguing (there is a dullness, even, in their high-minded absence of morals) and Mussolini, Isadora Duncan, etc., did not do much, in my view, to gin them up. Still, I did pursue the tale to its cryptic end. We are clearly due to hear more of the Lanny Budds.

Osbert Sitwell, *Open the Door*, December 3, 1941

I have been told—in fact, I have noticed—that quite a number of fiction lovers have a lively prejudice against short stories. This seems to be specially true of readers who go to the trouble of fetching their books from libraries, or to the expense of having books posted them—not to speak of the labor of posting books back again. At the end of all that one wants, naturally, solid value, "a book one can lose oneself in," as the saying is. From this point of view, collections of short stories are apt to look pretty doubtful—nothing but a succession of dead ends, of snappings out of it, of dirty turns played on the reader who had just been comfortably settling down. Also, the reader is apt to feel that the author is earning a doubtfully honest penny by collecting his pieces from magazines, and by serving up, in a deceptively coaxing jacket, nothing but a collection of odds and ends. The reader forms a picture of the author with his tongue in his cheek, murmuring cynically: "These ought to do again."

For whatever reason, I have seen ladies in libraries, yes, and in bookshops too, dropping attractive volumes as though they were hot potatoes, with a cry of outrage: "But these are only short stories!" Publishers, who have the public taped, receive short stories from authors with extreme gloom; young ladies in libraries, however persuasive, and young men in bookshops, however discreet, take up a deprecating attitude towards them. In fact, it seems to need the tongue of the serpent to put short stories across—and, even so, be prepared for an ugly comeback if the reader has not enjoyed himself. Far be it from me, who write short stories myself, to attempt propaganda for fiction in this form. Now that I come to think of it, rather too much propaganda may have been done already: the public has been confirmed in its prejudice by being told that the short story is an "art form." This is enough to put off any seeker for pleasure.

Actually, all that this should mean is that an unusual amount of the artist's technique goes to giving any good short story its form. But the art, if the story *is* good, is concealed art—so deeply concealed that you never might notice it. "Artiness"—an entirely different thing—rules any story right out, in my view. So does that awful cryptic coyness that some short story exponents consider smart. The writer who leads the reader right up the garden path, then breaks off with a "?" and walks away is not only failing to deliver the goods, he is helping to give the short story a still worse name.

My principal claim for the short story is that when it *does* come off it is preeminently good work. It cannot afford to misfire. It is out to produce a certain effect, and must. There is no room anywhere in it for muzziness—and look how muzzy some novels can be! It must have—and, if it succeeds, does have—point, punch, and pith. I should like—while still foreswearing all propaganda—to point out that some of the best as well as the most entertaining of our modern or recent English writing has been in the short story. Look at Kipling, Saki, Somerset Maugham—

the works of these three are already classics that any home should be sorry to be without. One more word to those who may perhaps be persuaded to depart from a lifelong prejudice and at least "try" short stories as reading fare—don't bolt the whole collection in one sitting. Short stories that are worth reading at all should be read not more than two or three at a time. Ideally, they should be allowed to "dissolve on the palate" one by one. For this reason: they are immensely compressed; they are designed to have a delay-action effect on your imagination. Give each story a chance to work in its own way. If possible, get up and walk round the garden between each. In this way you will find that your weekend book of short stories does last you the whole of the weekend. And not only this, you will find that it will amuse you even while you are not actually reading. But, of course, be careful *what* short stories you read.

Emphatically, go for Mr. Osbert Sitwell's. In *Open the Door* he has given us short stories at their and his own best. In fact one, "Defeat," is, I say in all sobriety, one of the finest, if not the finest, stories that I have read in the English language. It may be said that "Defeat" owes much to the poignancy and irony of its situation—but it took faultless feeling both as a man and an artist to write such a story without one wrong note or lapse. In this collection, all along the line, Mr. Sitwell has freed himself of that slight over-fantasticness, that slightly too inner laugh that was his only danger. He now shows a grand, simplified feeling for human dignity, even at its most pitiful; he shows more tenderness towards the grotesque—without any loss of height in his own high spirits, or any loss of edge to his fine and capricious wit. As a writer of wartime stories his taste is excellent: he distinguishes (as all our writers do not do) between obvious pathos and implacable tragedy.

Not that all the stories are war stories; neither are all sad—the sad and the merry are about fifty-fifty. Some—such as "Primavera," "Touching Wood," "Plague-Cart Before Horse"—are grim chiefly; some—such as "The Woman Who Hated Flowers"—show a sardonic tenderness; most have stings in their tales. While continuing his steady growth as an artist, Mr. Sitwell has not relinquished small and special delights—the veracities of the rich, the vanities of the apparently chastened old, and, above all, the quirks and pretensions common to human nature continue to put their spell on his pen—or, should one say, come under the spell of his pen? He sets, as he always does set, his scenes brilliantly: "the shires of England to San Salvador, from Sweden to the Riviera, from Southern Italy to China, from Mediterranean islands back to the Yorkshire Wolds" is, as his publisher indicates on the wrapper, the itinerary of this collection of tales.

James Agate, *Thursdays and Fridays: A Book for Everyday People*, December 31, 1941

Critics seem to have it all their own way—how rarely anybody criticizes the critic! Yet how important it is that he should be up to the mark. The wrong kind of critic not only wastes one's time, he really does more than anyone else to put art itself in a bad position. He can create, where books, pictures, and plays are concerned, what one might call bad visibility. He can conceal his subject behind a perfect smokescreen of high-class hanky-panky, catchphrases, misleading statements, and muddled thought. His superciliousness and his *nous autres* attitude can combine—have combined, in many unhappy cases—to put the general public right off art.

My opinion is that this kind of critic bothers the artist (who is usually a fairly straightforward person) just as much as he annoys the public. The artist expects his work to be understood, and—if he is a real and not a phony artist—he works harder than most people to this end: in his own way he is as plainspoken as possible. He is, above all, a person with a good deal to say. (The so-called or phony artist who has almost nothing to say but says this as mysteriously as possible may be ruled right out of this discussion.)

In the long run, we may thank the wrong kind of critic for any public hostility towards art. And the artist may thank him for the consequent isolation in which, entirely contrary to his nature, he (the artist) has often to live and work.

When people tell you they have no time for art, what they really mean, in nine cases out of ten, is that they have no time for all the nonsense about it. And those with a trend to art are made skeptical by critics who claim to find a new genius on every bough.

The real test of the artist is that he should be a person of good faith. He is also—and this is very important—using his medium, be this words, notes, or color, to say something that has not been said before. In many ways, he is in the position of the small child that, though already packed with ideas and feelings, is still in the process of learning how to talk. Both the child and the artist, for the same reasons, do sometimes express themselves rather funnily, or let us say, unexpectedly, in their efforts to tell us just what they mean. It is a help, in both cases, to the outsider if a third, understanding person is at hand to interpret. The critic, halfway between the artist and the public, should, at least to my mind, play exactly this part.

The person who knows about children knows well when the child *is* really trying to say something, or when, on the other hand, the child, excited by strange company, is simply showing off or trying it on. And the person who knows (genuinely) about art is able to make exactly the same distinction in the case of the activities of an artist. The critic should know just this. He should — in fact, he must, if he is to be any good — be, equally with the artist, a man of good faith. Because one man of good faith instinctively recognizes another: on this one subject he can never be fooled.

We give the critic authority on the understanding that he will deal fairly with us; on the understanding that, while knowing the language of art, he will speak to us in language that is our own. It is his business to simplify, not to complicate or falsify, the relations between the public and the artist. What I call the bad critic creates confusion by his wish to do an act on his own. Whereas the good critic, though he may admit to being an egotist, still always loves his subject more than himself: zest for his subject adds drive to his pen. Though he may admit to a number of prejudices, he never attempts to disguise these as principles. So, though you may disagree with him flatly on some points, you will always retain your respect for his point of view. When he says "Don't miss this," or "You need not bother with that," you have reason to feel, as he has reason to feel, that he does know what he is talking about.

All this has been my sidelong approach to Mr. Agate's critical excellence. That excellence is so fully recognized that I feel shy of adding comment to it: in calling Mr. Agate an outstanding "good critic" am I not restating the obvious, or even running the risk of being impertinent? So I shall confine myself to trying to show at least a few of the many reasons why Mr. Agate *is* such a good critic. And his *Thursdays and Fridays*, subtitled *A Book for Everyday People*, gives ample matter on which to work.

The book, divided into two parts, consists of reprints of his critical writings. His Thursday book pages for the *Daily Express* make the first half. In the second appear his Friday theater articles for *John o' London's Weekly*, which came out over the nom de plume, "Richard Prentis."

The Thursday pages, as Mr. Agate shows, were written for an enormous public with no initial bent towards books for their own sakes. The Friday articles were addressed to readers with a strong general feeling towards the theater, but perhaps certain gaps in their appreciation of it. Both Thursday and Friday readers would thus be "ordinary people" in the good, solid, unspoiled sense. They deserve—do we not all?—from the critic a straight deal. And they certainly get one from Mr. Agate.

He takes it—I feel sure rightly—that ordinary people are, at the same time, people of fundamentally sound good sense. It is to this good sense that he addresses himself. He is out to expose nonsense that, by fair or foul means, may have been put across. He is the arch-debunker: to the deflation of nonsense about, or in the name of, books and the theater he brings a needle-pointed, unfailing pen. Not a fad or a fashion gets by, with him. He is the relentless enemy of the highfalutin. How many exponents of fancy writing must have buried themselves after these attacks! And yet "attacks" is hardly the word—there is something imperturbable, disinterested, as well as astringent and vigorous, about Mr. Agate's delivery. You could never say that he had it in for any particular type or group. He cannot stand the *faux bon*—it is simply that.

So much for what one might call his destructive side. He comes out, to my mind, as strongly—even more strongly—in his power to build up appreciation. Though he writes disengagedly, often colloquially, he has behind him a background of intellectual pleasure got from the abidingly good in art. One might call him a *bon viveur* of the arts—but this has left his values both true and stern. He is, in the literal sense, the most attractive of critics: he can rivet one to whatever he likes to say. He makes every play with his personality—anecdote, confession, and prejudice—but behind this one feels that his principles are impersonal.

The book articles are brilliant; the theater articles, though equally stimulating, have a profounder quality. The theater is, clearly, his own ground. On the subject of the theater his knowledge—both his memory and his reading—goes so deep that it has been absorbed completely. He wastes no time tilting at anything that, while it merely bores him, may be excellent in its own way. Here, for instance, is Mr. Agate on ballet:

If I want to hear a symphony of Tchaikovsky, Brahms, or Berlioz and none is playing at the Queen's Hall, I have no objection to closing my eyes and hearing it at Covent Garden. That a number of young people should at the same time be scampering about on the stage seems to me to be neither here nor there, and, anyhow, it is entirely their own business. Presumably it pleases them, and I can arrange for it not to annoy me.

With the manias of the balletomanes he deals, however, less tolerantly . . . The range of *Thursdays and Fridays* is very wide: all sorts of biography, criticism, good and bad novels are covered in the first half; all kinds of productions, as well as theatrical memoirs, in the second. Apart from the other qualities I have touched on, this is the most entertaining book I have read for a long time.

Maurice Richardson, *London's Burning,* January 28, 1942

London "blitz" books continue to come from the publishers: there are now so many, one hardly knows where to turn. For months, since what one should guardedly call the first, or the 1940, phase of the home-front "blitz," many such records have been appearing. Many civilians—some professional writers, some not—have felt an imperative need to get on to paper their experiences as one kind of combatant.

One cannot fairly say that these "blitz" books are too many: each bears the mark of a profound experience and has the ring of implicit courage. And, to come to regard the "blitz" as a "stale" subject would be not only unworthy on our part, but extremely rash: all this may begin again—there is much we may learn meanwhile.

All the same, one must sift through this "blitz" literature to see how much *is* literature, how much no more than journalism. The books I should class as journalism (though of an excellent kind) give the impression of having come hot from the press while some of the ruins of London were still hot; through word-pictures, they supply information for which there was an immediate immense demand. They describe "blitz" experience as a special experience, not possible, through its fantastic nature, to relate to the rest of life. Such special, fantastic experience must, of course, take some time to digest, and many of the "blitz" books did not attempt to digest it; they wrote at the height of their feeling; they did not give themselves time.

The writer of the "blitz" book that is to have permanent value should, I think, have had the time and the faculty to digest his experience — also, to compare and to balance it with other happenings in his own life.

What the future England will want to know is how the *ordinary* man lived through *extraordinary* times. At present, it is necessary to sustain ourselves by taking the ultra-heroic view. We must point out, first of all, how wonderful everyone was. This may be carried — I must say, at the risk of offending readers — to the point of misleading sentimentality. While we *think* we depict the ordinariness of the ordinary man, we very often paint him in roseate hues.

To those accustomed to the "blitz" books in emotional language, Mr. Maurice Richardson's *London's Burning* may ring cold. For instance, Mr. Richardson opens, with perfect candor, by saying: "I joined the A.F.S. to dodge the Army. I have always had a peculiar horror of the Army, due to cowardice, hatred of discipline, phobia of scratchy uniform dating from school O.T.C. days." And the whole of his book is a record of what one might call involuntary courage, marked throughout by an anti-heroic tone.

London's Burning is an account of the writer's experiences in the A.F.S., from the middle of the summer of 1940 to the October of that year, when, in the course of a hellish night, he was knocked out and disabled from further service. It shows just how short a time it takes (under "blitz" conditions) to make a young fireman (or fireman young in experience) into an old soldier — disabused, canny, up to all tricks, taking no chances, saving of courage and energy.

If the A.F.S. recruit got a kick from his first "blitz" fire, that was the only kick he got. Roughly speaking, these fighters hated the job — but did it. In them survived, underneath their acquired toughness, the strength and the weakness of their civilian makeup — love of habit, of comfort (even the sparsest comforts), of safety itself.

The account of the training — with an instructor who was, one must hope, a bully of a rare type — is followed by an account of life in the unit: a London A.F.S. substation.

Recruited from many classes and types of worker, Mr. Richardson's fellow A.F.S. men still bore the stamp, and spoke in the idiom, of the different ways of life from which they came. The idiosyncrasies of each fireman, whether on furious duty or in off-times, were heightened by "blitz" conditions. There was little that they did not know about each other—and, on the whole, wonderfully little they did not like. Kindness and ruthlessness mingled in the congested station—in which there were not enough bunks to go round, so that, blind with next-morning fatigue, one had to wait for one's turn.

Mr. Richardson is not a writer for nothing. His accounts of fires are terrible and superb. Also, he can describe—and this needs disciplined language—nervous and physical tiredness at the nth degree. And, again, the ecstasy, blurred by exhaustion, of forty-eight-hour leaves—the sleep between sheets, the eating of food you like, the gimcrack amenities of a Maida Vale hotel—a hotel itself not immune from "blitz": he gives us one excellent chapter here . . . .

Every page of this book shows the benefit of reflection, digestion, and time. The cold exactness of the language makes the heat of the subject the more felt. I may say that no passages are "horrific."

I have already recommended, in these pages, two war books that rank (to me) as war literature—*Fighter Pilot* and *2 Survived*. To these I would add *London's Burning*—a book for now *and* the future, whose value is sure to be more than topical.

Evelyn Waugh, *Put Out More Flags*, March 25, 1942

Mr. Evelyn Waugh is never shy of his subject. In this he differs from many novelists who give one the feeling, halfway through, of being committed to something they do not quite like. Just as a person in a restaurant who has inadvertently ordered the wrong thing pushes the food halfheartedly round his plate, so does one kind of novelist push his subject around. Mr. Waugh is never in this position.

In his latest novel, *Put Out More Flags*, Mr. Waugh has settled down to a subject of which our novelists *have* been shy—people's private, uncensored reactions to the outbreak of war.

The book opens on that sunny Sunday morning, September 3, 1939, and covers the first (or Bore War) phase of hostilities. The main scene — with one or two breaks — is England. You may say: "Yes, but this has been done before." It has been attempted, but not done — that is exactly where shyness has come in. So far, this has been a bad war for contemporary novels: all the best productions have been "escapes."

There *have* certainly been a number of wartime novels, but these struck me as being inhibited. On the whole, our novelists have played safe; they appear to have imagined into existence a censorship such as never was, or could be. Against this, they are anxious not to offend. Consequently, they work hard to be bright, and at the same time to represent all their English characters as being, in wartime, inflexibly noble.

Orthodox topics for comedy, such as evacuees, servant-shortage, and ill-assorted relatives moving in on each other, have been played on till one could nearly scream. I respect the good intentions of novelists who hope, by their work, to contribute to good morale. But I cannot feel it a good thing, even in wartime, to overlook so much of reality.

As a reader, I feel I should like a pause in the list of smiling-through novels of English middle-class life — blitzed or un-blitzed, billeted upon or not billeted upon. We have been given many, and they were nice.

But, after all, when England became the Home Front, she did not cease to be a diversified society, full of crooks, cranks, rakes, sillies, and egotists. On Sunday, September 3, we did not all change our spots — as though we had gone into church, and never come out again. War has, if anything, heightened our foibles. One has heard a good deal of free, ruthless, and racy talk — after all, it is freedom that we are fighting for. Those nice, orthodox, smiling-through novels have only told us the half. For some time we have awaited the novelist who could reflect, in a book, the truly fantastic scene.

This has been done by Mr. Evelyn Waugh. *Put Out More Flags* seems to me to hit the nail right on the head. So much so that any reader lulled by conventional wartime fiction may receive a series of slight shocks. As to the pre-"Churchillian renaissance" England, Mr. Waugh has no illusions at all. He writes as most of us thought, felt, talked — though, need I say, much more brilliantly.

It may be argued that Mr. Waugh, from the time he burst on us with *Decline and Fall*, has always created a special world — or, in fact, that

Waugh characters are a race apart, a race so individual and so stylish that a generation of humans grew up to imitate them (which would not be the first case of Nature following Art).

Actually, the thing about Waugh characters is that they are superhumanly natural: they behave as they feel. They appear sophisticated because one is unaccustomed to seeing people behave as simply as this. In their willingness to try anything once, they preserve an incorruptible naïveté. The young things and the old buffers, all highly idiosyncratic, all seem, in one sense, the same age.

At the same time, with each novel of Mr. Waugh's they have been, as a race, perceptibly growing up. And either they have been growing more like us, or we have been growing more like them. Either we have become more extraordinary, or Mr. Waugh's characters have become less so.

It is, therefore, with a far from impersonal interest that we watch these Waugh people take 1939. Its forecast shadow had long been felt in their world. There were butterflies (if they *were* butterflies) of an uneasy, drafty, and clouded summer.

It is Basil Seal (of *Black Mischief*) who, present or absent, strings together the country and London scenes of *Put Out More Flags*. A cool hand, he does not cease to worry, and to be loved by, with degrees of exasperation, three women—his sister, Barbara Sothill; his mother, Lady Seal; his mistress, Angela Lyne. Barbara, alone, since the war, at Malfrey, has the restless pleasure, for some time, of housing Basil, who not only finds a way of milching her neighborhood, but is soon *au mieux* with the local bride.

At the start, all three loving women had hailed the war as a heaven-sent solution of the Basil problem; they had dedicated his life to his country with a mixture of solemnity and relief. But Lady Seal's attempts to maneuver Basil into the Bombardier Guards are not, for reasons shown, a success.

Sir Joseph Mainwaring, too often Basil's unhappy sponsor, expects the worst, and is justified. In their London flat, among bottles and needlework, Alistair and Sonia Trumpington—these days very happy out of the limelight—wonder what *this* war will be like. In London, Basil, before his reverse with the colonel and his get-out to Malfrey, has been converging with the intelligentsia, in the person of his reigning silly, the artistic Poppet Green.

More deeply, and with a profound repugnance, is that unhappy aesthete of the Twenties, Ambrose Silk, involved with the same youthful, dreary, and earnest set: passionately does he fail to share their concern as to the futures of Parsnip and Pimpernell, two poets who have fled to New York. Peter Pastmaster reappears, woos, and marries. Ambrose Silk, through his publisher, Mr. Bentley, becomes involved with the Ministry of Information.

Angela Lyne, alone, goes through a bad time in her flat. Basil, having built up a tidy sum in the Malfrey neighborhood by means I will not reveal, returns to London and makes the War Office, but not Susie, who is the preserve of Colonel Plum. Cedric Lyne, Angela's husband, goes to Norway, not to return.

Put Out More Flags is at once implicitly somber and brilliantly funny. I do not really think that any living novelist writes better than Mr. Waugh. In this book, as well as everything else, there are pages of a nervous, reticent beauty. His range of feeling, as well as his powers as a writer, continue to amaze me. He has placed, in *Put Out More Flags*, that first phase of the war—a phase so negatively tragic in its futility—in the perspective of judgment, as well as time. We and his people know better now. He implies a hundred ironies that he does not state.

I call this our first war novel because—though in the light of my summary this may seem odd—it is the first grown-up and serious one. Mr. Waugh has done more than cut the cackle; he has spoken—though with apparent lightness—the truth. No wonder he is not shy of his subject: only inefficacious people are shy.

Warren Stuart, *The Sword and the Net,* April 8, 1942

The Sword and the Net is a really superb thriller, with a good deal more to it than just that. By the end of the story the Nazi hero has been through not only physical dangers and agonies, but extreme spiritual vicissitudes. Mr. Warren Stuart has created, in Otto Falk, a man of honor forced to sacrifice honor to what he believes (till the belief snaps at a crisis) to be the one and supreme cause. Otto is a young German airman who has been shot down in England, who has escaped, made a sensational return to occupied France, and presented himself to Berlin. His reward is to be entrusted with an exacting mission: he is to serve in the inner Nazi spy and saboteur ring in America.

Otto has, from childhood, spoken English and Swedish. He is therefore told to disguise himself as a young Swedish carpenter, Nils Jorgensen. The disguise must go deep; it must be a psychological one. In affecting to be the simple, good-hearted Nils, fanatical enemy of the Nazi idea, Otto, at moments, almost *becomes* Nils—for Nils does indeed correspond with one underlying part of his character. The other Otto, the Otto his friends admire, is by contrast sophisticated and ruthless and a flaming devotee of the Nazi cause.

The spy arrives in America in a rather disconcerting glare of publicity: the atrocity program to which he finds himself committed, the strain of deceptions practiced with friendly people, and the conflict within him of the Nils and the Otto get him down. To crown everything, he falls deeply in love—and has to confront the American girl's horror when he tells her the truth.

But by the time he tells her, that truth is a thing of the past . . . Otto's fight to undo the evil that he has fostered, the closing-in on him of implacable enemies, and the ordeals shared by the girl Clare, provide the most exciting part of the book—a book in which the excitement standard is high. I shall be surprised if *The Sword and the Net* does not soon make a film. But it has subtleties the camera might miss: scenarios allow little place for the soul.

Virginia Woolf, *The Death of the Moth*, June 24, 1942

It was good news when we heard that another Virginia Woolf book was to appear. *The Death of the Moth* is a collection of essays—the essays were written from time to time during the last twenty years. Most of them have appeared in periodicals; a few have not been published until now. Before her death, Virginia Woolf had planned, and begun to work on, the making of this collection: her husband has now completed her work for her. *The Death of the Moth* is the third of her books of this kind; it follows the two volumes of *The Common Reader*.

With some novelists, criticism is no more than a by-product. We know that with Virginia Woolf this was not the case. In fact, I know there are many people who find her more simple, more sympathetic, perhaps more lovable as a critic than as a novelist. Possibly her feelings about books were more direct and less complicated than her feelings about life. Having known her, I know it is wrong to see her as a sort of Lady of Shalott, who could only bear to behold life when it was reflected into a mirror—the mirror being the mirror of art. No; actually she was a woman who was in love with every sensation connected with being alive. She loved no book better than she loved the living of a quite ordinary day. To read, to enter the world of a book, was to her like passing from one room of her house into another. But perhaps one is happier in some rooms than in others. And perhaps she found books less perplexing than she found life.

In her novels, what may be unfamiliar or even frightening is the perplexity of her characters. Her people are *not* complex, but are perplexed. Though they are outwardly quite prosaic men and women, living in London or staying at the seaside, they seem to be incapable of a quite prosaic experience. Their problems are the problems of visionaries: even the simplest acts they have undertaken—the taking of a taxi, the buying of a bunch of flowers, the entering of an unknown room, the keeping up of a conversation at dinner—make them constantly hesitate, question themselves, reflect.

Do we ourselves never feel—yes, even at the most inappropriate moments—this rush of questions and dreams? I am certain we all do. But we prefer to deny them: we are frightened of feeling silly or of losing our way. That may be why Virginia Woolf's insight, as a novelist, into the irresponsible, unpractical human mind makes some readers uneasy. Perhaps—should this be a new idea?—it made her a little uneasy too. It is tiring to know too much about human beings.

On the whole, the great attraction of novels is that while they make life seem more interesting, they do also appear to simplify it. We expect the novelist to put this and that in its place. Virginia Woolf, who was above all a truthful writer, could not perform this trick of making life seem simple, because it never did seem simple to her. But she wished, like many of us, for simplification, and books did to her seem simple—in the great sense. Therefore, when she was writing about books (in fact, writing her critical essays), she was at rest from the perplexities that she felt when she was writing about life (or writing novels). Her truthfulness permits her to show that among books she is very, very happy. These essays in *The Death of the Moth* communicate, above all, intense happiness.

I think the first reason for one's love of these essays is that they are never, in the frigid sense, "literary." They are full of burning ideas, but contain no dogma about the arts. They vary very much in tone; some are detached and impersonal—for instance, the essays on Henry James, George Moore, the novels of E. M. Forster, the art of biography—some are very personal, even intimate, and give the effect of confidences or of idealized, happy gossip. Examples of this second manner are the essays on Walpole and Cole, on Madame de Sévigné, on Sara Coleridge, and above all, the "Reflections at Sheffield Place," which opens some thoughts about Gibbon of the *Decline and Fall* with a dazzlingly lovely picture of rhododendrons reflecting their colors into a lake.

Those rhododendrons flowered how long ago? The spell of the writing makes them flower today. For Virginia Woolf the past was never sterile or dead; it was as near her senses, and as alive, as the present. Everything that had ever happened—that had been thought, felt, desired, or dreamed about—belonged, where she was concerned, to Today. Neither the coldness of print nor the stretch of time separated her from anyone who had lived. Books were to her, above all, invaluable keys to other people's experiences—experiences that her own imagination could enter into and enjoy to the full. Also, because she was a writer, all other writers, however long dead, were at once her contemporaries and her kin. Her writing about other writers, with all their queernesses, is thus, above all, very sociable. Like somebody who enjoys having many friends, she is at once generous and inquisitive. She likes to know what people think of each other.

Not all the essays in *The Death of the Moth* are about books and writers. There is the lovely and tender title essay itself. There are village and London pictures; there is "Evening over Sussex—Reflections in a Motor-Car." There is the closing "Thoughts on Peace in an Air-Raid"—the most moving picture that we have had yet of human malevolence threatening natural peace, the throb of engines high up in the silence over the old, small village and the calm, sleeping downs. A bomb drops, then there is silence; then we hear an owl hoot and an apple drop on the grass.

Siegfried Sassoon, *The Weald of Youth*, November 25, 1942

To write the story of one's own life should be easy—nothing need be invented; from the real scenes and real characters crowding the memory one need do nothing more than select. The plot has provided itself, and is seldom dull. And one's interest in the subject is not likely to flag—for oneself *is* a subject of the first interest.

So one might think. All this might appear true—to those who have either not tackled autobiography-writing, or not been exposed to the output of those too many people who, with too artless confidence, *have*. The fact is that the first-rate autobiography, able to stand on its own as a work of art, is rare. I should like to invite readers to make a list of autobiographers, of whatever country, whom they consider to be of the first rank. Compared to two other lists they might make—of major biographers and of major novelists—I feel sure they would find the first remarkably short. One might say, of course, that *concealed* autobiography is present in most forms of creative writing: many novelists make their own lives their material; many biographers turn to their own experience in order to translate that of their subject. The honest biographer may, even, confess to you that he feels most drawn to the character who in some way (though only he may perceive this) resembles himself.

The "straight" autobiography, of true value, is therefore, let us agree, rare. Both shyness and pride must be overcome before one can deal with the direct "I," before one can write about oneself, tell one's own story, with detachment, authority, and simplicity. Also—the first rule for all writers—"one must interest."[1] To be interesting needs great selective skill. The memories must be given an order that shall be intelligible to other people, as well as genuine to oneself. Sensibility—in the writing of autobiography, as in the writing of poetry—is the ultimate guide. But the critical faculty comes into play, too. And one must not lose sight of the fact that one is telling a story.

Mr. Siegfried Sassoon is one of our few born autobiographers. As a poet, he felt the force of moments as they occurred—but also, he has been able to revive them. His *The Weald of Youth* is full of vital recaptured moments, for the years covered are those of his very young manhood: the book ends with the start of the 1914 war. The first chapter opens in 1909, with the elation of seeing an early poem in print. In charm, in variety, and in interest, the book gains much from the writer's two-sided life. Here we have no tale of the orthodox literary aspirant, deserting the open air, despising outdoor activity, and seeking some cultured fastness, full of an inky gloom. Hunting and cricket played as great a part in Mr. Sassoon's youth as the writing of poetry and the meeting of intellectuals. One feels that English literature might have gained if, in the lives of more writers, either this, or an equivalent balance, could have been as truly kept. The breach between Heartbreak House and Horseback Hall occurred, I suppose, towards the end of the last century, and its effects are not ceasing to be regrettable. On the whole, we have to turn to the Russian novels for really living accounts of sport. English sport has not yet the literature (I really do mean *literature*) it deserves. On the other hand, much of our literature is impaired by having an indoor, finicky atmosphere.

Mr. Sassoon, in the different parts of his autobiography—in some, as you will no doubt remember, he thinly veils himself as "George Sherston," but in *The Weald of Youth* he no longer uses this veil—does much to close this breach between indoor and outdoor life. Over every scene he describes, therefore, hangs a sort of eagerness and exhilaration. The riding of a race and the tea party at the Gosses' in Regent's Park, the cricket match and the breakfast with Rupert Brooke, the young people's dance in the Kentish country house, and the interview in the daunting editor's office are all stamped with their first youthful zest for experience—for its own sake, of whatever a kind. This is, in fact, a fine book about being young. Those ambitious, shy, lonely months in London haunt one. There are memorable portraits of writers—each with his mild affectation—seen with youth's eager and sometimes puzzled eye. And over the country home, as over the Weald, hangs perpetually an early morning light. That the prose style is beautiful, simple, fluid, and evocative does not need to be said.

Leo Tolstoy, *War and Peace*, December 23, 1942

Tolstoy's *War and Peace* has been called the greatest novel in the world. Its reappearance today is an event: for too long it has been unobtainable in this country, at first because of, later in spite of, the increasing demand. Supplies of both the English translations—Constance Garnett's and Aylmer Maude's—ran out: the bookshops and libraries had to give thousands of would-be readers the same disappointing reply. Messrs. Macmillan have now been our benefactors in bringing out (by arrangement with the Oxford University Press) this fine one-volume edition of the Aylmer Maude translation, complete with notes, maps, list of principal characters, and table of historical events, priced at 12s. 6d. Nothing, however, is perfect in this imperfect world—unhappily, I may have to warn you that your particular copy may not be in your hands until next spring, and more, to be certain that *that* shall happen, you should put down your name for it with your bookseller *at once*. What has happened is that the first printing (30,000 copies) has been sold out before publication date. A second large (though, remember, not inexhaustible) printing should be ready by May 1943.

"Present conditions" are certainly not kind to us. Some of us, unable to wait till next spring, may successfully beg, borrow, or steal—but let me not inculcate bad book morals! Meanwhile, it is interesting to study our present-day need—call it hunger—for *War and Peace*. For the reasons for this, we must turn to the book itself.

Other writers (for all I know) may have attempted, but no one but Tolstoy has carried off, a novel of this magnitude—a novel that relates as well as embraces such diverse kinds of human experience. The first part of *War and Peace* was first published in Russia in 1865; the second in 1869—and yet, as one reads, these dates seem to mean almost nothing, for no novel remains more *contemporary*, more completely without a touch of "period" oddness or the very slightest grain of the dust of time. Each character, as one turns the pages, comes nearer to us than we are to ourselves. Each situation—be it in a drawing room or battlefield, young girl's bedroom or generals' council chamber, hunting lodge or state anteroom, threatened city or quiet country estate—is of momentous interest. What happens *matters*. Tolstoy imbued each scene he touched with the most convincing kind of psychological truth. To this truthfulness, I believe, are owed the book's harmony and its triumphantly right proportion. One passes, that is to say, without any sense of discrepancy, from some decision made by Napoleon to some hesitation of the man or woman in love.

War and Peace opens with 1805: that June, Russia, under the young

Tsar Alexander I, is on the eve of war with Napoleon. Books I, II, and III deal with the campaign waged by Russia against the French in Austria, which ended with the Battle of Austerlitz. In 1807 we have the meeting of the three emperors at Tilsit. The final war phase is the fateful 1812 — Napoleon's invasion of Russia, the French entry into Moscow, the burning of Moscow, the French retreat. With 1812 closes the main action of *War and Peace*.

There are, however, two epilogues: one deals with the after-lives of the principal characters. In the case of these characters there is no fixed "conclusion." Some have died, in the course of the story, but those whom we leave living seem as though they were likely to live on in a curious perpetuity of their own. We first met them, in most cases, young; we part from them middle-aged. They have grown, they have deepened, they have in some cases altered. But while life lasts, one cannot write "finis" to anyone.

The fine pattern of individual lives is placed against the heavier pattern of history. Yet, in *War and Peace*, history dwarfs nothing—one cannot call any one of these lives "little." The first greatness of the Tolstoy of *War and Peace* is—I maintain—his greatness as a creator of men and women. This is a novel crowded with major characters—and one should hardly say crowded, for that suggests confusion: in fact, each man and woman, from their very first appearance, has his or her own orbit, follows his or her own course. Paths cross, natures conflict, destinies affect one another—and all this goes to make a dynamic pattern that, though complex, is somehow never involved.

Five families, all aristocratic—the Bezúkhovs, the Rostóvs, the Bolkónskis, the Kurágins, and the Drubetskóys—dominate, at least on one plane, the novel . . . Pierre Bezúkhov (recently legitimatized son of the old Count) marries first the beautiful Hélène Kurágin, then, after her death, Natásha Rostóv. Natásha had been engaged, before this, to Prince Andrew Bolkónski (whose touching young wife has died in childbirth early on in the story), but has lost Prince Andrew's love through a passing infatuation for the dissolute Anatole Kurágin, brother of Hélène. This Anatole was once the unwilling suitor of Prince Andrew's sister, Princess Mary—but that match had come to nothing. Princess Mary finally marries Nicholas Rostóv, Natásha's elder brother. Handsome Boris Drubetskóy, first introduced as the object of Natásha's childish affection, becomes a hanger-on of Hélène's, and is in the end to marry the heiress, Julie, whom Nicholas failed to court.

Tolstoy paints youth and old age with an equal genius. The young-girlhood of Natásha Rostóv (whom we meet first at thirteen), the ardors of her officer-brother, Nicholas, the optimistic, recalcitrant innocence of Pierre Bezúkhov—stout young outsider with spectacles, suddenly much too wealthy—are unforgettable. Facing these stand those of aging or dying men, bound up in their pride, their personal fantasies, or the memories of their sins. Old Prince Bolkónski is implacable, often cruel; genial Count Rostóv is to be broken by circumstance; Count Bezúkhov is only seen as a dying figure; Prince Kurágin's intrigues are contemptible . . . Again, in his depiction of feminine beauty—whether it be the shallow but superb glitter of Hélène or the adorable vitality of Natásha—Tolstoy has been seldom approached and never surpassed. He not only shows the face, he penetrates to the spirit. It is by that test applied to the spirit that the plain, shy, awkward Princess Mary Bolkónski begins to shine through the novel, towards the end.

War and Peace is most often written or spoken of as an epic. As such it may sound intimidating. In reality, it could not be friendlier. I know no such pictures of delicious and happy scenes. I remember, for instance, best of all the Rostóvs' country Christmas in Otrádnoe, with Nicholas home on leave—hunting, wild dancing, sledge rides, and dressing up. No English novelist, of any century, has painted English country and fashionable city life with the fullness with which Tolstoy painted the Russian. And I think that, in reading *War and Peace*, it is by the likeness rather than the unlikeness of the two ways of living that you will be struck. One seldom breaks off to exclaim "How Russian!"—whereas, in reading even the greatest of the French novels, one frequently does break off to exclaim "How French!" These people seem no more foreign than they seem distant in time.

The historical portraits—most notably those of Napoleon and of Alexander I—are on another, though not unrelated, plane. The pictures of war—of battles, minor engagements, and movements of troops about countrysides—are of startling, majestic vividness. And between these come the discussions of strategy, either between the characters or direct from Tolstoy's own pen . . . And the vast canvas holds military figures of every sort—the wild officers of Pierre's playboy days, Nicholas Rostóv's seasoned brother-campaigners.

These are a few of the many reasons to enjoy *War and Peace*. But why do we almost *need* to read, or reread, it now? I think because this novel, with its comprehensive plan, its handling of time and space, its at once intensely human and superhuman vision, affirms the power of mankind to live out its destiny. One is enriched by what happens, though one may suffer. Great art, like religion, imposes form on the chaos into which life, at times like the present, might seem to merge. In the long run, I believe that we dread futility more than we dread tragedy. It is too easy, at the height of momentous times, to despise our own lives—and yet in our hearts we do not want to despise them. Tolstoy, in *War and Peace*, shows that though much may be pitiful, nothing is futile: in the range of human experience everything has its place . . . *War and Peace*, you may say, is nothing more than a novel: for the greater part its characters are fictitious. But *no*; they are real—for the feelings that go to make them are the feelings that go to make you and me. History, in the literal sense, plays a great part in *War and Peace*. But, in another sense, this whole novel is history—the history of a number of human souls who saw through a day not unlike our own.

Ethel Vance, *Reprisal*, April 21, 1943

One tends to think of the thriller and the psychological novel as being two utterly different types of fiction—poles apart. In the thriller much happens, and happens at breakneck speed; the characters are so built as to travel light; they are not allowed (so to speak) much psychological luggage, for fear this should slow down or hold up the plot. What they do is more important than how they feel. Their moral coloring is, as a rule, marked—though, perhaps, *one* character, "X," a person of mystery, may remain an enigma until the end. In the main, the men and women who keep the plot going are either courageous or cowardly, generous or mean, idealistic or rankly unscrupulous.

In the psychological novel most of this is reversed. Action is slow, and there is not very much of it: it[2] has been sacrificed to the interest in character—or is, at least, only used to illustrate character. What is felt is made more important than what is done. Reading a novel of this kind in the wrong mood, one might complain that the people endlessly dither about. Most of the men and women are enigmatic, and description and analysis loom large.

I have always felt that the thriller and the psychological novel (both of which, at their *best*, I greatly enjoy) suffer from the extremes to which they have been carried, and are each impoverished by the wide gap between them. I welcome any sign that the gap may close, and salute any writer who works to close it. Feeling and action are *not* incompatibles (as, indeed, these years of the war show). Why should we treat them as if they were? The novels of Conrad and Graham Greene, the magnificent subtle detective stories of Simenon (many of which are now to be had in English) are outstanding "mergers." And from America comes the work of Ethel Vance, whose *Escape* was one of the finest *exciting* books that I know.

Miss Vance's *Reprisal* is a worthy successor to *Escape*. You will not have forgotten how, in the former novel, private life was shadowed, threatened, and to a degree poisoned by a political atmosphere, by public events. That was in prewar Nazi Germany. In *Reprisal* the scene is laid in occupied France. In the charming Brittany *manoir* of Rusquec, life, for André Galle and his son and daughter, is gradually running down. These are a trio of French people of the most enlightened, honest, and charming kind. But the fall of their country has broken something in them. Winter lies on the landscape, and in their hearts.

In addition to this, the Galles have to face an acute crisis. A noncommissioned officer of the German army of occupation has been murdered on a road outside the village: twenty hostages, held by the Germans, are destined to be shot if the murderer is not found within three days. The hostages have been drawn from the village people, from among families well known to the Galles: one is their own servant's brother. André Galle, as a former minister—he is a disappointed left-wing idealist, who, in the good faith of despair, threw in his lot with Vichy, was soon disillusioned, broke with Vichy, and is now at the end of his career—is working desperately to gain time, to hold up the executions from day to day, to patch up the matter, somehow, with the German authorities whom he detests, and who mistrust him. Hoping for help from a more influential quarter,

André has sent for his former secretary, Edouard Schneider, now a man of power under the Vichy-German regime.

To Françoise, André's twenty-five-year-old daughter (through whose eyes we see the greater part of what happens), the coming of Edouard to Rusquec is both distasteful and sinister. The Galles, in their desperation, must flatter Edouard, but Françoise feels sure he does not mean well. To herself in one way, to her weak and tormented father in another, Edouard's attitude has been, for years, equivocal. And, worse, she has every reason to suspect that he was one of the *Tatler* men who had plotted to sell France. For Françoise, the tragedy of the fall of her country has gone with a personal tragedy—the apparent loss of her lover. Could she believe otherwise than that Simon Astley, the young American with whom, when the dark days began, she had been on the verge of happiness, had deserted and repudiated her when she most needed him?

The plot of *Reprisal*, which could not be more exciting, works itself out in a very short space of time—though we are given flashbacks into the past. The characters, and their complex, often uncertain relations to each other, are drawn with perception and certainty. The whole of *Reprisal* is saturated in the atmosphere of a particular place and time. And Miss Vance's style has a sheer and dazzling distinction, still new to the thriller, still too rare in other fields.

Sergei Eisenstein, *The Film Sense*, June 16, 1943

Russian genius, in the nineteenth century, showed Europe how great the novel could be. In the twentieth, it has captured the cinema—and Sergei Eisenstein is one of the giants, perhaps *the* giant, among Russian cinematographers. His *The Film Sense* should be read by those who still have hopes of the cinema as an art.

I say "still," because there has been, since the end of the 1920s, a decided drop in what used to be high hopes. Before that, the Germans, and then the French, had been pioneering in remarkable silent films, and young English and American enthusiasts began to take fire and to experiment. But the introduction of sound, for some reason, checked all this: the "talkies," though lively, were not original. Language set up the difficulties of Babel—the cinema lost its international quality, and, while gaining technical power with every year, fell under the rigid conventions of Hollywood. Preoccupation with the box office and the "star" system blew blightingly on the experimental film. Hollywood, be it noted, did once make a bid for Eisenstein's powers, but was too frightened to use them once it had got him there.

The Soviet Russian films—which for quite a number of years could not be shown in England, except by private societies—were born of dynamic new ideas and ideals. Financed by their government, the Russian film-artists could ignore the box office, and did not need to use "stars." They learned to embody sound in what had hitherto been a purely visual medium without halting the development of their art. Their aim was to express the poetic-heroic in mankind; instead of romanticizing the individual, they romanticized the mass movement. Their themes, at the outset, were revolutionary—but also they could make lovely dramatic films on such stolid subjects as cooperative farming, for example, Eisenstein's *Old and New* (called also *The General Line*). Eisenstein is still better known as the maker of *Potemkin, Ten Days That Shook the World*, and *Alexander Nevsky*.

I cannot pretend that *The Film Sense* is easy reading. It is the intellectual book of an intellectual man who knows, and cares for, his subject from A to Z. Eisenstein holds, with Miss Edith Sitwell, that the arts relate to each other, and can learn from each other. In poems and pictures he finds the potential film script—he even gives an analysis, from this viewpoint, of one passage out of *Paradise Lost*. And Leonardo da Vinci, by his showing, had made notes for what could have been an epic film of The Flood.

Samuel Richardson, *Pamela*; Jane Austen, *Sense and Sensibility*; Ivan Turgenev, *Liza*, July 28, 1943

Right away in the country, out of reach of the new books, and not yet reached by any of them, I have celebrated a week of summer and holiday by roving round the shelves of my own library and remaking the acquaintance of old friends. There is something timeless-looking about these rows of book-backs: sunshine coming in through the big windows has faded reds, blues, and greens to a monotone—oddly enough, it is the old calf bindings (some of them left the booksellers nearly two hundred years ago) that show their age least. Which made me ask myself, is this an appearance only? Or, can it be that some of our oldest books remain, everlastingly, up-to-date?

Perhaps it was this question that sent me to *Pamela*. Reviewers, unless they are very set in their ways, are generally interested by a first novel—they like to discover "promise." Now, *Pamela* is not only *a* first novel—the work of Samuel Richardson, London bookseller, of the respectable age of about fifty—it is *the* first novel: that is to say, the first English novel, in the sense in which we think of the novel now. First published in 1740, *Pamela* (with the subtitle *Virtue Rewarded*) fell into four volumes. The first two, one might say, depict the Virtue, the second two, the Reward . . . I must say that my own edition of *Pamela* is not the first (which would be worth its weight in gold) or even a nearly subsequent one: I possess—and should advise you to seek—the novel in the excellent Everyman's Library, in which it is No. 683 reduced to two volumes, each volume 3s 6d.

What does this first of all English first novels promise, both for the art of Richardson (who was to follow it with *Clarissa Harlowe*, in 1748, and *The History of Sir Charles Grandison*, in 1754) and for the English novel in general? Samuel Richardson, whether or not he knew it, was making a big experiment. For the first time in the history of storytelling he was setting out to *convince*, not just to amaze. He was sitting down to present a *lifelike* picture of life, from which the unlikely must be altogether omitted. His story, in the long run, would stand or fall by whether it was believable. He dealt, it is true, with passions—passion must spin the plot—but the characters belonged to the recognized social order, and the plot must be set in strictly familiar scenes: the contemporary English countryside and just such eighteenth-century houses as those in which readers lived. He was interested—and was out to interest his readers—in how different people behaved, and why, rather than in what *happened* to happen to them, more or less by chance. He showed men and women as making their own destinies. You may say that all this had already been done by Shakespeare. Yes—but in prose fiction it had never been done before.

A thoroughly moral man in his private life (he had been the good apprentice who married his master's daughter, he had had many children, and he had enjoyed, since boyhood, blameless friendships with a number of young ladies who asked his advice during love affairs), Richardson was a moralist as a writer. Or, strictly, one should say that he thought he was. Actually, to the modern eye, the morality is *Pamela*'s dubious part. The true moralist paints virtue as being admirable for its own sake; the second-rate moralist suggests that virtue ought to be sought because virtue pays— and the Samuel Richardson who wrote *Pamela* belonged, I am sorry to say, to this second, or salesman, class. To be fair to him, he moved out of it: in the succeeding *Clarissa* he shows a heroine consistently virtuous, but unfortunate to the end. So, while *Pamela* (skipped discreetly) is a rattling good story, *Clarissa* is sometimes majestic—it made me weep.

Who is Pamela, in what way is she virtuous, and how is her virtue rewarded? She is—at the start of her story—a pretty little serving-maid of fifteen; in fact, by a series of chaste but luscious touches, Richardson intimates that Pamela is a peach. She is the daughter of poor, aged, and honest parents, with whom she unceasingly corresponds. (The novel, throughout, is in letter form; Pamela, dutiful girl, writes everything home, even when her adventures are of a nature to raise the white hairs on those honest heads.) The story starts with the death of the good, rich lady who had treated her little maid as, almost, her own child—hence Pamela's excellent education. Pamela, her protectress gone, is left at the doubtful mercy of the son of the house, "Mr. B.," who, she finds, has had his eye on her for some time.

Mr. B.'s ideas in the matter were those of his day, but by the ideas of any day he could not fail to be found a boor, a bore, and a brute. Pamela's virtue consists in her rebuffing his dishonorable advances, and her reward consists in her gladly marrying him. From the very moment of the betrothal she appears to regard him as wholly admirable. Knowing all that we know, by now, about Mr. B., we cannot praise her adaptability— though, clearly, Richardson means us to. Letting bygones be bygones is, of course, one thing. But have we not grown accustomed to think of Pamela as, above all, a very idealistic girl? And really, by the most indulgent standards, Mr. B.—who has lied, bribed, abducted, eavesdropped, cheated, and resorted to extremes of physical cruelty throughout his lengthy pursuit of Pamela—is *not* a promising person with whom to set up in life. This is where the dubious morality comes in—and few but Richardson remain blind to it. Pamela's complete volte-face is only credible if we are content to regard her as a designing hussy. Minx she certainly was.

The second half of the book is "Pamela Married"—and in this half (I think only) one may be excused for skipping. The marriage—with one brief break when Mr. B., during a London season, becomes mixed up with a society enchantress—is an unqualified success. With Mr. B.'s relations, with the country neighbors, and in London, Pamela wins all hearts. Not only do children multiply, but she, in conjunction with Mr. B., sets out to write a treatise on her young's education. But "Pamela Married" contains, among certain reaches of dullness, one or two really brilliant and touching scenes—Pamela's intercession with Mr. B., during the worst phases of the enchantress period, and her interview (very simply dressed in white muslin) with the lady herself.

So summarized, the whole novel may sound absurd. But in spite of its few absurdities it is fascinating. Richardson, pioneer novelist, could command that essential for every novelist—the power to *interest*. He knew how to bring his characters so near up that, even today, they seem to move and breathe. While we quarrel with Richardson's view of his people, we accept the reality of the people themselves: it is simply that we see through them while he does not. To quarrel with a novelist about his characters is really, though we may not know it, a tribute to what has been his consummate art. Richardson was, in spite of himself, an artist— too much of *Pamela* happens indoors, for the gardens and glimpses of English Midland landscape that he does allow us are delicious. He shows feminine love of detail in dress and furnishings, and a highly romantic susceptibility to the atmosphere of a place. Minor characters—at least in the first half of the novel—are extremely successful; there is the sympathetic, adoring curate, the cozy old housekeeper in one country house, the sinister housekeeper in another . . . *Pamela* set a great ball rolling. If only by its unrealized possibilities it showed what the novel could do, might be. What matter if some of its values seem false now? Its realities stand the test of time.

Poor one-idea-ed Mr. B., with his lack of charm, would not get very far today. But Willoughby, of *Sense and Sensibility*—amusing, sympathetic, adaptable, and with such charming manners about the house—could be a menace still. He comes, it is true, a good deal later in time, and Jane Austen's world is more like our own than Richardson's. Also, Jane Austen's judgment of character is of an acuteness that remains ahead of our own—therefore, comfortably, we call it "modern." She would not have been so much interested in showing just exactly at what point Willoughby got off, if she had not, before that, been interested in showing how attractive he could be.

Sense and Sensibility (which I have in the attractive Oxford Press edition) was begun by Jane Austen in 1797, recast and finished at some intermediate period, and published in 1811. If not the most nearly faultless, I find it, after *Emma*, the most purely enjoyable of her novels—and I ask myself why it is so much less often read and talked of than *Pride and Prejudice*. Charming, vague Mrs. Dashwood, taking her three young daughters, after her husband's death, to settle in the Devonshire cottage in the grounds of her relatives, Sir John and Lady Middleton, seems to me a most promising subject. "Sir John was a sportsman, Lady Middleton a mother"—here we have the Barton Park couple summed up. Sir John—a kindly soul with time on his hands—is constantly dropping in at the cottage, and loves to gather round his hospitable table bevies of young ladies, with no young men; while Lady Middleton tolerates any guest who makes much of her exceedingly spoiled children. Unchanging aspects of English country-house life are painted here, with a laughing brilliance that must delight one. Jane Austen has likes and dislikes, but she is fair.

From naive, bourgeois London Richardson to Turgenev, the cosmopolitan, aristocratic Russian, seems a far cry. *Liza* (alternatively titled *A House of Gentlefolk*) is one of the loveliest of the Turgenev novels—I have just reread it for the fourth time. The W. Ralston English translation (again in Everyman's Library) is good. Here we have the leisurely, graceful lives of the mid-nineteenth-century Russian gentry, set in country estates and in country towns. Here is a story with no villain: its hero remains the victim of an early mistake. Lavretsky, at thirty-five, returns to take up life at his country house—he wants to catch up with the wasted years, when he was being dragged by his wife round fashionable spas. Believing his wife dead, he allows himself to declare his love for his young relative, Liza—and she returns it. Then, without warning, Lavretsky's wife, who had betrayed him, returns . . . Those who saw his play, *A*

Month in the Country, will remember how exquisitely Turgenev renders a quiet scene.

Eudora Welty, *A Curtain of Green*, August 11, 1943

Eudora Welty, born in Jackson, Mississippi, has a talent no less remarkable than her name. In fact, the name is so very much of the kind that Miss Eudora Welty might herself have invented that I was surprised when the introduction vouched for its being the author's own. Having read *A Curtain of Green*, I salute with joy an almost demonic originality. This, a collection of short stories, is the young Mississippi American's first book. One story, "Petrified Man," has appeared over here in *Horizon*, and subsequently in the *Horizon Stories* (which I reviewed in these pages some weeks ago). Except for this, I imagine Miss Welty's work will come as entirely new to the English reader.

Like all collections, *A Curtain of Green* has its inequalities. But I shall be surprised if, with at least four or five of the stories, you do not feel: "Something is happening that has not happened before." And almost every page has a quality that reminds me of a hot-flavored, powerful drink, iced cold. Brainstorms—some justified, others not—are, roughly, Miss Welty's subject; sometimes these are photographed from the outside, sometimes from the inside. When the photography is from the inside, the effect is so excruciatingly disturbing that one wonders if one is right in one's own head; when from the outside, the effect is devastatingly funny. "A Piece of News," "The Hitch-Hikers," "Flowers for Marjorie," and "A Curtain of Green" are examples of the first class; "Lily Daw and the Three Ladies," "Petrified Man," and "Why I Live at the P.O.," of the second. The last-named, with its semi-lunatic view of small-town family life, is one of the funniest stories that I have ever read.

On the other hand, I think it is arguable that "The Whistle," with its absolute moonlit starkness, its unspoken pity for all humanity (as typified by that pair of tomato growers), is the finest, as well as the strangest, story in the collection. This is a study of the sublime patience of man, when climate wages against him relentless war. The frost-announcing whistle, to Jason and Sara Morton, sounds as fatefully as the siren that we know.

No brainstorms here: reality is enough . . . You may find it hard to "take" Eudora Welty: if you wince at the vulgar subject you will not like her at all. Her attitude to vulgarity is surgical. Like all Southern writers, most notably William Faulkner (whom she resembles in no other way), Miss Welty is a great painter of decay. Her stained-glass windows and musty draperies, rain crashing down outdoors, are unforgettable. In the long run, I find her totally innocent of facile youthful mockery of humanity's weaknesses. No, she does not mock at such things; she understands them—with an odd, ageless, pitiful smile.

G. Fortune and W. Fortune, *Hitler Divided France*, August 25, 1943

Not long ago, business took me into a restricted area—a strip of the Kentish coast I have known since childhood. Here, west of Hythe, Romney Marsh begins, and one sees the great curve of the coast out to Dungeness. Inland lie the chalky South Downs. Leaving Folkestone, one almost drops from the high plateau—then, above the coast road, run those smiling hills, with woods, sun-bleached grass, and big-windowed houses perched on the slope like chalets, facing across the sea. This edge of Kent has always seemed to me beautiful because of the melodic relation of extreme flatness with rippling, varying height. On the June day when I came back again, Caesar's Camp, in the distance, quivered blue with heat; there was a dark-green silence along the tree-shaded, almost empty Folkestone streets; on the lawns of unoccupied houses the grass had grown into noble, bronze-tipped hay, and in the gardens the Kentish roses were at their fullest bloom.

I felt a dramatic strangeness about this area, cut off from the rest of England by an invisible line—for the non-resident to be allowed to enter is an adventure, as well as a privilege. But, above all, I had a most happy sense of return: I had not been here since the war began, and I must have been more homesick than I knew. There was only one disappointment—today, one could not see France; a heat haze, charged with sunshine, veiled the horizon. It was from the Leas at Folkestone that, as a little girl, I had first been shown France—a low-lying, violet form, distinct in the crystal air of that March morning. I still remember that moment—for I believe that, till then, I had not really *believed* that France existed. I had heard so much about France, it appeared too good to be true—might it not, after all, be a sort of fairy-tale land? . . . Gradually, as my years on that coast went by, I settled down to the idea of France as a neighbor. It was true, she did not often reveal herself. But each clear day, when one could see her, was an event.

This physical neighborliness with France, even the similarity of the two coastlines, adds something, I think, to the character of seaside Kent. On the June afternoon this summer, as I sat on a seat on Hythe Hill, staring into the heat haze over the sea, it came over me that France was many miles nearer than the familiar London where I belonged. And yet—for all one knew of the neighbor country, since 1940, it almost might have been Mars. To the romantic mystery France had had for my childhood had succeeded the tragic mystery of war—the iron silence that locks an enemy-occupied land. In these Kentish towns—themselves, in one way, cut off from us since the fall of France—I had found the happy, familiar pattern of existence still going on, only changed in a few, superficial ways. But what of the life across those few miles of water? How vitally had it altered? The ordinary French civilian, the man and woman—how were he and she living? How did they feel?

Hitler Divided France, by G. and W. Fortune, answers, in a practical way, a good many of the questions I had asked myself. The authors of the book are two British subjects who returned to this country in the autumn of 1942 after having lived in France for nearly three years. They are not writing their own reminiscences—in fact, they write with an impersonality that could be colorless were not their matter so interesting and the manner in which they handle it so direct. Their acquaintanceship among all classes of people in France appears to have been exceptionally wide: they have been able to quote all sorts of instances of behavior—without, for obvious reasons, naming people or places, or giving details that could compromise anyone. They appear, also, to have moved about France with a freedom that is, in view of the regulations, surprising. Their personal story, when it *can* be given us, should add, one may expect, to the documents of this war.

Meanwhile, they limit themselves to observed facts—no domestic detail, I am glad to say, has been found so minor as to be beneath their notice—and to a detached and careful analysis of the changing internal

French political scene. "The object of this book," they say in their post-script, "has been to depict life in France between the Armistice of 1940 and the total occupation of that country in November 1942, and, above all, to represent the views of various sections of the community prevailing in France during that period." At first glance, some English readers may resent an apparent defense of the Vichy government. The authors' aim, it is true, is fairness, and, while they seek no defense for "collaborationalism," they are concerned to show that French loyalty to France, though it took, in some cases, forms we find antipathetic, has a claim to be regarded *as* loyalty. Among the genuine traitors and sellers-out, there were, they say, apparent ones—men who at least did not act in their own interest, whose judgments were queered by the chaos of 1940, and who, if they did act mistakenly, acted in good faith. The authors no further commit themselves than to suggest that the Vichy "attentiste" policy may yet, in the long run, prove not unjustified. They would ask us to withhold judgment till facts are more fully known. One lives as one can.

Hitler Divided France is, as its title suggests, concerned to show the psychological, as well as domestic and political, effects on the country of Hitler's dividing line. About the whole principle of the division there was, the authors suggest, a devilish cleverness. The two zones—the Occupied and the Unoccupied—were by it made, virtually, foreign to one another: at the time when stricken France most needed the strength of unity, inter-zone jealousies, hostilities, and misunderstandings could not fail to spring up. The authors therefore regard the *total* occupation by the Germans (in November 1942) as for France an almost unqualified benefit—for with it vanished that crippling dividing line.

The pith of the book, however, is not theory but straightforward fact. The chapters on "Propaganda," "Collaboration and Resistance," "Rationing," "The Black Market," and "Transport" are particularly interesting. The resilience of the French spirit, among the ordinary people, the tough fiber of the French courage, are well shown. So, too, most of all in the chapter "Treatment of British Subjects," is an abiding, decent goodness of heart . . . The French have always shown a great gift for living: they have been the first exponents of the *douceur de vivre*. These days when, down to bedrock, they must live how they can, that gift seems not wholly lost to them. Style is a great support.

Sacheverell Sitwell, *Splendours and Miseries,* January 12, 1944

Within the last four years more has happened than the imagination can contain. I mean by "imagination" nothing boundless or abstract, but that faculty that exists, in greater or less degree, in each individual human being. It is indeed, I suppose, in this very faculty that our distinctive *humanity* resides: it is by our power of envisaging things, of calling up to our vision or keeping present what is not at the moment actually there, that we are made conscious of our identities. We may dismiss the man or woman with whom we feel out of contact as "unimaginative," but in fact I believe that the totally unimaginative man or woman to be very rare — outside the subnormal class. One cannot, however, deny that, from person to person, imagination varies in power as well as range; for some it plays its recognized part in living — indeed, living would hardly *be* living without it — by others it is outlawed and seldom named.

In normal, or so-called normal, times, one's imagination exceeds what actually happens: one can amuse oneself by finding a wider meaning for some apparently quite prosaic event by building up, from some chance observation, a drama for one's own inner theater. Children, whose lives are equably ordered by the grown-ups, or grown-ups who, whether from chance or choice, lead uneventful existences, are, in the main, the most "imaginative" — they supply what they find lacking in color, danger, and movement in this way. But even the active, out-in-the-world adult is accustomed, more often than he knows, to add to the bulk of his general experience something particular to himself. These days it is different. How often do we exclaim: "There is no time to think, no time to feel! Really, one cannot take in what is happening!" And is one disconcerted by hearing some truthful voice reply: "Perhaps that is just as well?"

Perhaps it *is* just as well. After all, we have got to live, to see this through; therefore we dare not let ourselves be weakened as imaginative suffering might weaken us. Our battening down of hatches is instinctive. When we say we "cannot imagine" we mean, also, that even if we *could* do so we might refuse to try. For the ordinary man and woman in extraordinary times, the refusal not only is possible, it seems to work well. But for the creative artist, who by temperament, habit, and training not only lives, but works through imagination, the refusal is impossible, and would not work at all.

So from time to time we have been given, throughout these last four years, works of art that are great because they attempt the impossible. Painting and literature, in order to rescue the ordinary man from the apathy that threatens him, stand up and look world war straight in the face, forcing themselves to assimilate what we refuse. Artists at least attempt to visualize what is happening—not to cities and armies, but to the human spirit. The artist, like the religious person, can bear to see what others dare not look at, because he has a courage founded on faith. He sees the immortal element running through mortal fate.

In *Splendours and Miseries*, Sacheverell Sitwell has translated from facts into images the experiences of these last four years of war. These unexpected images—gathered from painting, from myths, from the distances of the memory, from music, from travel, from the statement of the lunatic or the outpourings of the lover—penetrate us as facts, because[3] their dreadful familiarity no longer can. As in dreams, they have more power than the waking reality, because they are reality brought close up.

Splendours and Miseries is a majestic and daunting book. To read it is to see war reflected, not in a mirror, but in the glass over an old, great, dark picture. The changing reflection, still unresolved into a picture of any kind, is superimposed on the unchanging picture behind the glass: what is transient blends with what is already there, and is, somehow, blended into its pattern. Today, after all, is not disjointed from yesterday: all that is happening has its prototype in the past, and has been already foreseen in the sublime vision of the prophet or artist, the horrific vision of the demonic lover or the mad. All through time, there have been those who knew more than was good for them—and Mr. Sitwell leads us to these "Illuminati."

> We live but once [he says] and our lives are what we make them. There has never, in that sense, been any golden age, for the opportunity is always there. Six years is long enough in which to prepare for total war. Even in happier times ugliness and misery have always been. If we consider what to ourselves must seem a golden age, it is to admit that the idealism and sense of poetry of

the painters concealed its sordid truth. Mantegna, Gian Bellini, Carpaccio, no more than Botticelli, or Benozzo Gozzoli, sought out the leper, or took the likeness of the dying.

Now, in this long dark night of the spirit, that must end one day, we turn in memory to the dawn light upon the hills.

And again:

We are seeking for someone in a world of shades, and our way is barred by phantoms. It is not necessary to be a follower of any faith or religion in order to believe this. We have passed through among the damned, in their different sorts. The poisoner and the poisoned, and have seen the burning pyre. The reality of the phantom has been proved, in the sense that the dreaded figure has come to life, and moves. The thing most feared has happened.

. . . Dumb humanity waits for its interpreter. While the dead world waits to be woken to life again. The love and beauty that we have lost must be restored to us.

Who is this "someone" we seek, whom we must go down to hell itself to reclaim? In each man's case, his own soul. Without that, and breathing the air of a civilization that has culminated horribly fitly in the present war, we are, Mr. Sitwell believes, lost and dying. "There were times when mankind was not condemned to wars. But we have allowed our soul to die, and now we must search for her among the shades."

And who are these "damned" among which, in the course of *Splendours and Miseries*, we have made our journey? Antichrist, three mad women, Fuseli, painter of evil, Madeleine Smith, and her death-embracing lover—others, of many races and times. "These are the shadows of our subconscious souls." Alongside our intimidating path to redemption, the modern and ancient terrors merge: we see a steppe battle in terms of a Brueghel scene, the bombed ruins of the sordid modern town in terms of the medieval Hell. Two figures give a double theme to the book—one is Antichrist, the other Orpheus. I have called *Splendours and Miseries* daunting; it finds out the cracks in one's armor of apathy. The very pictures, with their dreamlike beauty, are frightening—there were some that

I could not bear to look at again . . . Mr. Sitwell rides full-tilt against the idea that we save ourselves by lack of imagination. If we refuse to feel, we shall soon be unable to. In which case, by his showing we shall be totally lost.

Barbara Nixon, *Raiders Overhead: The Record of a London Warden*, February 23, 1944

Raiders Overhead: The Record of a London Warden, by Barbara Nixon, is a first-rate account of the London air raids from the A.R.P. point of view. This is the first book by a warden that I have come across, and I recommend it not only to Civil Defence people, but to the ordinary citizen who may care to have a warden's inside account. Mrs. Nixon, already the author of several books, commands a vivid, though utterly calm, style. "The borough of which the story is told was among the more heavily bombed areas of London, but the experiences recorded are not claimed as being anything exceptional." Sketches of fellow wardens (particularly the toughs of Post 13, who were anti-woman, and had ejected their last) and of shelter characters abound. And the author is likeably funny about herself. But *Raiders Overhead* is also a serious study of A.R.P. organization, and of some of its weaknesses and defects.

Conditions differ, of course, from borough to borough . . . There are poignant, though few horrific, passages: the wardens' funeral, and the chapter called "Aftermath," should take their place among literature of this war.

J. L. Hodson, *Home Front*, March 1, 1944

Home Front is another—the fifth—installment of J. L. Hodson's *War Diary*. Its immediate predecessor, reviewed in these pages, was *War in the Sun*. These diaries of Mr. Hodson's seem to me to have double value: at once contemporary and for the future. Why? Because they provide a continuous running record of the years onward from 1939, and because they are, to a rare degree, comprehensive. The author, obviously, could not be everywhere at the same time; but he has a way of letting any scene he describes reflect what is happening elsewhere. His imagination grasps, firmly, the concept of world war, and he makes the most random incident or brief scrap of dialogue appear in its relevance to that whole. The apparent attractive inconsequence of his entries might be, at the first glance, deceptive. He does certainly note things down because they amuse or intrigue him, and because they may well amuse or intrigue the reader. But he never notes down anything that has not a point, or that fails to illuminate character or events.

One can realize, looking back, that each year of this war—in fact, each one of each year's four seasons—has had its distinctive temperature and color. These can be partially, but not wholly, accounted for by successes and reverses, our ups and downs. Our susceptibilities have been, in themselves, variable. It has been interesting to move about among people—even, as most of us must, in a fairly small way—and see how incalculable their reactions are—to a major headline, to a speech, to a new restriction, to an irrepressible rumor. Mr. Hodson has moved about in a big way—not only from front to front, but from man to man. He has by now acquired far-reaching terms of comparison. Both by nature and training observant (this might go without saying), he is at the same time disabused, shrewd, and frank. His frankness I find especially reassuring: he does not hesitate, in his wish for the all-round picture, to record the less shining side of human behavior, and his accounts are, therefore, a first-rate corrective to idealized official pictures of us British at war. Human nature remains human nature—and well we know it. The grumbler, the slacker, the skeptic, the self-pitier, the maker of reservations on his or her private behalf are always with us, and, perhaps, even latently within many of us. Some of the dispassionate entries in Mr. Hodson's pages make one look rather sharply into one's own heart.

This *Home Front* comes, in all senses, nearer home than preceding volumes of Mr. Hodson's diaries. It is subtitled *Being Some Account of Journeys, Meetings and What Was Said to Me in and about England during 1942–1943*. It is a crowded (without being incoherent) book, on a crowded scene. It renders both the density and the intensity of this embattled island, and captures the moods, the stresses, and the characteristics of an island race—the British—engaged in a world war.

As it takes all sorts to make a world, it takes as many to wage a modern war. On countless men and women, boys and girls, in our docks, factories, shipyards, hospitals, the forces and Civil Defence, Mr. Hodson shows the impact of world ideas. Masses of British people, of the less traveled sort, have cherished their own, unconscious isolationism. There have been many things that they have not wanted to know. Mr. Hodson makes it quite clear that, as an ally, Russia has fired the working-class imagination most; America, with her standards of creature comfort, appeals more, he suggests, to the middle class. As to our nearer Continental neighbors, with the exception of Germany, opinion, if any, would seem to be negative. In the main, war routine has civilians well in its grip: outside long working hours, the young seek romance, on or off the screen; their elders are more than occupied keeping the home going. Talk, however, abounds. Fatigue and, still more, boredom are menaces not to be overlooked—both could have adverse effects on production as on morale. The effect of blitzes on England has been, on the whole, stimulating. Overoptimism or undue pessimism, according to news from the fronts, both leave their marks on output. As interesting as anything in *Home Front* are the remarks on courage—its psychology, its inconsistencies, the qualitative (rather than quantitative) difference between courage in men and in women.

All Mr. Hodson's journeys, as extensive as the size of England allows, were necessary: they were made with the object of collecting material for his broadcasts. And none of his reflections are out of the blue—all arise from a definite incident, a remark, an extract from a letter or from apparently enigmatic behavior on the part of some person that he describes. His power of painting in words is well to the fore here—the park of the country house as the scene of a training battle; docks, shipyards, a bomber station, a submarine base, factory interiors, an East Anglian "deserted village," homes of all sorts, and the varying discomforts of provincial wartime hotels: all these should go straight to the reader's imagination and, as surely, remain in his memory . . . If you, tied to your own responsibilities and your own routine, want to know what and how the rest of England is doing, you cannot do better than *Home Front*. And the book would do well for the men abroad who like to know how we make out at home.

Frank O'Connor, *Crab Apple Jelly*, May 17, 1944

"O'Connor," once said W. B. Yeats, "is doing for Ireland what Chekhov did for Russia." In my reading for this week, I passed from the Slav to the Celt in taking up, with an anticipation that was not disappointed, Frank O'Connor's new book of short stories, *Crab Apple Jelly*. It would be too much to say that Russian writing has handed across to the Irish a ready-made key to their nature; but it has, I think, encouraged the Irish to find, or rather to forge, a key of their own. Within the last fifty years Ireland has built herself up a magnificent prose literature: a literature that does not deny weakness, that rises clear of sentiment to an august pity; that is at the same time racy, realistic, objective.

Those who like Ireland least must still admit that she is a fertile breeding ground for character. Even in her few big cities the mass-produced individual is rare: the level of idiosyncrasy is high. Even when packed tightly among his fellows, in the city, the country town, or the crowded farmhouse community, each man (and, for that matter, most women) lords it over his interior world of fantasy. Talk is as erratic as private thought; behavior veers before impulses. There is fatalism, not only with regard to oneself, but with regard to one's neighbor, who is as unaccountable. The English, I think, are always a little put out if somebody does not do the expected thing; but though there are many more reasons for rage in Ireland, the above has seldom been one of them. Crabbed, independent folk, wild growths, solitaries, and the oddnesses of their solitary behavior have been the ingredients of *Crab Apple Jelly*—translucent and firm as a well-set jelly, and as pungently flavored, is Mr. O'Connor's art. The opening story, "The Bridal Night," drew my tears; the others remain in balance between the tragic and comic, with, on the whole, a cheerful trend to the latter. "The House That Johnny Built," "The New Teacher," "The Star That Bids the Shepherd Fold," "Uprooted," and "The Mad Lomasseys" seemed to me above all to be praised. These are not tales of bog and mountain and lake, but of Cork city, of watersides, and of the square and parlors, pubs, shops, and school-rooms of country towns, whose psychological atmosphere is as rich as a plum cake.

Mulk Raj Anand, *The Barbers' Trade Union*, August 2, 1944

The Barbers' Trade Union is a collection of short stories by Mulk Raj Anand, whose novels (*The Village, The Sword and the Sickle*, and others) are already well known. Art, I feel certain, is the best, most peaceful, and most pleasant interpreter of one race to another. As such, Mr. Anand's writing has, from the first, qualified—it has good art's pre-essential: that of being guiltless of propaganda. His comprehension of his own people is at once smiling and pitiful, but, above all, astringent. Mr. Anand writes about the Indians much as Chekhov writes about the Russians, or Seán O'Faoláin or Frank O'Connor writes about the Irish. At the same time, his manner is quite his own.

Though only a few of the characters in these stories are actually children, I noticed that *childishness* is a recurrent theme. Under fussy or pompous façades—those of the petty official, the policeman, the government clerk, the maharaja, the terrorist, the usurer, and so on—almost touchingly infantile motives operate. On the whole, and outstandingly in such stories as "The Maharaja and the Tortoise," "Lottery," and "A Pair of Moustachios," this makes for comedy. But also, as in "A Confession," "The Cobbler and the Machine," "The Terrorist," and "A Kashmir Idyll," there is profound pathos, and often grimness, in the lengths to which self-delusion or daydreams run. Or sometimes, as in "A Rumour," we are shown innocent victims of other people's speciousness and unrealism. Mr. Anand's writing has an attractive, sensuous quality: he somehow charges his pages with heat, color, scents (or smells). He has most of all, though, that power which makes a writer great—he can give human weakness a dignity of its own.

James Joyce, *Stephen Hero*, August 16, 1944

Stephen Hero is James Joyce's original draft for *A Portrait of the Artist as a Young Man*. Even the adventures of the manuscript are in keeping with the character of its author-hero—it was cast into the fire after its rejection by (some say) the twentieth publisher. This act of haughty despondency was, however, to an extent undone by Mrs. James Joyce, who, "at the risk of burning her hands, rescued these pages"—about one-third of the whole. The destruction of the rest of the novel I do, having read *Stephen Hero*, most intensely regret. The interest of comparing this first draft with *A Portrait of the Artist* is, obviously, endless. But also, from the portion we have here, one is able to guess at what might have been James Joyce's first novel's value in its entirety. *Stephen Hero*, had it been published when it was written (which was between 1900 and 1903), might have gained for James Joyce a circle of readers of the kind who could not fail to be alienated by his later unfriendly obscurity. This increasing obscurity (present in *A Portrait of the Artist*, marked in passages of *Ulysses*, and dominant throughout *Finnegans Wake*) cannot but have been, in part, the artist's defense against a world that apparently did not want him. Joyce pursued (some say elaborated) his own art inside an intellectual solitude that is, for a writer, neither natural nor good. Isolation, by every showing, was forced on him: he was a great writer (one of the greatest in English) *not* because of, but surely in spite of it.

Stephen Hero pictures a young man at odds, like Hamlet, with his surroundings, obsessed, like Hamlet, with the idea of his personal destiny, but also, like Hamlet, potentially sociable. To an extent, this student at the National University, Dublin, is the undergraduate of all time. It is true that, for young Daedalus, the strongly Catholic and petit bourgeois character of his environment present extra problems, and that a good third in the catalogue of his irritations is the complacent nationalism of his contemporaries. We see a natural heir to the outside world fuming in a narrow, provincial sphere—Stephen's great stand for Ibsen, for instance, scandalizes the college debating society no less than it bothers his busy mother.

The world teems with young Stephens—though all, alas, do not grow up to be James Joyces. By these thousands, *Stephen Hero* may well be read as a manifesto. The language—as compared to that of the subsequent *A Portrait of the Artist as a Young Man*—is juvenile, the thought straightforward, the narration conventional. There are action and movement outside as well as inside the hero's consciousness; there is first-rate character-drawing (such as that of the pompous, shifty, and incorrigible Daedalus senior, some young ladies, and some of Stephen's student friends) and there are simple, lively, poetic, or realistic descriptive passages. Most important, and not to be overlooked, is James Joyce's theory of art in embryo. I do strongly recommend *Stephen Hero*—to appropriate readers; not, I must say, to all—as a clue or key to the novels that followed it. I mean, if you have not yet read A *Portrait of the Artist*, read *Stephen Hero* first—it may clear the way. Apart from everything else, this young novel by a great writer has outstanding merits of its own.

Noel Barber, *Prisoner of War*, September 20, 1944

Yes, this has been a long war. In the course of these five years every one of us, probably, has faced out his or her darkest hour, in which it seemed impossible to go on. This had to be wrestled with all alone, as Jacob wrestled in the dark with the angel. But everyone has gone on: in every spirit lies hidden a far from small individual victory. Help came, grace was granted—or, if you like more prosaic terms, one got one's second wind.

We have had more intimate enemies than the Axis. Weariness and separation—from those we love, from our preconceived plan of life, from so much that was happy and normal—have been perhaps the chief. Our principal weapon against these has been activity. Hard work has sought us; and we have sought it. I have heard so many people say, "It is just as well one has not too much time to think." Yes, for us free ones life has been hard enough, but always, just somehow, tolerable.

I say, for us free ones, because it is impossible not to wonder about our prisoners of war—those men who remain so acutely "missing" from their families, from their circle of friends. It is impossible, if one has any imagination, not to realize that the psychological struggle of which we are conscious must be doubled for them. Weariness and separation, from which we find our escapes, could so easily dominate their entire days. If the war has seemed long to us, what must it seem to them? We make out somehow; we have found our solutions. What are their solutions; how are they making out?

Each of us whose husband, son, brother, or friend is a prisoner of war has the evidence of his courageous letters. Receivers of such letters seek one another out, exchange any information that can be got from them, try hard to arrive at a complete picture. Such a picture, of life in a prison camp, is wanted—not only emotionally, in order to envisage the day-to-day life of individually dear men, but practically, one might say, sociologically. For those years of captivity, and the way in which they have been spent, will be ever-present factors in the existence of the men who are—we hope soon, now—to return. A picture, more nearly complete than one could have believed possible, has been given us in Noel Barber's *Prisoner of War*. Here, told for the first time, is the full story of how British soldiers, sailors, and airmen live when they are taken prisoner by the enemy. How has it been arrived at? Mr. Barber has had access to reports on the various prison camps; also, he has read, sifted through, and collated some thousands of letters. Every detail supplied here has its authentic source. The close, careful work of notation, comparison, checking, must have been endless; but I can think of no work more worthwhile. The result is a book that will not only be of evident value to all whose relations or friends are prisoners of war, but of interest to every thinking and feeling person.

Getting up in the morning, meals, work, exercise, recreation, going to bed again—that remains the frame of daily life for us all. The hour at which we rise, the sort of food that we eat, the nature of the work, the degree of enjoyment we get from the recreation, the mood and hour in which we go to bed—all that determines the day's color. First, Mr. Barber supplies—allowing, meticulously, for the variations between camp and camp—the prisoners' version of that routine. Aided by a fine assembly of photographs, he helps us to envisage the camps themselves—everything from medieval castles to hut cities. Climate, surroundings, landscape are contributory factors, for worse or better, to the different characters of the different camps. Sleeping quarters, washing arrangements, and the space and facilities for exercise are described fully—castles, for instance, though generally having a fine outlook, are least satisfactory in this regard. Then as to food—the official weekly menus are given: this allowance could just sustain life, but the dependence of prisoners upon their parcels is made clear. Of the cooking and preparation of food by the prisoners themselves, we are told in detail: the contents of parcels are put to uses whose ingenuity brings a lump to one's throat. "Biscuit pudding," for instance, is a popular feature. Often the nature of the dish is not determined till the cooking is done — if it emerges soft, it is pudding; if hard, it is a cake: in either case, it is much enjoyed.

Work in the fields is, on the whole, popular: it entails open air, extra rations, pay, a view of the country, and the natural pleasure man gets from contact with the soil. This pleasure is, naturally, at its highest where the prisoners make their own camp gardens, raising flowers and vegetables. They have also been active in leveling playing-fields.

So much for the body. But Mr. Barber deals fully, even more fully, with the ever-important question of the mind. While some prisoners of war are men at the height, or approaching the height, of their powers, many others are very young men, just at the start of life. Are these years of captivity to be a total, dead, embittering loss? Is the prisoner's best hope to be somehow to get through time? The answer has been a triumphant "No!" Food for the mind is traveling into the camps as steadily as food for the body. With what they have asked for and have been sent, the men have brought into being within the camps libraries, universities, and orchestras. The young prisoner can fit himself for his future career, not only by study of a proscribed course, but, now, by taking examinations. The older prisoner may develop cultural interests for which life, so far, has not allowed him time. Not only musical instruments, but "self-instruction" courses in the playing of them are being sent to the camps.

The inner, individual struggle of each man is ever-present in Mr. Barber's, as it must be in the reader's, mind. Though he does not dwell on it, this is, of course, the crux. He does say:

> The psychological strain on a prisoner of war is more serious than most people imagine. No man can live two or three years in a compound and not change mentally; the conditions are bound to bring either the best or the worst out of his character. It is therefore vitally important that the people of Britain should do everything possible to combat this deadly effect on men's minds, to make certain that, when the prisoner returns to normal life, he has lived an experience and not a tragedy; and that he is fitted for the life that spreads before him, and is not, by his very sacrifice, doomed to start late in the desperate struggle for existence which the world may well see when this war is over.

Rosamond Lehmann, *The Ballad and the Source*, October 11, 1944

English novelists, since the novel began, have packed their pages with "characters"—comic, resplendent, or sinister. So gladly do we enter this gallery, so much entertained are we by these personages and by the super-life with which their creators endow them, that we seldom ask how *deep* characters go. These fictitious men and women more than play their required parts—what more do we want?

Nothing more, perhaps. Should I seem to be quarreling with the English novel if I were to point out that, while it deals superbly with *character*, it tends to fight shy of *personality*? And what is the distinction between the two? Character is definable, personality not. Character works itself out in external action; personality is something slumberous, deep-down, and so slow, oblique, or tricky in its effects that it might appear to be inactive. But the very fact of its being what you might call nebulous makes it all the more powerful. Again, personality is rarer than character: you cannot be alive and human without having some kind of character; but in only (say) one out of fifty men, women, and children do we meet that enigmatic, dynamic, disturbing force that we have agreed to call personality. Once met, it is unmistakable. Do we like or dislike it; are we repelled or attracted?—we never quite know. We all know the man or woman whom no cap quite fits, who can never be finally pinned down or accounted for. Over your or my relationship with any one such person a sort of perpetual query hangs. The story is never totally satisfying; but, at the same time, it is never totally finished. One might say that people with personality attract complex love rather than simple friendship—for one thing, to know them takes a good deal of time. And it is impossible to come in contact with personality without being profoundly affected by it, in ways that one cannot gauge and one may not like. Nothing is more dire than the misuse or waste of this semi-voluntary, semi-involuntary power over other human beings: it needs, above all, to be canalized by clear intellect and scrupulous will. Personality finding a major channel has given us saints, statesmen, geniuses in the arts: as against this, personality running riot makes in the main for destruction, confusion, loss.

If personalities are troublesome in real life, one can see how they must be troublesome to the novelist, and may excuse him for fighting shy of them. They tend to hold up, rather than further, plot. If they are to enter a book at all, they demand to be *the* subject, belittling any others. How much more obliging, for the novelist's purpose, are pliable, colorful, active, more superficial "characters"—always either good or bad, black or white! And how infinitely easier—as well as often more repaying—are these to present: *if* your aim be a story that, unlike "Frankie and Johnnie," has both moral and end.

So novels dealing with personality as opposed to novels employing character have in this country been, as I said at the start, few. What have we? The range of the novels of Henry James, but he was an American. Some of the novels of George Eliot. Richardson's *Clarissa* and Jane Austen's *Emma*—for, indeed, Emma Woodhouse demands attention as something more than what she patently is, the star semi-comic feminine character of all English fiction.

And now we have Rosamond Lehmann's long-awaited new novel, *The Ballad and the Source*, which deals, wholly and brilliantly, with personality, its self-created environment, and its endless effects. The personality is that of Mrs. Jardine, who is, when the story opens, and remains when it closes, a mysterious lady. Mysterious to whom? First and last, to Rebecca, the little girl who is the "I" of the book, but not to Rebecca only.

Mrs. Jardine, with her husband Harry, returns from abroad to occupy The Priory, a long-shut-up house, thereby becoming the neighbor of Rebecca's family. Having been a friend of the children's grandmother, she sends a note asking that they may be allowed to come and pick primroses in her park, then stay to tea with her. The reception of this note by their parents shows that, with regard to Mrs. Jardine, the social situation is abnormal—however, Rebecca and Jess are allowed to go. This is the first impression, from which so much follows—

> As we crossed the lawn, a french window in the front of the long, low, creeper-covered house opened, and a woman's figure appeared. She waved. She gave the impression of arms outstretched, so welcomingly did she surge forward to meet us. She was dressed in a long gown of pale-blue with wide sleeves embroidered thickly with blue, rose, and violet flowers. She had a white fleecy wrap round her shoulders, and on her head, with its pile of fringed, puffed, curled white hair, a large Panama hat

trimmed with a blue liberty scarf artistically knotted, the ends hanging down behind. She was small and rather stocky, with short legs and little feet clad in low-heeled black slippers with tongues and paste buckles.

When she came up to us, she said:

"I must kiss you, because I loved your grandmother."

We lifted our faces, and she gave us each a kiss. Her lips and cheeks were dry, warm, the skin so crinkled all over with faint lines it seemed a fine-meshed net. The most noticeable things about her were the whiteness of her face, the paleness of her large eyes, and the strong fullness and width of her mouth. Her teeth were regular, splendid, untouched by age.

The period of this opening part of the story is, I should make clear, pre the 1914 war: extravagant, luscious oddness of dress would, one feels, always have been a perquisite of Mrs. Jardine's; but, as seen by the children on that spring afternoon, she was odd in the manner of her day. Her eyes, her idiom of speech, her jewels, the furniture and objects surrounding her (such as the mauve watered-silk couch), all go to build up this effect. Then there is the childhood portrait of her lost daughter, Ianthe, and the scarcely more living presence of her husband, Major Jardine, Harry—red-faced, thin, almost speechless, uncontrollably trembling. Her grandchildren—on that afternoon still unknown to her—are to enter the scene gradually; first by their banal Christian names (Maisie, Malcolm, and Cherry), then when they actually come to stay.

Ironically (though wholly characteristically), Mrs. Jardine feels drawn to her dead friend's grandchildren—principally to Rebecca—but can never fully accept or digest her own. It is into the little, eager, still unflawed mirror presented by Rebecca that she projects the first of those many and contradictory images of herself and her relations with other people that are to make up *The Ballad and the Source*. It is to Rebecca that she gives *her* version of the Ianthe story. And what a story! Have we a monster mother, or monster daughter? Mrs. Jardine and Ianthe—which was the other's victim? Mrs. Jardine's behavior, as maternal behavior, had been, by all but her own showing, preposterous. But had she a right, as she claimed, to super-vision, to the overruling prerogatives of genius?

Miss Lehmann, with supreme art, has surrounded her central figure with mirrors (of which Rebecca is only one) so placed as to reflect into one another. Tilly, an old servant common to both families, Maisie Thomson, and the young sculptor Gil by turns take up and further the extraordinary story — a story so drenched, so pervaded (whoever tells it) by Mrs. Jardine's atmosphere that in its forest-like depths one loses all ordinary landmarks of right and wrong. It is impossible to enter Mrs. Jardine's world without being saddled with a myth (contributory to her own myth) from which it is almost impossible to escape.

Nonetheless, it is not the least of Miss Lehmann's triumph that she has supported her Mrs. Jardine with a cast of characters whom she never quite overpowers, and whose own reality remains strong. Maisie Thomson, for instance, is a masterpiece. In the construction of *The Ballad and the Source*, a difficult — one might have thought almost impossibly difficult — method has been used with memorable success. You will almost certainly find this novel, as I found it, very hard to put down. But more: it has qualities of truth and imagination that demand something better than rapid, excited reading; and you should probably read it at least twice if you are to begin to realize how good it is. The only thing I could wish less of is the protracted painfulness of the final scenes with Ianthe, as told by her schoolgirl daughter.

Charles Morgan, *Reflections in a Mirror*, January 17, 1945

The essay is, I believe, the most difficult form in literary art. One's inhibitions on the subject of essay-writing, and, often, one's shyness of essay-reading, may date from unwise teaching at school. At the age of about twelve one proceeded, in English lessons, from the unalarming "composition" to the essay — ringed round with prohibitions and with its stern invitation to abstract thought. The exclusion of narrative, of out-and-out description, and of the word "I" was enjoined. How pathetic were one's classroom attempts at essays, swollen, to the point of elephantiasis, with abstractions, bristling with quotations, callowly didactic! Does the practice of essay-setting persist, in the best schools, still? For really, how hopeless to set very young people to a task which many mature and accomplished writers would prefer not to attempt, or have, anyhow, never successfully achieved!

The main psychological rule, I suppose, of an essay is that it should be reflective. Young people are not reflective—they are too busy registering impressions; they deal in vivid, emotional reflexes. Reflection implies maturity. The child and the young person—as, also, a number of people in after-life—only seek for their own reading, and read with genuine pleasure, those essayists who break the schoolroom rules. These delightful, unacademic sinners multiply. For, since the early nineteenth century, English literature shows an unbroken romantic trend. The classroom's iron definitions of form show a time lag. Progressively, the essay has loosened up.

This, like all forms of romanticism, can go too far. Let us not lose the distinction between freedom and anarchy. Form, in art as in all things, we *must* have—form only becomes despotic or over-rigid when the creative spirit flutters, slackens, or pales. I admire much in Charles Morgan's *Reflections in a Mirror*; I admire most that this writer has reanimated the essay in its most classic form. No early rule of the schoolroom is—as a point of interest—broken here. Yet the remoteness, the didacticism, the abstractions associated with the essay in the schoolroom are missing.

Yes, one rule *is* broken, and that with deliberation and good effect. This was done at second remove, when these essays became a book. For originally they appeared, one by one, as that unsigned series, "Menander's Mirror," so well known to readers of the *Times Literary Supplement*. The *Times* and its daughter the *Supplement* forbid "I"—for reasons both traditional and conclusive. Who indeed is to question that stronghold of the dignities of journalism? Nonetheless, I am glad that, during their revision, Mr. Morgan admitted his "I" to the essays. The gain in intimacy is great, the loss in dignity none. The "Menander" mask—how baffling it was to readers, or to how many readers, I do not know—being now removed from Morgan's face, there seems no reason why he should not speak as himself.

"Menander's Mirror" was "a series of essays on contemporary values in life and literature." The pessimist might say: "How write essays on what barely exists?"—for, indeed, these times are unfriendly to evaluation of any kind; and "contemporary values" often seem nil—or scant. But remember, no value exists till it is defined; so that, to define the values of any day is, at least to an extent, to create them. You may quarrel (though, in most cases, I doubt it) with Mr. Morgan's definitions: you cannot but be glad that they have been made.

Aggressiveness, provocation, was never the essay's province; and never— here the classic control comes in—was essayist less aggressive than Mr. Morgan. He has, all the same, a way of saying, calmly, what has not been said before and was overdue to be said. Objections to our dear friend, the Common Man (or, his alter ego, the Little Man), may by now have been stated, but never quite, I think, with just this fairness. (His essays "On Being Born Now" and "The Uncommon Man" are, in this context, certainly to be read.) Mr. Morgan's absence of anger is itself an asset in these stupefyingly angry days. How some of our younger but not-quite-so-young-now literary figures will like being referred to as "the stale van-guard" I do not know; but the comment is made in sorrow, not in the other thing.

The first essay, "In Search of Values," provides a key to the design and intention of *Reflections in a Mirror*. Of the essays, as a collection, their author says:

> Their range is wide. A reader who comes upon one by chance may see in it only a discussion of a particular subject, and may for that reason be the better entertained; but there is, neverthe-less, a free relationship between them, which will, I hope, appear gradually, as it might in the continued conversation of friends. In discussing the rise or decline in public favor of an author or an idea, I have tried not only to note the fact and comment on it, but to inquire how much of the change is to be dismissed as a swerve of fashion, and how much of it is more deeply significant as a pointer to an enduring change of values. If the essays are concerned with literature, they avoid coteries like the plague; if with war, they are innocent of strategy; if with social problems, they are, at any rate, not an arsenal for any party. That prejudice will be found in them is certain and even desirable, provided that the writer admits, as he does most freely, that his, like all opinion, is, in part, emotional. Finally, these papers ask more questions than they presume to answer.

Mr. Morgan's essays on other countries—"The Return of France," "The Idea of Europe," "Italia Irredenta"—should supply a worthy directive to thought and feeling. On life as an art he is excellent—as "La Douceur de Vivre," "A Leisured Civilization," and "On Unrelated Knowledge" show. His anti-materialism is something stronger than emotional prejudice. In the literary group, the essay on Emily Brontë takes first place, but those on Turgenev, Hardy, and Tolstoy stand out for qualities of their own. "On Picking Sides" comments on changing literary fashions.

T. S. Eliot, *What Is a Classic?* March 7, 1945

The title of this new book—even apart from its author's name—is likely to catch the roving eye. *What Is a Classic?* is the text of the first Annual Address to the Virgil Society, delivered by the society's first president, T. S. Eliot, on October 16, 1944. Are we to take it, from the context, that Mr. Eliot will only discuss "*the* classics" in the Greek-and-Latin sense associated with school? Or may we hope that he will be coming to grips with the question his title raises for the ordinary reader?

We may. The last line of the very first page is reassuring. The address—the book—really does set out to establish (and, to my mind, establishes) what *a* classic is. It is high time: nothing could be more welcome, in these days, than this kind of suggestive, directive criticism. Why in these days specially? Because, since the war, people have *read* more and been taught *about* books less. For young people, the peacetime lecture room, with its rows of attentive notebooks, has given place to direct, avid, enjoyable, often omnivorous, spare time in wartime reading. In this, the chief guides are interest, feeling, and natural taste. That this should be so is excellent. But, at the same time, the wish to arrive at standards, to be certain of values, is inevitable. What are the tests that one should apply? Popular critics of past and reviewers of current literature tend, I am afraid, to create confusion by their unconsidered use of classifications and terms. The word "classic"—as Mr. Eliot points out—can have a least half-a-dozen connotations.

What Is a Classic?, I should make clear, is not, and is not intended to be, a foolproof, domestic remedy for those suffering from literary indigestion. It is an address delivered by a great living poet, on the subject of a poet of all time, to a learned society. It is couched in language worthy of speaker, subject, and hearers—and more, the language shows a compression, and an intensity—if, at the same time, a lucidity—that are Mr. Eliot's own. Mr. Eliot's theme, to which he has given thought, demands a response of thought from the reader. To make this response is well worthwhile.

The book—in itself, in a sense, a summary—deserves better than to be summarized, with doubtful correctness, in a review. And it might be misleading to isolate any of Mr. Eliot's points. Myself, I found I reflected longest on what he says about maturity:

> If there is a word on which we can fix, which will suggest the maximum of what I mean by the term "a classic," it is the word *maturity*. I shall distinguish between the universal classic, like Virgil, and the classic which is only such in relation to the other literature in its own language, or according to the view of life of a particular period. A classic can only occur when a civilization is mature; when a language and a literature are mature; and it must be the work of a mature mind. It is the importance of that civilization and of that language, as well as the comprehensiveness of the mind of the individual poet, which gives the universality. To define *maturity* without assuming that the hearer already knows what it means, is almost impossible: let us say then, that if we are properly mature, as well as educated persons, we can recognize maturity in a civilization and in a literature, as we do in the other human beings whom we encounter . . . . No reader of Shakespeare, for instance, can fail to recognize, increasingly as he himself grows up, the gradual ripening of Shakespeare's mind.

"Maturity of mind," he says further on, "this needs history, and the consciousness of history . . . . Virgil's maturity of mind, and the maturity of his age, are exhibited in this awareness of history." Absence of provinciality—and read closely Mr. Eliot's close, just analysis *of* provinciality—is a sine qua non of the mature-mindedness necessary for the classic. Again, the classic is stamped by its "common language"; and, by that which it has in common with all kinds, and with the sum, of human experience.

Mr. Eliot thinks it arguable that English literature has not produced "a classic" in the sense he means: he questions, however, "whether the achievement of a classic . . . is, for the people and the language of its origin, altogether an unmixed blessing—even though it is unquestionably a ground for pride." A classic, apparently, may exhaust a language—and exhaust, even, the potentialities of a people. Like one great crop raised, it impoverishes the field. Mr. Eliot finds it significant that, after Virgil, Latin poetry showed a steady decline. "We may," he says, "be inclined to ask, then, whether we are not fortunate in possessing a language which, instead of having produced a classic, can boast a rich variety in the past, and the possibility of further novelty in the future."

Bill Naughton, *A Roof over Your Head*, March 21, 1945

Too many true sayings come to be worn threadbare—so threadbare that nobody dare repeat them—before we have ever quite grasped their truth. That "one half of the world does not know how the other half lives" is a case in point. We may agree in theory that we are ignorant, or at least poorly informed, as to our fellow creatures' lives. In practice, it generally takes some incident, some apparently quite slight revelation, to make us *feel* our ignorance. We are then surprised.

In a sense, of course, we are not so ignorant as were our forefathers. The war, by shaking us out of our own grooves, by throwing us into working or living companionship with all sorts of strangely assorted people, has been an eye-opener—and for those of us who remember 1914–1918 this is happening for the second time. Even before 1939 few of us were quite lacking in social conscience. Reports, leading articles, documentary writing, and, here and there, a case in the newspapers, brought to our notice what are called "bad conditions." Unemployment, with its stagnancy and frustration; inadequate housing (long before bombs began) and the inadequacy for life, in the proper sense, in industrial cities, of what houses there were; the effects of overcrowding and underfeeding on millions of working-class people's lives—these, as facts, have been far from unknown to us. But have they, perhaps, been facts that are difficult to comprehend imaginatively?

A single appeal to the imagination does more than table on table of statistics, volume on volume of reports. Dickens's novels, for instance, broke down, in our well-to-do Victorian forefathers, a complacency against which the social reformers might have continued to thunder in vain. To us, less comfortably armor-plated, some of the Dickens pictures of social misery may well seem mawkish or over-melodramatic—but they spoke the language necessary for their own time.

Bill Naughton's *A Roof over Your Head* speaks to us in the language of our time. It is a cry from the heart, rather than a complaint; it is less a muster of harsh facts or study of bad conditions than a picture of the effect of those facts and conditions on a group of individual human lives— those of a young man, his wife, and their two small children in a Lancashire industrial town, in the years just before this war.

A Roof over Your Head is an autobiography that ranks high as a work of imagination. Does this sound contradictory? It should not—for autobiography is more than the enumeration of the events that have gone to make up a life: it is a contemplation of those events in relation to one another and to the man who lived through them all; it is a search made by imagination through memory, to discover the inner meaning of what has happened. This process of imaginative search is present in all great autobiography, be it that of soldier, statesman, financier, traveler, or artist. In this case, we find it in the autobiography of a young working man.

Mr. Naughton is Irish peasant by birth, Lancashire working class by upbringing. It may be felt that his nationality sets him, to a degree, aside, by making a special case of him. In fact, it does not disqualify him to write of what he writes; but it does empower him to write in a particular way. He owes, for one thing, I think, to his extraction, a strong, traditional peasant feeling for what one might call, in the high sense, propriety. He is Irish in the strong Catholic influence that surrounded his childhood; in his idealistic, almost religious, feeling for family life, in the quickness of his emotional reflexes, in his self-questionings and capacity for remorse. Say, if you like, that he has a sense of sin. Not feeling himself without sin, he does not cast many stones.

That innate family feeling is a strong factor in a book concerned with the struggle to maintain a family life. Also, we find an underlying un-materialism, even anti-materialism—a model kitchen, a drying-cupboard, an upstairs heating do *not* represent the height of his aspirations. He desires—yes—a roof over his and his children's heads; but that roof is to cover a strong, sweet, natural growth. What he wants might be summed up as *douceur de vivre*. He wanted to be the father, as he had been the child, of a good home. He shows, from time to time, the child of the good home's expectations of life; the belief, so hard to detach oneself from, in the existence of benevolent "grown-ups." As here:

> A man imagines there is a protective Society grown strong around him. A great tree of civilization: Law, Churches and Pastors and Bishops, Wealth, Books, Buildings, Newspapers, Institutions, Democracy and Decency, Public Opinion, Good and Famous Men. He feels safe against injustice among all these. They wouldn't see a family dragged down in starvation. But when the man goes to speak to this Society it is not as he imagined. The nearest he can get to it is the meeting of little individuals. These are fierce, busy, and helpless. They have no time for him. He can yell, scream, moan, or cry—Society does not hear. He might break windows; then they will lock him up.
>
> This knowledge is inclined to take the cockiness out of him.

Mr. Naughton was born to make himself a writer. I put it like this because I feel it is how he would wish it put. He was born with a certain awareness, vision, susceptibilities, and with also the Irish capacity for expression—but all these he developed by sheer hard work. (The sanity and austerity of his attitude towards writing might well be a lesson to many young aspirants who can afford to "sprout" and experiment under easy conditions, unlike Mr. Naughton's own.) His self-education was carried out in the (often midnight) intervals of working in a mill, heaving coal, or driving a lorry, or during the long and otherwise deadening interludes of unemployment. The sum total is that he has enabled himself to make *us* feel what it feels like to lead the life that he, and thousands of other youths of his age, led.

He can describe, for instance, the sensation of weeks of more or less nonstop hunger—more felt in the head, in aches and dizziness, he says, than actually in the stomach. He can describe what might be called the *climate* of continuous and extreme poverty. He can do full justice to the escapades, the light-headed nonsense devices, by which one keeps one's balance, or into which one escapes. (One of his most excellent chapters is called "Fiddling.")

One main impression left on me by A Roof over Your Head is that to be very poor is to be very near to life. No veils of sympathetic, discreet "arrangement" divided this young man from the physical processes of birth and death—he assisted, in fact, at the birth of his third child. He had married and was the father of two children at an age when other young men, in peacetime, are still at the university. We may denounce him for marrying without means of support. But—dare we? Life has imperatives that, to the simple soul, may still seem to be stronger than economics. We belong to, or are watching, a generation that for faith's sake is not hesitating to die. Can we blame a man who, in faith's name, has not hesitated to live?

Roland Penrose, *In the Service of the People*, April 18, 1945

In the Service of the People, by Roland Penrose, has been compiled from books, newspapers, and reviews published during and immediately after the German occupation of France by the intellectuals of the Resistance movement. It answers, I think, the charge once leveled against the intellectuals of France—and, less directly, of other countries—that they are selfish, dwellers in ivory towers, unconcerned with the welfare of the community in which they live or with the fate and the honor of their country. The fanatical isolation of the study, the studio, the laboratory, before this war, may or may not have held good. But in 1940 the terrible call was heard: the best brains of France offered the best of their services to her freedom. It was as Frenchmen, simply, that these French poets, scientists, lawyers, professors, musicians, painters entered the secret fight. Of their achievements, much has been put on record; but much more still remains to be known. Risks, ordeals, and martyrdoms build up, one by one, into the noble story of the liberation of France. These men feared, and acted against, what has power to hurt the soul.

The stories here are brief and are sparely told; the documents speak for themselves. I shall not forget the closing phrase in the letter Jacques Decour wrote to his parents before his execution: "I consider myself rather like a leaf that falls from the tree to make mold. The quality of the mold depends on the leaves. I am thinking of the youth of France, in whom I put all my hope."

Honor, one feels, is due to those of whom it was asked to sacrifice the honor of their names. Mr. Penrose instances one or two prominent people who agreed to pass as collaborationists in order to give cover, under their roofs, to the secret, vital activities of their friends.

Stephen Spender, *Citizens in War—and After*; Rumer Godden, A *Fugue in Time*, June 6, 1945

Stephen Spender's *Citizens in War—and After*, though, technically, it deals with the wartime subject of Civil Defence, seems to me to be one of the first important books of the peace—a peace which, though not yet total, has implications that have been facing us since (and indeed since before) VE Day. We enter this peace, as we entered war, soberly, and with considerable resolve. At the same time we are tired and not a little dazed. We have lived through what, apart from everything else, has been a period of nonstop activity: indeed, we should all be very glad to rest. Rest, yes; but stop off, no. For many of us still feel charged-up with powers and energies of which, six years ago, we should not have thought ourselves capable. Can we switch these over into some other output; or must they run down to a full stop, or go to waste?

War has given us nearly six years of intensive human experience. Not the least part of this has been service—and service alongside other people: people, in many cases, superficially very unlike ourselves. We have not only come to know them, but come, in the course of that, to know ourselves in a new way. And such knowledge—because this has been a total war—has extended outside the forces, and has enriched almost every civilian man and woman. Are we to lose it with the return to peace?

It would be insincere to pretend that the stand-down of the Civil Defence services has not been, in one aspect, a relief. It sets free many who undertook night duties in addition to all-out daily work. But do some of us, perhaps, feel a slight vacuum? Do we miss the camaraderie of our stations and posts?

Mr. Spender stresses the underlying link, rather than the break, between peace and war. His feeling for continuity gives background to his admirable account of the activities of the various branches of Civil Defence — the N.F.S., the Warden's Service, the Ambulance Service, the Light and Heavy Rescue, the W.V.S.[4] Now the tin hats are being put away. Must we say goodbye to the spirit in which we wore them? Mr. Spender argues no — a hundred times no. The "— and After" parts of his book make no less inspiring reading than do his accounts of citizens still at war.

This is a full, able, and brilliant piece of work. The background argument throws into relief the concrete, informative, and pictorial passages. (The actual illustrations are colored photographs.) I do not think that either the former Civil Defence worker, or the interested onlooker wanting to know more, will find anything lacking. Mr. Spender himself is an ex-fireman; and in his sections about the N.F.S. — and also about the Fire Service before it became the N.F.S. — experience shows in every line. As an ex-warden, I am in a position to check up on what he says about wardens, and I have no fault to find with, and nothing to add to, his picture. He has rendered, excellently, both the collective temperament of each of these two services *as* services, while suggesting and allowing for variations in each, from station to station, post to post. And he voices, in a brief, personal passage, a feeling many of us had, a feeling intensely secret, but not shameful — sheer *Boy's Own Paper* excitement at finding oneself in action. "*Can* this be me?" (I know the grammar is wrong; but in the internal exclamation grammar is seldom above reproach.)

Smooth-running interaction between the different services was essential at a large incident. The firemen, wardens, Light and Heavy Rescue parties, and ambulance personnel gained, literally, a working knowledge of one another during raids, and, as the Civil Defence technique adapted itself to the changing technique of the raiders, the W.V.S. played an ever larger part, before and after incidents were declared closed. The collaboration was bound, however, to be at high pressure: between-times, back again at their posts or stations, the services could not continue to be in touch, and therefore remained ignorant, however amiably so, of each other's interests and routine. Not the least valuable thing about *Citizens in War — and After* is that it provides a needed link-up — retrospectively, it is true, but not too late. The mobility (against all odds), the resource, and the courage of "the ambulance people" were well known: here we have filled in for us their routine background. The highly skilled and, to put it mildly, somber work of the Heavy Rescue parties was more often taken for granted than studied. Mr. Spender shows how a collapsed building, with possibly living people underneath it, presents, in an awesome way, the same problems as a game of spillikins.

Heavy Rescue, for reasons which imagination can supply, proved to be the most taciturn of the services. With an East End warden, a Civil Defence doctor, and two ambulance girls, Mr. Spender had, on the other hand, conversations which he has built up into vivid and solid portraits. Though much of the action part of the book has a London background, the author has not confined himself to London; by traveling, he has collected material from members of this "army without arms" all over the country.

What of those who stood by faithfully throughout the war in areas on which few or no bombs happened to fall? They too deserve their laurels; incidentally, many came to London, during the capital's bad times, as volunteer reserves. London "lulls" presented—and perhaps in a more acute form—the same problems that in non-blitzed areas had to be faced throughout: how to convert long spaces of inactivity for Civil Defence into some sort of gain, instead of demoralizing dead loss. Wardens, as Mr. Spender points out, had their training lectures, in a progressive series, to keep them going. (Even so, I know cases where much was owing to post wardens' powers to keep their posts, during inactive vigils, cheerful centers of life.) In the N.F.S., vacuums were badly felt, until group discussions were introduced. As to the value of these discussions, Mr. Spender is in a position to speak with both authority and conviction. In the good sense, it seems more than possible that they have "started something." I should like to draw your attention, particularly, to the sections about discussion groups . . . And there was another resort in this enforced leisure—increasing production in arts and crafts.

When you have read *Citizens in War—and After*, I think you will see why I count it as not the last of the war books, but the first of the peace. It lays stress less upon the idea than upon the actual *sensations* of democracy. It reminds us how in the midst of death we were in life. Let us not lose life now that we may hope to live it.

Rumer Godden's *A Fugue in Time* is a novel of imaginative distinction. Its idea is one that might have appealed to Virginia Woolf, though the carrying out is Miss Godden's own; indeed, I do not think that the author of *Black Narcissus* and *Breakfast with the Nikolides* could at any time owe anything to any other writer. Her art is a curious—and, to me, very attractive—blend of sublimity and despair, lyricism and something just short of harshness.

The Dane family have, for the whole term of their ninety-nine years' lease, occupied 99, Wiltshire Place, a London house. To this home, completed in the year of their marriage, John Dane, in the early 1840s, brought his seventeen-year-old bride Griselda. Now, halfway through the World War, the lease is just running out, the owners will not renew, and the aged, unmarried Sir Roland Dane, K.C.B., D.S.O.—the youngest and now the only surviving one of John and Griselda's nine children—is to be evicted. To her great-uncle, during his last days in the house, arrives young American Grizel Dane, in London with a U.S. ambulance unit and with, apparently, no other place to live. These two occupy the silent, once-teeming, and humming house; and, together, watch the Wiltshire Place sands run out.

I say "now." Actually, there is no fixed "now" in the book: past, present, and future mingle; or, rather, interweave like themes in a fugue. Hence the novel's name. Everything that has ever happened in this is still happening, and is happening simultaneously. We have the original couple, Grizel and John Dane, their servants, three of their children—Pelham, Selina, and Rollo—and the foundling Lark, whom John Dane brought home to his grown-up family after his wife's death. All these we see at different ages and stages of their existence. Times of day in the house bring to life these people, sometimes at a crisis, sometimes in the accustomed flow of the family routine: they pass up and down stairs, sit by fires, talk on the balcony, light the candles on birthday cakes or on Christmas trees, ring or answer bells. Any arbitrary time sequence is broken up—we pass, without warning, to and fro through the years. Is this confusing for the reader? At the beginning I found it so, but gradually the different characters, with their inherent destinies and their buried wishes, so gained a hold on me that the musical intermingling of everything became as interesting as it was strange. The end, with its reconciliations, is like a final chord.

Evelyn Waugh, *Brideshead Revisited,* June 13, 1945

Evelyn Waugh is a novelist who can exert the exact degree of power that his subject requires. This is rare. One has become familiar with what might be called the puffing-and-blowing school—those who lay bare rippling outsize muscles, or even import a steam crane, in order to do what amounts to nothing more than the shifting of china ornaments on a mantelpiece. Equally, we have the underestimators of their task—those who genuinely do not know the difference between the Himalayas and a rock garden; and who, having committed themselves to a theme that really does demand they should move mountains, hope for the best with a series of dainty touches. No novel of Mr. Waugh's till now, has, I feel, required that he should go all out. *Brideshead Revisited* does; and he, therefore, has. The effect is not one of roaring engines, but of the extreme, it could be sinister, quiet of never-more-necessary control.

To say that *Brideshead Revisited*—subtitled *The Sacred and Profane Memories of Captain Charles Ryder*—is, accordingly, his greatest book would seem to me incorrect. There is no question of his having "at last," as it were, brought off something. Each of his novels has hit its intended mark. He has not, up to now, aspired to write a great book. This time he has; and he has done so.

Inside the wrapper, in place of the usual anonymous "blurb," we find a column headed "Warning" and signed by Evelyn Waugh. Of *Brideshead Revisited* he says—

> There are passages of buffoonery, but the general theme is at once romantic and eschatological.
>
> It is ambitious, perhaps intolerably presumptuous, to trace the workings of a divine purpose in a pagan world, in the lives of an English Catholic family, half-paganized themselves, in the world of 1923–1939. The story will be uncongenial alike to those who look back on that world with an alloyed affection, and to those who see it as transitory, insignificant, and, already, hopefully past. Whom then can I hope to please? Perhaps those who have the leisure to read a book word by word for the inter-

est of the writer's use of language; perhaps those who look to the future with black forebodings and need more solid comfort than rosy memories. For the latter I have given my hero, and them, if they will allow me, a hope, not, indeed, that anything but disaster lies ahead, but that the human spirit, redeemed, can survive all disasters.

Uncertain as to the exact nature of the science of eschatology, I turned to the *Oxford Dictionary*. For any who share my ignorance, may I quote?—Eschatology is "the science of 'the four last things: death, judgment, heaven, and hell.'"

How, you may ask, are "the four last things" involved, or, how is Mr. Waugh to show them to be involved, in the living fortunes of the Flytes, children of Lord and Lady Marchmain and inhabitants of the great house Brideshead, and in the interknitting into those fortunes of Charles Ryder—first, through his romantic undergraduate friendship with Sebastian Flyte, then through his reciprocated love for Sebastian's sister Julia? Opening and reopening, at random, *Brideshead Revisited*, you might say that no one passage shows any special tension, ominousness, or weight. There is no rhetorical writing; there are[5] no inked-in foreshadowings of fatality and no outstandingly strong scenes. There is dialogue—some of it in the vein of which Mr. Waugh has long shown himself master. There are passages charged with compressed action; and there are characters who make one feel, instantaneously, and anew with every gesture or word, that they have been endowed with fullness of life. There are scenes of gaiety, illusion, romance, distress. No one given moment appears momentous—and yet a feeling of apprehension is gradually and inexorably induced. Is there—the reader may ask, halfway and more than halfway on his course through *Brideshead Revisited*—is there to be an earthquake, in which this whole bright surface will crack across? No; rather this is an affair of a rising tide. The surface is not to crack; it is to be submerged.

The time is the past. The story is finished for Charles Ryder when he begins to tell it. Or rather, its events have come to an end: its implication waits for the epilogue. In the prologue and epilogue, we have Captain Ryder, thirty-nine years old, in an early year of the war. Under orders, he moves troops from a camp in Scotland to an unknown, unnamed destination in the south of England. Arriving in the dark of the small hours, under every un-ideal condition, he finds the new camp to be in the grounds of a mansion that has been taken over since the war began. And this is Brideshead. In such a manner, unknowing, has he returned (or, one might say, been returned) to a place he had expected never to see again. Brideshead and its people have been the core of his former, finished inner and, in a sense, only life.

Inside this grim Army frame, between the prologue and epilogue, lies, or rather extends, like Brideshead valley, the story, in a forever romantic and elegiac light. For the story's start, we are back—a transition itself so startling and so effective that it seems to involve more than the physical turning-over of one page—in the glowing and easy Oxford of 1923, where Charles Ryder, an undergraduate in his first year, makes friends with the charming, lyrical, unaccountable Sebastian Flyte.

It is as undergraduate friend of the younger son that Charles first comes to Brideshead, turns in at the gates, looks up the valley. It is early summer; the two have escaped for the day from an Oxford devastated by Eights Week; from Brideshead, the family are away. Lord Marchmain has, anyhow, left the scene: he is living in Venice with his mistress. It is Lady Marchmain, we soon discover, who is the presiding genius, whether benevolent or otherwise, of Brideshead. This daughter of an old Catholic family, adored by her friends, fled from by her husband, devoted to and fatal to her children, is Mr. Waugh's masterpiece—and she is something more: she embodies the question running right through the novel. Even her glum, correct elder son, Bridey, and her disconcerting, straightforward, youngest child, Cordelia, are not in a happy relation to her; she queers Sebastian, who takes to drink, and she mishandles Julia—who first makes a marriage that is, in the eyes of her church, no marriage with the Canadian success-boy, Rex Mottram; then, ten years later, returns Charles Ryder's passion.

Time, in *Brideshead Revisited*, is more than an element; it is a dramatic factor of which Mr. Waugh has made the fullest and boldest romantic use. We watch Julia flower from a "spidery" débutante into a woman whose stature, variability, and capacity for tragedy make her a heroine on the grand scale. We watch the (apparent) decay of Sebastian, from a golden boy into a sly drunk—but apotheosis is waiting for him beyond that. Time adds irony to Bridey's preposterous marriage, and refines the comedy of the debunking of Mr. Samgrass—the over-agreeable Oxford don. Time throws a somehow exalting light on Cordelia's unaesthetic maturity. Time (for the purposes of the novel) culminates in Lord Marchmain's return to Brideshead, to die there. Lord Marchmain's death itself is, eschatologically speaking, the climax and the end, in all senses, of *Brideshead Revisited*.

Whom, Mr. Waugh has asked, may he hope to please? As a reviewer, I speak for the first of the two sorts of readers he has in mind—one may or may not, also, be of the second; but that is a matter of private life. The wording of this novel, its textures, its beauty, and the faultless working of its concealed mechanics are a delight.

J. B. Priestley, *Three Men in New Suits*, July 11, 1945

J. B. Priestley's new novel, *Three Men in New Suits*, is the story of three men just out of the army. It will be much discussed, and possibly quarreled with. Admirably and masterfully written, it is as easy to read as it is, in parts, hard to swallow. I expected Mr. Priestley to have a better judgment than his three young men—surely he has had wider and longer opportunities to form one?—and I almost doubted, in places, whether he had. The number of snap judgments with which he appeared to concur—if only by not dissenting from them—rather staggered me.

Alan Strete, Herbert Kenford, and Eddie Mold all come from the same part of England, have all been through the war in the same regiment, and all, the war being over, come home again at the same time. Alan is the younger son of the late Sir William Strete, of Swansford Manor; Herbert is the son of a prosperous farmer; Eddie is a quarry worker—and, he is to find, the husband of an unfaithful wife. Eddie's homecoming *is* tragic: the returns of Alan and Herbert are not more than inharmonious and disconcerting. As a novel, *Three Men in New Suits* suffers from the people in it all having to be cases or types, in order to give a context to the discussions that carry the message of the book. Swansford Manor and its inhabitants seemed to me unconvincing—which would not matter if the social opinions Alan promulgates were not based on the unlikely behavior of his mother, brother and sister, and their friends.

First meetings—meetings again—are devastating: too much attaches to them. There are bound to be oscillations and disappointments; they have a strained phantasmagoric quality. Any two people, if they are wise and wish to continue to love each other, do not allow any first meeting to count for too much. If they tend to do so, they should be counseled not to. Could nobody have suggested to these three, or even one of these three, young men that a little long-term tolerance, with regard to their families, would not have been too bad—and, still more, need *not* have represented seduction to the corrupt ways of the bad old world?

A psychological study of a man's first three days at home, at the end of war, could make a novel of preeminent human value. Such a novel, Mr. Priestley is fully equipped to write. But it should, I think, include the emotions and sensations of those who are returned *to*, not only those of the returning. To be returned to is—for any but the most blockish parents, brothers, sisters, and, most of all, wives—an ordeal in itself: to the effect of the ordeal on *their* behavior justice should (I say sternly) be done. Alan, Herbert, and Eddie are human enough; but Mr. Priestley has surrounded them by stock figures incapable of the most elementary reflexes. Because he has not done justice to individuals, his criticisms of society as a whole (for they are his, through the mouths of his three young men) sound to me one-sided and hollow. Without charity, and without perhaps a touch of irony, the road of human progress seems to me likely to be as arid, and inevitably as competitive, as the Brighton Road on a prewar Sunday afternoon. Yes, this novel implies we should all learn to like each other better. But it suggests no point at which this could well begin.

Cyril Connolly, *The Condemned Playground,* January 23, 1946

The Condemned Playground is a collection of essays, satires, and critical pieces by Cyril Connolly. It offers an open view of the mind, and displays the extraordinary range of powers of one of the most important critics of a generation—the generation now in its young maturity. A generation that has, for a long time, been regarded as one of precocious children—disrespectful, experimental, and brilliant—but which must now be recognized as having moved forward into its due place, that of the grown-ups.

England—I sometimes feel, in the darker moments—would rather raise, and tolerate, crop after crop of playboys than honor, and take seriously a savagely serious and original mind. There has been a policy— quite, of course, unadmitted and unconscious—of "Keep the children at play, so long as they don't break anything valuable, until, one morning, they wake up and find they are old men." England is equally kind to the golden lad and the noble silver head—both voices are listened to with attention. Maturity and its claims, on the other hand, almost always create an awkwardness, a predicament. It seems one too many, in almost all fields of action. In fact, there appears to be little demand for it.

Or there *has* not seemed to be much demand for it. Surely, now, in the crucial days, the demand for maturity—of mind, of judgment, of feeling— has become immediate and pressing? The imperative to be grown up is upon us all. Those who have hesitated to grow up should pull themselves together and do so; and those who have been grown up for some time, but whose grown-up-ness has been ignored, should be recognized.

Mr. Connolly is by a few years younger than this century—a century whose violences and convulsions have been more noted than, and have perhaps helped to obscure, its accession, by this year, to middle life. He was one of what was collectively called the youth of one postwar period; he represents the maturity of another. The pieces in *The Condemned Playground* cover the years 1927–1944. His first published article, on Sterne, is here; also, critical writing that was his most recent at the time of the book's going to press. What lies behind the selection of the pieces and, at the same time, inspired their arrangement, is significant: read through, *The Condemned Playground* is the reverse of scrappy—the book, in fact, is as continuous as a story. The story is the relation, from year to year, of a mind with its own times.

Of his title, Mr. Connolly says:

> *The Condemned Playground* signifies for me the literary scene of the 1930s, the period of ebullience, mediocrity, frivolity and

talent, during which I wrote most of these essays and my first two books. I also chose the title to refer in a more limited sense to that leafy, tranquil, cultivated *spielraum* of Chelsea, where I worked and wandered. But there is another sense in which *The Condemned Playground* refers to Art itself; for Art is man's noblest attempt to preserve Imagination from Time, to make unbreakable toys of the mind, mud-pies which endure; and yet even the masterpieces whose permanence grants them a mystical authority over us are doomed to decay: a word slithers into oblivion, then a phrase, then an idea . . . .

This feeling of evanescence has always been with me as a critic; I feel I am fighting a rearguard action, for although each generation discovers anew the value of masterpieces, generations are never quite the same and ours are, in fact, coming to prefer the response induced by violent stimuli—film, radio, press—to the slow permeation of the personality of great literature.

"Like most critics," he goes on to say, "I drifted into the profession through lack of moral stamina." He suggests that criticism—or, as he at one time felt it to be in his case, "the interim habit of writing short-term articles about books"—was the outcome of, or the one road left open by, drastic *self*-criticism: the high standards set by his reading made him abandon his own creative work. This cut both ways; it may be remembered that, from the time of his very first appearance, Mr. Connolly has been recognized as a creative critic. His earliest book reviews—of which there are examples here—had a richness, force, angle, and, above all, unpredictable course which made them works of art in themselves. If they were an apprenticeship to writing, they showed no characteristic of prentice work. And the two books he did write in the 1930s—*The Rock Pool* and *Enemies of Promise*—show that he did not lower the standards that, at the start, had been so forbiddingly high. Rather, he found himself able to approach them. Since then, there have been rumors of his association with "Palinurus," of the famous *Unquiet Grave*.

Most of the pieces in *The Condemned Playground* were written concurrently with the writing of the books; and those dating onward from 1940, concurrently with the editing of *Horizon*.

The expression "literary scene" means something. Literature is like a landscape: its foreground, the present, packed with moving figures, sometimes too close up to be judged; its background, the past, showing those mountain ranges which are the classics—but even these seem to change, seem more or less distant, higher or lower, as mountains do, in the varying, changing lights of our own day. Mr. Connolly registers, in his writing, those changing lights. He can also, when his subject is modern writing, fix, by a sort of magnesium flash from his own temperament, figures, here and there, in the chaotic foreground. Where he is concerned, art and life are inseparable: he is fascinated by the interplay between the two. This fascination he communicates to the reader. He does not shun or dread, but rather explores and uses, his own susceptibilities.

The essays in *The Condemned Playground* are at once just and savage, somber and frivolous—Proust said, frivolity is an intellectual quality. He has a religious regard for "the saints of art." *Kind*, he is never—those who have seen salt dropped on a slug may have some image of what he does to the reputation of the middlebrow novelist. The trend of the middle part of his book is to discourage feeling young persons from writing feeling novels unless, absolutely, they must.

The book is in three sections. The first, essays on Sterne, Swift, Chesterfield, and on some of the recognized great moderns of the interwar period—Joyce, Gide, Thomas Mann. We have the "Imitations of Horace"; also, the A. E. Housman controversy, which raised Cain. In the second section, we watch Mr. Connolly out with salt after slugs. An exquisite parody of a mid-period Aldous Huxley, and three hair-raising satires— "Year Nine," "An Unfortunate Visit," and "Ackermann's England"— supplement the chase. The third section is the most personal, the richest, the most dignified and most interesting: it contains fragments of direct autobiography; the "Barcelona" piece stands out strongly by having been placed in juxtaposition to the earlier, jaded, blasé "Spring Revolution." "The Fate of an Elizabethan" touches the seat of a malady; and "The Ant-Lion" is unforgettable. "Writers and Society" would, for the purpose of wide circulation, merit publication in pamphlet form.

I cannot omit, yet hesitate to embark on, comment on the brilliantly funny "Where Engels Fears to Tread." I know of no living English writer, in any field, who commands more admirable, one might say more enviable, prose than does the author of *The Condemned Playground*.

Robert Henrey, *The Siege of London,* February 6, 1946

With *The Siege of London*, Robert Henrey gives us the third of a magical trilogy. First came A *Village in Piccadilly*; then, *The Incredible City*—I cannot suppose that readers will have forgotten either. This third book, I think, is the best of all: the most concentrated and the most poignant. I call the trilogy magical because it achieves something more than sheer good writing, observation, and sensibility can account for—it captures the very air of wartime London. Air (I mean, the element) is almost impossible to describe—it is breathed in, it fills one's being and colors one's whole mood; its intoxication, when it is intoxicating, is so strongly felt that it creates intimacy even between strangers. One says of close friends or lovers that "they breathed the same air"—and perhaps *they*, only, know what that particular air is.

In the same sense, all London lovers who stayed in London throughout these last years have breathed the same air. It has been an unaccountable factor in every experience. "What is London like, these days?" friends at a distance asked; and every answer one gave, every picture one attempted to paint, seemed to oneself, somehow, unsatisfactory, falsifying, out of the true proportion. The fact was that wartime London was "like" nothing else—she had air, light, proportions of her own. The things that mattered and that did not matter must, to the rational outsider, seem so extraordinary. To try to convey what one did mean meant the search for a language.

Such a language Mr. Henrey[6] has found, or, perhaps, is happily formed to speak. His system of notation is quite his own. The 1940–45 London of his trilogy is, somehow, so much nearer the psychic mark than the London of the so many more thorough, careful, documented accounts we have had. He accents nothing; his manner is apparently flitting and discontinuous. Yet, under his touch, slight incidents bear the weight of a world of feeling, elusive moments become immortal, and continuity, like a deep-down current, knits up moment and moment, scene and scene, face and face.

In London, each year of the war was as unlike the other war years as are the different seasons to one another. Different developments of the war, bad news, good news, reflected themselves so strongly that no two

Junes or Septembers (for instance) seemed to have much in common. Mr. Henrey's vivid, reflective writing registers each emotional change. *The Siege of London* takes up where its predecessor, *The Incredible City*, stopped; and though the ground it covers is geographically the same, everything else is different: we are in a further phase of experience; everything has advanced. Characters met before (most notably, the Lavoisier family) reappear, but their fates have taken another turning. In the parks, the grass has worn a little thinner. After the mid-war immunity, air raids have begun again, and the reaction to them is totally different from the reaction to the 1940–41 blitz.

Mr. Henrey still writes from that light-colored, towering block of flats that (as he says), like a huge docked liner, overtops the low roofs of Shepherd's Market. Soho (of which he gave us an inside picture in his intervening novel, *The Foolish Decade*), Piccadilly, the parks, with their birds and bands and people, and the riverside are still his favorite haunts. The block of flats, with its personnel, residents and visitors and market neighbors, is, as before, a microcosm of the world. In a delightful passage he shows the block's *inside* similarity to a liner—we have the long lit passages, the fellow-passenger feeling between the dwellers at times of stress, the engine-room depths, the flag flown.

All through *The Siege of London* a crescendo is felt. Indeed, the just more than a year chronicled here—February 1944 to April 1945—is, as the war's climax, really the supreme test of a London chronicler. First, we have the mounting tension of the pre-D-Day months; the everywhere palpable but mute and utterly secret preparations for the invasion. Then, D-Day; followed by the (as it appeared) military emptying of London; and the extraordinary sensation, throughout the city, of a great bolt shot. Then the V1s—and never, in any book I have read, have I found those drizzling, overcast summer months, with their sinister droning skies, better rendered. To this, the Saturday in the Kentish country house is a sunny preliminary, or overture. Then the reverberations of the liberation of Paris; the lift of the blackout; the drop in spirits after Arnhem; the relentless succession of the V2s to the V1s. The cold and anxious Christmas of the German breakthrough; the lights in the Abbey; the obsessing vision of the Ardennes . . . The crossing of the Rhine; and the departure—with which the book movingly closes—of one of the first boat-trains from Victoria, with, once more, civilian passengers to France.

In the Lavoisiers' tragedy and courage is incorporated the spirit of French resistance. Pitched on a gentler, but no less intimate note is a variety of incident all through. In this book the author's son, delicious and imperturbable child of besieged London, is, like the city, a year older. Again, through rifts in the texture of the present we have gleams from the past—indeed, did the Londoner ever feel the past more strongly than in these years? Interknit, for instance, with the story of Gay's Christmas tree (which would have delighted Barrie) is the comet-streak of Gaby Deslys's white car, and the long-ago face of Dick Steele of the first *Tatler*. One could weep at the pathos of the plain little Soho waitress whose only romance went wrong.

V. S. Pritchett, *It May Never Happen*, February 13, 1946

The short story has for some time been demanding wider attention. More, it expects to have its own recognized place in literature—and this, most critics would tell you, it has gained. The short story's literary prestige has gone up; but it has not, I fear, felt a corresponding rise in popular favor. Possibly one cannot have it both ways.

Our friend the average reader objects at the start to short stories simply because they *are* short; he is likely to be further intimidated by the growing rumor that they are "literary." This means to him—and he may not be wholly wrong—that he is going to be confronted by page after page over-packed with words, crisscrossed by tenuous fancies, and fogged by some high-class feeling he does not share. His own not unnatural requirements in the way of plot and character will not be met.

Looking back at the reading of his young days, our friend will remember the stories—which nobody even troubled to call short—of Kipling, Wells, and W. W. Jacobs.[7] Through those he roved at large, in the happy days before the expression "art form" had been invented. *Those*, he feels sure, weren't literary; they were just well-written. Chiefly, however, they were just damned good stories.

G. K. Chesterton said in one of his essays that the artistic temperament is a disease that afflicts amateurs. In the same sense, I should say that literariness is a disease afflicting the well-meaning but insufficiently high-powered writer; also, that literary writing is an unconscious device, an attempted cover, where there has been incomplete, or too specialized, experience of life. None of our great English storytellers have been, in this sense, literary: in most cases they have loved literature with passion, but that is another thing.

V. S. Pritchett, whose collection of stories, *It May Never Happen*, I am considering this week, is one of the most admired, and admirable, of our critics: if you do not possess, you will recollect his last collection of essays, *In My Good Books*. In saying that he keeps his literary criticism and his storytelling miraculously apart, I do not suggest that he has a dual personality. His criticism has, possibly, something of the directness, swiftness, and vitality that make his storytelling so good: his storytelling, on the other hand, is unmarred by any kind of a carryover from the critical mood.

In fact, Mr. Pritchett belongs to that English mainstream that gave us Defoe, Fielding, and Dickens. He has something in common with these three—as, indeed, had Kipling, Wells, and Jacobs. He has the zest, the faculty for touching life at the point where comic and tragic fuse, the sympathetic addiction to thieves' kitchens. In a way, as a writer he seems to have skipped a century: he is without the synthetic sentimentality and jocosity to which Dickens, as a Victorian, could be prone, and towards which Kipling and Jacobs showed an inherited tendency.

Mr. Pritchett writes about, and belongs to, the twentieth century, our own. But he seems to have been born with, and he keeps unspoiled, the sort of undoctored vigor of Defoe and Fielding.

Obviously, life has become, since *their* day, very much more complicated and febrile—both in itself and as a subject for writing. The contemporary writer, describing the contemporary scene, can no longer—if his object is to be truthful—deal in primary colors and unwavering bold lines. To be human, in our day, means to carry a whole load of the sensibility and anxiety that has accumulated since the days of our ancestors; a load of which they knew nothing. One cannot, therefore, depict the modern man without depicting his struggles under the modern burden. And the best modern writing—such, for instance, as I consider Mr. Pritchett's to be—registers this accumulation of sensibility.

Take, for example, the first story in *It May Never Happen*: it is called "The Sailor," and is about the author's (or "I's") encounter and subsequent dealings with a discharged seaman. Such a theme, one might say, is timeless: men from the sea, or old sailors—farouche, aggressive—appear in almost all our classic English picaresque novels. But Mr. Pritchett's sailor, together with the country in which the main part of his story is set, are seen as they could only be seen *now*. This is the country:

> The bungalow where I lived was small and stood just under the brow of a hill. The country was high and stony there. The roads broke up into lanes, the lanes sank into woods, and cottages were few. The oak woods were naked and as green as canker. They stood like old men, and below them were sweet planta- tions of larch where the clockwork pheasants went off like toys in the rainy afternoons. At night you heard a farm dog bark like a pistol and the oceanic sound of the trees, and sometimes, over an hour and a half's walk away, the whistle of a train. But that was all. The few people looked as though they had grown out of the land, sticks and stones in cloth; they were old people chiefly. In one or two of the bigger houses they were childless. It was derelict country; frost with its teeth fast into the ground, the wind running finer than sand through a changeless sky or the solitary dribble of water in the butts, and the rain legging it over the grass—that was all one saw or heard there.
>
> "Gawd!" said Thompson when he got there.

Not thus, and not thus felt, was any English landscape across which Moll Flanders or Tom Jones made their venturous ways.

The happy foreigner (or, should one say, sadly, once-happy foreigner?) has always considered the English mad: our behavior abroad, our habits at home, give rise to this impression; and our literature, should the for- eigner seek so far, at once documents and confirms it.

It May Never Happen is soundly in this tradition: almost all the stories focus on English peculiarity. Mr. Pritchett taps the rich vein of English middle- and lower-middle-class life—offices, shops, factories, the prov- inces, the suburbs. Phobia, of one kind or another, dominates many of his characters: the son's astounding discovery in "The Lion's Den" is an ex- treme case. Again and again, the façade of respectability is pierced—we look through, not at, point-blank scandal or ruin, not at vice or cruelty, but into the twisting Gothic underlights of human nature. The happenings in these stories are, to put it mildly, odd.

Sometimes Mr. Pritchett's people, like Dickens's people, are grotesque; often they are neurotic. Yet, in the main, they are people of goodwill. Kindliness is absent from almost none of them—some of the stories, such as "Aunt Gertrude," "Many Are Disappointed," "The Fly in the Ointment," and "The Night Worker," are, consequently, extremely moving.

A favorite angle with Mr. Pritchett is that of the adolescent boy— grown-up, or so-called grown-up, behavior in business, love, or domestic life is rendered with the semi-distorted clearness it would have for a young observer. "It May Never Happen," the excellent title story, is a case of this, as are "Aunt Gertrude" and "The Chestnut Tree." The adolescent's over-acute sense of people's physical peculiarities plays a part in the portraiture—Mr. Phillimore (as described in the paragraph on p. 58) is unforgettable: one would recognize, and avoid, him on any train or bus. And each scene is set with no less sharpness—one feels its charm or oppression; one breathes its air . . . To return to my original point: *It May Never Happen* contains a set of rattling good stories, tragicomic, 100 percent English, which are literature without being "literary."

François Mauriac, *A Woman of the Pharisees,* April 24, 1946

A Woman of the Pharisees is the first of a collected edition of the novels of François Mauriac, to be published by Messrs. Eyre and Spottiswoode; translation into English by Gerard Hopkins. This project of giving us, in our own language, the complete works of a novelist who is by general consent the greatest living French writer is an important one: moreover, in engaging the services of Mr. Hopkins, with his faultless sensitivity to style, the publishers have guarded against the incalculable damage that can be done to an author, outside his own country, by bad translation. The rendering of a literary work of art from one language into another should not fall far short of being a work of art in itself. In these years, as we know, it is hoped that the circulation of books from country to country may do much to build up, not only between former allies but between former enemies, a mutual psychological understanding of one another.

Incompetent mauling by bad translators might well undo much of the good of this. Let us hope that British books going to Europe may be, in this matter, at least nearly as well served as M. Mauriac has been by Mr. Hopkins.

Inevitably, when a foreign book is read in one's own language, the more curious qualities of its foreignness stand out—when read in the original, these qualities are to a greater degree absorbed in what one might call the atmosphere, or the tonal color, of the sentences and paragraphs that went to the page direct from the author's brain. The impact of a Mauriac novel on an English reader able to read French will be immense; if the novel be read in English it will probably, rightly or wrongly, be still greater. The total originality of Mauriac, his force, and the dynamicism of his characters have the effect of shaking a page of English prose—as a thunderclap, or the explosion of a bomb in the distance, makes a familiar landscape seem to quiver and rock.

This is not to say that Mauriac is a violent writer: he mines down deep, but seldom explodes the mine. His handling of themes has the gentleness necessary for an extreme precision: this is most marked when he is dealing with dire passions or with actual or potential crime. Why has he been accorded this place, as the greatest living French novelist, or even, as it is felt by many, the greatest novelist living in any country now? I should hesitate to answer this question arbitrarily, in a few words— but I would suggest that Mauriac's greatness lies in dealing with men and women as, primarily, creatures of the soul. The aridity of almost all twentieth-century novels, however brilliant, however apparently comprehensive, may be due to their authors' narrowing of the human range, to an insistence on treating the characters as creatures, only, of sense and of intellect. This leaves something lacking from the depiction, even, of directly passionate love, and gives a sort of minority unimportance to the pursuit of the hero's or heroine's thought-streams. The character in the sense-and-intellect novel bears about as much relation to a human being, as we would feel him or know him, as does the dehydrated to the fresh-plucked fruit.

Mauriac is a Roman Catholic: he has a sense of sin, and much that is terrible in his novels comes to us as a communicated terror in the beholding. Are his characters, then, divided into blacks and whites? Certainly not: each of them is subject, from the first page to the last, to at once profound and momentous spiritual alternations and changes. They act as they act because they are what they are; and yet each act is found to have altered the actor, to have changed his relations not only to people around him but, one may feel, to God. The appalling idea of predestination meets a flat contradiction in the Mauriac world. In its place we have a ceaseless tension, and pity.

In *A Woman of the Pharisees* the Curé says to the boy, Jean de Mirbel, who has stumbled upon a revelation as to the life of his idealized mother:

> "It's no use trying to force one's way into other people's lives, if they don't want one there: remember that, my boy. Never push open the door of another person's life, for it can be known only to God. Never turn your eyes upon that secret city, that place of damnation, which is the soul of another, unless you wish to be turned into a pillar of salt . . . ."

A Woman of the Pharisees (*La Pharisienne*) was written during the German occupation of France, and is the latest novel of its author. Like other Mauriac books, it is set back in a period (the years preceding the 1914 war) in which history and living memory overlap. The scene is sometimes Bordeaux, sometimes a country house in La Gironde. The central figure is Brigitte Pian, second wife of a weak-willed landowner and stepmother to his children, Michèle and Louis. It is Louis Pian, a schoolboy during these years, who, looking back as an adult man, tells the story. Mme. Pian, contrary to conventions, is not an unkind stepmother; her treatment of Michèle's adolescent love affair with the boy Jean de Mirbel is no harsher than that of a real mother's (of her French class and type) would have been; to Louis she is, in a preoccupied way, indulgent. It is in her relations with other people—with the children's father (still in love with the memory of his first wife); with her unfortunate couple of protégés, who, defying her will and, she believes, God's will, marry; and with the innocent, inspired, sometimes mistaken Curé of Baluzac—that the horrifying aspects of her character appear. No novelist other than Mauriac could have given us the complexities, and, for all her awfulness, the inherent tragedy of Brigitte Pian—religious, dominating, and apparently unscrupulous—a woman of whom the Curé once says: "There are some who choose God, but God does not choose them." Jean de Mirbel, with his contradictions of temperament, M. Puybaraud, the former school usher, and the Curé himself play a no less important part in the plot. The atmosphere, created in so miraculously few words, is extraordinary: rooms, gardens, streets, and stretches of countryside have a density that could be cut with a knife. The characters, down to the last physical trait, have a sometimes almost unbearable close-upness to one's vision.

Richard Aldington, editor, *Great French Romances*, May 15, 1946

To review *Great French Romances*, edited and with an introduction by Richard Aldington, is, in effect, to review a library. Of the four masterpieces reprinted, in translation, here, each left its mark on a generation; the reading of each should, I estimate, ideally occupy a month; and a year's pause on the reader's part for digestion should, again ideally, intervene between the close of one story and the start of the next.

Here are the titles, authors' names, and first publication dates of the four romances:

La Princess de Clèves. Madame de Lafayette. 1678.
Manon Lescaut. The Abbé Prévost. 1731.
Les Liaisons dangereuses. Choderlos de Laclos. 1782.
La Duchesse de Langeais. Honoré de Balzac. 1834.

As you may see by the dates (and as, should you fail to have seen, Mr. Aldington points out in his introduction), these novels appeared at intervals of approximately fifty years: the first was written during the reign, and, in fact, at the court, of *le roi soleil*; the last just after the Revolution of 1830—the revolution that terminated the brief, ultra-reactionary period of the French Restoration. These four have been selected by Mr. Aldington for their intrinsic value as literature: the equalness of their spacing-out in time is, he tells us, a matter of chance purely. Nonetheless, the fifty-year intervals *are* worth noting:

There is no absolute rule about it, of course, but that is just about the length of time needed for a fashion, an epoch, even a novel to be about at its nadir—old-fashioned without being quaint, vaguely remembered without being familiar, grandmotherly without being venerable . . . I have no wish to stress the point, but I think it not unreasonable to say that each of these novels illustrates a change in the sexual fashions of France, which, without having any sort of monopoly, has certainly in the past gone in rather enthusiastically for that sort of thing.

No analogy to any one of these novels exists, one may say for certain, in English writing. Richardson's *Clarissa* is probably the nearest. *Clarissa*, published in 1751, comes, roughly, halfway in time between *Manon Lescaut* and *Les Liaisons dangereuses*—and traces of Richardson's masterpiece (which swept France and was possibly liked better there than it was in England) appear, the reader may find, in Laclos's book. Reciprocally, these French novels not only reached us, one after the other, but were enjoyed in polished circles in England. The polite world, when truly polite, was small; the aristocracy of Europe was international—so much so that, even when a state of war existed between two countries, the grandees of one could continue to visit the capital and be entertained in the large country houses of the other. If England looked to Italy for art and the delights of antiquity, the winds of fashion, all kinds of fashion, have since the sixteenth century blown to our shores from France.

Our ancestors found these books absorbing, striking, moving, and sometimes shocking. These are love stories. They deal with love in the grand manner, with authority, and to the exclusion of almost everything else. What remains foreign to us in French writing is not so much its frankness in the treatment of love (which our own younger novelists have, by now, easily and somewhat clumsily exceeded), but the frankness of its *interest* in the matter. It is theory, analysis, dissection, applied to what we here regard as a tenderly elusive emotion, that makes us gasp. No Englishman could have written, and not many Englishmen can read, Stendhal's *De l'amour*. (Lurking in most Englishmen's breasts is the feeling that that sort of thing should not take up too much of one's time.) Stendhal's interesting distinction between *amour passion* and *amour vanité* is illustrated by these contrasting stories. The third is pure vanity, the fourth almost pure passion. The first two are sentiment—but on a high plane.

I take it that these four romances are already known to the reader by reputation—*Manon Lescaut* and *Dangerous Acquaintances* (to give the title of the translation) being the most famous. Equally, I take it as probable that all four, perhaps even a single one, may not, so far, actually have been read. With this Pilot Press compendium comes a good opportunity. The translations—are they Mr. Aldington's?—are irreproachable.[8]

Elias Canetti, *Auto-Da-Fé*, July 10, 1946

Auto-Da-Fé, by Elias Canetti, is not a tale of the Inquisition, but could hardly be more terrible if it were. It is a novel set in modern times; the central character is a famous scholar, Peter Kien, whose mind gives way—under stress, one might feel, of every possible and impossible provocation. For years, Kien has secluded himself in his library, in his top-story flat in a large unnamed city, presumably Vienna: his only realities are books. Delusions begin to set in; he falls prey to his revolting housekeeper, of the ever-starched blue skirts; and, through her, to the sadistic ex-policeman who is the concierge of the block of flats. After his marriage to Therese, the housekeeper, the unfortunate scholar's position in his own home becomes untenable—his whole routine of life has been broken up, the sanctity of his library has been violated. He turns out, takes to the streets, cheap hotels, and the underworld of the city—in which he falls into company with a hunchback pickpocket dwarf, Fischerle. Coaxed by his enemies back to the flat again, he receives a well-meaning visit from his brother George, a successful psychiatrist from Paris: George's attempt at treatment miscarries and only serves to precipitate Peter's end: now raving mad, he burns himself with his books.

It can be seen that this is not a cheerful story—nor is it anywhere relieved by a touch of beauty or tenderness. I read *Auto-Da-Fé* with difficulty, awe, admiration, and, sometimes, out-and-out reluctance. So close-packed is the writing, so direly faithful the analysis of Kien's tortured mind, so unclear the distinction, in some places, between actual happenings and hallucination, that I should find the plot difficult to summarize, even roughly, were it not for help from the book's wrapper. This is a Continental novel—it appeared, under the title of *Die Blendung*, in Vienna shortly before the *Anschluss*: it was, then, acclaimed by critics as one of the major novels of this century. Then, almost at once, there descended on central Europe, with Nazi domination, the cultural darkness which has remained till now. This must have been very hard on authors, such as Elias Canetti, whose reputation was just approaching its zenith. The republication of *Auto-Da-Fé*—in this excellent English translation, work of Veronica Wedgwood—is not only an intellectual enterprise but a reparation. Possibly Continental novels are more grown-up than ours: I feel an immense respect for the very relentlessness of this Canetti book—at the same time, I find it difficult to "take." Possibly, again, our nerves are more sensitive than they were in 1938. Since then, we have lived through much; but what we have lived through makes pain, vileness, and squalor more rather than less poignant. One is shy of books which come rather too near the bone.

Rémy, *Le Livre du courage et de la peur,* October 9, 1946

Le Livre du courage et de la peur, by "Rémy," has impressed me so deeply that I am moved to break what I feel to be an unwritten law—that of not reviewing foreign books (except in their English translations) in these pages. Whether *The Book of Courage and Fear will* ever be translated, and published for us in England, I do not know—frankly, I think quite possibly not: it is a book about French people, for French people; intimate, detailed, and not in the more obvious sense dramatic. At the same time, it is a book that belongs to humanity: fundamentally, its subject *is* humanity—its endurances, its capacity for faith, its power to rise to sublime heights. I must say, I do very much hope that some English publisher may be emboldened to give it to us here.

Meanwhile, for English readers who can read French, it is a book very much worth obtaining. I have not, by the way, in my heading, put the price in francs, as this had been removed, with the cover band, from the copy given to me in France. The book has been recently published here (in France) and I know the price to be not forbiddingly high.

"Rémy" (with, as alternative, "Jean-Luc") is the Resistance pseudonym of Gilbert Renault, leader and organizer of a Resistance "ring." He has compiled *Le Livre du courage et de la peur* from the memoirs of men and women who survived imprisonment by the Gestapo in France and, in many cases, subsequent deportation to Germany. These people not only gave him their own stories but were able to fill in a picture of the last days of those who did not survive—who died in prisons in France or camps in Germany, who were executed, or who "disappeared." "Rémy" has in the main confined himself to the adventures of characters in his own Paris ring, and their families—though he does here and there mention members of other (for instance, Bordeaux) rings with whom he came in contact in the course of his work. Also, we have Brittany characters, fishermen, and quiet, small-town folk, who helped with the secret, desperately dangerous journeys to and from England.

The book contains one corrupt, and memorably corrupt, character: the traitor, Pierre Cartaud (pseudonym, "Capri"), who, almost gratuitously, denounced to the Gestapo a long list of his former fellow workers in the Resistance. This young man seems to have done evil for evil's sake: his mentality and twisted motives have a sort of horrible fascination— even the Germans, whose tool he was, despised him. His first victims were his own adopted parents, in whose friendly Bordeaux house he had lived like another son. From his photograph, "Capri" looks a gigolo type. Summoned by the Gestapo to identify arrested persons, he would brazen the situation out—though it is on record that "Capri" writhed, at moments, under the eyes of his former friends.

This one case of vileness does serve, however, to throw the good faith of others into relief. The arrests, the Gestapo ordeals, were not confined to those who were *active* members of the ring: their mothers, wives, sisters were swept in, and, in default of the wanted person, imprisoned and put through grueling interrogatories. It is the behavior and feelings of *those* people—quiet, elderly ladies, sheltered and formerly somewhat conventional girls, home-loving young wives—which is really the most moving part of *The Book of Courage and Fear*. Many of the families in this group were of the middle class, conventional, law-abiding—not families which, normally, turn out either emancipated or adventurous women. These mothers, daughters, sisters, and wives, snatched from their homes under terrifying circumstances, had nothing but their wits and their unbreakable loyalty to France and their loved ones to fall back on. Their loneliness was complete, and despair threatened—but never quite gained ground.

There is something almost biblical about the stories of these people: in the prison scenes, one is reminded of the early Christians. The adventures of Maisie and Isabelle Renault, the author's eldest and youngest sisters, first in the Fresnes and then in the Santé Prison, their interrogations by Kramm, their communications (by the bizarre and unsavory "telephone") with their unseen fellow prisoners, provide some of the most moving pages in the book. The "telephone" conversations are on record. Many of the Fresnes prisoners—of whom a proportion were executed—were very young, and their talk has a sort of heroic childishness.

The quiet manner of this book makes its contents still more impressive. It is full of little touches of human nature—such as the affair of Isabelle's stockings. Accounts of secret journeys and tight corners also have their place.

Josephine W. Johnson, *Wildwood*, January 29, 1947

Wildwood, by Josephine W. Johnson, is an American novel about an adopted child. Its opening enticed me by its purely chance resemblance to that of *Anne of Green Gables*, a long-standing favorite of mine: in both books we have a scared female orphan, nothing much yet to look at, but full of character, on her journey towards an unknown home and uncertain destiny.

Anne, as you may remember, soon won all hearts: Miss Johnson's Edith is less fortunate. Her adoptive parents are not a good proposition—Mrs. Pierre is a neurotic; her husband cares only for birds. Mr. Pierre had, in fact, consented to adopting the child under the impression that it was going to be somehow like a goldfinch. Poor, dark, gawky, thirteen-year-old Edith, on her arrival, is a bad disappointment, grasps this and never properly rallies—she lavishes her affections on a cast-iron dog in the gardens of Wildwood (this being the Pierres' house).

The story is elaborately written, and so drenched in sadness that it ceases to be sad. There is beauty in it: I imagine it must be for the beauty of her style that Miss Johnson won (as I see she did win) the Pulitzer Prize for another novel of hers, *Now in November*. But I must say that I think even beauty in writing needs the addition of excitement or humor, or even both. The only part of this tale that is near-funny is Mrs. Pierre's funeral. In the main, were a Gloomy Book of the Month Club to be instituted, I should consider *Wildwood* a safe bet for the January choice.

Edmond Buchet, *Children of Wrath*, March 5, 1947

Children of Wrath is the work of an already well-known French novelist, Edmond Buchet: since its appearance, last autumn, in France, under its native title of *Les Enfants de colère*, it has enjoyed in that country a distinguished success. To the average British reader this novel may seem a trifle French—not merely because it hinges upon the triangle, the husband, the wife, and the lover situation (which is, in fact, becoming almost glumly familiar in fiction here), but because of the priority it gives to specialized, and all-exclusive, emotion.

The husband is, in this case, a psychiatrist—the novel cannot but, as its publishers point out, bear a certain resemblance to Nigel Balchin's *Mine Own Executioner*: the predicament existing, chiefly, inside the mind of one who, professionally, doctors the minds of others. The wife, Valentine, and the lover, Walter, are, in fact, well, and comparatively early, out of it: she is murdered; he—but this I must not reveal.

As a matter of fact, I thought the mutual passion of Valentine and Walter (a German-Swiss) somewhat, if anything, Teutonic, in its blend of humorless exaltation, sadism, and infantilism. Such a couple did seem to me better dead. As for Theodore, the husband, he is to come upon a strange, stark redemption during the flight from Paris in 1940 . . . The translation, which would appear good, is the work of Marjorie Gabain.

Jean-Paul Sartre, *The Age of Reason*, April 16, 1947

The Age of Reason is the first novel[9] of Jean-Paul Sartre, most discussed of the younger French writers. Sartre's name is inseparable from Existentialism—the new school of philosophy which has appeared in Paris since the war, is spreading to the intellectual life of other cities, and is already affecting literary art. Sartre plays are the sensation of Paris: only one, *Huis clos*, has so far been performed in London—as *The Vicious Circle*. Short stories of his appeared before the war, but have not so far, I think, been translated. *The Age of Reason* was published in France in 1945: it is excellent that we should now have a chance of reading it—and, still more, that we should owe this English version to Eric Sutton. None of the force, flexibility, and occasional colloquialism of the writing have been lost.

The idea of a novel by a philosopher may be alarming. Actually, *The Age of Reason* is at once engaging—more sheerly "readable" than many books of less intellectual content. The action takes place within forty-eight hours, in Paris, in 1938. The group of characters pass swiftly in and out of each other's lives—Mathieu, professor of philosophy, whose mistress Marcelle tells him she is going to have a child; their friend, Daniel, tormented by the secret of his emotional life; Ivich, the White Russian girl student, to whom Mathieu feels an irritable attraction; Ivich's brother Boris, who is having an affair with the nightclub singer Lola.

All these people are aware with intensity of their own existences: for Mathieu, the question whether his child is or is not to be, should or should not be, born brings about a crisis of the personality in which his whole past comes surging to the top. In the background, all the time, is the Spanish war; on the horizon mount up the world-war clouds of 1939.

The Age of Reason has been criticized, in this country, as harsh and sordid. You may, apart from any of the incidents, find something repellent in the egotism of the characters, who are, whether or not you like them, drawn with superb craft. (The girl Ivich, badly as she may have needed a slap, is a masterpiece.) Let me leave it that this is a dynamic, deeply disturbing novel, and that *not* to have read *The Age of Reason* (which is, I note, the first book of a projected trilogy) is to have an incomplete view of the modern literary scene.

Mary Renault, *Return to Night*, August 20, 1947

Return to Night, by Mary Renault, has been awarded the £40,000 Metro-Goldwyn-Mayer prize as the outstanding novel of the year, and will shortly be filmed. Unfairly, this may somewhat queer the book for the English reader, who will inevitably be seeing it in terms of screen-worthiness. Actually, Miss Renault has put some excellent writing into this tale of a thirty-four-year-old woman doctor's passionate love affair with a beautiful, tormented, mother-ruled young squire ten years younger than herself. The Cotswolds landscape, the doctor's work in the village, and the cottage hospital are well done. Only, for some reason, I do find several of the love scenes embarrassing. However, all may not.

Elizabeth Taylor, A *View of the Harbour*, September 24, 1947

A *View of the Harbour* is Elizabeth Taylor's third novel. Young, she has reached the stage when one exclaims, "Good—a new Elizabeth Taylor!" This does not mean that her novels have settled into a type—apart from anything else, there have still been so few of them: how could they? It means, rather, that here is a name which stands for something distinctive in novel-writing, and which guarantees pleasure.

Yes, pleasure. I somehow get the impression that a good many novel-readers' attitude to the novel is somewhat fatalistic and dreary. "Can you," they say, "recommend me something not too frightfully bad?—of course, one does not expect much." I, on the other hand, *do* expect much from a novel, and consider myself justified in doing so. If the reading of fiction is not to provide pure, exquisite, and transcendental enjoyment, why read fiction at all? There are ever so many facts one ought to find out about: if one does not hope to enjoy oneself, why not improve one's mind?

I cannot feel that it is the business of novels to be "improving"—but, on the other hand, they can and should exhilarate. They should give one the feeling that human existence is a fascinating (if maddening), irides-cent, quivering, mysterious, and, above all, exciting affair.

Miss Taylor, as a novelist, fulfills my exacting expectations—so much so that I cannot believe she will not fulfill yours if you still allow your-selves any. She does not, as a novelist, make any attempt to bypass the fact that she is a woman—none of the best women novelists, from Jane Austen on through the Brontës, Colette (in France), "Elizabeth" of the *German Garden*, Virginia Woolf, and the now promising Eudora Welty in America, ever has. It is woman's fate to be closely involved with small things; it is the woman writer's business to see through them—something not short of vision, better than mere perspicacity, is wanted: this Miss Taylor has. She deserves, and has gained, attention from critics—but, still better, she pleases ordinary readers.

There is something infectious about the interest her characters take in themselves and each other. They are egotists, but they are never bores. In *A View of the Harbour* we have a group of assorted people, with nothing (in most cases) in common but the fact that their houses stand side by side. The scene is constant: a small English fishing harbor, overlooked by dwellers along the waterfront. Small boats slap about, gulls skim; there is the white lighthouse which, after dark, swings its rotating beam over shabby façades and into windows of rooms. Miss Taylor's art is not unlike the beam from the lighthouse—it brings a scene or a face into momentary brilliant illumination, then moves on, picking out something else.

There is something tantalizing but effective—perhaps the more effective for being tantalizing—about this manner of storytelling. For, a story *is* definitely being told: much has happened between the beginning of *A View of the Harbour* and the end. Robert Cazabon, the doctor, and his novelist wife Beth; their daughters, Prudence and Stevie; Mrs. Bracey, of the secondhand clothes shop, and *her* daughters, Iris and Maisie; the war-widowed Lily Wilson, of the Waxworks Exhibition; Mrs. Flitcroft, the charwoman, and her nephew Eddie; Mr. Pallister, of the pub; charming, restless Tory Foyle, the Cazabons' next-door neighbor, who has divorced her husband; Edward Foyle, whom his mother remorselessly describes as "an ordinary little boy"; Prudence Cazabon's two highly strung cats—with all these we become uncannily intimate.

To an extent we have the outsider's view represented by Bernard Hemingway, retired naval commander, who is staying at the pub. Bernard, all his life, has aspired to be a painter—if his harbor paintings are now a doubtful success, he does show himself at least a born confidant. Pottering about the waterfront all day, posted in the bar in the evenings, Bernard has soon taken stock of all that is going on—among Rabelaisian, paralyzed Mrs. Bracey, lonely Lily, and moody, fascinating Tory he divides his attentions. He is misleading—an apparently bluff type whose sympathy is, at the same time, insidious.

Bernard Hemingway, Tory Foyle, and Beth Cazabon are, decidedly, Miss Taylor's masterpiece characters. The agonizing situation created by Tory Foyle's and Robert Cazabon's discovering that they are in love is delicately handled both by the participants and Miss Taylor—here, I think, her method shows its value: whenever the high point of any one scene has been reached, we are given no more of that. Nothing goes on for too long; nothing lags or drags. There are no lengthy descriptions, and very little analysis—the dialogue, which is brilliant, is elliptic. The day-to-day conversations between Beth and Tory, friends since they were at school, wandering vaguely in and out of each other's houses, are, I think, as good as anything here—*how* unconvincing, as a rule, are women's friendships in novels. In Stevie, whose eyes go slightly out of focus as she drinks milk, and Prudence, mooning round with her cough and cats, we have the young at their most frenzying.

Some readers may find Miss Taylor's manner too fragmentary—though even they, I think, can hardly be proof against the queerly transparent atmosphere of this novel, which is like spring twilight at the seaside. Myself, I think that that very fragmentariness is a form of artistic honesty. Novelists of Miss Taylor's young generation have their own problems: life these days *is* an affair of snatches and moments, of combinations of oddly assorted people. For the novel of today and tomorrow some new pattern or other will have to be found—Miss Taylor seems well on her way to finding one of her own.

Frank O'Connor, *The Common Chord*, December 17, 1947

The Common Chord is Frank O'Connor's fourth book of tales. On the wrapper there is a drawing of two deer in vain flight across the course of an arrow; and, though the marksman is pictured as being Cupid, there seems an appropriateness, in quite another sense, of this motif to Frank O'Connor's work. This Irishman, whose reputation is European, is more than a master of ringing and true prose; he shows, particularly as a short-storyist, the power of sighting, piercing, and bringing down the most shy or elusive subject. None of the plots or situations in his stories are obvious; and more, it is often nothing but his art which could have made them plots or situations at all.

Under his treatment, they become concrete, clear-cut. All these tales in *The Common Chord* have in common one same theme: love in Ireland. Some are comic, some deal with tragic deadlocks. In the main, we are to infer from Mr. O'Connor, love in Ireland is on the run: an awkward and inordinate intruder, not well seen. This may surprise those who associate Mr. O'Connor's country with soft skies and sweet songs; and indeed how Ireland herself is likely to react to the far-from-soft impeachment of these stories I do wonder. The British reader may ask if they can be true; the Irish reader, if honest, can have very little doubt. This is an instance of *toute vérité n'est pas bonne à dire.*[10]

We are given studies of the withering effects on human hearts—and, indeed, on human destinies—of muffishness and puritanism. These are most inexorably run down in the longest and grimmest story in the collection, "The Holy Door." At the same time, there is material for comedy—and to what splendid comic use is it put!—in the mixture of naïveté and effrontery with which some of the characters pursue their own courses in spite of all: "The Custom of the Country" (in which an Englishman changes his religion in order to marry the Irish girl of his choice, and, having been married in the full blaze of public approval, has then to mention to her that he is now a bigamist) and "Friends of the Family" are good examples of this.

"Judas" is a picture of that too-common type, the mother-dominated young man, consumed by self-reproach, because he has been away from home all the evening in pursuit—which, ironically, is unavailing—of a young woman. "Babes in the Wood" shows us a sturdy little boy, who happens to be a love-child, stranded with a foster mother but always hoping to be swept away into an idyllic existence with the young, vital, so-called "aunt" who from time to time visits him.

In fact, none of these stories are *depressing*—depressingness in a story (or in a novel) seems to me more than a bad fault, really it is intolerable. There is, here, a bite and a raciness, a sustained and, in spite of everything, exhilarating high tension, the infiltration of queer, romantic light into what could otherwise have been the drabbest scene—there *is* no drabness. Gaiety and somberness interweave like the light-and-dark in a quick-flowing river; there is a poise and shrewdness about the most unexpected characters which draws one to them; many of the stories consist in a great part of dialogue, and the dialogue, as always with Mr. O'Connor, is superb. *The Common Chord* is literature, and should not be missed.

William Sansom, *Something Terrible, Something Lovely*, April 28, 1948

William Sansom, one of our leading imaginative short-storyists, gives us a new collection—*Something Terrible, Something Lovely*.[11] My use of the word "imaginative" may seem vague: obviously, it requires imagination first to devise, then to write, *any* short story. All the same, I think that the story in which the imaginative element preponderates is to be distinguished from, and is to be judged apart from, the story which is a pretty direct transcript of what could easily *have* been normal everyday life.

In Mr. Sansom's earlier work, imagery and fantasy loomed large— they only did not run riot because he is an extremely controlled writer. He showed a strong, and for some readers occasionally alienating, trend to allegory. This time, in this new book, he can be seen to be making a marked attempt to focus his camera on reality.

For, it goes without saying, any artist is a walking camera—sometimes consciously, sometimes not, he is forever making exposures, then developing, in his internals, the results. As your reviewer, I can but warn you that you may still find some of Mr. Sansom's photographs—that is, some of these stories in *Something Terrible, Something Lovely*—disconcertingly odd. He can take a promising, honest-to-God theme, such as a tripper or hiker looking down from a cliff, seeing a nice-looking girl sunbathing in a cove beneath, and descending in order to investigate, and make out of it an apocalyptic nightmare, in which every kind of neurosis comes racing across the screen. "Thinking," in fact, "makes it so." (I refer to the second story, entitled "The Cliff.") I cannot, also, think of anything more unnerving than the second, hallucinatory episode in "The Little Fears," in which the "I" of the story, standing in a small public park blazing with roses, finds himself speed-encircled by a motorcyclist roaring round and round and round the park railings. The fact is that Mr. Sansom uncovers, remorselessly, the seeds of exactly such irrational, dreamlike dreads in *us*.

He can, as against this, summon up the fundamentals of humanity when he sets himself to the telling of a straight, fact-y story: the first in this book, a tale of two little girls, is a good example. And also, grim as the theme may be, there is an oddly convincing, domestic touch about "Various Temptations"—in which a plain, wistful, thoroughly nice girl handles, and all but masters, a sex-murderer. "Displaced Persons" is a

Sickert-esque, sundown scene in a pub; "Building Alive" is a Sunday morning V1 episode from the N.F.S. angle; and in "Journey into Smoke" we have a nice, school-roomy anticlimax to the adventures of firemen coping with a blitz blaze in a toffee factory. "How Claeys Died" is perhaps the finest here—a redemptionist's sublime, if practically futile, end, among the horrors of immediately postwar Germany.

There is one story for which I feel Mr. Sansom *should* be called to order—it is unpardonably and barrenly horrible. I mean "The Little Room"—in which we have the last moments of a delinquent nun, walled up alive, to suffocate, under (hypothetical) twentieth-century conditions: electric light blazing on pretty pale-green walls, an instrument recording, from minute to minute, the approaching exhaustion, by the victim, of the last of the air . . . This *may* be an allegory: even so, I find it to be an allegory we could do without—the writer, in this case, seems to abuse his art. Please, Mr. Sansom, do not do this again!

Graham Greene, *The Heart of the Matter*, June 2, 1948

The Heart of the Matter shows Graham Greene at the full of his stature as a novelist: which is to say, towering above his contemporaries and setting a high mark for younger writers who are to follow. François Mauriac, in an essay, spoke of that one book of which every novelist feels himself capable, which foreshadows itself in the work that he does achieve, and continues to make his achievements, though they may satisfy his readers, faintly dissatisfying to himself. The potentialities of that still-to-be-written book continue to inspire, afflict, and haunt him. In the end, who is to know but the man himself whether that book *is* ever written, whether it is, when it comes to the fact, writeable? It may have been the hard fate of many successful men to die with their real capacities unrealized.

Whether *The Heart of the Matter* is the book that Graham Greene has up to now been always moving towards, only he can know. Certainly to the reader it would appear to be the culmination of something. At the same time, this author is still young in the sense that he may be expected to have decades of work still ahead of him; so it may be taken there must be much more to come.

All, then, that need be said is that Mr. Greene is happy enough to have written a novel by whose value he should not fear to be judged, either by the present day or the future. As for ourselves—our unhappily fluid century has not had, so far, so very many landmarks: we should be glad of this one.

This novel's having an awe-inspiring theme does not prevent its being supremely readable. Stories on a far smaller scale have been told with far more fuss. Dense chunks of prose and portentous dialogue have come to be associated with the large concept; readers have been bludgeoned into believing they must be being uplifted because they are being more than half bored. The unboringness of Graham Greene may be a minor virtue, but it is a true one: he heads—and is, I am glad to say, being followed in—an important break away from obscurity, long-windedness, and analysis that goes round and round in circles. For some time, his novels have been showing the well-built compactness and mobility of the ideal thriller. One may, in passing, apply to *The Heart of the Matter* the seldom justified statement that here is a book impossible to put down.

One becomes, thus, engaged almost insidiously painlessly with a novel which it is an ordeal to follow through. Ordeal, that is to say, in the sense in which tragedy worthy of the name must be an ordeal: pity and terror. The story opens with a satiric blandness: the scene is a port on the West African coast, in wartime; we find ourselves among a colony of British officials and their wives. Everything steams; everyone sweats; the gin is warm; vultures scrabble on the iron roofs; there is a nightly blackout; from time to time sirens scream.

To this scene, enter two newcomers—at the beginning, the apparently egregious clerk Wilson, minor public school man and secret poetry addict; and, halfway through, nineteen-year-old Helen Rolt, brought in, half-dying after four weeks in an open boat, with other survivors from a torpedoed ship. Her husband, after four weeks of their marriage, has been drowned.

Major Scobie, deputy commissioner of police, is the central figure: more, it is his soul which is the battleground of the book. We are to watch his progress to what, in his own eyes and the eyes of his church, is damnation—watch him through the crisis of his relations with his dreary wife, his cheerless young mistress, and, above all, with God: even in his official virtue there is to set in, by every sign, an irreparable decay. At the same time, here is a creature, surely, exalted no less than he is betrayed by the sublimities of his own pity? If ever there were a picture of a good man, here is a picture of a good man. Or not? The verdict remains open.

The inner content of *The Heart of the Matter* is, I find, impossible to discuss lightly in a review. I leave it, that the rather grandly presumptuous title of the novel justifies itself—individually, we are loath to touch what is, for the full-range human being, "the heart of the matter"; and the majority of our novelists condone, embroider, and flatter just this repugnance. Mr. Greene, on the contrary, has been inexorable.

Scobie is—to return to the easy plane—something rare in present-day fiction: an adult character. His integrity—cracked though *he* may feel it to be—his simplicity and his unsentimentalized quality of "touchingness" can but act strongly upon the reader.

Surrounding Scobie, at different removes from the foreground, are his awful but, in her way, not untouching wife Louise, the mysterious Wilson (aforesaid), Yusef the shady Syrian merchant, Harris the cockroach hunter, Scobie's boy Ali, the priest Father Rank—all set in motion forever. As to Helen Rolt I was doubtful—hers is, however, a bleak, unrewarding part . . . The structure and working-out of the plot—in which nothing is there for nothing, everything interlocks—can but be noted, and envied, by fellow writers: by the reader it may, and should, be taken for granted—the best plots are.

Neil Bell, *The Governess at Ashburton Hall,* July 28, 1948

Neil Bell is so well-known and so long-established a writer that in reading a novel of his for the first time I feel myself to be a person arriving late at a party already in full swing. I experience, therefore, diffidence in confessing that I did not enjoy *The Governess at Ashburton Hall* as much as I had hoped to. This novel is a period piece (1898) with a thriller background. The heroine, Barbara Pascoe, a girl brought up in comfortable circumstances but finding no money after her father's death, goes as governess to a wealthy but inexplicably uneasy family in Devonshire. Somehow Barbara did not entirely win me—perhaps she had just too much common sense—and I flagged under the length of the letters the characters wrote each other and their inexhaustible gift for delivering monologues. However, *The Governess at Ashburton Hall* is a well-rounded-off (as to plot) and certainly ample tale.

Guy de Maupassant, *Bel-Ami*, August 4, 1948

Guy de Maupassant's *Bel-Ami*, translated into English by Eric Sutton, appears in Messrs. Hamish Hamilton's "Novel Library," price 6s. This appearance is an event: it places Maupassant's masterpiece, for judgment, alongside the fiction literature of the world—with the works of Voltaire, Jane Austen, Defoe, Henry James, Gogol, Swift, Walter Scott, Dickens, Turgenev, Flaubert, Balzac, and Fielding. The occasion, I think, demands reconsideration of an admittedly fascinating but, some would say, hateful novel.

Maupassant is, in fact, being offered the position that he deserves. In this country—as, indeed, in some parts of his own—the idea that he is a "naughty" writer has evaporated only extremely slowly. *Bel-Ami* certainly does, in its plot and flavor, correspond with the Victorian-British abstract idea of "a French novel"—the type of thing toyed with by profligate younger sons on the road to ruin. (In fact, in a British novel of the day, any character with an addiction to the reading of French novels might almost always be known to be marked for vice.) Balzac, Stendhal, and Flaubert were not excepted—it was recalled that even the French themselves had taken exception to *Madame Bovary*.

At the same time, the reading of *those* three masters involved a sternish intellectual effort, from which corruptible British young were likely to be deterred by slackness. Maupassant was another kettle of fish—he was dangerously easy to read. That he could be sought out, read, and highly esteemed for anything but the lowest reasons remained, for quite a long time, inconceivable.

Maupassant still is shocking, but not in the old sense—he is shocking to the heart. His pictures of cruelty and ruthlessness take one's breath away. It is the cruelty of Georges Duroy, hero of *Bel-Ami*, rather than his amorality, which seems terrible now. He is the businesslike and matter-of-fact seducer, or would-be seducer, of almost every woman who crosses his path; he is incapable of love; his campaign of so-called love has a double root of self-interest and vanity. What is damnable about him in the modern view is that he outrages other people's feelings. Is respect for feeling, perhaps, the base of our new morality?

Since Maupassant's day, the Anglo-Saxon language has given birth, here in this country and in America, to novels far more licentious than *Bel-Ami*—we have tale after tale of which the heroes and heroines consider they owe it to themselves to romp through as many love affairs as possible. Such novels, into which, no doubt, commendable effort goes, are often marred by an absolute lack of grip—of the subject, of the characters, of what is happening. Though earnest, they are fundamentally unserious.

Maupassant *is* serious—though he writes so impassively, so objectively, though he may seem to be taking as his subject nothing more than appetite or frivolity, he is all the time driving in the full, dire implication of *what is happening*. His insatiable love of life, his uncontrollable fear of death are both to be felt, at their strongest, in *Bel-Ami*—story of a lusty young Norman not, perhaps, unlike himself in youth.

"George Duroy, nicknamed Bel-Ami, is," says the writer of the preface, "the supreme cad of fiction." We first meet him as a demobilized noncommissioned officer, back from French North Africa, prowling about the glittering boulevards of Paris of the 1880s on a hot night, with big ideas and no money in his pocket—his wretched weekly salary as clerk in a railway office has long ago been spent. A chance encounter with an old friend is to set Duroy upon the road to fortune. Morally, Maupassant "places" Duroy, from the very first:

> His native Norman conscience, rather coarsened by the daily round of garrison life, strained by the example of African peculations and dubious dealings, stimulated also by military ideas of honor, army bravado, and patriotic sentiment, dashing exploits as recounted by subalterns, and the swagger inseparable from the profession, had become a sort of three-bottomed box in which a little of everything was to be found. But, above all, he wanted to succeed.

And succeed he does—mainly, though not entirely, by exploiting his fascination for women. This is a success story calculated to inspire a revulsion against success. It is a story magnificently told in terms of sensation; full of unforgettable pictures—Duroy confronting himself, in his hired tailcoat, in the mirror on the Forestiers' landing; Madeleine Forestier, in her white wrapper, smoking and gesturing with her cigarette on a sunny morning; Charles Forestier's death in the south of France; the honeymoon in Normandy; the terrible conversation in the church; the spectacular evening party at the Walters' . . .

It is a story, at the same time, mercilessly without illusions, in which the stale and tawdry underside of pleasure is reproduced. And it is, I think, an indictment of what we do still feel constitutes sin: unlovingness. To an extent, it is a period piece—in a sense that perhaps the greatest novels are not. Decidedly, *Bel-Ami* is a book for adults—though the very young of today could easily find it no more than comic or dull.

Simone de Beauvoir, *The Blood of Others*, September 15, 1948

The Blood of Others, by Simone de Beauvoir, has been described by its publishers as "the greatest novel to come out of the French Resistance." It is, at the outset, to be distinguished from the by now typical, though admirable, "Resistance novel," in that the Resistance theme is submerged— the greater part of the story happens before the war. We have, shortly, a group of young Parisians, whose relations with one another—up to 1940 pursuing a heated but somewhat aimless course—are precipitated by the German Occupation.

This is an excellent subject. Did we not often wonder, during the war, *what* effect enemy occupation would have had on our own devious private lives? Subtly but strongly, our personal relationships would have been changed—some of our friends would have lost value, others gained it: quite dim or frivolous persons might suddenly have soared up into heroism; others, hitherto ranking high, might have just perceptibly panicked, faltered, failed, or made compromises for which one could not forgive them.

The characters in *The Blood of Others* are, deliberately, not cast in the heroic mold. They are—up to the summer of 1940—in the main ineffectual; one is downright frivolous. They analyze their sensations, drift in and out of love affairs, are tormented by ideals which they cannot fulfill. At the same time, they are not heartless, for they are nagged at by a feeling of responsibility for each other. "Each of us is responsible for everything and to every human being" is the text, one might say the doctrine, round which Mlle. de Beauvoir has built up her story.

We begin and end with a girl dying: inside this tragic frame are set back the happenings leading up to the moment. Helen is succumbing to a wound received in the course of a wild, brave act—the rescue of her former fiancé, Paul, from the Germans. Jean Blomart (the lover for whose sake Helen had, a year ago, thrown over the faithful Paul) watches, now, by her deathbed. Jean Blomart's sense of guilt is acute—not only was he, as leader of a Resistance group, responsible for Helen's having gone on the expedition, but he is conscious of having wrecked her life (while she still had life) by his doubts and scruples. Her gaiety had confounded his seriousness; her lack of principles had shocked him. Ruthlessly, therefore, early on in the war he had broken off their affair—an affair which, in its best day, had looked like culminating in marriage. When Helen came to Jean Blomart, in his capacity of Resistance leader, to volunteer to help, he and she had ceased to be anything in each other's lives. Only now, too late, while Helen lies dying, does Jean comprehend how much she had loved him, and how deeply he really had loved and needed her.

This might sound like an obvious sentimental theme; it is, however, given fire and strength by Mlle. de Beauvoir's way of telling the story, and by the extraordinary livingness of her characters. Helen, the little shopgirl, wild as a hare and with the morality of a pirate, is, from her first escapade with the stolen bicycle, enchanting. She is a live wire. She makes a dead set at Jean (her fiancé's friend), engages his unwilling affections, suffers but never whines. Jean himself is the typical problem child of the late 1930s—the rich man's son with socialist leanings; he has left home, upset his mother (who remains, throughout, remarkably sympathetic and adaptable), and insists on playing the part of an ordinary worker in his father's factory.

He lives in a cheap little room—to which his mother insists on adding luxury appointments—and his friends are all, now, drawn from the workers. At the root of his mind remains the fear that the rest will think he is no more than playing at socialism, and that the middle-class taint cannot be got out of his blood. Already he blames himself for the death of a comrade, Jacques, killed in a riot after a demonstration. It is, in fact, his suspicions of himself which make him so suspicious of Helen—he mistakes her gaiety for lightness . . . The rest of the group, Paul, Marcel the painter and his unhappy mistress, Denise, are touched in with the same almost magic sureness—one becomes involved, up to the hilt, with them: can one say more of characters in a novel?

"Simone de Beauvoir," her publishers tell us, "clarifies many of the existentialist doctrines upon which she and Jean-Paul Sartre have set such store." This novel of hers does, certainly, bear some resemblance to Sartre's *The Age of Reason* and *The Reprieve*: its plot is, for instance, occasionally difficult to follow owing to switches-about in time, and a tendency to write of the central personage (Jean Blomart) sometimes in the third person, sometimes in the first. Mlle. de Beauvoir is, however, considerably less grim than M. Sartre, considerably more given to rendering moments of tenderness and gaiety. I find it possible to enjoy this novel without knowing anything whatever about Existentialism: here is an authentic touch on the nerve of life.

The translation, by Yvonne Moyse and Roger Senhouse, is good.

Ivy Compton-Burnett, *Men and Wives* and *More Men Than Women*, February 9, 1949

"It is given to few authors to become classics in their lifetime . . . ." This true remark is culled from the uniform wrapper of two volumes of the collected works of Ivy Compton-Burnett, now being issued by Messrs. Eyre and Spottiswoode. *This* author, who has from the first continued upon her own totally original course, has proved an exception to the rule.

Recognition of Miss Compton-Burnett's genius has expanded slowly but surely, in widening circles. Her readers, of which more and more have been acquired with each novel, have been up to now thwarted by a situation: they desired to read their way backwards through her earlier works, but could not. The earlier works, snapped up and snuggly tucked into shelves by the earlier cognoscenti, could not be got by those joining the party late.

Messrs. Eyre and Spottiswoode—already doing good work in the matter of Miss Compton-Burnett's French opposite number, François

Mauriac—are to be thanked for putting this matter right. Actually, the resemblance between Miss Compton-Burnett and M. Mauriac, superficially, is extremely slender: it would be foolish to force the analogy too far. M. Mauriac, by inference when not by direct statement, infers religion; Miss Compton-Burnett does not. Her novels are on the surface (mind you, the *surface* only) as cozy as his are drastic: in her case, we are dealing not with primitive squires or calculating businessmen of the Gironde, but with English gentle-people in English settings, in the last, best-behaved decade of the nineteenth century.

Just as surely, however, as M. Mauriac, does she plumb down into an underworld of the soul. The polite carpet of her family conversation-pieces heaves and ripples with subterranean forces. For this very reason, Miss Compton-Burnett has been found baffling by English readers, who expect to know where they are from a novel's first page. Her novels consist almost entirely of dialogue: this being so, it has been at times objected: "But English people of this kind do not *talk* like this."

No, but they feel like this—the alarming thing is that they feel like this without often knowing it. To enjoy Miss Compton-Burnett's art—and to fail to do so is, *I* think, really to forfeit something—one must accept one thing that she always does: she deliberately jacks her characters up on to a higher level of consciousness, *and* of articulateness, than the equivalent persons would have in real life.

Men and Wives (first published in 1931) and *More Women Than Men* (first published two years later) could not be better examples of her method. In *Men and Wives*, we have a group of well-to-do families in a neighborhood surrounding a country town—the Haslams, the Hardistys, a trio of sisters headed by widowed Mrs. Agatha Calkin, the rector Ernest Bellamy—who is divorcing his young and beautiful wife, at her request, in favor of other claimants—the doctor Dufferin, who aspires to Camilla Bellamy, and the solicitor Dominic Spong, a lugubrious new-made widower.

In *More Women Than Men*, the scene is set in a girls' school, and dominated by the terrifyingly powerful figure of the principal, Mrs. Josephine Napier. The pupils do not appear: it is the staff (superbly pictured, with their forlorn inanities), Mrs. Napier's husband, nephew, and trying contemporary Elizabeth Gifford, who contribute the passions which spin the plot.

Benjamin Constant, *Adolphe*, February 16, 1949

The publication in this country, in English, of Benjamin Constant's *Adolphe* is an event: Messrs. Hamish Hamilton offer this short classic, in the gay decor of their Novel Library. A brilliant (if, with regard to Constant, somewhat disillusioning) "Introduction" comes from Harold Nicolson. The translation of *Adolphe* itself is by Carl Wildman (who approximates, *I* think, almost faultlessly to Constant's lyrical-classic style). The *Cahier rouge*, appended, has been done into English by Norman Cameron, who has less perfect material to work on but does also give an impression of truth and grace.

I had not read the *Cahier rouge* (or, here, *Red Notebook*) before: on the other hand, I almost grew up on *Adolphe*—which should, I hold, be handed to all women as a cautionary tale. But how much more than a cautionary tale it is—an exquisite, nerve-racking, retrospective view of a love story. Constant wrote *Adolphe*, from an earlier draft, in 1807: this rewriting was accomplished in fifteen days. The novel was not printed till 1816.

The effect, however, is timeless: parts of the story might have been written yesterday. *Is* it, can it be, possible that a generation who knows not *Adolphe* has grown up? If so, I should state that this novel, with its changing, lightly lined-in Continental scenes, is about two people, two people only—Adolphe himself, restless inside the bonds of a love affair, and Elénore, his clinging, too tender mistress. To anyone whom love has ever made claustrophobic, *Adolphe* will speak: these two characters ruin, consume one another; yet, all the time, one kind of love *is* there . . . *The Red Notebook* is a rather jagged (though nonetheless stylish) autobiographical sketch, covering the earlier years of Constant's life. He was French Swiss.

Aldous Huxley, *Ape and Essence*; P. H. Newby, *The Snow Pasture*, March 2, 1949

Ape and Essence is the new Aldous Huxley—a short novel, pinpointed by its publishers as "a cautionary tale, a satire, and a prophetic nightmare: a warning to Mankind of what will happen if we persist in our present follies." This drastic picture of the future has been, by Mr. Huxley, cunningly cast into the form of an imaginary film script—rescued, from a lorry-load of rejects on the way to the incinerator, by two Hollywood worthies of this time last year.

That the day of the find should be that of Gandhi's assassination adds, for one of the finders, a double significance to the Tallis manuscript. Having reacted violently (how, indeed, could they not?) to the crumpled pages, the "I" of the story and his friend Bob Briggs pursue the prophetic author to his up-country lair, only to find that Tallis died some months ago, and has been interred, by his own wish, in the sands of the Californian desert.

Upon this introductory first half of *Ape and Essence* follows the second, which is the script itself. Mr. Huxley has, I should say, done well in placing his postwar tale (the war in question being atomic World War III) at that one more remove from reality given by script technique. Bearability for the reader may, I should like to think, have been his kindly aim in this decision: that aim has been *just* achieved—one cannot say more. The script (or main) portion of *Ape and Essence* remains bearable, really, for quite another reason—Mr. Huxley can but, from time to time, remind one of a devilish bespectacled little schoolboy setting out to make his sister or aunt scream. Like the youthful horror-monger, he lays on horror too heavily, till one's impulse is to turn and say, "Oh, shut *up!*"

As it stands, seldom since Flaubert wrote *Salammbô* can bestialities, cruelties, have been set out so remorselessly by a master pen. *Ape and Essence*, also, reminded me here and there of one of our classics, Sir Rider Haggard's *She*, in which a savage tribe conducts its revolting practices in the shadow of a great ruined, deserted city, once-imperial Kôr. And, as a picture of a world reduced to barbarism by one war too many, I am not sure that Edward Shanks's *The People of the Ruins* (published here some time back in the 1920s) is not, in its lesser violence but greater subtlety, more lasting in its hold on the imagination. However . . .

Hollywood, one must say, does not make noble bones. It is Hollywood's ruins, rather than London's, which Mr. Huxley has caused Lord Macaulay's hypothetical New Zealander to view. Dr. Poole, hero of the script story, comes from a land intact—New Zealand has, we are told, by reason of its remoteness, escaped obliteration in World War III; its inhabitants retain our present-day outlook, susceptibilities, amenities, way of life—in fact, what we know as civilization.

We meet, therefore, on the Californian beach of two hundred years hence, a party of New Zealand scientists who have just landed: they have come to rediscover America. Dr. Poole, a young and serious botanist, unwisely falls behind the rest of the expedition: he is forthwith captured by natives and marched off. He is reprieved from burial alive on the plea that he can show his captors how to correct soil erosion and raise crops.

It is, from then on, Dr. Poole's fate to be a (virtually) present-day participant in this future nightmare. I refuse to transcribe to *The Tatler*'s cheerful pages some of the scenes he witnesses. What, however, predominates over physical horror (which, as I said, sometimes defeats itself by sheer over-lavishness) is the stink of spiritual degradation—*that*, Mr. Huxley has rendered awesomely well. Belial has conquered: Belial-worship (modeled into a detailed travesty of the Christian practice) is the flourishing religion of the land. Dr. Poole, it turns out, has arrived on the eve of a high feast day, whose ceremonials provide some outstanding cases of scenes on which I refuse to dwell.

All this, of course, is not for nothing: the object of *Ape and Essence* is to drive home a moral. Mr. Huxley's moral, I think, is most clearly worded in a dialogue between Dr. Poole and the Arch-Vicar of Belial: they are, retrospectively, discussing the total victory of the Evil One (who is, of course, the pious "He" of their talk).

> The Arch-Vicar nods.
>
> "Yes, it was a pretty close shave," he says. "If they'd stuck to the personal and the universal, they'd have been in harmony with the Order of Things, the Lord of the Flies would have been done for. But, fortunately, Belial had plenty of allies—the nations, the churches, the political parties. He used their prejudices. He exploited their ideologies. By the time they'd developed the atomic bomb he had people back in the state of mind they were in before 900 B.C."
>
> "And then," says Dr. Poole, "I liked what you said about the contacts between East and West—how He persuaded each side to take only the worst the other had to offer. So the East takes Western nationalism, Western armaments, Western movies, and Western Marxism; the West takes Eastern despotism, Eastern superstitions, and Eastern indifference to individual life. In a

word, He saw to it that mankind should make the worst of both worlds."

"Just think if they'd made the best!" squeaks the Arch-Vicar. "Eastern mysticism making sure that Western science should be properly used; the Eastern art of living refining Western energy; Western individualism tempered by Eastern totalitarianism." He shakes his head in pious horror. "Why, it would have been the kingdom of heaven. Happily, the grace of Belial was stronger than the Other One's grace."

He chuckles shrilly . . . .

"Turn back, before it is too late!" intones Mr. Huxley's voice, down the horror-megaphone. "Think, feel, check yourself, think again, reflect!" You and I may feel that this solitary mystic and prophet's path has carried him, years ago, clear of our British course, and that he and ourselves are not in the old close touch. We may feel, in fact, that *Ape and Essence* was written with the primary and noble object of terrifying America—which object (for it has, I gather, already appeared in that country) it has no doubt achieved. Fewer of our lady-skeletons would be wearing nylons; nor could we, at present, expose to annihilation such a universe of bijou homes. We may feel, too, that the secondary solution—i.e., that 'tis love makes the world go round, and that love may send the world twirling again back into a saner course—is a little trite.

For Dr. Poole and his reclaimed inamorata Loola are last-but-one seen necking, on the sublime plane set by Shelley-quotation, in the back seat of a decaying Super de Luxe Chevrolet, in the skull-strewn garage of one of the ruined bijou homes, lit by sunset. They are last of all seen legging it off across the desert to take refuge in an authorized lovers' colony. But there, again, Mr. Huxley has his Mr. Tallis alibi—this aimed to be a big-box-office Hollywood film, of course.

After the above, there is something cooling about the very title of P. H. Newby's new novel—*The Snow Pasture*. Mr. Newby emerged as, and will remain, a leading and representative novelist of the 1940s; just as Mr. Huxley, grandly and forever, carries the stigmata of the 1920s. No fantasy, though many visionary touches, enters into *The Snow Pasture*—a quiet story, when it is all told, though throughout one feels crisis immanent in the air.

The scene is a Monmouthshire mining valley, not only darkened by coal dust but rattling with tinplate works, and, after dark, red with furnace reflections. In this community, urban between the mountains, the young doctor Robert Pindar (who, upon his release from the army, has bought a practice here) and his wife Evelyn are uneasy, non-indigenous dwellers. Their twelve-year-old son Benjamin, on the other hand, has taken to everything round him like a duck to water, and is zestfully—and, from the point of view of his mother, deplorably—running wild. Clem Johns, a miner's son, is Benjamin's inseparable companion.

Ironically, young Clem is more and more attracted into the Pindars' civilized orbit—from which their own son is more and more in flight. Meanwhile, a gulf is widening between Robert and Evelyn: she wilts in the harsh, glowering atmosphere of the valley; he is in the grip of a curious state of soul—to himself perplexing, forbidding to her. It is Clem, with his turbulent vitality, who, child though he is, makes the triangle's third point. The Pindars are forced, by a whim of Evelyn's rich, eccentric father, to accept the Johns's boy into their home.

This novel resembles a modern building—outwardly ultra-simplified, but having a complex inner structure of tensile steel. And, as on the white walls of such a building, every change of light reflects here itself, every shadow registers. The behavior of the characters is of a lifelike incalculability which may perplex the reader accustomed (more than he knows) to see life in novel-convention terms. Unconsciously, I believe, the public asks of the novelist that he should, while constructing a tricky plot, *fundamentally* make life appear straightforward. Mr. Newby, though as a storyteller he could not be clearer or less ambiguous, refuses just that concession. His people's *actions* are simple, but the motives behind them have been so (humanly) split and mixed as to make those actions the last that one might foresee.

No "scene"—and there are many in *The Snow Pasture*—ever does quite break as one might expect. All the time, the emotional weather-quarter changes: clouds which have looked most ugly dissolve in peace—storms, when they come, blow up from what a minute ago had been tranquil, unthreatening patches of sky.

In short, Mr. Newby captures inside his novels life at its most elusive, most contradictory, and, therefore, most itself. In *The Snow Pasture* does impulse, then, spin the plot? Really, each impulse is a sort of convulsion, on the part of one or another person, due to some deep-down state. Clem Johns's tough parents and Robert's race-going partner Tim, together with his wife Erica, are no less lifelike, in this way, than the four central people. They are, for this reason, baffling, as they would be in life.

The scene painting, as in other Newby novels, is magnificent, haunting—we leave Monmouthshire, for intervals in the story, for the Cotswolds, setting of Evelyn's father's home. (Incidentally, that graceless old stage-Irishman is to me the most nearly tiresome, and least convincing, personality in *The Snow Pasture*.) Robert Pindar, as a war-shaken young man desperately set on adjusting back to life and saving his marriage, and young Clem, unsettled by new prospects, are important—both in their own rights, as sharply cut individuals, and as outstanding problem-types of our time.

Elizabeth Taylor, *A Wreath of Roses*; Angus Wilson, *The Wrong Set*, April 6, 1949

Elizabeth Taylor, whose ever-unfolding powers are to be watched with joy, gives us as her fourth novel *A Wreath of Roses*. This has been awaited with confidence by those who remember *At Mrs. Lippincote's*, *Palladian*, and *A View of the Harbour*—and few who read those three can have forgotten them.

Why?—I mean, why should some novels be memorable, others not? One can always, of course, fall back on the hackneyed reviewers' phrase: "Miss X (or Mr. Y) strikes a distinctive note." But a note, however distinctive, cannot hang all by itself in the air for long. A novel may have some of the qualities of music—as, indeed, of painting—but first and last it is, it must be, a story: a story told.

Therefore, it is for the story that the reader looks, and it is the manner of the telling that he judges. Today is difficult: events roar heavily past us like priority traffic along a main road; we individuals, picking our ways along the curb, feel like pedestrians on sufferance. There seems to be nothing on which to fix the eye. Where is *the* story, the individual story, to be found? How is it to be disentangled from all this rush? For the novelist these days, the finding of the story needs more than ingenuity; it needs faith.

Miss Elizabeth Taylor has the first thing required: certainty of vision.

Her stories are therefore convincing; they remain with one, indelibly, as though they had been some turning point in one's own experience. And, like equivalent events in one's own experience, they have a greater significance than one can account for.

She takes into account, indeed, to a great degree, she takes as her subject, the irrational element in people: therefore, there always is in her novels an element not subject to reason, and which cannot be rationalized away. As against that, there is a beautifully concrete *practical* accuracy about her writing. As, for instance, in the apparently humble matter of kitchen sounds—a kettle being filled at a tap; the sound of "water drumming into the kettle." Miss Taylor's writing never goes drifting off into a subjective cloudland: we are firmly anchored, throughout, to small, tactile, banal, sensuous things.

She is, in fact, a paradox, being at the same time flawless domestic novelist and poet. In A *Wreath of Roses*, Liz with her first baby and Richard with his lie-clouded inner vacuum are equally true. This novel is of a quiet extraordinariness which at the first reading may not appear: I recommend two readings; then, perhaps, a return. The first time, one is carried along fast by excitement, by a tension owing to something more than mystery. The second time, when there is nothing further to be discovered— that is to say, in the way of *plot*—one reads more deeply. And it is from that point on that a whole new range of discoveries will begin.

What is the situation? Two young women, Camilla and Liz, are spending an August holiday with Frances, formerly Liz's governess, now a painter of genius, austere and retiring. This month together in the flint cottage outside a country town has been for years, for all three, an event on which the rest of the year turns. Camilla and Liz have been friends since their schooldays: for Camilla—a creature of otherwise frozen feeling, unrealized beauty, reluctantly making her living in a girls' school— the friendship still comes first: almost too much has come to attach to this August meeting.

For Liz, there is conflict. Camilla means no less, but Liz, now, has married—now there is Harry, her baby, in her charge at the cottage. A subtle sense of difference, a threat of change, casts itself over the trio now they are face to face. And, another intruder. This is, too, a heat wave, which accentuates everything.

And the other intruder? On the train journey here, Camilla has fallen in with a young man—speciously good-looking, blatantly not her type, and, as Liz and others are to perceive, bad, mad, and possibly dangerous. Richard Elton is one of the postwar lost boys; but something worse is the matter—what, what, *what?* Camilla and Richard have been cast, at the outset, into a sort of unspoken, unseemly intimacy by being joint witnesses of a tragedy, a suicide at a wayside station. But something more accounts for the hold Richard gains on Camilla's fancy, and on everything that that comprehends. Exclusion, desperateness, jealousy of Liz's baby drives Camilla, more and more, into Richard's orbit. He is staying in one of the inns in the country town. Their meetings, tacitly deprecated by Liz and Frances, become more frequent.

There are two other characters: Liz's husband, that too-good-looking, too-pleasing, apparently hollow clergyman Arthur, with his unsettling way of suddenly popping into the cottage; and Morland Beddoes, the humdrum, humble, and shrewd film director, who, having been for years inspired by Frances's paintings, takes the great risk (as the girls see it) of coming to visit her. Beddoes, like Richard, is putting up at the Griffin.

Nor, having set out to name the cast, must I ignore Mrs. Parsons, the help from the village, nor Hotchkiss—enormous, perfectly awful dog. Mrs. Parsons and Hotchkiss are among several pointers to Miss Taylor's sense of comedy which, along with her sense of beauty, floats through *A Wreath of Roses.* Never was novelist less "intense" or daunting. Light, offhand, gaily preposterous is the running dialogue between Camilla and Liz—and, indeed, the scenes between Liz and Arthur, that married pair so often just out of tune. In novels, I tend to find the depiction of friendship between women either inept or out-and-out embarrassing: Miss Taylor gives us an enchanting example of the reverse.

A Wreath of Roses holds other discords and melodies on which I have not left myself room to touch, and upon which, at the best, I should touch with diffidence. These I leave you to find. *A Wreath of Roses,* in fact, is far from being that set piece known in literary circles as "a reviewers' joy." It is a readers' novel: as such, I pass it to you.

* * *

The same cannot be said of Angus Wilson, whose collection of short stories *The Wrong Set* is, I understand, his first published book. How, it may be asked, can one tell from a first book whether the writer might or might not have written better? I can only say that *The Wrong Set*, though not a success, makes one feel that here there *is* talent—misused.

"The first thing one notices about these twelve stories," assert the publishers, "is how they make one laugh." This I did not notice: the effect, in the main, is a seediness as to subject, and an outdated anger, monotonous, in the manner. The drunks and nymphomaniacs and sadists and have-beens who drool through these stories are no more funny than dead flies shaken out of curtains.

What is more, they seem to have lived so long ago that they no longer matter: these stories *date*. If one is to be a satirist, one must be of the moment or of all time: it is fatal to fall between two stools. I do wish Mr. Wilson could dislodge from his system the resentments of circa 1932; I wish he could eliminate from his style the over-thoroughness of a cement mixer; and I wish he could realize that nauseating physical detail is, apart from other things, an offense against art.

The title story is by far the best: one really does get to like poor old Vi. "Fresh Air Fiend" is grimly true; and "Crazy Crowd" and "Mother's Sense of Fun" have good moments. "Realpolitik" is lively and efficient. The effect of the stories—the publishers further, hopefully claim—"is to purge us of our hypocrisies." If that be the author's object, let him open his eyes and glance at the present-day scene. Hypocrisies have become more rather than less interesting since they acquired the New Look.[12]

Norman Mailer, *The Naked and the Dead*, May 18, 1949

The Naked and the Dead, by Norman Mailer, is for the reviewer a bit of a proposition. Here is an American war novel which has swept its own country, and whose appearance here has been preceded by sensational rumor. Like *Elephant and Castle*, *The Naked and the Dead* is extremely long; though, in this case, the action occupies less than three months and the scene—the South Pacific island of Anopopei, on which the Americans make a landing, and on which they finally mop up the Japanese—is geographically small.

The size of the book is accounted for by its structure: the story fans out into the prewar civilian lives of the soldiers, their interior images and monologues during the time on the island, and their hopes for or fears of postwar days. The characters pinpointed by Mr. Mailer are not, once one has sorted them out, many—we have General Cummings, Major Dalleson, and Lieutenant Hearn, and the "non-coms" or G.I.s Croft, Gallagher, Brown, Wilson, Martinez, "Red," Roth, Goldstein, Minetta, and one or two others.

The author requires for his purpose uncensored reproduction of talk and thought. One must be fair to readers at the possible cost of being unfair to him: I must say, therefore, that by the majority a number of pages of this book will be found repellent; they employ a vocabulary at which the most hardened can but blench. I equally feel, however, I should add this: *The Naked and the Dead* should not be denounced on hearsay, or on the strength of "skimming." Mr. Mailer is a serious artist who has embarked upon a large, important design, in the execution of which he has stopped at nothing: I cannot doubt this to be what he intended, a comprehensive picture of war, though based on only a segment of the world battle-front. It is also a master picture of action: the passage towards the end, the platoon attempting the mountain, is magnificent. A second purpose has been the reflection, in this handful of men, of chaotic, cosmopolitan, and in the main still voiceless America. I cannot regret my survival (for it was a case of that) of an entire reading of *The Naked and the Dead*: ultimately, something was added to my experience. What is likely to be this novel's future in this country, I cannot say.

George Orwell, *Nineteen Eighty-Four,* July 6, 1949

George Orwell's *Nineteen Eighty-Four* is a terrifying follow-up to his *Animal Farm* of three years ago. Almost everybody read *Animal Farm* if for no other reason than that it was about animals (to whom in Britain we are kindly disposed) and the pill of the moral slipped down rather painlessly. With *Nineteen Eighty-Four*, Mr. Orwell—one of the best independent brains we have today—comes right into the open: there are no genial allegorical ambiguities about this story set in the England of the future. Subject, the extinction (humanly, rather than physically, speaking) of the last potentially free man, one Winston Smith, under pressure of a totalitarian regime called Ingsoc ("Newspeak" for English Socialism).

Aldous Huxley's *Ape and Essence* pales, where I am concerned, beside *Nineteen Eighty-Four*. Mr. Orwell, for one thing, never overshoots his mark: there is a nerve-racking *possibleness* about his England of less than forty years hence. Masochism, defeatism, fatalism, and all-round loss of standard have done their work: the race survives, but survives under conditions so poisonous that atomic bomb wiping-out would seem the lesser evil.

Every individual is spied upon by the Thought Police: into the wall of every room is set a telescreen, giving out propaganda, but also televising the inhabitant's every movement for the watchful Party. Detection in "thoughtcrime" means a hauling off to the subterranean torture chambers of the Ministry of Love.

The world is, in 1984, divided between three powers—Eurasia, Eastasia, and Oceania. Of Oceania, England is Airstrip I. War has remained continuous throughout human memory: in fact, its continuance serves the Party's purpose. The three governing slogans are "War is Peace," "Ignorance is Strength," and "Freedom is Slavery."

Mr. Orwell has made this novel, for all its dire content, acceptable—in fact, impossible to put down—by riveting us to the individual fortunes of the solitary would-be rebel, Winston Smith. *Don't* funk this book—though to read it is an excoriating experience. Read it—then, watch and pray.

François Mauriac, *The Desert of Love* and *The Enemy*, December 21, 1949

The Desert of Love, with which is included a second short novel, *The Enemy*, should further substantiate the claim that François Mauriac, author of these two, is the greatest living European novelist. His publishers in this country, and his first-rate translator, Gerard Hopkins, are to be thanked for bringing his work to us. "The Collected English Edition of the Novels of François Mauriac" is now about midway upon its course.

M. Mauriac's novels may have, for the British reader, certain intimidating characteristics. We who read for pleasure are used to more easygoing fare. And yet, *as* a novelist, this great Frenchman is preeminently "readable" — his work as a whole, I think one may safely say, contains not one single abstruse, flagging, farfetched, or dull patch. His occasional dauntingness has the same two sources as his undeniable strength — he is a deeply religious Catholic, and he is a regionalist (which is to say that his stories, though they have scenes elsewhere, begin and end in Bordeaux and the country round it). The region from which he himself springs provides a more than purely physical background for his novels. Many of his characters come to Paris, but they remain haunted by the sounds, smells, and way of life of their birthplace. They are (to use a word in the least derogatory sense) impassioned, as well as fated, provincials.

As for religion, it is by the very force of that that M. Mauriac plumbs down — remorselessly though (paradoxically) never without pity — into the most tormented depths of the human soul. Most of all, he deals with the torments aroused by love.

The Desert of Love and *The Enemy* (in French, and I think better, *Le Mal*) both have the same theme — an adolescent's passion for an older woman. In the second story, the passion is "realized"; in the first, not. Which fares the worst, Raymond Courrèges, scarred and warped for life by a humiliating rejection, or Fabien Dézaymeries, well-nigh devoured by his mother's friend? The subtle thing in these stories — nay, more, the essence of their majestic justice — is that in neither case are the women shown as monsters: on the contrary, Maria and Fanny are both, in their own ways, victims. The stories are so written that every moment in them seems to be part of one's own experience — one *becomes* Maria, pacing the shabby-finery villa, hearing the rain fall; or one becomes Fabien, casting Maria's letter, in his intense revulsion, unread and torn up into the stream.

Above all, *The Desert of Love* and *The Enemy* are not cynical studies of futility. Their message is this: inescapably, one is responsible for the soul of a fellow human being with whom one has been involved as one is involved in love.

Books and Occasions

Paris Bookshops

Anyone back again in Paris for the first time since 1939 probably—after one general, dazzled look round—makes for their old haunts. Your reviewer made for the bookshops. As to these, conflicting reports have been brought home by those who, since 1944 and the Liberation, have had reason to travel between England and France. Accounts of a book boom, no less lively than ours, came in side by side with depressing pictures of Paris bookshops with tables and shelves bare, of editions exhausted before distribution was complete, of black-marketing in the works of popular authors. The discrepancy between the two pictures was puzzling—if everybody was reading, where did the books come from? This month I could go and see for myself.

Staying in a hotel on the Left Bank, in one of the quiet, provincial-type little streets running downhill out of the Place de l'Odéon, I was in the heart of the book world. The Boulevards St. Michel and St. Germain make an L round this quarter; and from the top of the Luxembourg Gardens the Boulevard Montparnasse is within easy reach. The Odéon Theater, itself closed for the holidays, offers the hospitality of the arches along its two sides to a variegated selection of bookstalls. The narrow bystreets of the quarter, twisting, turning, intersecting each other at unexpected angles, have for years been no less kind to the book-seeker than are the boulevards in whose angle they lie. And on the *quais* of the Left Bank, opposite the Ile St. Louis, the magical, dazzling, cloudless weather of early August permitted the vendors of secondhand books to display, from early morning till late evening, the wares on their cases and tables without fear of rain.

Easy access to books has always been one of the charms of Paris. In the open air—at the quayside stalls, at the outdoor tables under the awnings—and no less indoors, inside the wide, ever-open entries to the shops, one may handle, gaze, sip, browse, philander with literature endlessly without buying. There is nothing odd or suspicious in spending an entire morning or afternoon in this manner. Incidentally, I was interested to learn how this bookshop habit, recognized even by the Germans as inseparable from the Paris manner of life, lent itself to the maneuvers of Resistance people during the Occupation: often did bookshops make cover to vital meetings, in which a half-sentence (on which many lives or the success of a sabotage project might depend) could be exchanged between apparent strangers, brushing up against one another, it seemed by chance, in desultory progress around a table of books. How far this went—whether, for instance, pages of cypher were actually slipped between the pages of books in remote shelves, to be collected later—I cannot with authority say: the entire story of the Resistance methods is yet to be known. The possibilities would seem to be endless.

Are the Paris bookshops of summer 1946 empty? At the first glance, one would say decidedly, no. This first glance, however, would be deceptive: the bookshops, out of professional pride, succeed in giving a brave impression. (In this, they are in line with the rest of the shops in Paris: there is not much of anything—what there is is attractively, gallantly set out.) Compared with the abundance of spring 1939, book stocks *are* low: there is, or seems to the stranger's eye, a fascinatingly wide variety of titles and authors, but there are few copies, quite often not more than a single one, of any one book. If you have set your heart on anything particular, this may involve a long search from shop to shop. In each, the bookseller, entering into the spirit of the chase, will give advice and suggestions, directing you further on. The chances are that, unless you are remarkably strong-minded, you will be deflected from your first idea, making so many fascinating purchases en route that by the time you do find the book you started out after you discover, also, that you have no money left.

What, to judge by the bookshops, is Paris reading? What is being published and (as long as supplies last) sold? First, as might be expected,

I was struck by the results of the psychological release caused by the departure of the Germans and their censorship. The lid has been lifted: out into print are coming all the French thoughts, feelings, and experiences of the last years. Or, I should rather say, beginning to come: the speaking of truth must still be only at its start. The Resistance gave France a whole new gallery of heroes, many of them young: and the annals of their struggle are in demand. There are some books about Paris during the Occupation, but these seemed to me to be more sought by the British and Americans than by the French themselves—*they* remember only too well, without books.

The present spirit of France, it struck me, is towards recovery: what one feels most in the Paris air is a vigorous resolution with regard to the future rather than a tendency to brood over the past. This reflects itself, in the Paris bookshops, in all sorts of works on development and planning (not unlike our own). Also—due to the fact that under the Occupation people were more or less immobilized, unable to move without difficulty, discomfort, and humiliation about their own country—there is an intense interest, on the part of the Parisians, in other, outlying, regional parts of France. Guides to and local histories of such regions, fine books of photographs of their landscapes and architecture, were much in evidence: many of these, I saw from their publication dates, were prewar, many were shabby from having been long in stock, but in all bookshops they occupied prominent positions—evidently they are what is wanted now. In the old days, one would have thought that these books on regional France were planted to catch the eye of the foreign tourist: this year, it may be remembered, foreign tourists are so few as to be negligible—Paris bookshops cater for the French book-buyer, and what is shown reflects his demands and taste. Once (it now seems a long time ago) for the Parisian Paris was a sufficient world: now, at the end of the years of trial, he is keenly aware of his country, France, as *a whole*.

And the same feeling applies, it would seem, to the French past—not the past of the last few years, but of the glorious aggregate of French history. To the forefront in all the shops were fine books on French literature, architecture, and painting. Given the number of illustrations and excellence of the production, the prices of those art books were surprisingly low: the average price was the equivalent of 12s. All round, French book prices still are, as they always have been, considerably lower than ours—the habit of paper binding makes for economy. Also, it is my (favorable) impression that in the main French books are shorter than English ones; therefore, even under austerity conditions, larger print and more open spacing is possible.

In our own present English taste for biography we are evidently at one with France. The range of French biography—prewar, reprints, and postwar output—is, to judge by the bookshops, wide. And, at the moment a rather important point, it is by no means confined to outstanding *French* figures. One may take it that there is in France today the desire to get a cross-section of European life, achievements, and trends of thought. And most particularly, there is an interest in England. I was struck by the popularity of English writers, both standard and modern, and by the prominence of their works in the shops. A new-looking book on Dickens (by a French author whose name I unhappily failed to note) caught my eye in every window and on every counter: it must be on France's summer bestseller list. Dickens's novels tie with the Kipling stories in a wide and established popularity: I am told that the average French reader now knows his Dickens as well as, or possibly better than, does his British brother.

I do not know how good the translations are—I hope they do Dickens justice. Kipling, they tell me, goes into French well: in every second window I was confronted by a gay-covered *Simples contes des montagnes,* which it needed an effort of cerebration to identify with *Plain Tales from the Hills.* Not less in vogue was *Wuthering Heights* (no attempt made, I was glad to see, to translate the title). A brief book survey on the other side of the river gave me a Rue de Rivoli bookshop with an entire showcase devoted to translations of Jane Austen and Henry James. French people who spent the war in England did not fail to note the Trollope revival; Trollope, accordingly, is to be "tried" on France—his better-known novels are in course of being translated, though I did not yet see any actually on sale. I should predict, in the present mood of taste, a considerable boom in Trollope, for this reason—he is 100 percent English. And never (at least, such was my impression) can the English good qualities have been rated more highly than they are in France today, or the English limitations more kindly seen.

I could not but be conscious of this good feeling, moving about Paris and in the country round. My redoubtable and incurable British accent opened floodgates of conversation and inquiry whenever and wherever I made it heard. How were we, over there in England? How was London? Films about London, in her present state, have recently been shown all over France, and have obviously made a deep and sympathetic impression. After twenty-four hours in Paris this time, I began to feel, like dear Miss Bates in *Emma*, "Everyone is so kind." Everywhere, this enveloping atmosphere of well-behaved and neighborly curiosity.

This curiosity as to England, which I, as a single person, could only go such a very short way to meet, finds its outlet in an omnivorous reading of modern as well as classical English novels. I was surprised, surveying the bookshops, at how quickly our new books, in translation, seem to be reaching France. They come out in light, bright, cheap, and attractive form. Not only our established successes, such as J. B. Priestley and Somerset Maugham, but writers so young, new, or eclectic as to be as yet barely known to the English public are represented. In fact, I came away with the feeling that it will behove the English reader to keep his eyes open and his socks pulled up, or it may happen that his brother across the Channel will be the more up-to-date with contemporary English writing. I hope, equally, that we English writers may not disappoint French expectations of us; and that we may give a psychologically true, not belittling or falsifying, picture of our own country—its postwar ways and manners and feelings—to the French eye. At present, as I say, the French seem to be reading as many English novels (translated) as they do French. Prominent among native output I noticed Aragon's *Aurélien* (reviewed in these pages last week), and a prize-winning novel, *La Vie des morts*,[1] which will, no doubt, be reaching England soon.

But Once a Year

"But once a year"—and, some say, often enough. All rhyme, no reason, Christmas comes round again. Out with the silver-glass bells and the tinsel stars! We gore our thumbs on holly, risk our necks on ladders, skid on the berries pattering to the floor. Christmas cards crowd the chimney-piece—robins and reindeer, skaters and Santa Clauses, snowy sunsets and sheep, coaches and carol singers, yule logs and olde-worlde inns—shy-making verses inside; red cord bows. Mr. Pickwick and all his company are back with us. Advance resistance to Christmas was so much bluff—we are for it: we let ourselves go again.

Is any heart completely closed to Christmas? If so, pity that heart. This Christmas nonsense confounds every clever saying. We grow older; the years fly round so fast; we think we know all there is to expect—yet, every time, Christmas takes us by surprise. A forgotten chime breaks out. Memories?—yes, but more. This is a birthday, and a re-birth day: something renews itself in the world and us.

Children know the secret: they understand that life *must* overflow the bounds of the everyday. It was in the expectation of something tremendous and inordinate—their eyes remind us at this season—that they consented to be born. You tell your child, "It cannot be always Christmas"—it assents; but a look of profound unconviction crosses its face.

Oh, it will learn sense, it will learn sense—but pray it may not lose gusto! It is wonderful how obstinate gusto is: cynicism conceals but cannot undo it. Christmas card language repeats, every year, a truth. By the first, the Bethlehem Christmas, humanity forever was lifted up: there is something sublime about being human. We know noble moments—yes, but there is more than that: our childishness, our company-lovingness, our sheer desire for fun are hallowed by the divine goodwill . . .

This is the country season. Rare is the "white Christmas"—outside the daydream, the annual, and the Christmas card!—but lanes, plowlands, and the brown depth of woods will be crisped by frost or mellowed by curdling mists or soughing mildly under our island rain. Not for nothing does our Christmas come at midwinter: an elemental kindness reaches us from the sleeping earth; something stirs in us as we draw our first waking breath of the early silent darkness of Christmas morning. The country house is full: everyone has been busy—last night's late bustle had not long died down before this morning's early bustle began. This year, to make the party, everybody in it has lent a hand—we have all made ready; now we shall all enjoy. Wood has been chopped and stacked throughout last week; fires will burn prodigally today. Everybody has been going without *something*, to build up Christmas—today, let us all the more enjoy the illusion of absolute plenty. Let us take it all for granted, like the birds touching down on the lawn for their Christmas crumbs.

Mist-muffled, gale-blown, or glass-clear in frosty blueness, bells from the village church will begin to sound. Outside windows the landscape, etched with bare trees, seems to stretch away in the Christmas-card country; if there be snow, it will be cotton-wool snow dusted with glitter-powder, the bird prints on it touched in with a blue paintbrush. If the sun shines, the evergreens will be glossy, rimmed with a special light.

Indoors, the fires, still palely brilliant, purr: the rooms hold a festival climate of their own. Christmas Day has a great ceremonial shape—every hour around the face of the clock is to be important: the clocks know it. In the kitchen, the range is being stoked with saved-up coal for the great roasting. The Christmas dinner, in *your* house—is it early or late? That is to be decided by the majority age of your Christmas party.

And the present-giving, the parcel-opening, the big surprise event—are you, as a family, of the breakfast-plate school, or do you hold off the presents until Christmas tree hour? That does, of course, key up enchanting suspense. But, myself, I love the dementing breakfast—the litter of untied ribbon and gaudy wrapping-paper in morning light, the buried[1] toast, the forgotten coffee, the neglected sausage, the ultimate chattering rush for church.

One tradition of Christmas Day in the country is the afternoon walk—it does not matter to *where*. On the return, dusk falls—pause for a moment longer out on the wintry lawn and look in at the rooms you are coming home to. Think, as you watch the firelight through the glass, of the homeless. Sweetness, decency, peace—God gave us strength to preserve them. What we have, we hold in trust on behalf of a queered and a battered world. Happiness, always sacred, becomes the more so for being rare . . .

As the evening deepens, the house will seem to be fuller than it is. Most unghostly, most natural at Christmas is the presence amongst us of the distant or the dead. Christmas calls across space and back through time: whether it is our ancestors or the young men who did not come back from wars, we cannot believe that those who loved life before us, who loved this life we love, are not with us now.

All Christmases cannot be country Christmases; however, it is a phenomenon of this season that the country comes to town. There is something primitive about the silence of the streets once the last rush of Christmas Eve has subsided. Squares with trees in them become winter mysteries: the suspension of the abstract roar of the city allows us to hear birds. Out from the houses in rows and the flats in blocks comes something vital: each is a core, a home.

Indoors, over Christmas, life inside the town home becomes self-enclosed; there sets in a cozy, cave-like independence—some few neighboring streets, holiday-somnolent, become one's whole terrain. In this, there are no strangers: from front-door steps, greetings are called across: for us all, the "local" has decked itself out in holly. The afternoon walk is taken over the grass of parks.

In hotels, Christmas trees flowering over with electricity, revolved about gravely by hotel children, bring a lump to the throat. Decidedly it is better to be at home; but restaurants, even, take on a steamy homeliness. Tomorrow, the pantomimes will be opening . . . All through a Christmas afternoon in London there is an old-fashioned smell in the air—chestnuts roasting, gunpowder from the crackers. Dusk, coming earlier here than in the country, makes windows spring one by one into orange light. Christmas London has, also, its friendly hauntings—the ear might fancy, down Victorian streets, the staid clip-clop of the cab horse, the more irresponsible jingle of the hansom bringing guests to the Christmas party.

It comes but once a year.

Old America

For the Old World, there is a fascination in the idea of the New. Fascination is complex in its effects—by no means does it always make for liking; it may have in it elements of hostility. This perhaps accounts for Europe's mixed reactions to America: a country to which we never can, apparently, fail to react in *some* way. Criticism, mistrust, or, in these trying times for us, nagging envy has[1] fascination latent at their root. Has this, perhaps, a romantic source? It may be to be traced, centuries back, to the lure of the "undiscovered country." The idea of America as adventurer-land dies hard (nor should America wish it may ever die). We envisage the elemental rawness, if also the elemental poetry, of something beheld for the first time—a map not yet completely filled in, a terrain still in the process of being opened up. And, what is more, this basic illusion overrides all we learn to the contrary—trans-Atlantic movies and magazines, for instance, show that America's concrete civilization is not only long past the improvised stage but has, in fact, by far overshot our own. Buildings, interior decoration, house and dress accessories, book jackets, plastics, textiles, highways, and swimming pools and, it may seem sometimes, even figures and faces express something finished, adept, and realized—America's style, her own. And that style is, for many of us, emblem of an extreme modernity.

America, it is evident, has made her own the twentieth century. She proclaims herself almost too much at home in it—whereas we, in our way of living, still seem unadjusted or astray. America epitomizes size, speed, facility, and overpowering brightness, indeed glare: most of all, we tend to conceive of her as arid, utterly open, and unhaunted. To an extent, she may share this view of herself; more or less contentedly she exports it; and on our side, restrictions upon travel make the picture difficult to correct. We therefore start for America (we who go there) with the expectation of something alienly novel, something never-before, in the very taste of her air, light from her sky. We prepare to enter a Today so overpowering, so void of anything of the past as to seem to *our* senses more like Tomorrow. The Manhattan skyline, soaring knife-sharp above the incoming ship, the phantasmagoric ground plan tilting beneath the incoming plane do, it is true, yield the foreseen impression; and it may be that for minutes after arrival the ultra-contemporary illusion lasts. But then, to the abstract verge of the highway, grandmotherly dwellings begin to crowd, or New York's Victorian streets engulf the taxi. What steals upon one is America's oldness.

This oldness, age, consists in more than the contrast with what *is* very strikingly new. It is palpable as something in itself—brought, perhaps, rather more into prominence, by the absence of out-and-out antiquity. It has to stand up against nothing actually ancient, but does not depend upon that for its reality. It is a matter of weathered living and gathered silence—not the virgin silence of "undiscovered country," but a hush in which experience is contained, at work. New York's pockets and backwaters, into which the past has run, to remain in depth, cannot but be come upon by the visitor—cynicism may tell him that Sutton Place, with its gardens down to the river, has been preserved expensively, or that Greenwich Village must owe its survival to oversight. It remains that areas of the city are not merely outmoded, shabby; it may occur to him that what is given out by these is a sort of virtue, for here it is that New Yorkers choose to stroll; it is here that in fancy they come to live. New York—as we have been and may need to be told repeatedly—is not America; is New York only. Its apparent phenomena are the commonplaces of other eastern cities, as of the smaller towns; just around urban corners, as across whole pastoral tracts of country, there hangs the blue-grey softness and bloom of age. New England, with its white classic façades, demure wide streets, and little seaports pickled in splendid history, and the South, with its colonnaded Colonial mansions, moss-hung estates, and Wren-like churches, are—as America's visitors know, or should—accredited repositories of the past; or, as the hostile would say, lived-in museums. In these regions are found vintage eccentricity, aristocratic shabbiness, intellectual disregard for fashion. But the deeper surprise, the actual eye-opener, comes when the visitor travels further afield, across the vast, blunt, moneymaking, avowedly blatant Middle West, to California's populous showy coast. For here, also, upon the brand-new surfaces, condensations of yesterday have begun to form. The yesterday of the Middle West and the West is not yet remote, nor is it yet avowed: so far, there is little more than a touch of desuetude and perhaps dismay about the set-back building, the tangled garden, the indiscriminate counters of the junk shop. But all the same, here is the birth of a past: one sees in how short a time, in how new a place, yesterdays run together to make a background. America's growing-oldness is contradictory, out-of-the-picture, on the whole inadvertent.

For, of course, great parts of the country do denounce age, and keep up a war against it, in any form or manifestation, as women do against wrinkles in the face. The adjective "old" is, for numbers of people, fatal, at least derogatory—it implies the outdated, therefore the doomed. In such an America, natural and charming people apologize for receiving one in "this poor old house," and as, perplexed, one looks round the calm, large exterior (for American home planning, fifty years ago, could have taught much to contemporary Britain), they make haste to tell one, they're on the point of moving, and that *this* near-ruin, is to be, rightly, torn down. There are progressive cities in which no apartment block or office building dare hope to outlive its first phase of youth; it must be replaced by something far more dynamic. But these clean sweeps, this automatic junking, show more than mere blind aspiration to the bigger and better. They reveal, for one thing, the illusion that there may yet be permanence, *if* the ideal permanence can be found; and, for another thing, a mistrust of the past's insidious, detaining power. The America which is in this frame of mind sees European past-consciousness as a decay, a malady—yet the incontrovertible truth is that her own past mounts up, gains ground, refuses to be denied. That is the unlooked-for presence which strikes the stranger to the American scene. He reacts to what he did not, of all things, expect to find.

What may also be come on by him, and with delight, are forms of grace in danger of being lost to Europe—the polished, proper upkeep of homes, the secluded, timeless silence of villages, leisure, uncalculated enthusiasm, and, above all, boundless and kind civility. Best American manners combine an archaic beauty with their living simplicity; and in the same sense speech (as apart from slang) conserves, in wording and turns of phrase, an English now known to the English only in literature. History speaks in place names, taste in the glaze of china, moldings of friezes, flutings of doorways; in such things works the tradition which we share. Nor, after all, is America unhaunted—ghosts there may or may not be; what matters more is the pressing surround of forefathers, their hopes and fears, their triumphs or their defeats. Heredity seems, here, an unsleeping force. Not less elegiac than ours are country graveyards, with their naive stones; and former races, the Indian and his vanquishers, seem never very far underground—at night, the blotted-out hills seem tense with danger. Civilizations leave their deep-down mark—California, New Mexico recall a heroic Spain; Louisiana bears the imprint of a royal France; New England's sturdily high mind, the South's worn pride and lingering feudalism stand for extremes of an England in conflict once. But America is no more the unknowing child of an ancient, mixed stock. She has mastered, she has exceeded what went to make her. She inherited much, but one cannot inherit age. Oldness she had to, and did, by herself attain to. America's oldness is her own.

The realization of America's age, the kindled sense of the meaning of her past, inspires her contemporary artists. In writing, as in painting and music, there is now a new, aware American school. No longer, for instance, does the American novel express discontent with the crude homeland and an aesthetic lust for the joys of Europe. There is a vogue for America in America—and this has produced, one is bound to say, not so much complacency as analysis. New American writing may seem to us forbidding—we do not know, and cannot be blamed for not knowing, exactly what it is all about; we are put off by something which seems savage in its intense, continuous self-concern. American books, more than ever, seem "too American." All the same, to broach them is worth our while; they may at least in part enlighten us, help to break down our idiotic, conventional, commerce-engendered fantasies. Since the New World *is* to fascinate us, we do well to do what we can to know it. What is newest about America is her discovery that she is, by now, old.

Preface to *A Day in the Dark*

If this selection of stories does not please, I can blame nobody but myself—in the first place, for not having written better ones; in the second, for choosing wrongly from those there are. There could have been more in this volume had some been shorter; only twenty, it came to be found, were possible. I threw out several from my original list, sacrificing them to lengthier pieces which, rightly or wrongly, I like better. These twenty do at least range through time: the first story I wrote and the last I have written so far are both here. Thirty-six years stretch between the two.

At the end of each of the stories, its date is given. It may be noticed that in arranging them I have broken up their chronological order. This I did not to cheat or annoy anybody who might try to trace my development *were* the stories in chronological order, but to preserve that hypothetical person from waste of effort. As I see it, a writer of short stories is at his or her best sometimes, and sometimes not; and this is true equally at any age or in any year at which he or she happens to be writing. "Development" may appear in any one writer's successive novels; in successive short stories I hold it to be a myth. The short story is a matter of vision, rather than of feeling. Feeling (which is important in the novel) does or should mature as one grows older. Of vision, one asks only that it should not lose its intensity—and I would say that if vision is there at all that wish is usually granted.

There of course is the question of technique: as to that one does learn more, the more stories one writes. I would willingly call technique simply craftsmanship, but that it involves something further. As to each new story, once it has been embarked on, a number of decisions have to be made—as to size (or length), as to treatment (or manner of handling), and, most of all, as to what is this particular story's aim? What is, or should be, this particular story's scope? What is this particular story really about, and how best can what it *is* about be shown? To an extent, such decisions are made instinctively, but intellectual judgment must come in also. The first thing the writer must learn about technique is that there is no such thing as technique in the abstract or in vacuo. Neither is it something to be arrived at for good and all. Each new story (if it is of any value) will make a whole fresh set of demands: no preceding story can be of any help.

At the beginning, I overwrote—as "Breakfast," 1920, will show. Delighted to find I could write at all, I was aware of no reason to hold my horses; the idea of doing so came to me later, slowly. Looking back, I wonder, with due gratitude, that my first two collections of stories, *Encounters*, *Ann Lee's*, were as kindly treated by critics as they were. The chief hint of reproof with regard to *Encounters*, that I was an imitator of Katherine Mansfield, was as a matter of fact not merited: I had read nothing of hers (though I can't think why) when *Encounters* went to my first publisher. But I see that I was in her debt in another way: her lovely performances, early in the 1920s, created a place for and interest in the short story, and at my beginning I profited by that.

I also gained from, and was encouraged by, the acceptance of the short story as "a free form." Impressionism lightly laced with psychology bought one out of needing to have a plot. At that time that suited me, as it did others. But by now, the 1960s, I think the "free form" short story has run its course. That is, I suppose that it has with the world in general; I do know that it certainly has with me. I now prefer narrative short stories, with a beginning, a crisis, and an end. I admit that many of mine—and several here—continue to terminate with a query: exactly what happened next (or in some cases, exactly what *had* happened) is left for the reader to conjecture. Can I defend this? I can at least explain it by saying that I expect the reader to be as (reasonably) imaginative as myself. And I would point out that a number of my stories, such as "The Demon Lover," "The Cheery Soul," "Hand in Glove," "The Happy Autumn Fields," have a supernatural element in them, which makes some of the happenings unable to be rationally explained. I do not make use of the supernatural as a get-out; it is inseparable (whether or not it comes to the surface) from my sense of life. That I feel it unethical — for some reason? — to allow the supernatural into a novel may be one of my handicaps as a sincere novelist.

Fifteen of the pieces in this volume I chose from existing collections of my stories. To them are added five others, more recent work. "A Day in the Dark, "I Hear You Say So," "Gone Away," and "The Dolt's Tale" have seen daylight, so far, only in periodicals; "Hand in Glove" was written at the request of a friend who edited books of ghost stories.[1] (Years back, the same friend, then editing "horror" tales, elicited from me "The Cat Jumps.") . . . Running my eye over these twenty, as a whole, I can think of no general remark to make on them — and now that I come to think of it, why should I? In their different ways, they stand for some of the greatest pleasure I have had out of writing, onward from 1920 . . . I note that nine of them have a wartime setting, a "today" whose air, at times, seems still in my lungs; and I note, there are[2] six which are set in Ireland. (The locale of the Victorian family in "The Happy Autumn Fields" is, though not stated, to me unshakeably County Cork.) Ireland, being the country of my birth, may account, at times, for my manner of seeing things?

Autobiographies

Biographical Note

Elizabeth Bowen was born in Dublin. Her permanent Irish home is Bowen's Court, County Cork: an eighteenth-century house built on land granted to her ancestor by Cromwell. Being an only child, she succeeded to this house on the death of her father, Henry Cole Bowen, barrister-at-law, in 1929.

Education, at Downe House School, Kent, during the First World War. From childhood up to the age of twenty, Elizabeth Bowen was not certain whether she wanted to write or paint. A short time at an art school showed her what she could *not* do: she then sat down to write stories—as she has been doing since. Her first collection, *Encounters*, was published in 1923. She still sees pictures, though now never tries to paint one.

After writing, travel is what she cares for most. France and Italy are her two favorite European countries. Since the Liberation she has revisited France several times; and also, in the winter of 1947–48, toured in Czechoslovakia and Austria. She has been twice in America; her last visit was in 1933.

Since her marriage to Alan Cameron in 1923, she has divided her home life between England and Ireland. The Camerons lived near Oxford for ten years, then moved to London, where they have a house in Regent's Park. Here they have lived since 1935. Experiences in London throughout the war, with further sidelights got from half-time work as an A.R.P. warden, have gone to the making of *The Heat of the Day*.

It is ten years since the publication of Elizabeth Bowen's last novel, *The Death of the Heart*. In the interim she has written short stories, criticism, broadcasts, an autobiographical fragment, the history of Bowen's Court, *English Novelists* (for the "Britain in Pictures" series), a play (in collaboration with John Perry),[1] and reportage for the Ministry of Information during the war.

I Love Driving at Night

I find driving or being driven stimulating to the invention of stories. Best of all, I prefer driving myself. If not, I like to be sitting beside the driver, who should, ideally, be an old friend or someone I know well.

I like driving in the very early mornings; by the light of the sunset (though not, of course, straight *into* the setting sun), or by night—I particularly enjoy driving myself for long distances in the dark.

I enjoy the sensation of speed and seeing the contours of the country change and new distances open up.

Normally, I prefer driving fast; I find that I always tend to drive fairly fast when I am by myself. On the other hand, I sometimes like going very slowly indeed, but the thirty miles an hour average always bores me.

I like best a winding upland road, bound only by low banks or hedges, and crossing a great expanse of open country—for example, such country as one traverses on the A40 road between Oxford and the Welsh border. I also like driving through the streets of small old-fashioned market towns: crowded city traffic is irritating. I always far prefer to leave my car in a garage at the outskirts of any large town—that is, if I want to "explore."

The kind of car that it is *does* matter to me. I only like a "luxury" car for luxury occasions; otherwise I like one that seems to me familiar, shabby, and easygoing.

I greatly prefer a tourer to a saloon car, and I shall be exceedingly sorry if no more tourers are made. Motoring (from the point of view from which I see it, as a sensation) is rather spoiled for me in a saloon by the view being cut off across the top.

My own and favorite car is a 1929 Morris Oxford tourer which I still have in Ireland. I consider this kind of car ideal for country life.

It is delightful to have a sympathetic companion to whom one can point out anything that is amusing, beautiful, or interesting along the road. But a sustained, formal conversation throughout a long drive seems to me to spoil all the pleasure.

It always strikes me that a good driver in a sense *interprets* the character of the country through which he is passing. Quite apart from questions of traffic, etc., he knows when to speed up and when to slow down in order to obtain the greatest enjoyment for himself and his passengers.

How I Write My Novels

Q: Does the whole story come in a flash?

A: No. I think that I see a story—or rather, that I suspect a story—then I follow it up.

Q: Do you conceive characters who then almost write themselves?

A: Yes, decidedly. If my characters are to live, I allow them to take command of me and of the entire story.

Q: Do you write a regular number of words per day or only when the mood takes you?

A: I write for a regular number of hours a day; but in those hours I write a varying amount of words. But regular hours I *do* keep.

Q: How do you do your research?

A: Being an imaginative writer, I don't need to do research. I have to do all my work through imagination.

Q: How did you become a writer in the first place?

A: I just made up my mind that I wanted to be one and went on writing and writing until somebody—or anybody—took notice of the fact. Then I was published . . .

Q: What advice would you give to budding writers?

A: Do more or less what I did. Stick to it and don't be too easily discouraged. On the other hand, don't reject criticism. Take any that comes along, because it's certainly a great help.

Q: Do you write by hand, dictate, or type your stories?

A: I always write straight on to a typewriter—I like the noise!

Q: Are there any other writers in the family?

A: No—not one!

Q: On what writer, if any, do you think that you have modeled your style?

A: That's difficult to say. If I knew, then I wouldn't hesitate to tell you; but I think that a style forms gradually out of all the styles of the different writers one has admired. It's a sort of composite achievement. I know that I admire the precision of various styles—Jane Austen, for instance; but I don't think that I've consciously styled myself on any other writer.

Q: Has any writer, more than any other, had an influence on your work?

A: I suppose the only way to teach oneself to write is to pick up something here and something there, and I've probably picked up something from every author I've ever read, from ever since I was a child to recent years when my own style developed.

Q: Which, in your opinion, is your best work and why?

A: *The House in Paris*, because it immediately took command of me and seemed to insist that I should write it.

Q: Who is your favorite character and why?

A: A little boy called Leopold in *The House in Paris*. There was something grand about that one little devil against the world.

Q: Which novel gave you the most trouble?—and which the least?

A: A novel published just before the war—*The Death of the Heart*. The technicalities troubled me. As for the easiest novel, I should say *The Last September*, which was almost autobiographical.

Miss Bowen on Miss Bowen

I was born in Dublin on June 7, 1899. I am an only child and was meant to have been a son, and should have been called Robert. My father had the finest, most able, and balanced mind of any man I have known. He was profoundly intellectual in his outlook on life, but kind-hearted, percipient, and tender in his relations with people, as the intellectuals often are not. My mother had very great charm, sweetness of character, spirituality, and a touch of endearing perversity. She was, I believe, very beautiful. On their honeymoon he taught her Greek.

The summers we spent at our family home, Bowen's Court, County

Cork, a big Italianate eighteenth-century light grey stone house, standing in open pastoral country under a range of small mountains, in the arms of a semicircle of trees. When I was seven my father had a breakdown from overwork. While he was under treatment my mother took me away and for some years we lived in the south of England. At first this seemed to me a delightful adventure, and the small brittle English seaside houses, the seaside tamarisks, and the chalky Kentish downs were like something out of a book. But my attitude toward England became, with a child's arrogance, rather indignant and patronizing.

This happy life with my mother in our succession of small houses, in a delicious companionship which our difference in ages hardly affected at all, came to an end with a shock: her death, of cancer, when I was thirteen. I had known she was ill, but not so ill, and when she died I felt I should never trust life again.

When I was fourteen, I was sent to boarding school at Downe House, in Kent. I distinguished myself in no way; I was untidy, indolent, bad at games, and my essays, reeking with the pretentiousness of adolescence, attracted a good deal of severe but salutary criticism from the headmistress—as far as anyone can teach anyone else how *not* to write she, I think, taught me.

I wrote my first short stories when I was twenty. These were subsequently collected and published under the title of *Encounters*. From the moment that—as it were—my pen touched paper, I thought of nothing but writing, and since then I have thought of practically nothing else. Which is not to say I have been industrious: I have been idle for months, or even a year, at a time. But when I have nothing to write I feel only half alive.

Q. Did the work on the book change your original plan for it?

A. No, I think I wrote the book more or less as I had projected it. To an extent, as the fundamental idea gains more and more force in the course of writing, I always find that a novel shapes itself as it goes along. In this case, particularly, the characters took command of me.

Q. Do you keep notebooks of events, conversations, etc.?

A. No. Phrases of talk, visual impressions seem to pigeonhole themselves automatically in my memory. As for ideas for stories, they seem to rise slowly to the surface (or conscious) part of my mind, out of my subconscious, when I put myself into the necessary passive state. I think all my characters are "composite." Sometimes the faces, or physical personalities are lifted from people I barely know by sight—sometimes from people I have only seen once. I envisage my characters only cloudily when I first think of the novel. I acquire the necessary information about them as I go along. If, for instance, one of my characters were a lawyer, I would frequent the company of lawyers as far as possible. But, unlike Sinclair Lewis, I am not a documentary novelist. I write my novels straight ahead through from beginning to end. No scene or incident is written in advance—that is to say, before I come to it in the course of the story. Before starting I only know (1) the central idea, (2) the nature and trend of the plot, (3) the desired shape of the story.

Q. When do you write? What sort of room, etc.?

A. From 9:30 to 1:00, 2:30 to 5:30. I mistrust working late at night. I need a great deal of sleep. My room should be a silent room. A large writing table. Outlook, if possible, on trees and/or green space. Ideally, nobody coming near me, no calls to the telephone. Ideally, no social engagements before 6:30. After that, a drink, a bath, a dress that's fun to put on, and a little gaiety.

Q. What is your technique of working? How much do you do in a day?

A. Up to 1935 I wrote in longhand. I always, now, work straight onto a typewriter. I type badly, so final versions go to a professional. I think in advance, but really think mostly on paper; my writing brain gets properly into gear only when I sit down at my table. I am a great rewriter: each page represents from two to ten discarded drafts. On the whole I am a slow worker. Part of each day's work goes to revising work done the day before. On an average, I should say that I write about 600 words in a (full) working day.

Q. Which of your works do you consider the best?

A. Artistically, I have been most nearly completely satisfied by some of my longer short stories, such as "Summer Night," "The Disinherited," "The Happy Autumn Fields." Of my previous novels, *The House in Paris* gives me most pleasure. Though I think perhaps the *human* content of *The Death of the Heart* is more important. I consider *The Heat of the Day* my best novel so far.

Q. What comment about your work do you like most?

A. Someone once said I was "a muffled poet"—that I transposed poetry (or rather, what might have been poetry) into terms of the short story or novel.

Q. Who are your favorite modern writers?

A. I am never sure how far back the word "modern" goes. Among living fiction writers, some of my favorites (*not* in order of preference) are Henry Green, Graham Greene, Mauriac, Montherlant, Sartre, Colette, Evelyn Waugh, Camus, Eudora Welty, Rosamond Lehmann, Bemelmans, I. Compton-Burnett, Faulkner, Elizabeth Taylor, Elizabeth Jenkins, E. M. Forster, Frank O'Connor, Seán O'Faoláin, Rumer Godden, P. H. Newby, Dorothy Parker.

Q. Who among the writers of the past?

A. Proust, Turgenev, Tolstoy, Chekhov, D. H. Lawrence, Firbank, Henry James, Virginia Woolf, Hardy, Emily and Charlotte Brontë, James Joyce, Jane Austen, Fielding, Richardson, Meredith, Stendhal, Flaubert.

Q. Have you any hobbies or avocations?

A. I collect scraps to make scrap screens. I should like to collect china if I could afford it. I wish I had started collecting matchboxes early in life, but it is too late to begin now. I like decorating and arranging rooms; and, when not actually doing so, daydreaming how I *would*. I like arranging flowers, especially when I have a large and crowded garden to pick from. I like scrap-work.

Q. What work are you contemplating?

A. Four *long* short stories, each representing a season of the year.

Elizabeth Bowen, of Cork and London

I was born in Dublin, but belong in County Cork—where my family, coming over from Wales, settled in the seventeenth century. My later schooldays were spent in England, but I used to go back to Ireland for the holidays. I left school at eighteen, and never went to college—any "further education" was picked up by me as I went along: by means of reading, travel, and knowing all sorts of people. Having hoped in childhood to be a painter, I attended a London art school for a term or two; but what I chiefly learned there was that I could not draw. Possibly I have carried over the painter's eyes into the visual element in my writing.

I began to write at twenty (having abandoned the art school) and my first book—a collection of short stories—was published when I was twenty-three. I married, in that same year, Alan Charles Cameron. For ten years we lived outside Oxford, where he administered public education for Oxford City. We had a number of young, brilliant friends in the university—some professors, some students. That was a pleasant life. After that, we left Oxford and came to London, where my husband took up a post in connection with the BBC's educational broadcasting. He now acts as educational adviser to the Gramophone Company (EMI).

Our London house is in Regent's Park—which has been the scene of several of my stories. I have a particular, almost countrified love for this locality—a love strengthened by the experiences of war. Our house, patched up again after drastic bomb damage, is now once more its own urbane, Regency self. I divide my life between it and the house in Ireland.

For my work, I keep regular hours. Ideally, 9:30 A.M. to 5:30 P.M., with a break for lunch. I find I'm greatly helped by routine—the same hours, same room, same table. I *can* work in any place where I can be for long enough to set up a routine—for instance, I find a small, friendly hotel, in a locality where I don't know too many people, ideal. Attempts to work in a friend's house seldom prosper; somehow, the atmosphere is too personal.

Out of working hours I like to be "out of school"—i.e., to amuse myself. Generally, when I'm working hard at a book, I don't read much: I like better to be in the open air, walking, gardening, or motoring. Or, if indoors, I like to go to the cinema. Really, I like any kind of easygoing gaiety. I think hard while I'm writing—*away* from writing I prefer sensation to thought.

Like all Irish people, I love talking—though not to the same person too long. I think my idea of the purest pleasure is travel—not hurrying, not keeping to schedule, free to linger in any attractive place. I've been three times to America, and loved it each time. In Europe, I know France and Italy best; but have also spent time in, and greatly enjoyed, Austria, Holland, Czechoslovakia, Switzerland, Hungary.

I don't think I have any hobbies, in the exact sense. I am fond of both my London and my Irish house, and both of them take up a good deal of my time. I *can* cook, but don't enjoy it—which probably means I am not a good cook. I am not particularly fond of any animal, except cats. My relaxations are looking at picture books (such as *New Yorker* albums), playing the gramophone, or reading either poetry or detective stories.

I have no children, and am an only child: so is my husband.

My Best Novel

It's exceedingly difficult—or so I find—for an author to be objective when comparing his or her different books. One of them may be dear for subjective reasons; another may rank as the nearest possible realization of a concept. Again, is an author's "best" novel to be taken to be his most honorably ambitious or his most successful? The degree of success is, of course, a matter for the outside world to decide.

My recently published novel, *The Heat of the Day*, is the one of mine I esteem most: I have put into it, as into no other, my sense of the world, and of the world at a particular time. As far as I am concerned, it is still too near to me to be judged by me; and, as a "new novel" it is still in the course of judgment by readers . . . I am most fond of an early novel of mine, *The Last September*, of which the scene is laid in Ireland. I think, if it be not presumptuous to say so, that *The House in Paris* appeals to me most as a work of art—perhaps because of all my novels it seems to me most foreign to myself; almost as though someone else had written it. I have, on the whole, been given to understand that *The Death of the Heart* is the novel of mine for which readers feel most affection. Oddly enough, perhaps, I now find it rather too sad—apart from the riotous middle seaside section, which I confess to rereading occasionally, with amusement. I always enjoy comedy, whether by myself or anyone else.

I think I get most certain and lasting pleasure (of the kind one seeks in a fellow author's work) from four or five of my longer short stories—e.g., "The Disinherited" (published in the collection *The Cat Jumps*), "Summer Night," and "A Love Story" (published in *Look at All Those Roses*), and "The Happy Autumn Fields" and "Mysterious Kôr" (published in *The Demon Lover*). Like many prose writers, I probably would wish to have been a poet, and it is agreed that the short story, with its unity of mood and possible[1] lyricism, approaches most nearly to the condition of poetry.

Autobiographical Note

I was born in Dublin, at 15 Herbert Place—a terrace of small brown brick Georgian houses facing on the canal. For the first seven years of my life, we spent the winters in Dublin, the summers in our family house, Bowen's Court, County Cork. My ancestor, a Welsh squire who had come to Ireland as a colonel in the Cromwellian army, was granted the lands on which the house stands in the seventeenth century. Bowen's Court itself was built by one of Colonel Bowen's descendants (and my ancestor). The house bears the carved date 1775. Like most eighteenth-century manors, it is built in the Italianate manner. It has belonged to me (as I am an only child) since my father's death in 1930, and has been a continuous influence in my life.

Much of the later part of my childhood was spent in England. The Kentish coast has been a second home to me, and is still the part of England I love best. My mother and I lived in Folkestone, Hythe, and the Elham Valley for about five years, up to her death in 1912. I have put this part of Kent into two of my novels—*The House in Paris* and *The Death of the Heart*. In the latter novel, Folkestone and Hythe bear the concealing names of Southstone and Seale-on-Sea.

After my mother's death, I lived with one of her sisters, in England, till I was grown up. My holidays from school were spent in Ireland, with my father. I went to three schools: a small day school at Folkestone, another day school in Hertfordshire, and the boarding school Downe House, then at Downe, Kent. (The school was in a country house which had been Charles Darwin's: the house has since been converted into a Darwin Museum.) This third school, Downe House, was the one that left the determining mark on my character: English subjects were very well taught there, and the headmistress encouraged me to become a writer. She, Miss Olive Willis, had a close friendship, dating from Oxford College days, with Rose Macaulay; and she introduced me to Rose Macaulay—to whose help and encouragement in the early phases of my career as a writer I owe so much—after I left school.

As a child I was fonder of drawing than I was of writing, and had made up my mind I would become "an artist." I drew pretty well at that time. But actually my powers of drawing stopped short when I was about fourteen: I have never been able to draw any better than I did at that age. Two terms at a London art school when I was twenty finally disillusioned me as to my drawing powers: I discovered myself to be bored, and an art-school dunce. So I gave up. But I often regret that lost gift. It seems to me that often when I write I am trying to make words do the work of line and color. I have the painter's sensitivity to light. Much (and perhaps the best) of my writing is verbal painting.

I began writing (poetry at first) when I was about nineteen. I was at first very cagey about my efforts. Really I was luckier in my start than many young writers: my first book, a collection of short stories called *Encounters*, was published in England when I was twenty-three. It contained several stories written when I was twenty. Though the book hardly sold at all, it had an encouraging press—very friendly reviews from the leading English critics of that time. I often wonder, if the reviews had been scathing, or if the book had been ignored, whether I should have had the courage to go on.

I spent[1] the years between leaving school and my marriage in London, in Ireland, and abroad. I traveled with one of my Irish aunts and her family in what do now not seem very recondite places—the Italian Riviera, the Italian lakes, Switzerland. This, however, inculcated my lasting love of Italy. A winter at Bordighera inspired, subsequently, my first novel, *The Hotel*. (Before the appearance of that novel, I had published a second book of short stories, *Ann Lee's*.)

In 1923 I married Alan Cameron, a highlander by descent. Between us we have a good deal of Celtic blood, as his mother was Cornish. Having been demobilized from the army after the First World War, my husband had entered the Public Education Service. He remained[2] interested not only in education but in all forms of administration, and in local government. We spent the first two years of our married life at Northampton, on account of his work, then moved to Oxford, where he became director of education for Oxford city. At Oxford we remained for ten years, which were very delightful. We had a small, old house, converted out of the stables of a manor in the old-fashioned village of Old Headington, about one-and-a-half miles from Oxford city. During this period, we used to spend our summer holidays traveling about France—usually, we took our car. We generally headed, at an easy speed, for the southwest: the Dordogne or the Auvergne. Also, I was usually lucky enough to spend three weeks every spring in Italy.

In 1935 we left Oxford for London: my husband had taken up the appointment of secretary to the Central Council of School Broadcasting at the BBC. He held this post up to 1945, when he had to resign from the BBC owing to eye trouble; this, dating from the 1914–18 war, had become aggravated by the amount of reading his work involved. He did once more, later, return to work as educational adviser to the Gramophone Company (EMI), carrying through a very interesting scheme of educational gramophone records.[3]

We lived, in London, at 2, Clarence Terrace, Regent's Park.[4] I fell in love with this house at first sight: it is in one of the famous Nash, Regency, terraces, overlooking the lake and trees of the Park. The rooms, though not large, were[5] high, large-windowed, and stylish. It was a miracle that this house, and its neighbors, survived the war, as Regent's Park was pretty heavily bombed, both in 1940 and during the V1[6] summer. In fact we did suffer pretty severe damage: I had hoped the worst was over after the night of May 10, 1941; but in the summer of 1944 a V1, landing across the road, blew the poor house hollow inside, wrecking every room.

I would not have missed being in London throughout the war for anything: it was the most interesting period of my life. It was interesting to see the quiet old English capital converted into a high-pressure cosmopolitan city. I became an A.R.P. warden. Air raids were much less trying if one had something to do. Also, the Warden's Post, where one spent so many evenings on duty, became a fascinating focus of life. We wardens were of all types—so different that, but for the war, we would not have met at all. As it was, in spite of periodic rows or arguments on non-raid evenings, most of us became excellent friends.

When the women in my age group began to be called up for National Service, I wondered what would happen to me. However, as author and journalist, and in view of the fact that I was doing writing work for the Ministry of Information, I was allowed to continue my normal life. I was therefore writing continuously throughout the war—the only interruption being the necessity to clean up my house from time to time, when it had been blasted. (Nobody who has not cleaned up a house in which every ceiling has come down and every window has been blown in knows what cleaning-up can be like: glass dust and plaster from old ceilings are most pervasive.) As a housewife, I was more fortunate than the majority of Englishwomen, as, owing to my husband and myself both being full-time professional workers, we were allowed to keep our excellent Irish housekeeper. I often think of dedicating the novel at which I am now at work (and which I began in the war years) to her, as but for her it could never have been written.

I have now been writing for thirty years.[7] I have published six collections of short stories, seven novels, a biography of my Irish home, *Bowen's Court*, and, in England, a fragment of autobiography entitled *Seven Winters*. I have written a number of prefaces to books; and I collected and wrote a preface for *The Faber Book of Modern Short Stories*. In the last fifteen years, I have also done a good deal of literary journalism. I do not really consider myself a critic—I do not think, really, that a novelist *should* be a critic; but, by some sort of irresistible force, criticism seems to come almost every novelist's way. I write, at intervals, for the *New Statesman*, *The Listener*, *Vogue*, *Harper's Bazaar*; and do request articles, from time to time, for papers too diverse to enumerate. For nine years, onward from 1941, I did a weekly book page for the *Tatler*.[8] For six months, before the war, I was theater critic for Graham Greene's short-lived but interesting weekly, *Night and Day*.

I have written a number of "feature" broadcasts for the BBC. One on Jane Austen, one about Fanny Burney, one on Anthony Trollope. The Trollope broadcast has been published as a booklet by the Oxford University Press. I have also written two "place" broadcasts—one on the Kentish coast (in a series entitled "Return Journey"); one about Bloomsbury, London.[9] Writing for the air frenzies me: it is such a new and different technique—all the same, its problems are fascinating.

The novel on which I am at work at present, and which is nearing completion, is to be entitled *The Heat of the Day*. The setting is London during the war. It is not about blitzes, etc.; but about the peculiar psychological climate of those years, and the problems set up in people's personal lives. An espionage theme comes into it.

Now that the war is over and Europe "open" again, I am filled, like almost everyone else, with an insatiable longing for more travel. I was in Paris this August and September, attending the Peace Conference in the capacity of a freelance journalist. During the weekends I managed to see something of France. I find I love France more than ever. I wonder when I shall be able to return to Italy. I find myself pulled two ways—half of me longs to be on the move again, after the immobilization of these war years; half of me longs to stay quiet (preferably in County Cork) and write and write all the books that I have in mind.

In January of this year, 1952, my husband retired from work with the Gramophone Company, owing to ill-health. We gave up the Regent's Park house, left London, and came to live permanently at Bowen's Court. My husband died here, on the 26th of August.

Selected *Tatler* Reviews: 1954 to 1958

Denis Johnston, *Nine Rivers from Jordan,* January 20, 1954

Nine Rivers from Jordan, by Denis Johnston, is a book which has long been due to come. It is, that is to say, one of those books to which World War II was due to give birth some ten years later, when reflection should have had time to work. Man in action hardly has time to think—he reacts (as we saw from brilliant reportage) sharply, from day to day, but the search for the meaning must come later. Yes, for the long-term evaluation one must have, evidently, the long term.

Also there is the question, a vital one, of placing one thing in relation to another—can it be failure to do this (failure, perhaps, to have time to do this) which has left, in the case of so many people, a sort of lasting, puzzling gap between wartime experience and civilian life?

The author, as who can fail to remember, served through the war as BBC correspondent in the field, working first in the desert, then in Italy, and, finally, with the Americans in Germany. He was the first person to deliver a commentary on a bomber raid from a participating aircraft; he found himself all unawares (not having known what he was approaching) inside the gates of Belsen; he beheld the meeting of the two armies, the actual closing of the pincer, in the Brenner Pass. One of the great merits of *Nine Rivers from Jordan* is that not one of the accounts in it has lost its almost uncanny, momentary sharpness: one reads about everything with the sense that it is actually happening, here and now. A journal, or Mr. Johnston's scripts, surely must have provided this vivid detail—no quite unaided memory could be so clear-cut, so minutely factual.

But what is important, what makes this book literature, is that the author has put what *was* contemporary material to what *is* a contemporary use—he is writing not about *a* war (however worldwide), but about War, and his treatment is at once imaginative and philosophic. What goes to make up War?—how, fundamentally, is it to be differentiated from Peace? Are not the same impulses, compulsions, desires, passions present, though outwardly taking a different form? Does not the same vast, slowly evolving pattern underlie everything?

Mr. Johnston is an Irishman, an Anglo-Irishman, gifted with the ambivalence and detachment peculiar to that race inside a race. An Irishman, of whatever kind, is a born freelance. Yet it is impossible to be in a war and be not embroiled in it—why else, indeed, does an Irishman seek a war? I should say that his semi-detachment gives virtue—that is, a fearless veracity—to his accounts of World War II as seen by him.

He has been a barrister, which gives impersonality to the mind; and before and after the war was and is a dramatist—first, probably, known to London through his play *The Moon in the Yellow River*. The distinction between dramatist and "dramatizer" could not, I think, be better illustrated than it is by this book: the "dramatizer" inflates, and thereby falsifies; the dramatist instinctively reaches down to the essentials and implications of human conduct.

We must listen, therefore, when (at the close of the splendid section dealing with the time in the western desert) Mr. Johnston delivers a frank, it may seem shocking, verdict on War:

> Fear, in its proper place, can serve to heighten the perceptions and quicken the emotions. It is a bond that can link men together in a brotherhood that will outlast all other bonds. Once you and I have shared the same Fear, we have something in common that transcends Class, Race, and Creed.
>
> This is one of the things that we can learn from War, and it brings home the meaning of the creed of the fighting men—that War is not really such an evil thing at all. How can it be evil

if, in it, one lives more abundantly, and experiences a deeper sense of the meaning of life? . . . War, as these men play it, need not be some sordid squabble into which we are drawn weeping and with reluctant feet. It is a game to be played according to certain fixed principles and assumptions. And for that reason I beg to utter one more heretical and anti-social statement which must be kept from the ears of Winston Burdett: that as War appears to be inevitable in this life, it is more important to keep it the good thing it is, than to win or lose it.

Nine Rivers from Jordan opens, characteristically, with a picture of our army in at once roaring high spirits and full retreat. Desert encounters include the then General Montgomery, fascinatingly first met in Australian headgear; desert friendships rank high.

One of Mr. Johnston's enterprises also plunged him into the heart of Tito's fierce, singing, young boy-and-girl partisans. Sympathetic, to those who have shared his hopes, may be found his attempts to go gay in a Paris under American Army rule. The Italy the Allies fought their way up, the Rome of immediately after her liberation are no less clear, though they may be less terrible, than the Germany conquest was to disclose. And the metaphysical effect left by Belsen upon this one man is shown as deeper, more lasting, than the physical horror.

He blundered into Belsen when not unromantically driving through German forests in patient search of a German girl who had continued to haunt his imagination: naive letters from her to a fighting lover, left behind in the debris of a German retreat, had happened to come into his hands. Annaliese for him had been the sweet and patient spirit of Woman, transcending War, and redeeming Germany.

Appalling, ironical, and for him conclusive was it to come on Belsen where he should have found the girl: he makes clear, indeed, that that mis-arrival constituted a spiritual turning point . . .

The allegoric side of *Nine Rivers from Jordan* must not be overlooked, if the book is to have for the reader its full value. Real figures loom large, symbolic figures still more so. The title derives from a prophecy; interposed passages are in the descent of James Joyce.

Above all, this is *not* "another war book."

G. M. Trevelyan, *A Layman's Love of Letters*, March 31, 1954

A Layman's Love of Letters is, as a stimulus to the pure enjoyment of reading, second to nothing likely to come our way. This book reproduces in printed form the Clark Lectures delivered in Cambridge in the autumn of 1953 by Dr. G. M. Trevelyan, O.M., master of Trinity College, formerly Regius Professor of Modern History in the University of Cambridge.

The Clark Lectures, provided year by year by Trinity College for the university, may deal with any subject connected with English literature — the field is wide, the inspiration considerable, and the choice of the actual subject, in each case, is left to the speaker. For some time past, the lectures have been delivered by persons distinguished as professional students or critics of literature: last October, Trinity made a brilliant departure from custom by persuading the great historian who is its master to take the platform for these half-dozen talks.

Dr. Trevelyan describes himself as a layman (or as Chaucer, he says, would have called him, a "lewd man"), because literature never has been, in the specialized sense, his subject — it has, rather, been his abiding pleasure! It could well be for this reason that his approach is so spontaneous, personal, untrammeled, and, in a magnificent way, lighthearted. This book of his — so unbookish, for each page has the gusto and resonances of natural talk — should be the ideal reviver for those of us whose wish or power to read has begun to fail. Some of us, it may be, have been scared off from the masterpieces which should be our natural heritages because these have begun to reek of the classroom or, still worse, have become encrusted in critics' jargon.

Dr. Trevelyan pays tribute to the critics — though he occasionally, in a good-humored way, joins issue with one or another of them (Matthew Arnold's verdict on Shelley; Raymond Mortimer's on Kipling; E. M. Forster's on Sir Walter Scott). Ideally, criticism is the product of love and learning: how much it *can* do to illuminate, widen, and deepen a natural pleasure these talks certainly demonstrate. What perhaps Dr. Trevelyan does not allow for is the unlearned person's fear of didacticism — we resent being told what is good for us — or, at least, what is good for us comes to sound unattractive. Totally lacking in the didactic spirit, the genial master of Trinity simply tells us *what* he has enjoyed, and how and why.

Would we enjoy more if we had studied less? Does to be *taught* English literature endanger our intuitive liking for its flavor? "The study of English at our universities is," the speaker considered, "indispensable in the present state of society, which is very different now as a patron of Letters from what it was sixty years ago. . . . In general, the whole background and atmosphere of thought and knowledge was more literary than today. There was less specialization and more culture." Indeed, to the undergraduates of Dr. Trevelyan's day the idea of making a study subject out of what to them was sublime experience appeared fantastic. The study of literature *now* preserves what might, Dr. Trevelyan shows, be an only too easily lost tradition.

For one thing, there are far fewer literary periodicals than there used to be; and moreover, shortage of space necessitates considerably less, and less full, reviewing—whereas, as things formerly used to be, "literature was kept before the nation's eyes and discussed very fully in public from different points of view." Secondly, there used once to be more and larger private libraries; more people could afford to buy books, and they lived, not in flats, but in houses with space for bookshelves. Books played not only a social role; they enriched, in homes, the domestic atmosphere. And, above all, there was leisure—one not only read in the evenings, one talked by day, and what *had* been read added character to the conversation. As recreation, reading was still unrivaled . . . Young people now grow up in a thinner air. So it has come to be that our universities must rouse, train, and foster literary taste—which might, it seems, otherwise fade and vanish.

Here, in the first of Dr. Trevelyan's talks, is a lively discussion of Lord Byron—poet to honor but never to overrate; more striking, perhaps, in his temperament as a man. How could one critic claim (as indeed he did) that Byron was a better poet than Shelley? And was it Victorian priggishness which caused Matthew Arnold to write off Coleridge as "a poet and philosopher wrecked in a mist of opium"? What of "The Ancient Mariner," "Kubla Khan," the first part of "Christabel," and "Frost at Midnight"? And, to contend that the poet Gray ever wrote anything better than the "Elegy Written in a Country Churchyard" is, our speaker considers, perversity . . .

The fascinating theme of book illustration engages Dr. Trevelyan next—how well *is* the poet or novelist served by "pictures"?

Instances were Cruikshank, "Phiz," and Seymour—three men who "did much for Dickens by giving ocular reality to his incomparable menagerie of characters." Lesser novelists, such as Lever and Ainsworth, were, our speaker is of the opinion, practically "made" by the work of Cruikshank and "Phiz"; and Surtees owed much to the Leech drawings of Jorrocks. As for Lewis Carroll's Alice, our conceptions of that prim and immortal child are practically inseparable from the Tenniel pictures— attempts to re-illustrate *Alice,* by later pens, seem to most of us not only impious, but unsuccessful.

From illustration, we pass on to translation—how near can translation be?—how much is bound to be lost? A translation can itself be a work of art; but, alas, many are little more than distortions. For those of us who are wide readers but poor linguists, the translator's function is, clearly, very important—of the novels reaching us from abroad, too many versions in English seem slipshod or creaking: in versions of this kind the inept translator cheats both author and reader!

Dr. Trevelyan on Kipling is magnificent; as he is, again, in defense of Sir Walter Scott (for defense, in some quarters, does seem required). In discussing Browning, he shows an equal sense of the soaring genius and curious limitations. His views on the historical novel, as those of a great historian, are of first importance, and should at no cost be missed by addicts of that particular type of fiction. Place-names in poetry give him a further subject; elsewhere, he is eloquent as to mountain poetry, which is a particular taste of his. George Meredith, as novelist, man, and poet, should be restored to the readers he well deserves by Dr. Trevelyan's warm though critical tribute; and no less attention goes to A. E. Housman. On the border ballads, macabre and fierce, I am not sure that our speaker is not the best of all.

A *Layman's Love of Letters* is a slim volume—unalarming, human, kindly, colloquial. Exiles from literature should seek it out. For to read again, we find, is to ride again.

Elizabeth Jenkins, *The Tortoise and the Hare*; James Baldwin, *Go Tell It on the Mountain*, April 14, 1954

Elizabeth Jenkins is to be numbered among the most distinguished living English novelists. By no means is she among the more prolific—her books, each one memorable, have indeed been few: here is a case of achievement and reputation built up on quality more than quantity. Her biography of Jane Austen became a classic; and, though in no sense a disciple, Miss Jenkins does in one great particular resemble the woman whose life she wrote—she takes joy in, and gives us, out-and-out novels.

Rare is that gift today—we have much "fiction," but what, we may sometimes ask, has become of the magic art and the ancient spell? The ideal novel draws us into its world; it turns upon some crisis or situation which rivets and delights us by its importance, and, best of all, it brings us into the company of characters who are not merely lifelike but intensely and superabundantly *living*. Life itself, as shown us in such a novel, takes on an interest it lacks in so-called reality.

Today, the novel is "used" for too many things—outlet for self-analysis, social diatribe, daydream fabrication. We are rich in shockers, thrillers, and spellbinders, costume affairs, or nostalgic pictures of childhoods. Much of our fiction suffers from over-flavoring—either too much sugar or too much spice. And, above all, there has been a certain loss of solidity— of that four-squareness we associate with the great Victorians. The work of Elizabeth Jenkins (among whose earlier novels, you may remember, were *Harriet*, *The Phoenix' Nest*, *Robert and Helen*, and *Young Enthusiasts*) is at once solid in content and light in touch. As novels should be, hers are enjoyable.

This latest, *The Tortoise and the Hare*, has an at once timeless and contemporary subject—the thieving away of one woman's husband by another. In fact, the eternal triangle. Miss Jenkins, however, has given the situation a startling twist—for *here* we have no patient housewife of fading charms losing to a lovely young interloper. On the contrary: Imogen Gresham, in her middle thirties, is as lovely as ever she was—is indeed, though in silence, adored by another man. And her rival? Miss Blanche Silcox, a country neighbor, is fifty: she is (or appears to be) the typical "good sort"—downright, ungainly, good-humored, capable, and without a shred of feminine attraction. The type most men like—like, but no more.

Can one wonder that Imogen, at the outset, is nothing more than a little puzzled when she finds that the admirable Blanche is taking up more and more of Imogen's husband's time? And the husband? Evelyn Gresham, Q.C., is now at the peak of professional success, for which he pays in strain and fatigue. He is cold-natured, intellectual, fastidious, and—as a man to be married to—alarming. Separation during the war years has ended the original idyll with his young wife; and, though the Greshams are once again together, in a lovely riverside Berkshire house, Imogen is inhibited in her marriage by a slight loss of nerve, an anxious uncertainty. Nor are matters improved, from her point of view, by the standoffish scornfulness of Gavin, her and Evelyn's only son.

But that is the worst, so far—no fear of being supplanted has yet entered Imogen's gentle head. Evelyn, weary and critical, has at no time shown any wish to philander; he is courteous to but easily bored by women. How, in that case, will such a man react to a spinster's gruff but violent passion for him? Miss Silcox, it begins to appear, is not only a good sort, but a good sport—she fishes, goes racing and knows the form, drives a mighty Rolls; in which, with increasing zeal, she chauffeurs Evelyn up and down from London. (Imogen is unable to drive a car.)

She is wealthy, knows how to order a first-rate dinner, and is the mistress of an uncharming, tasteless, but supremely comfortable, well-run house—whereas Imogen, though she creates an enchanting atmosphere, is subject to aberrations as a housekeeper.

Can a woman—well into years, and of such a type as to seem in no possible sense desirable—win, and hold, a difficult man by flattery? This question has been posed in *The Tortoise and the Hare*, and answered all too convincingly. The answer is in the characters of the three persons— Imogen, Evelyn, Blanche. And, of the three, Blanche is Miss Jenkins's masterpiece: grotesque as she is, this woman is given dignity—she has been evoked for us with uncanny insight, rendered for us with consummate art. What *could* have been incredible in the situation is, by the end, not so.

The country and village setting has been beautifully drawn; and, dire though the story is, comedy is never far round the corner. The "progres-

sive" Leepers (neighbors), their neglected children, and Mrs. Leeper's siren sister, Zenobia, give outlet for Miss Jenkins's sense of absurdity—her
satirizations, like Jane Austen's, never decline into caricature.

* * *

Go Tell It on the Mountain, the first novel of a young Negro author,
James Baldwin, has already had an exciting reception in America, and
can hardly fail to leave its mark upon us. Son of a Harlem clergyman, and
himself at the age of fourteen for some time a preacher, Mr. Baldwin has
taken as his subject adolescence, plus religious experience. Genius glows
through this book, from the first page—whereon we meet the fourteen-
year-old hero Johnny in procession with the rest of his family down "sin-
ful" Lenox Avenue, on their elect Sunday way to the church called "The
Temple of the Fire Baptized."

The author is in no special sense concerned with the color question;
rather, it is the universality of his theme which gives his story its wide
appeal. Inevitably, interest must attach to this picture of a family's life in
New York's colored quarter, and to those evocations of the South which
come through in the older characters' flashback memories. For experience is not confined to the youthful Johnny: his father Gabriel, his aunt
Florence, his mother Elizabeth all, in the course of the Sunday service,
relive their lives in the form of anguishing prayer.

Something Old Testament-like, dire, and majestic inhabits these persons turning from doom to God: never blacker has loomed up the sense
of sin. Like fire, ecstasy sweeps through the ranks of worshipers: at the
core of the story, throughout, something stays sane and true.

I note one American critic says: "It is a cliché to say that a first novel
shows promise. But what does one say when a first novel is a fulfillment?"

Sir Compton Mackenzie, *Echoes*, May 12, 1954

The art of the broadcast, what does it take? Above all, of course, personality—voice, wit, "approach," intimacy, and mellowness. Individual outlook, sense of life, love of learning are blended by suppleness of mood.
These days, when so many persons go on the air, for such a variety of

reasons (when, in fact, much broadcasting is "informative" and can claim to be little more), the artist-broadcaster stands out—*he* is the man heard for his own sake; he calls the tune; he decides the subject.

He does much to refresh, in this jaded age, what should be our aural delight in language. Such is Sir Compton Mackenzie, whose *Echoes* now brings to us, in printed form, twenty-eight of the most memorable of his talks.

I take it these are unaltered scripts. One reads what was written to be heard, and it is fascinating to study how the effects are built up. For the broadcaster, always, must sound spontaneous; his aim is to evoke not only brilliantly but immediately. However subtle his subject may be, he must not risk over-subtleties: he must be direct. These pieces in *Echoes*, though they may read like essays, show the accomplishment of the speaker rather than the author—that is, they command a style of their own. Beautifully literate, they are "non-literary": they are, I think, models of what prose for the air should be—short as to sentences, vivid, concrete.

Echoes, which has a horse omnibus, together with the back view of a four-wheeler, inset upon its bright pink jacket, is well titled: echoes indeed these are. Sir Compton, for our delectation and, we may feel, his own, has captured much of the magic of the past. He conveys not only experience but its nimbus of sensation: for instance, some of his subjects are "Going to the Pantomime," "Old Omnibuses," "Old Snapshots," "Delights of Old Sweets," "The Vanished Color and Scent of London." What a deeply romantic sense of London he has! For youthful countrified readers, themselves knowing the metropolis only as a chaos of large stations, taxis, shopping, perchance a matinee with an aunt, his now long-ago novels, *Sinister Street* and *Sylvia Scarlett*, created a glinting picture with haunted depths. He is steeped in London—by now in decades of London—as few are.

Not less satisfying are the portraits in *Echoes*: Sir Edward Elgar, Ellen Terry, and Henry James (having an agonizing conversation with his housekeeper on the subject of marmalade from the Army and Navy Stores) are among them. "Royal Encounters" features a youthful confrontation with Queen Victoria, carriage brought to a halt in an otherwise unfrequented London bystreet, going on bowing and bowing to the lad who was to be Sir Compton Mackenzie, owing (he only afterwards understood) to the ceaseless activities of an air-cushion.

Also, in this same piece, we have a courtesy visit to "the Kaiser," the long-retired Wilhelm II at Doorn.

On the subject of that overall experience which is life, its value to each of us, and what it has in particular held for him, Sir Compton Mackenzie is at his wisest, his most humane, his least sentimental (which says much), and nonetheless at his most moving. Into this "Life" group fall the pieces entitled "People," "Places," "Things," "Living," "My Time of Life," and "A Week on the Way to Seventy." "When a man ceases to be curious," he says, "his life is finished." And later, he once again recommends, "Curiosity, zest, memory, a perpetual search for experience, a perpetual delight in people, books, trees, flowers, music . . . ."

Incidentally, he debunks "The Naughty Nineties."

Eudora Welty, *The Ponder Heart,* October 13, 1954

Progress fosters many excellent things—does it, however, produce genius? Countries, or parts of the world which are most enlightened, most mechanized, most cleaned-up and abreast of the new ideas seem, sometimes, lacking in the creative urge.

Whereas Spain, Wales, Ireland, the depths of provincial France—still tradition-bound, still in the shadow of the past—give out, where the arts are concerned, giants, as did, prior to 1917, the still-feudal Russia. Great Scottish writing comes from the unmodernizable fervor of Scottish temperament.

The literary output of the United States—prototype, surely, of the progressive country—may seem to give the lie to this argument. But it is a fact that, in northern America's deep South, it is the nominally "backward" state of Mississippi that has given birth to two of the most outstanding writers of our time—William Faulkner and Eudora Welty.

In the South, to judge from Miss Welty's art, there has been no impoverishment of the human air. There is a richness of idiosyncrasy, as shown in her beautiful short book, *The Ponder Heart.* Narrator of the story is Edna Earle—that is, Miss Edna Earle Ponder, proprietress of the Beulah Hotel in the small town of Clay. The predominating figure is Uncle Daniel, *her* Ponder uncle, though also contemporary. For:

"My papa was Grandpa's oldest child and Uncle Daniel was Grandpa's baby. They had him late—mighty late. They used to let him skate on the dining-room table. So that put Uncle Daniel and me pretty close together—we liked—to caught up with each other. I did pass him in the seventh grade, and hated to do it, but I was liable to have passed anybody. People told me I ought to have been the *teacher*."

Nothing lessens, however, Edna Earle's sense of respect, due to precedence by a generation: Uncle Daniel remains her marvel and pride. Nor, when he presents her with a seventeen-year-old aunt-by-marriage, Bonnie Dee Peacock, is her attitude to the bride less impeccable. This solution of Uncle Daniel's love life should have been permanent, but for a tragedy. Before that had been the infatuation for intrepid Elsie Fleming, death-riding motorcyclist at the fair, and the short-lived marriage to Miss Teacake Magee (née Sistrunk, relict of Professor Magee, killed by a train) who'd insisted on singing at her own wedding.

Uncle Daniel's noble and generous innocence soars above the norm of common humanity. So high, indeed, did it come to soar that Grandpa, "to teach him a lesson," had once consigned him, for a spell, to the Jackson city asylum. For it came to look as though, in a short time more, Uncle Daniel would have given away everything. No sooner would he meet you than he would start trying to give you something. Things Edna Earle could think of that he'd given away began with a string of hams, included two trips to Memphis, a field of white Dutch clover, innumerable fresh eggs, a pickup truck, even his own cemetery lot—but they wouldn't accept it. "He's been a general favorite all these years."

Grandpa's sudden death (a case of the Ponder heart) having removed one check upon Uncle Daniel, Edna Earle takes over the watchful role. To and fro between the Beulah Hotel (which, by the way, Uncle Daniel had given *her*) and the Ponder mansion—which, at some distance from Clay, stands alone in woods full of hoot-owls—plies this fond and ever-elated niece . . . Edna Earle is not writing the Ponder story, she is *telling* it, breathlessly and with emphasis, to a stranger who's dropped in to the deserted Beulah. How has the Beulah come to be dead-empty? The climax of the court-scene drama explains.

So we hear the whole. Any further attempt at summary could only knock the bloom off *The Ponder Heart*. For the joy and magic are in Edna Earle's vocabulary, and her way of seeing things. You'll know the Clay community—the ubiquitous Sistrunks, the Clanahans, and so on—deliriously and thoroughly by the end. Also poor little Bonnie Dee, with her batting eyelids, and her run-down tribe, the Peacocks of Polk—"Of course, Polk used to be on the road. But the road left and it didn't get up and follow, and neither did the Peacocks." A climate, an atmosphere, and, I do not hesitate to say, a civilization are forever embodied for us in *The Ponder Heart*. The Joe Krush illustrations do justice to architecture and furniture. Rare are books like this, so lovely and lively. In fact, this seems hardly a book: it's a lease of life.

Somerset Maugham, *Ten Novels and Their Authors*, November 17, 1954

Ten Novels and Their Authors, by Somerset Maugham, is, *I* find, a refreshing sweeping-away of nonsense on the subject of the novel, by a master entitled to speak out. If anything's the matter with the novel these days, it's a matter of what is the matter with the novelist—and the only thing that can be the matter with a novelist (that is, from the point of view of the public) is the inability to write quite such a good novel as he or she should. "Is the aim of the novel," Mr. Maugham asks, in his introductory chapter (rhetorically, for he well knows the answer), "to instruct or to please?" It may be because so many novelists in these days have opted for the instructive side—or, at any rate, are eager to diagnose what appear to be the evils of our age—that the poor thing seems to be putting up such a joyless show, or that so many critics proclaim its funeral.

Mr. Maugham knows that if a novel does not please—that is, if, however tragic its theme, it does not still produce within the reader a sensation that is in the main agreeable—it has failed. On page 12, he puts his cards on the table—saying outright what are the qualities which, in his view, a good novel should have. This chapter, entitled "The Art of Fiction," should be read not only by those who hope to write but by those who hope to enjoy themselves when they read.

The ten novels selected here for discussion comply, each in its own way, with what has been set down. They all, also, come under the heading

of "the world's great novels": in fact, they are classics. Four are English —
Tom Jones, Pride and Prejudice, David Copperfield, Wuthering Heights.
Three are French — *Le Rouge et le noir, Le Père Goriot, Madame Bovary.*
Two are Russian — *The Brothers Karamazov* and *War and Peace.* One is
American — *Moby-Dick.* These are, as you will recognize, all famous;
around each one, libraryfuls of criticism have gathered. Mr. Maugham's
book is a stimulating — though also alarming — innovation: in each case,
with the novel he links its author. And for those who regard "great" authors as occupying a Valhalla of their own, he may be found somewhat
iconoclastic.

For the effect is that he leaves these ten authors — that is, as human
beings — hardly a foot to stand on. Henry Fielding and Balzac (I'm glad
to say) come out of it best. But the other eight unfortunates stay on view
as snobs, neurotics, personal exhibitionists, would-be but unsuccessful
amorists, psychological "queers," egotist cranks. Mr. Maugham is not
really being so cruel as I may make him sound: all he points out is in support of his argument (or, at any rate, so I read it) that (a) a great novel is a
sort of leveling-up with life on the part of an otherwise subsidiary human
being; and that (b) the novel actually profits by, and draws strength from,
its author's inherent malformities and weaknesses.

The effect on me of *Ten Novels and Their Authors* is that I cannot wait
to read these ten novels again — but also that I never again wish to meet a
novelist — that is, with the exception of Mr. Maugham!

C. V. Wedgwood, *The King's Peace,*
February 9, 1955

To relate history — that is, to tell the story — is only part of the work of
the historian. What we look for is not merely a series of events but their
causes, outcome, and, above all, meaning. It *is* always possible to place
an arbitrary modern interpretation upon the past, or make it seem to illustrate some theory. But this may be, and too easily is, done at the cost
of falsifying it. Surely it must be better when there is a showing of events
in the light which they had in their own day — while, also, they are made
clear to us in ours?

If we are to enter into the spirit of a time, we must know its conditions and way of life. We should be able to form at least some idea as to how like, and again how unlike, it was to our own. In that sense, not the slightest practical detail is irrelevant. And it is by means of detail that C. V. Wedgwood builds up her picture (a living picture) of seventeenth-century Britain and Ireland in the impressive opening chapter of *The King's Peace*. This was the realm over which Charles I reigned—and reigned, for years, in apparent sunshine. He believed himself to be "the happiest King in Christendom." And indeed, said as much, in June 1637, to his less fortunate nephew the elector palatine.

The King's Peace is the first volume of what is to be Miss Wedgwood's comprehensive study of the Great Rebellion. This opening, itself so well proportioned, makes us confident as to the architecture of the whole—its scale, its scope, its scrupulous balance. For in her account of these four years, 1637–41, Miss Wedgwood brings us to the eve of the Civil War. She shows us a prosperous kingdom, a smiling surface; yet, nonetheless, four years more intensely critical than any one person living within them knew.

There was, as yet, no foregone conclusion; only by degrees did there emerge the issues which were to be at stake. The situation developing to crisis might yet have been saved. Miss Wedgwood's picture of Charles I shows us a man by no means rushing headlong upon his own doom but, rather, advancing upon it by a series of slow, considered, dignified, and misguided steps.

Austere ideals, no less than shining illusions, motivated the unfortunate king. His obstinacies, if sometimes petty, were often noble. His people, law-loving and for long content, neither envisaged nor desired "an upturning." Shyness, formality, unapproachability made Charles less loved that he might have been: all the same, monarchy rated high. The king's sacerdotal idea of his own position need not, it seems, necessarily have led to conflict: what mattered more was his inability to act upon sound advice (Strafford's), his readiness to be ill-advised, and, sometimes, his inability to act at all. In his blindnesses, his hesitations, and his rashnesses, one sees what at this distance of time appears to be the inexorable workings of a fatality.

One only too simple, radical cause of trouble was, from the outset, shortness of money. Charles governed for years without the parliament which could have raised funds by constitutional means. What could have been reasonable levies came to be, only too soon, extortions; and worse, the hope of loans from abroad led the king into European entanglements which were not well seen.

He was accounted lukewarm in his support of the Protestant cause abroad, and over-tolerant to Roman Catholics at home—the plight of his sister, Elizabeth of Bohemia, and her son the elector palatine (now living as refugees at the Dutch court) was, it was considered, a reproach to him. Miss Wedgwood emphasizes the immense part played by religion, in that day, in external affairs: it seems clear that the king's weakness in foreign policy (if, indeed, he had one at all) roused as much feeling against him as his blunders in government. To the greater part of Britain the Reformation, still so recent, remained a burning reality.

Would Archbishop Laud, the High Churchman, and Strafford, with his uncompromising vision and fearless will, have carried the day for Charles, but for Charles himself? These two indomitables were stronger than the king they served. The revolt of the Covenanters not only led to the king's ignominious wars against Scotland, it was quick to arouse an echo in England. And over the challenged, uneasy people hung the threat of the army raised by Strafford in Ireland—ready, one heard, to strike on the king's behalf. *Could* Charles, ultimately, have saved Strafford? The tragedy of the stern man's fall, as recounted here, is intensely moving. Miss Wedgwood says: "The wasted life of Strafford, more even than his wasted death, is a reproach to the memory of King Charles I."

On a book of the magnitude of *The King's Peace*, your reviewer can offer but few remarks: it merits far more thorough discussion. Miss Wedgwood has the art, one might say genius, of bringing long-ago characters to life. Deep in her comprehension of the human enigma, she can also deal in small, smiling, intimate touches . . . This Civil War period has, as a subject, for a long time suffered from over-popularity: fiction has loved it less wisely than well. One can hardly say it has been overdramatized; for, as Miss Wedgwood shows us, it *was* dramatic—it has, more, been dramatized wrongly. Partisans still gather hotly to either side.

As Miss Wedgwood puts it: "The idealization of certain figures in the Civil War has led, later, to exaggerated condemnations . . . . Human values can be fairly assessed only if an honest effort is made to understand the difficulties and prejudices of each of the people concerned." *The King's Peace* aids us in this direction.

The writing, beautiful in being clear, has, too, a grace and energy of its own. It is contemporary writing—yet one is reminded that Miss Wedgwood's frequentation of the seventeenth century has comprehended, also, its literature. Her own style carries the imprint of a time when the English language was at its purest.

Ivy Compton-Burnett, *Mother and Son,* February 16, 1955

Mother and Son is the new I. Compton-Burnett novel. This fascinating and altogether unique novelist—one of our greatest—gains more readers with everything that she writes: she is at once formidable and (if one may use the expression without vulgarity) spellbinding. As I have before remarked in these pages, one must not look to Miss Compton-Burnett for what might be called superficial realism—her children (in this case Francis, Alice, and Adrian) speak, for instance, with the sagacity and irony of particularly grown-up grown-ups, and servants (in this case Bates, the parlor maid) command the exact diction of ideal prime ministers. But her inner realism, her penetration into human psychology, is so startling as to make one catch one's breath.

Like her other stories, *Mother and Son* is written largely in dialogue. And, again, we are in the secure late-Victorian world, in which coal fires blaze, expeditions to lunch with neighbors involve train journeys along a branch line (with, of course, a carriage at either end), and it is unconventional for a lady to walk alone along a tree-shaded road at dusk. Rosebery Hume, in stepping forward to escort his mother's rejected companion to the railway station, does hardly more than is correct.

Miss Burke, applicant for the post, has unhappily failed to correspond with Mrs. Hume's notion of a companion. Having been interviewed in the presence of Mrs. Hume's son, husband, and husband's nephews and niece, she is not, understandably, at her best. Being given her tea by Bates in the next room she, however, hears of another post in the neighborhood: two ladies desire a working housekeeper. When next we encounter Miss Burke, she is ensconced with Miss Greatheart, Miss Wolsey, and their cat Plautus. Is dim Miss Burke the nigger in the woodpile?[1] For she extrudes (or so at least it appears) handsome and hitherto idle Hester

Wolsey—who, now compelled to earn *her* bread, becomes companion to Mrs. Hume.

So we have two groupings, two households—the Humes' and (some stations away down the local line) Miss Emma Greatheart's. Not a feminine character in the story—with, perhaps, the exception of the twelve-year-old Alice—is not, let me say at the outset, distinctly sinister. We confront an all-in battle for power, which is given a new turn by the hitherto dominant Mrs. Hume's demise. What is Hester Wolsey up to, over there at the Humes'? She has begun by driving a wedge, or trying to, between the middle-aged celibate Rosebery and his mother. Is she not now, since Miranda Hume's death, setting her cap at the widower Julius?

I should doubt whether it has ever been necessary for Miss Compton-Burnett to read Freud: her own view of parental relationships should suffice her. Rosebery (devastatingly known to his trio of young friends as "Rosebud") is a pampered egotist rather than a casualty. Though coldly, it must be admitted, the wind does blow on him when his mother's protective presence is removed. And to crown all, the past gives up two dark secrets regarding parentage . . .

Mother and Son has a plot which continues to develop with every page. It is a comedy written with the relentlessness of tragedy—and, personally speaking, each phrase in it gave me intense delight. I should add that one of the most operative characters is a non-speaker, the cat Plautus. To those of you who regard cats either with unwilling love or with respectful hatred, I commend (even apart from its other glories) *Mother and Son*.

Joyce Cary, *Not Honour More*, April 20, 1955

Joyce Cary's new novel, *Not Honour More*, concludes the Nimmo trilogy—the two others being *Prisoner of Grace* and *Except the Lord*. This time, we are to have Chester Nimmo, revivalist Liberal politician, seen through eyes which are charged with hate—Captain Jim Latter's. This is the man who was Nina Nimmo's first love, and who now, since her divorce, is her second husband. For some years, the Latters' marriage has been idyllic: a Devonshire cottage is its scene. But this dream of security, this balm of longings at last fulfilled, has ended. Lord Nimmo, the dastard, has reappeared.

Jim Latter tells the terrible story. And it is told with the extreme dryness and curtness of a statement. "Statement," in the police sense, in fact, it is. Captain Latter is writing under arrest, expecting, indeed desiring, the end in store for him. It is a part of Mr. Cary's genius that he has caused so much fire, so much emotion, and, above all, such blazing spiritual wrath to come through the apparently deadpan words. This is the language of the soul of a man—a man who could have forgiven (for love's sake) a wound to his own good name, but who feels that his country, England, has been betrayed.

Not Honour More is, like its predecessors, a political novel. The time is that of the 1926 General Strike—Tarbiton, the teeming West Country city on whose outskirts Palm Cottage stands, is presumably Plymouth. Around the docks, the factories, and the warehouses, infinite possibilities of danger are in the air, and both Communists and Fascists are exploiting them. Jim Latter, late Captain 21st Hussars and District Officer Nigerian Political Service, retired, is in the emergency a "Special," desperately trying to play an honest man's part, and to steer a course between two evil extremes. In his view, Lord Nimmo, moving in on Tarbiton in a blaze of publicity to campaign for settlement, is the arch-wrecker.

The straight-minded soldier's predicament is a hard one. For Nimmo, as all the world can see, has by no means finished with Nina, nor she with him—what are the two up to, at Palm Cottage? Finding the terrible old man with the old woman who is now his (Latter's) adored wife, Latter lets off a gun at him. So begins the story.

How far political detestation is colored by sexual jealousy, our hero (and he *is* a hero) must ask himself. Behind all his acts and decisions is a searching of his conscience. To Latter, democracy is a racket—and Nimmo's loud-mouthed democracy most of all so. He suspects conspiracy; and towards the end the depths of a vile conspiracy are laid bare. That, at last, is enough for Latter: he must avenge.

Mr. Cary is probably wider in scope and range than any other novelist writing now. He is exceptional in his power to bridge the gap between private feeling and public action. The strike scenes in *Not Honour More* are, for instance, concrete and memorable; at the same time, he is able to penetrate into the most shadowy interstices of character. Within his people, the battle of good and evil is never a straight flight. He is a wonderfully bold dealer in inconsistencies.

The woman Nina, one might say, is dementingly inconsistent—yet one believes in her. She is extraordinary; Nimmo (as the two previous novels had room to show) is almost shockingly extraordinary, and Latter himself in the end is driven to an extraordinary, as well as a dire act. Yet none of Mr. Cary's novels are ever bizarre: they convey to the reader what he must feel himself: an awe of humanity—of the heights to which it can sometimes rise, of the lengths to which it must sometimes go.

Anthony Powell, *The Acceptance World*, June 1, 1955

To embark on a novel sequence requires more—that is, of the author—than to write a novel which finishes with its final page. The extended design offers greater scope; but he must be sure that it *is* a large design. He must take a long-term view of his characters, whose fortunes are to be followed through chance and change for, it may be, any number of years. And the characters must be interesting in themselves, so that the reader is glad when they reappear.

Happily, Anthony Powell has what is needed. *The Acceptance World* now comes to us, being the third volume in the sequence he has called *A Dance to the Music of Time*. It links up perfectly with its predecessors, *A Question of Upbringing* and *A Buyer's Market*. In its own right, I am not sure that it is not the most excellent of the three—but this may be because its dramas and ironies are enhanced by our knowing what went before them.

One or two new persons are introduced—Mrs. Erdleigh, for instance, comes gliding into Uncle Giles's tea party in Bayswater, Quiggin beetles into the Ritz in his leather coat—but mostly we meet a number of former friends whose peculiarities continue to absorb us. These peculiarities (with the exception of Uncle Giles's) lie, in several cases, some way under the skin: Mr. Powell's people are "interesting" thanks to *his* way of seeing—outwardly, some could be called conventional, and a lesser novelist might have passed them by. Some are social, some are artistic, some are political. They are representative denizens of the London world of 1931–32, the period of the "great depression."

Jenkins, the narrator, and his contemporaries are by now in their middle or later twenties. He, with his Eton friends Templer and Stringham, and the ever-egregious Widmerpool (memorable since *A Question of Upbringing*), are in a mood for taking life as it comes: early experimentalism is past. Templer's half-hearted marriage collapses before our eyes; Stringham's already has been a failure. Jenkins meets again, by chance, Templer's sister Jean, and the two fall in love and have an affair—whose emotional climate and tensions are brilliantly pictured. Communism (though still in its prewar form) is represented by two self-seeking bores.

The Walpole-Wilsons—whose debutante dinner party we attended early on in *A Buyer's Market*—are, alas, offstage in *The Acceptance World*; so is Sir Magnus Donners. Intrigue, this time, centers around St. John Clarke, a respectable aging novelist anxious to keep abreast with aesthetic trends and wavering conscientiously to the Left. Mrs. Andriadis (siren of *A Buyer's Market*) has fallen under the influence of austere Herr Guggenbühl . . .

All these goings-on are related by Mr. Powell with a calm lucidity which does not lessen their phantasmagoric oddness—we have here, in fact, a foremost master of comedy. Above all, however, the fascination of this sequence of novels consists in the unfolding of the main pattern: this *is* how lives are lived—partly shiftlessly, partly in subjection to some fatality, partly in a series of forward spurts owing to energy, enterprise, or passion.

It may be found that, in order to keep his people together, Mr. Powell stretches the arms of coincidence rather far. His characters seem to be magnetized, quite by chance, to the same spots. But look at one's own experience—this does happen!

Evelyn Waugh, *Officers and Gentlemen*, July 6, 1955

The new Evelyn Waugh novel, *Officers and Gentlemen*, is a continuation of *Men at Arms*. Further, it rounds off—or, as the author tells us, completes—its predecessor. "I thought at first," he says, "that the story would run into three volumes. I find that two will do the trick. If I keep my faculties I hope to follow the fortunes of the characters through the whole of their war, but these two books constitute a whole."

Officers and Gentlemen is a Waugh novel rather than war novel. (The author's surname makes unavoidable what I hope will not be seen as a pert pun: I risk that for the sake of the statement.) The bite and quality of his mind, the fundamental charity of his judgments, and the dynamic energy he can inject into a story have seldom been more in evidence.

Whatever their fortunes, his characters remain themselves — incised with an extreme clearness. Much of the action in which they are involved is in the nature of a phantasmagoric dream; the personalities of those taking part remain distinct from it — whereas in the average war novel the theme itself tends to submerge all else.

Finally, *Officers and Gentlemen* is a comedy — a comedy which incorporates what is tragic without a jar to feeling or flaw in taste. I am certain that no writer other than Evelyn Waugh could have brought this off.

This is a savage satire, but at the expense of situations rather than of persons. As a criticism of the conduct of some parts of World War II, *Officers and Gentlemen* gains by the almost devastating lightness of its manner and the lightheartedness of some contrasting episodes. Throughout the story there is a liability to be struck by mirth, and successive pages are unbearably funny. But also there is — as in all the latest and I think finest novels of Mr. Waugh — a vehement, often-angered romanticism. He shows us the abuse and rendering-down of heroism by the negative forces of sheer muddle. One of his characters cracks outright.

Largely, we are this time with the Commandos — in training on the Scottish Isle of Mugg, in waiting at Alexandria, and landed too late for action on Crete. Guy Crouchback, recalled from Africa "under a cloud" (for the reason, turn back to *Men at Arms*), finds little in London except the blitz and low tempo at the Halberdier barracks.

An order to report at Hazardous Offensive Operations Headquarters opens a further chapter — temporary attachment for training purposes X Commando.

"Report to Colonel Blackhouse at Mugg."
"Tommy Blackhouse?"
"Friend of yours?"

"Yes. He married my wife."

"Did he? *Did* he? I thought he was a bachelor."

"He is, now."

Virginia, now Mrs. Troy, is to be landed with the inimitable Trimmer—met, in an idle mood, in a fog in Glasgow. Resourceful in war as he is lucky in love, Trimmer simultaneously McTavish—under which name he blazes into the headlines: just the hero wanted for propaganda.

Another of our former friends, Ritchie Hook, remains dramatically off-scene, for reasons beyond his control, during the greater part of *Officers and Gentlemen*. And no one character in this book has quite the magnitude of Apthorpe, unforgotten by Guy.

We gain, however, in Colonel Trotter ("Jumbo"), Major Hound, and the cryptic Ludovic. And there is the adorable Julia Stitch . . . The dialogue in this novel is Mr. Waugh's at his most superb: perfect. But the masterpiece is the Crete end. We have no more formidable novelist than this.

Ithell Colquhoun, *The Crying of the Wind*, August 24, 1955

The Crying of the Wind, by Ithell Colquhoun, is a travel book—subject, Ireland. The author's approach is personal: on the whole she followed her own way, and she has given us her impressions of it. As to these, she has a ready and often very beguiling pen: her book indeed may serve as a sort of guide to sensations which those arriving in Ireland may hope to share. I do not doubt that many may be tempted to follow the trail blazed by Miss Colquhoun. She is a painter and, I understand, a poet. To Irish landscapes and cloudscapes she brings a painter's eye, writing particularly beautifully about skies, twilights, river valleys, sea-frayed coasts, and the intensive atmosphere of remote places. To my mind, she is handicapped only in one way—by an aptness to swallow all she was told.

Ireland is subject to visitors with a pronounced pro-romantic slant, and Miss Colquhoun, by all evidence, has been one of them. Ireland, particularly the West, can be relied upon to lay on moods which cheat not a single expectation. At the same time, the country has a humdrum quality—lately, a sort of naive up-and-comingness—which romantic travelers either exclude from vision or refuse to digest. The ideal travel book would, possibly, take in everything—but with regard to Ireland it has yet to be written. True, domestic realities did obtrude upon Miss Colquhoun, and in a disturbing form: in almost every bedroom she occupied she found herself next door to noisy plumbing. So proud are we Irish to have plumbing at all, and of so recent a date is its introduction, that we do not mind its announcing itself, however stridently. For a visitor, however, this may be trying.

Such an honest book, in intention, is *The Crying of the Wind* that one could wish its author to have been more armored, by nature and temperament, against tall stories. She stayed mainly either as a paying guest in country houses, or in homes which had gone a degree further and made themselves over into guesthouses—in such, it is the custom to give full value by regaling guests with high romance over the tea and cakes. An ideal listener must have been Miss Colquhoun: in consequence, her version of Irish country-house life dates back to Miss Edgeworth or Sir Jonah Barrington—rats cavorting around amid chipped Crown Derby, and high sea tides sweeping in at drawing-room windows. (I do know one house in which this was liable to happen, but the ground floor is now fitted with iron shutters.)

The off-the-map parts of the travels are delightful—no hitches hold up Miss Colquhoun, who always gets where she wants *somehow*. She's good on the archeological angle also. Legend and lore appeal to her, and she has sifted out the fairy mythology fairly thoroughly. On the horse world she did not choose to impact. Immunity to religion kept her apart from Ireland's realities on Sundays: our country is, she mildly complains, no place for "a cozy old agnostic"—in fact, as church-time approached she found herself forced to take to the woods. Her remark on Maynooth might, I thought, have been spared. Ireland's main defects, from the visual point of view—mean architecture (apart from Georgian building) and the tendency of plantations of conifers to fur up formerly clean skylines— seem, oddly enough, to have passed her by.

Homesick for the days of the Irish Literary Renaissance, our visitor made do with Dublin-today bohemia. She took part in a tremendous romp in Ballsbridge. Speaking of the popularity the Somerville and Ross stories "once enjoyed," she seems unaware of their vigorous renewed vogue. Her remarks on weather may not ring true to those who know Ireland over a term of years—snow is *not* frequent: in general, our winters are moist and "soft," with pink mountains and brilliantly green moss. Her final chapter, "The Municipal Gallery Visited," is disfigured by sayings which I am certain she must regret: the ladies in question, dead lately, are still well-loved. To straightforward criticism of *art*, Miss Colquhoun is, on the other hand, well entitled—her own black-and-white drawings illustrate *The Crying of the Wind*, and should please all.

John Wyndham, *The Chrysalids*, September 28, 1955

The Chrysalids, by John Wyndham, takes its place in its publisher's series, "Novels of Tomorrow"—to which, I gather, this author's previous books, *The Day of the Triffids* and *The Kraken Wakes*, already belong.

All novels about the future—or, to be more exact, set in the future— seem bound to be either uncomfortable or utopian. Since the time of the earlier, scientifically optimistic H. G. Wells, we have been given far, far fewer utopias. Nightmares, at their extreme devised by the late George Orwell or by Aldous Huxley, have come to be more the thing for fireside reading. Mr. Wyndham is not a nightmare-monger, though I myself do not find him exactly comforting.

He is, from the evidence, American; he depicts civilization, some 2,000 years hence, as being about on a par with that of the earliest settlements in New England, or, alternatively, with that of the newly opened- up Middle West of the pioneer days. The community he describes lives in Labrador, whose climate has changed: this, now, makes good farming country.

Living conditions themselves are not too primitive, but ideas are. Rule is authoritarian; religion, so far as one can see, exists to promote and sponsor a form of witch-hunting. This handful of people, crouched in a cleared space, are maniacs on the subject of race purity and for this reason: in the surrounding zones, known as the Fringes, dwell deformed monsters, travesties of humanity. So the original orthodox human mold *must* be preserved: if not, it may be lost forever. Freaks, of any kind, meet no mercy.

Beyond the Fringes extend the Badlands—whole areas calcinated, left lifeless, by the hydrogen bombs of by now mythical wars. Seen by ships at sea, the coasts of the Badlands, after dark, still send out a radioactive glow: sailors speak, with awe, of luminous ruins . . .

The hero of *The Chrysalids* is a boy, David Strorm, who tells the story. He's a pleasant, natural, ordinary lad—only dimly interested in the lost past. Trouble breaks out, however, when David makes a playfellow of a little girl called Sophie, who turns out to have six toes. The poor child is, thus, a "deviant," or a "mutant"—against whom the ruthless extermination laws of the community may operate. Finally *The Chrysalids* becomes an exciting escape story.

This is a complex, not at all cozy book, perhaps somewhat overcharged with imagination. It ends on a more cheerful, utopian note. I recommend *The Chrysalids* to thoughtful readers.

François Mauriac, *The Lamb*, October 19, 1955

"Unrivalled by any living novelist in any country" has been an outstanding English critic's verdict on François Mauriac—winner of the Nobel Prize for Literature in 1952. Such an award means that a man's work transcends national boundaries. And it might, indeed, be found that this writer's genius is not wholly typical of his country, France. His books are less cerebral, more fundamental, and more impassioned than is most notable in French fiction. And their subject has universality: the soul. Of this M. Mauriac's latest novel, *The Lamb*, could hardly give a clearer example.

All Mauriac characters are lifelike, completely convincing, yet outsize. Their emotions and sufferings are on a giant scale. And the creations of this great Catholic master are formidable in their recognition of evil—or, sometimes, in their display of evil.

In *The Lamb* our central figure, Xavier Dartilongue, is a young man in a state of intense conflict, at once spiritual and human. He is on the verge of entering the priesthood. He takes a night train from Bordeaux (his native city) to Paris, where a seminary awaits him. On the train, however, takes place an encounter which is to deflect him from his immediate purpose and plunge him into a maelstrom of other claims.

Jean de Mirbel, a landowner from the forest-muffled country around Bordeaux, is Xavier's fatal traveling companion. Jean (already met in another Mauriac novel) is now, in early middle age, turbulent, difficult, and peremptory. Through the carriage window, while the train was still in Bordeaux station, Xavier had looked on at the goodbye between de Mirbel and a young woman—who is, it transpires, Michèle his wife. Xavier cannot rid himself of the idea that these two are at a crisis of their destinies. And during the talk on the journey, Jean lets fall that he intends on leaving Michèle forever.

That train conversation, alone in the carriage, surrounded by the rushing darkness of midnight, is a masterpiece such as only M. Mauriac could bring off. For in its course, something fantastic happens. Jean strikes a bargain with Xavier. If the young man will consent to abandon the Paris seminary and return with him (Jean) by the next train to Bordeaux, Jean will return to his wife in their country house—provided he is accompanied by Xavier.

In effect blackmail, this takes effect. For Jean trades upon Xavier's deep conviction that one is responsible, under God, for the fate of one's fellow human beings. In that view, there is no such thing as a "chance" meeting. And, once having met a person, one cannot part—one is involved forever in their destinies, one may even be, in however humble a way, the instrument of their salvation or damnation. Xavier's first duty (it comes to seem to him) is to save the marriage of the de Mirbels. Tormented and innocent, the young man—who is indeed the victim "lamb" of the story—consents to come, at the bidding of Jean de Mirbel, to Larjuzon, the lonely country house, perfect stage for the drama to follow.

Larjuzon is one of those estates whose atmosphere M. Mauriac renders so overpoweringly. Michèle de Mirbel is not alone here: with her are her stepmother, Brigitte Pian (central character in A *Woman of the Pharisees*), Mme. Pian's girl secretary, Dominique, and Roland—a miserable small boy who, adopted by the de Mirbels as an experiment, is on the point of being packed back again to a public orphanage. From now on the action of the story (which a few days brings to its violent end) is to concern itself with the effect of all these people on Xavier, and his effect on them.

Through every page runs an austere beauty and pity—there are the love scenes between Xavier and Dominique, his confrontations with the terrible Brigitte Pian, his unavailing solicitude for Michèle, and his attempts to succor the little boy. (Roland is, after Xavier himself, the most moving and haunting character in *The Lamb*.) Here's a novel which sweeps one into depths of experience such as one seldom braves and may little know. The rendering into English is the work of that master translator Gerard Hopkins.

Graham Greene, *The Quiet American*, December 28, 1955

Graham Greene's new novel, *The Quiet American*, is set in French Indo-china, during the fighting; most of the action centers around Saigon — city of danger, tense with intrigue and rumors, now and then paralyzed by explosions. Here are gathered the news-hawks; and Thomas Fowler, an old hand, British war correspondent, is as tough as his American opposite numbers. Fowler it is who narrates the story—and, give him his due, like him or not, seldom has story been better told. Here, indeed, is a brilliantly savage masterpiece.

At home and abroad, no novelist's reputation today is higher than Graham Greene's, and this book shows why. Here is a perfect case of objective trouble complicated by inner subjective twists. The superbly mechanized plot interknits outer and inner conflicts. At the same time, everything happens so close up that the reader becomes a magnetized looker-on, unable for a moment to turn away. The Saigon situation could be enough, but to this is added the grim fate and ever-ambiguous doings of Alden Pyle, the quiet American in question. The narrative opens with Pyle's death; next, we are to discover what led up to it.

Are there no lengths to which a wrong-headed idealist will not go? Pyle, from Boston, arrives in Saigon with a definite mission at heart, an impervious moral belief, and a head crammed with ideas from high-minded books (written by Americans for Americans). He personifies the well-meaning troublemaker. He has an "unmistakably young and unused face . . . . With his gangling legs and his crew-cut and his wide campus gaze, he seemed incapable of harm." Thus does Fowler first recollect the newcomer—at the start so mildly absurd, of so little interest. How, then, is it to come about that, upon the discovery of the body, Fowler is the first to be interrogated?

What is known, what is common knowledge, is that Pyle had recently taken Fowler's girl, the enchanting Annamite Phuong. The idyll, becalmed still further by opium smoking, seems to the boy from Harvard extremely shocking: he proposes to rescue Phuong from a life of shame, marry her, and bring her home to his mother, to be processed into the American Way of Life. The ingenuous project amuses Fowler, till the day when Phuong does, in fact, walk out on him.

Yet there is more than a question of love rivalry: the two men, preposterously unalike, one a skeptic, one an apparent simpleton, keep on crossing each other's paths. There is the argument in the room in the tower; there is the struggle at the edge of the marsh, when Pyle saves the unwilling Fowler's life. There is the incurable opposition, throughout, between the Old World and the New.

With the going-off of the bomb in Saigon square, crowded at midday, the crux comes. Fowler finds himself face to face with the unforgivable; from now on, there seems only one course to take. More of the story, I would not for worlds reveal. Its most startling aspect is that it *is* credible.

The Quiet American will, I fear, be considered anti-American. Is Mr. Greene unfair to good Alden Pyle, and all that he stands for? The youth is touching enough; he's magnanimous, modest, friendly; he shows courage. Yet innocence (of the wrong kind, in the wrong place) deforms him into a menacing monster. Is he, then, the victim of his own ideas? Alas, no; the cost must be met by others.

Pyle, I imagine it will be said, is not a character but a caricature; to me, I admit, he is not convincing—only the novel's genius puts him across.

Mary Lavin, *The Patriot Son*, April 11, 1956

Old Ireland, of song and romantic legend, and modern Ireland—are they leagues apart? An American lady alighting at Shannon Airport expressed a fear, with reference to the runways, that there was no place left for fairies to dance. That, we natives had not gone into. On the whole, Ireland adapts to change by the simple process of not changing. And most constant of all is national character. This, Mary Lavin captures as few can. Her new book of short stories, *The Patriot Son*, shows our ancient oddnesses in today's setting.

Short stories carry national flavor in the most concentrated form. Maupassant's could not be anything but French, Chekhov's anything but Russian, Hemingway's anything but American. Miss Lavin's are straightforwardly Irish—without a single conventional Hibernianism. Her people are neither bog peasants nor hunt followers—and she has steered clear, in *The Patriot Son*, of anything strikingly picturesque. Nonetheless, in her pictures of small-town people in the Irish Midlands (her own part) she gives us something formidable. She has great comic sense, good humor with, just often enough, bite to it. She touches on tragedy, but without too much dwelling—in "The Little Prince," tale of a banished brother, heartbreak *is* present, though it is muted. Unlike some realists, she is not depressing.

Many genial Irish small shops, I fear, conceal a Bedelia Grimes in the back parlor. This woman of iron, planning her own marriage, wrecking her sister's, packing abroad the too easygoing Tom, is as dauntless as anything Irish fiction has given us since Somerville and Ross wrote *The Real Charlotte*—true, she does not wear Charlotte's deceptive mask. Bedelia figures in "An Old Boot," "Frail Vessel," and "The Little Prince" aforesaid. In the title story, we have another example of sour caution—I could wish, incidentally, that Miss Lavin had not placed "The Patriot Son" first: it is her only story about "the Troubles," but it could give the impression that all the others are to share that theme. They have better-found ones.

Most charming, and indeed I think a masterpiece, is "Chamois Gloves": we live through the day on which three young postulants take their first vows. "A beautifully fine day, thank God!" There is bustle everywhere—and what of the three concerned? We enter the mind of Veronica—left, at the end, with her sister's forgotten gloves, last symbol of a girlhood in common. This is a lyrical, tender story, with more than one family comedy in the convent parlor. Hardly less touching is "Limbo," in which a small girl, back from the ends of the earth, is cheated, by her parent's choice of Ireland, of the English schooldays she'd pictured, hoped to enjoy. Poor little Naida, of the blonde plaits, sole and conspicuous Protestant in the classroom!

Another high point in *The Patriot Son* is "A Tragedy": a tale of young married life overshadowed by a third person. The title has, subtly, a dual meaning; for the return of unwanted Sis from visits away coincides with news of the crash of an Irish airliner. Town and village are humming with morbid rumors as Tom and Mary drive through the night to collect Sis from her long-distance bus. Mary's widowed sister, Sis, *must* be given a home: her chatter, her flighty silliness, her self-pity are driving Tom crazy with irritation.

Across the sea, in the Welfare State, this same Sis, young and perfectly able-bodied, would have been pitched out to find a job for herself—in Ireland, family pieties are stronger, and pity goes to lengths almost pathological. Which *is* right? "A tragedy" contains, in its few pages, more irony than goes to many a novel.

Twelve pieces, in all, make up *The Patriot Son*. Even if Ireland, in principle, leaves you cold, you can hardly fail to react to these twelve as *stories*. And let not the mouse wedged in the teapot spout put you off either mice or tea!

Rose Macaulay, *The Towers of Trebizond*, September 12, 1956

Rose Macaulay's latest (and possibly greatest) novel is *The Towers of Trebizond*. It is also her first since *The World My Wilderness*, published in 1950. Miss Macaulay is one of the few writers of whom it may be said, she adorns our century, bringing to it high qualities—style, wit, laughter, and learning—which on the whole we connect with happier times. Civilization, her work reminds us, is *not* over. The reissue, this season, of her *Potterism*, written in 1920, is well inspired—fresh, applicable as though it were written today, that early masterpiece merits renewed life. Miss Macaulay has dazzled more than one generation. And, better still, she has caused more than one generation to sit up.

No writer above a level can be classified. Terms such as "satirist" or "romanticist" seem, in this case, to be either misfits or so inadequate as to be misleading. Each novel coming from Rose Macaulay has shown more than one facet of her diverse genius: *The Towers of Trebizond* unites and gives play to them all. This is a novel in which travel plays a great part—travel indeed is a passion with the characters. Yet the narrator Laurie and her Aunt Dot are not submerged by the landscapes in which they find themselves.

Large in the cast looms a camel, of such a kind as to have stolen any story other than this. Religion is a theme; but, great as it is, it is not allowed to outweigh or displace others. And, in the same sense, the historic past does not wither the living moment. The love story gains in depth and force by being touched upon rather than fully told. And over much of the tale shimmers lovely comedy.

The scene, throughout the greater part of *The Towers of Trebizond*, is Turkey. Hither have come Aunt Dot, her niece (in the role of illustrator for a proposed book), the High Anglican Father Chantry-Pigg, and Dot's white camel, which is to be used for transport. This party, which has impressed into its ranks a Turkish woman doctor, Halide, is a self-constituted mission—object, the conversion of Turkish women to Anglican Christianity. There are, however, diversions along the way, some caused by the temperament of the camel, some by that of Father Chantry-Pigg, who is zealous rather than diplomatic. And Doctor Halide—who, back again in her homeland, proves less progressive than she had seemed in London—is also a brake upon activities: a somewhat touchy patriotism grips her.

To attempt to convey the dotty and noble charm of this escapade—or should one call it crusade?—would on a reviewer's part be a bad error. You *must* read, to see how Miss Macaulay has done it. And no less absorbing are the travels themselves, the scenes, the encounters, and the adventures. This novelist, without meaning to, will I fear put innumerable "straight" travel writers quite out of business. *The Towers of Trebizond* is, among other things, an enchanting skit on the present popularity of travel books.

> "How everyone gets about," said Aunt Dot. "I wonder who else is rambling about Turkey this spring. Seventh Day Adventists, Billy Grahamites, writers, diggers, photographers, spies, us, and now the BBC. We shall all be tumbling over each other. Abroad isn't at all what it was."

Dot's eye has been unavowedly fixed on Russia—if not for the reasons mostly ascribed in these days—and theological enterprise makes Father Chantry-Pigg her secret ally. The two, accordingly, slip through the Iron Curtain (with no more trouble, apparently, than if it were a bead curtain), leaving Laurie landed with the camel and a more than ticklish series of explanations. Asia Minor is now to offer the scene for Laurie's meeting with her cousin Vere, and for total happiness. Later Syria, then the Holy Land, enter the story; then there is London, and a lovers' Venice, before the heartbreaking end.

One can speak of *The Towers of Trebizond* almost endlessly, without touching—is a reviewer shy?—on this novel's poetry, humanity, spiritual import, intellect, and above all emotion. Trebizond, with its vanished, compelling towers, is the symbol on which everything turns—the center. Delicious as are the frivolities, nothing in this book is out of scale with the majestic conception.

François Mauriac, *Lines of Life,* January 23, 1957

An early work of France's majestic novelist, François Mauriac, *Lines of Life* is now published by Eyre and Spottiswoode. *Destins* was the title he gave it; the English version comes from Mauriac's gifted translator, Gerard Hopkins. Set, like most of this master's work, in the Garonne country, this moving, dramatic, and dire story deals with a château family and their village neighbors. The month is September, on the eve of the vintage. At Viridis, among the blue-sprayed vines, rules widowed Elizabeth Gornac, with, in the background, her austere father-in-law. Her one son, Pierre, a difficult young fanatic, goes and comes.

Only nominal is the bond between son and mother. The real disturber of Mme. Gornac's peace is Bob Lagave, a youth of more charm than is good for anyone—including, tragically, himself. In Paris, where he lives with his self-made father, Bob has thrown off all trace of his village origin—in his grandmother's Viridis cottage he feels a stranger. Here, when the story opens, he is staying, to recuperate after a nearly fatal attack of pleurisy brought on by one of his typical escapades. It is natural that the boy should drift to the château, for "only in Elizabeth's company could Bob breathe freely in this out of the way spot. The poisonous atmosphere of adoration which his Paris friends had provided had become more necessary to him than he knew."

But in that Paris "poisonous atmosphere," *what* exactly had happened? Paula de la Sesque, a young girl frankly in love, follows Bob to Viridis.

Late at night, the two announce their engagement. Naively, Mme. de Gornac acquaints her son Pierre (who has made a sudden return) with what she believes to be innocent, charming news. Pierre's reaction and the action he takes are terrible—Bob, he hints, is fit to be no girl's husband. Finally, challenged by Paula, he tells her why. To us (that is, the readers) the nature of the charges is not revealed. We may exercise our speculation as we will.

The most acute drama of *Lines of Life* takes place within Elizabeth Gornac—one of those middle-aged women M. Mauriac draws with, alternately, pitilessness and pity. Paula's horrified flight after Pierre's disclosure leaves Mme. Gornac alone with Bob, prey to feelings she dare not understand. And what of Pierre, would-be priest and tormented character? The story's climax is to lay bare *his* soul . . . François Mauriac is an unsparing novelist; yet somehow he gives humanity full proportion. You should not by any means miss this fine, if imperfect, example of his art.

Rebecca West, *The Fountain Overflows*, February 6, 1957

A springlike excitement in midwinter should be created by *The Fountain Overflows*. For this major novel is by Rebecca West—her return to fiction after twenty-one years. Since *The Thinking Reed*, published in 1936, she has been claimed, as a writer, by the astounding happenings of our "real-life" world; her *Black Lamb and Grey Falcon*, *The Meaning of Treason*, and *A Train of Powder* have been among the outstanding documentations of recent history. Had she, one began to wonder, deserted fancy for what is still more strange in the realm of fact?

Then came promising rumors to the contrary. Indeed, *The Fountain Overflows* must have been occupying its author for some time, for it is of the length its subject requires. Outwardly, this is a family story, domestic in its humors as in its drama. The period is the early 1900s, the background a southern suburb of London, the center a poverty-shadowed home. Four of the principal characters are children—one of whom, Rose Aubrey, tells the story (looking back from fifty years later on). Nor are Cordelia, Mary, Rose, and Richard the only non-adult dwellers in Lovegrove Place. Their difficult father Piers, their heroic mother Clare, live, too, in a quasi-visionary world in which grown-up conventionalities count for little.

Or count for little until the duns, in numbers, are literally at the door. Often does this happen, and each time it is the fine-strung Mrs. Aubrey who has to cope. Her husband (writer turned journalist by necessity) is as unstable as he is brilliant. Friend after friend, well-wisher after well-wisher has Piers Aubrey first let down and then insulted — one of the most long-suffering (near the end of patience) is a proprietor of a chain of suburban newspapers: in consequence Piers, fractious as a chained eagle, finds himself editor of the *Lovegrove Gazette*. For the children, reared in a climate of insecurity, the new start and new home are at least a harbor from the restless tossing of a disorganized existence.

Mr. Aubrey comes of Irish landowning stock; his wife has the other-worldliness of her Highland forefathers. Yet she it is (as has been already said) who must grapple with reality in its harsher aspects.

Again and again — as when it is found that, to pay a debt, the father has sold up the Edinburgh furniture — solid ground gives way beneath the poor woman's feet, and her children know it. Of Mrs. Aubrey herself, it is to be said that she is something greater than a great artist manqué — her career as a concert pianist having been cut short, in her girlhood, by a drastic illness, she now has invested her hopes and faith in the musical future of her daughters.

Relentless, intolerant of anything but the best, the mother is the piano teacher of Rose and Mary. The aesthetic tragicomedy of the family is, however, the eldest, very pretty Cordelia with her specious, *faux bon* playing of the violin. Miss West, as many will recall, excels in portraits of phoneyness — Cordelia has about her something of that ill-fated paragon in the short story "The Salt of the Earth."

The Aubrey children, to me, have points in common with those E. Nesbit children, whose adventures diversified my young days — they are of the same epoch, inhabit South London, and adapt themselves with the same nerve to domestic crisis, hardships, and sudden parental absences. They are lords of a universe of make-believe — the Aubrey home is alive with "made-up" animals: dogs, horses. (My love for the works of E. Nesbit is so great that I hope Miss West will not quarrel with this comparison.) And certainly, what happens to the Aubreys is, by any standards, out of the ordinary. Not only are they poor in a wealthy age (to well-bred Edwardians, poverty was among the more unmentionable facts of life), but they become involved first with a poltergeist, then with a murder trial.

How was Rose (for all her inherited Highland second sight) to know that her dull schoolfellow, Nancy Philips, whose dreary Saturday party she attended, would shortly be a refugee in the Aubrey home, with her mother charged with poisoning her father?

Yet the excitingness of *The Fountain Overflows* does not depend upon spectacular happenings; it is something generated within the story. This long, closely written book contains not a line one could bear to miss. Fundamentally, it is a novel about integrity—whether in mind or will, in the human affections, or in art. Mr. Aubrey, traitor to those who love him, shows a blazing fearlessness in defense of justice; Cordelia's pathetic success-mania shows up, by contrast, the uncompromisingness of the rest of the Aubreys . . .

It seems to me that this book, though so much a novel, is enriched by Miss West's experiences in other fields. She has sat in court through historic trials, delved into the pathology of many "cases." Here, back again to fiction, she pictures people who are neither treasonable nor perverted—we may note that, even in so doing, she raises well-nigh political questions of right and wrong.

Elizabeth Coxhead, *The Friend in Need,* April 3, 1957

Elizabeth Coxhead's novel *The Friend in Need* has a compelling subject: child welfare. The scene, London, around the Pentonville Road; the heroine, a somewhat high-handed young social worker, Isobel Fairlie. The "deprived child," and what is to be done for it under the Children's Act 1948, is Isobel's charge, care, interest, and endless problem. Under her administrative power come the little victims of broken homes, illicit unions, or parents negligent or downright criminal. With the children she shows her good heart, her instinctive sense. Adults bring her bossy side to the fore.

As child welfare officer, Isobel has the entrée into a seedy variety of homes. Her own, to which she returns in the evenings, is in a graceful though shabby Regency backwater, pitched on those northeast London heights. Her gentle father, who keeps house for her, is more perceptive than the young woman realizes. I wondered, myself, how the author really did sum up Isobel? At any rate, she does not idealize her.

The truth is, Miss Coxhead is too good a novelist to show her hand. *The Friend in Need* is something very much better than a social document given fiction form—though also, there's a good deal to learn from it. First and last, it was the character interest, plus the Pentonville scenery, which absorbed me.

John Braine, *Room at the Top*, April 10, 1957

A novel so telling as to be terrible is *Room at the Top*, by John Braine. It is also well—almost too well—written: once embarked upon it, the reader cannot break free. This is a careerist's view of himself; by the end, the "I" finds himself landed with a shocking, undesired reward. Walter, a young man at once class-conscious and aggressive, irked by his own poverty and obscurity, arrives to take up a post in a rich community—the prosperous residential outskirts of a big North Country industrial city. His own home town is seedy, "failed," and depressing; he is obsessed by the wish for a different life.

So that the ice he finds himself cutting among the *jeunesse dorée* impresses him—and, indeed, others. For Walter, for all his boldness, is nothing more than a new and minor Town Hall employee.

Sex, in the young man, is inextricably knit up with social ambition. Through the Thespians, an amateur theater company, he gets to know first Susan, alluring daughter of a powerful local magnate, then the unhappily married Alice.

Alice's reserve masks a dangerous temperament. The affair with her runs concurrently with the courtship of Susan—the formidable scenes of passion are not on the usual level of English fiction: there may be readers, indeed, who will balk at them. The Yorkshire setting, the heated provincial atmosphere are remarkably done; with Alice and her fate we have full-scale tragedy.

I don't know how old Mr. Braine may be, but certainly he has given us adult work. *Room at the Top* impressed me deeply.

Jean Cabriès, *Jacob*; Maurice Druon, *The Last Detachment*; Berthe Grimault, *Beau Clown*; and Minou Drouet, *First Poems*, April 17, 1957

French genius is many-sided. It can be practical: has it not raised dress and cookery to the plane of high art? From France emanates the idea that life is worth living well; with intelligence, style, care, attention to detail — no small pleasure need be too small to rate, no task too prosy to lack drama. But the national genius finds supreme release in the arts themselves: in painting, music, literature, the theater, and the cinema it has more than claimed its individual field; it has opened up an entire and splendid universe. So on this page one has most in mind, French writing.

One inclines to think of the French intellect as preeminently critical, analytical. But how giant is its creative side in the novel! Without those great nineteenth-century masters, Balzac, Stendhal, Flaubert, our view (through art) of humanity would be incomplete.

Technique, plus a gift for analysis — though not of the kind which thins down emotion — always has been a forte of French writing. In the twentieth-century masters, Proust, Gide, Mauriac, these qualities show their strength in a changing era. François Mauriac, by the death of the other two, is left to be France's outstanding living novelist. Yet important younger figures enter the scene: Sartre and Camus, whose Existentialist philosophy give their country's fiction fresh urge and startling direction.

Feminine performance shows itself worthy of woman's place in Gallic civilization. Colette (the unparalleled), Simone de Beauvoir, Louise de Villemorin, and the teenage prodigy Françoise Sagan are among those who bring to the French novel individual gifts — some greater, some less.

The health, vitality, and continuing promise of French fiction is shown by the constant occurrence of young, new names. Freshness of angle, originality as to subject show that though newcomers *benefit* by the great tradition, they are not by any means dwarfed or hypnotized by it: they have the confidence of their generation; they speak out. Four remarkable recent books I now offer you.

First, *Jacob*. The twenty-four-year-old author, Jean Cabriès, has been widely acclaimed in his country: and rightly. Here is a retelling, in terms of powerful modern imagination, of the Old Testament's—I think—most extraordinary human story. M. Cabriès's interpretation is masterful: his book, though extremely long, held me spellbound. The first-rate translator is Gerard Hopkins.

Maurice Druon, author of *The Last Detachment*, is also young, or at least in the younger group. (His *The Film of Memory* was reviewed in these pages some time ago.) *This* novel of his is a heroic, inspiring picture of the stand made by a group of Saumur cadets against the overrunning German forces in the early summer of 1940. Saumur, as you no doubt know, is France's great cavalry school, and these twenty-year-olds, scions in many cases of ancient families, show "cavalry mentality" in full timeless glory.

Precocity, in literary France, has a high incidence. Mlle. Sagan is thrown, by comparison, into the sunset years by Berthe Grimault, fourteen-year-old author of a hair-raising rural novel, *Beau Clown*. Principal characters, four escaped lunatics, four Negro soldiers in the U.S. Army, a bevy of very young ladies of easy virtue, and assorted livestock. Scene, central France. Mlle. Grimault, photographed feeding rabbits on the back of the jacket, clearly must have a future: she looks as tough as they come.

Mlle. Grimault, however, is well into middle age compared to eight-year-old Minou Drouet, whose *First Poems* reach us from Hamish Hamilton. The little creature, photographed clutching an overflowing armful of white poodle, was the cause—last autumn, in France—of a controversy only second to the Dreyfus case. The ins-and-outs you will find in the introduction. To *my* mind, an unmistakably childish vein does appear in this poetry, which is often lovely—see "I Only Had One Friend," or "My House at Le Pouliguen."

John Montgomery, *The Twenties*, May 1, 1957

What accounts, I do wonder, for this revival of interest in the Twenties? Why has that decade sailed into fashion? If you share the craze, here's the stuff you want—*The Twenties*, by John Montgomery. *An Informal Social History* is the book's subtitle; and emblematic objects—a cloche hat, a gramophone with a horn, an open motorcar like a bath on wheels, a lady brandishing a cocktail, and a Charleston-ing couple—are on the jacket. The author has done terrific research, and presents his material well and clearly.

The years covered are 1918 to 1930. We open with Armistice Night and close with "The Depression." The peace treaty and its aftermath, the international scene, and the political home front are pictured and, where necessary, diagnosed—or possibly one should say, postmortemed. Large sections of the book are, however, devoted to lighter subjects, of the kind which give color to daily life—sport, the theater, motoring, the movies, aeronautics, and speed-racing, literature, crime, and the Bright Young Things. Wembley Exhibition, the Irish troubles, and the General Strike have, deservedly, chapters to themselves—and another goes to the royal family: King George V and Queen Mary, the then Prince of Wales, and the birth of the Duke of York's first daughter, Elizabeth.

The Twenties, the author says in his forward, "is intended to appeal both to readers who do not remember the period and those who seek a nostalgic reminder."

Myself, with deference, I think the book likely to do better with the first group than with the second. True, the names and events in these pages do ring bells, but I don't feel Mr. Montgomery has quite got the *inside* feel of the thing. To judge by his agreeable photograph, how should he?—alive he may just have been in the 1920s, but how conscious? Some of the judgments he proffers, and his generalizations, cannot but seem slightly out of the true to those who do remember the 1920s. One could wish he had stuck to facts, made fewer deductions. Though he does the Twenties proud, I hasten to say.

Those of us who were in *our* twenties in the Twenties did rather more, I suppose, than take the thing for granted. I remember nobody brandishing a cocktail. It was gratifying to hear our mild good-timing described as "postwar recklessness" by our elders. As for "the spirit of the age" I believe that to have been not so much *reflected* (see Mr. Montgomery) as invented by the early Noël Coward, Michael Arlen, and—late entrant to the scene—Evelyn Waugh. The 1920s, thanks to brilliant artists, received a buildup while they were going on; now, they are getting a bigger one retrospectively. Sedulously, we lived up, as far as possible, to the dashing types put out by Coward and Arlen: but for those two, we'd have gone on muddling along much as young people do in any decade.

Sunday papers—as Mr. Montgomery points out—also contributed much to the hectic vision. Exhilarating, however, as it was to be stigmatized as the New Generation, in our heart we had to muffle a certain doubt: is not *each* generation, in turn, new? Today's parents—by now, indeed, grandparents—who were young in the Twenties should take reputed rocking-and-rolling orgies, and other much-written-up spasms of the mid-1950s, with a grain of salt, and indeed more.

It would be, however, unfair distortion to suggest that Mr. Montgomery's *The Twenties* exclusively centers on goings-on. His book is, in the main, an attempt to set the 1920s (as a whole) into perspective. He is fascinated by the period, and shows it. And let us gladly remember famous men—women, practically no children, and cartoon personalities—such as Suzanne Lenglen, Ramsay Macdonald, Pip, Squeak, and Wilfred, Jack Hobbs, Malcolm Campbell, Henry Segrave, Marie Stopes, Alan Cobham, Aimee Semple McPherson, Steve Donoghue, Ethel M. Dell, George Grossmith, Alice Delysia . . . The list is impressive, endless.

And, as might be expected, high points in *The Twenties* are the illustrations. Photographs are supplemented by *Punch* drawings, and (I think best of all) the 1920s advertisements. Back we go, into a world of Eton crops, Oxford bags. Neo-Tudor suburban housing may draw a shudder (though we've had as bad, and worse, since), "fascinating lingerie" an austere smile.

H. E. Bates, *Death of a Huntsman*, May 8, 1957

H. E. Bates's new book, *Death of a Huntsman*, contains four tales, linked by a sinister theme—the subjugation of man by woman. Each of the four is a well-nigh perfect example of the novella: a form more used on the Continent than here. A novella is not to be mistaken for a potted novel on the one hand, or an overlength short story on the other: it is a thing entirely in itself, and Mr. Bates is one of our masters of it. On this occasion, it suits his purpose well, and is also merciful to the reader. For I doubt if anyone could endure, for a full-length book, the company of any one of these fiendish ladies.

Glimpses and dark intimations are enough. By wonderfully economical constructions, Mr. Bates takes us straight towards the heart of the drama—at the same time allowing himself sufficient room to set his scene and build up his characters' backgrounds. His four men, if one may say so, are sitting ducks: if they had not met trouble in the form he shows, they undoubtedly would have met it in another. They are, respectively, a City man residing in "the stockbroker belt" country, a lorry driver, a shipping clerk, and a butterfly-loving bachelor of sixty. It is my firm conviction that Mr. Bates loves the country, landscapes, nature, and seasons of the year considerably better than he likes human beings—and why not?

Clear-cut as his characters are, they are always a shade less convincing than his scenes—which in this book, as in others of his, are forever exciting, poetic, moving, memorable. And this preference is probably just as well. If one were more deeply touched by his male sufferers, their predicaments would be too painful for words: as it is, they make nerveracking, first-rate stories.

Harry Barnfield, the "huntsman" of the first piece, is an exception— Mr. Bates is all for him, and so was I. His encirclement by a ghastly former charmer of the 1920s, with whose daughter he is on the point of finding happiness, really *is* tragic. One way and another, "Death of a Huntsman," with its comical opening and somber close, is for me the masterpiece of this volume—though "Night Run to the West," with its eerie nocturnal main road setting, runs it close. In "Summer in Salandra"—scene, the island off Portugal—I thought we were going to be in for horrible vulture trouble (as in this author's novel *The Jacaranda Tree*). As it was, the lady with the handbag, the steamy heat, the landslide, and the clerk's foot crushed to a pulp proved more than enough. In "The Queen of Spain Fritillary" (wonderful English Midland background) a nasty little seventeen-year-old plays fast and loose with an aging hermit admirer.

Why, oh why has Mr. Bates, one of the props and stars of good English prose, deviated into *American* language? Why does he call a lorry driver a truck driver? Why does the lady say "Nobody called much" instead of "Almost nobody rang up"—the context of the talk being a telephone? Why does the handbag maniac in the island story accuse her victim Manson of being "mad" with her, instead of "angry"? Not a single one of these characters is American! If *Death of a Huntsman* had reached us via the U.S.A., I still do feel that the author, or someone else, should have retranslated it into our native tongue!

Vera Brittain, *Testament of Experience,* July 17, 1957

Successor to *Testament of Youth* by Vera Brittain is the author's *Testament of Experience*. This second autobiography begins with Miss Brittain's marriage, in 1925, to G., a political philosopher—who had, in her own words, "inconveniently emerged, to remind me that the human relationships which I thought I had renounced were still there for the taking." The succession of blows dealt to herself and her age group by World War I (see *Testament of Youth*) account for Miss Brittain's attitude, which her suitor had difficulty in overcoming. And after the marriage, though all went well, adjustments were necessary. These her new book goes into, among other things.

Much devolves on a woman who feels called upon to be not only spokeswoman for her generation but sentry on behalf of the next. It was important, as G. realized, that Miss Brittain be in no way fettered, sidetracked, or cramped. She embarked on maternity after long discussion. Fate once more began to gun for her, and early: her and G.'s central European honeymoon was terminated by the news that one of her aunts had jumped off a high mountain in Wales.

There was then the departure for America, where G. held a post in a university. For the bride, trans-Atlantic existence did not work out—later, relations with the U.S.A. were almost unintermittent and very cordial. So the writer returned to London and set up house with Winifred Holtby (see *Testament of Friendship*). G. used to join them in Chelsea when on vacation.

Tributes to this singularly unselfish man occur, rightly, throughout *Testament of Experience*. So do testimonials to Miss Brittain, some from persons happy enough to know her, some from strangers in every part of the globe. Fortunately she never seems to have lost, or failed to file, any letter or press cutting. The reaction to *Testament of Youth* justified her sense of having a mission—and indeed that chronicle, gallantly written under domestic pressure, more than merited the success it had. Her fiction production, she tells us, had more vicissitudes: a novel to which she attached hopes was hit by the royal abdication in England and *Gone with the Wind* in the U.S.A. And later, Miss Brittain was to incur considerable—and, it does seem, unjust—unpopularity, owing to her connection with Christian pacifism. Of those harsh years she writes with courage and dignity.

It would be too unkind to accuse this author of self-importance. Humor is possibly not her forte. She does, no doubt inadvertently, give the impression that the moment she took her eye off the world (owing, in most cases, to the claims of maternity) something was liable to go wrong. She returned to London, for instance, after a holiday, to find her little girl with a raging temperature and in need of a tonsils operation. "I had just arranged for this to be done immediately after G.'s return, when Hitler marched into Prague." Little Shirley did have her operation: two days later, Italy raped Albania. One must, however, see Miss Brittain's point in making these and other juxtapositions: one of the aims of *Testament of Experience* is to interknit private life and public events.

Those with a mania for privacy, rightly or wrongly, may wonder how Miss Brittain does with so little. As against that, portions of *Testament of Experience* deal with sensations known to general humanity—being bombed, making arduous wartime journeys, making speeches, or talking to former enemies. My feeling is that this book would have more force if Miss Brittain had been rather more selective. What she says fills 480 pages—and the pages would be more were the print not small.

Evelyn Waugh, *The Ordeal of Gilbert Pinfold*, July 31, 1957

"Seeing things" is a recognized form of trouble. But what about hearing—and hearing *what*? Evelyn Waugh's new novel deals with hallucination, and very thoroughly. *The Ordeal of Gilbert Pinfold* has a ring of authority, for good reason—Mr. Waugh, we learn, three years ago underwent the same disconcerting experience as his hero. Mr. Pinfold, a novelist of fifty, hears voices. It is Mr. Waugh's belief that his and his Mr. Pinfold's passing affliction is nothing like so rare as may be supposed.

In fact, this unnerving comedy brings to the surface what may be your, my, or anyone's form of phobia—that of listening in (heaven knows, inadvertently!) on adverse discussion of oneself. There also are those bad dreams in which someone says: "I think, now, it's time to tell you what we all think of you." Such a nightmare one may not shake off for weeks. In waking hours, one staves off such an outrage; it may be that the cultivation of bland immunity is one of the arts implicit in growing up. Mr. Pinfold, however, is caught off guard; nor can he elude his tormentors by a change of location—he is mewed up in the cabin of a ship. His cabin must, he concludes, be wired for sound—therefore, that he is overhearing his fellow passengers the poor fellow does not for a moment doubt.

Mr. Pinfold's voyage on the SS *Caliban*, plying between Liverpool and Rangoon, has, ironically, been undertaken in search of calm. His country home life is pleasant, his reputation secure, yet for some time he has been feeling not quite the thing—indeed, far from it. A strong sleeping potion dissolved in crème de menthe has been causing him to come out in blotches; slight persecution symptoms declare themselves; his memory plays embarrassing tricks. His state has been not unobserved by his charming wife.

> "You haven't always been altogether making sense lately," said Mrs. Pinfold . . . "and you're a very odd color. Either you're drinking too much or doping too much, or both."
>
> "I wonder if you're right," said Mr. Pinfold. "Perhaps I ought to go slow after Christmas."

Hence, Gilbert Pinfold instated in the SS *Caliban*—a ship "middle-aged and middle-class; clean, trustworthy, and comfortable, without pretence to luxury. There were no private baths." The cargo, mixed; the passengers "more or less homogeneous . . . . Scotchmen and their wives mostly, traveling on business and on leave. Crew and stewards were Lascars."

Whence, then, the voices, and still more sounds—the more demonic for being lifelike? An amateur jazz band plays three-eight rhythm under the sufferer's cabin, a mutiny is quelled brutally on the deck above. A sex talk is administered to a sniveling seaman. A sadistic torture scene—every gasp too clear—is to be overheard from the captain's quarters. A Third Programme talk on the novel, excoriating himself, discharges into the ears of the fuming Pinfold. His political affiliations, his war career, his effective manhood are exposed (it seems) to nonstop searing discussion. Perversions are attributed to him, ad lib. Young toughs are, apparently, planning to storm his cabin. A breathless fan, one Margaret, offers him love; a she-fiend, Goneril, urges suicide.

And so on. The devastating and racking funniness of *The Ordeal of Gilbert Pinfold* comes from Mr. Waugh's genius for sheathing terror in mirth. Handled otherwise, this would be one more drab "case" story, or a contrived and over-ingenious fantasy. As it is, we are given pure entertainment, the better for getting the reader under the skin. Mr. Pinfold's sorties, to the bar or the captain's table, and attempts to pin down the evils he thinks afoot, give context for superb snatches of Waugh dialogue.

Ivy Compton-Burnett, *A Father and His Fate*, August 28, 1957

I. Compton-Burnett's latest novel, A *Father and His Fate*, also deals with excessive family feeling. Indeed, we now recognize that this great author has made blood relationship and its attendant psychological maladies her subject. Grim would be the result were it not for Miss Compton-Burnett's exquisite humor, and the breathtaking twists and turns of each household drama. This time, the central figure is Miles Mallory, a gentleman fairly advanced in years and blessed with a wife, Ellen, and three daughters—Ursula, Constance, Audrey. His property (like that of Mr. Bennet in *Pride and Prejudice*) is, unfortunately, entailed in the male line; therefore, Miles has taken into his house his nephew Malcolm Mowbray, perforce his heir. Also under his roof is Miss Gibbon, formerly governess to the girls.

Nearby, within constant visiting reach, dwells Malcolm's widowed mother, Eliza, with her two younger sons and her companion, Miss Manders. And Eliza Mowbray, almost without warning, introduces a further inmate—Verena Gray, a dynamic young person with wide blue eyes, high color, thin lips, and a strong chin. Verena has recently lost her mother: grief, however, has not numbed her powers—in a flash she becomes engaged first to Malcolm, then to his uncle Miles.

How to Miles, since the *père de famille* is already married . . . ? In this manner: he and his wife had set off for foreign parts; they were shipwrecked; Miles was saved, Ellen reported drowned.

Ellen Mowbray's return is preceded and followed by violent showdowns. Verena adapts to the situation and marries long-suffering Malcolm, after all. A splendid tea-table battle is to mark the homecoming of the honeymoon couple (for the preposterous plan is that *all* combatants shall continue to dwell together). And one last bomb, most shocking of all, is yet to explode . . . This is no more than the layout of Miss Compton-Burnett's, so far, most drastic novel. If I have not aroused expectations, I have done badly. Those I *have* aroused, the book will exceed — I swear!

Françoise Sagan, *Those without Shadows*, November 6, 1957

Françoise Sagan looks like becoming one of France's veteran novelists by the time she is twenty — or is she twenty now? Her third book, *Those without Shadows*, has the poise and assurance of her two first; and the assurance is more than justified. The theme is, so far, her most ambitious. In both *Bonjour Tristesse* and *A Certain Smile* the plot was centered upon a single figure: a tempestuous teenager. This time she plays her spotlight, flitting and impartial, over a group. What we watch is the interplay among several people.

Youthful indeed they are, these bright men and women who meet at the "evenings" given by Alain and Fanny Maligrasse. It is their youth which attracts and rivets their hosts; themselves a couple into their fifties. Alain and Fanny, elegant intellectuals, are negatively somewhat a tragic pair: they care for each other but there is a vacuum in their marriage, and instinctively they are seeking some consolation from the vivid, alert personalities who surround them. Confided secrets, dramatic meetings, momentous dramas key up the atmosphere of the Maligrasse salon.

Bernard, with his frustrated passion for Josée and, in the background, his miserable little wife, is a so far one-book novelist, at a standstill: he earns his living in Alain's publishing firm. Edouard, all innocence, is new to Paris, straight from provincial Caen. Josée, rich girl, is a rake with a heart to let: unaccountable to the friends who know her is her *tendre* for Jacques, a brutish medical student. Beatrice, the beautiful, stupid actress who lives in a haze of her own ambition, is the real wrecker — to Bernard (who has already had an affair with her) she is no danger, but she breaks Edouard's heart and, insidiously, ruins the older Alain.

These mercurial characters seem unsolid. And rightly, for it is their unsolidity which is Mlle. Sagan's subject. One is struck by the futility of their goings-on, the aimless senselessness of their acute suffering—and it is by this, exactly, that the author is *intending* us to be struck! Furthermore, the young men and women, being intelligent, are the victims of their sense of their own futility. The lightness with which *Those without Shadows* is written, the sheer effective brevity of the novel, all the more drives its point home—moral it has none.

The French title of this book is *Dans un mois, dans un an*. The effective translation into English is the work of Irene Ash.

Anthony Powell, *At Lady Molly's*, December 4, 1957

Anthony Powell's *At Lady Molly's* is the fourth novel in his *A Dance to the Music of Time* sequence. Some of you may find it the most enjoyable — it is a shade less aseptic, lighter in touch, and more largely written in dialogue than its predecessors. One should, too, take into account the fact that enjoyment, when books form a series, is cumulative: there is the pleasure (resembling that in real life) of meeting already-known characters in fresh situations. And the best of all is, one knows there is more to come.

Our narrator Nicholas Jenkins, first met at Eton (in *A Question of Upbringing*), in *At Lady Molly's* reaches the brink of marriage. His own courtship is, however, obscured by events in the personal circle round him — most notably the immortal Widmerpool's engagement to a tough Riviera widow, ex V.A.D.[2] of World War I. To relish the whole of that comedy one should, perhaps, glance back at the spoor of Widmerpool across the two intervening novels, *A Buyer's Market* and *The Acceptance World*. (You can, of course, if you enter the story late, read the Jenkins annals backwards. I recommend this, though *At Lady Molly's* is able to stand alone.)

Uncle Giles, hitherto a constant, is absent from this volume. Templer appears but briefly; Stringham remains offstage — though we have a view of him as a Steerforth to Miss Weedon's Rosa Dartle.[3] We meet for the first time the Tolland girls, ranging from Frederica, about the Court, to Norah, ambiguous in Chelsea, and Erridge, their troubled brother, a left-wing peer—who crosses the amorous fate-line of our friend Quiggin, till now unmolestedly living with Templer's ex-wife. But the dominating newcomer is Lady Molly.

The outstanding scenes in this novel (as the title suggests) take place in Lady Molly's Kensington drawing room. Here the human habitués, mixed in status and character—this is a house where you may meet anyone!— show themselves as jumpy and temperamental as the cats and monkeys crowding the nooks and stairs. The hostess, formerly Lady Sleaford, has married one Jeavons, an ex-officer. She herself is kindly, noisy, a tease. "There is no greater sign of innate misery," Mr. Powell remarks, "than a love of teasing." This is one of the knife-sharp generalizations with which this author constantly makes one sit up. His position in English writing remains unparalleled. The time of *At Lady Molly's* is (around) 1934; the main scene is London.

Storm Jameson, *A Cup of Tea for Mr. Thorgill*, December 11, 1957

The new Storm Jameson novel *A Cup of Tea for Mr. Thorgill* deals with Communism in Oxford, depicting a trio of Red cats set among academic pigeons. One should not perhaps say trio: the third defaults, and it is his predicament that we study. His more slick-tongued comrades get off scot-free—one, indeed, retaining a key position (which makes one's skin creep!) in a vital department of the university. Poor young Nevil Rigden, our don hero, is headed for trouble from the start: he is of proletarian origin, vulnerable to sneers from his ill-wishers, and accordingly forever on the defensive. Handicapped by a bumptious, uneasy manner, he is inwardly ravaged by guilt and conflicts—he feels out of contact with his working-class family. Extra edge is given his guilt by a dying mother.

Little nonsense is stood by poor Nevil's wife. Evelyn Rigden, a young woman of pedigree, slips out of all or part of her clothing with a willingness, speed, and frequency still not typical, surely, of the majority of North Oxford matrons. Her control of her husband is largely passionate; her more true mind-union is with her brother, one Thomas Paget— who, as a brilliant scientist, is shown as Oxford's white hope on the modern side.

Miss Jameson's view of Oxford is, I cannot but feel, lugubrious, not to say disapproving. She depicts, as the Senior Common Room of her favored college, a group of reactionaries steeped in port wine and cynicism. The master of the college is a slothful, snobbish hedonist with a corrupt sister. Of undergraduates there appears to be a shortage: only two of the species feature in this story—one, a genius, is on the point of being sent down because he *is* a genius (on a trumped-up charge of drinking and womanizing); the other, Jewish, is, we are to infer, suffering persecution for that reason. Oh dear, oh dear. However, there are many events in the plot: a suicide, a rape (which does not take place in Oxford), an attempted murder. Mr. Thorgill, a symbolic Yorkshireman, turns up only twice in the book he names.

Oxford, having so far survived, is I think likely to survive *A Cup of Tea for Mr. Thorgill*. But one thing does worry me: is not Miss Jameson doing a slight disservice to foreign readers? Everything this outstanding novelist writes is, very deservedly, much exported. And our ancient British institutions are always "news." Czechs, Germans, Swedes, Danes, Poles, Spaniards, Italians, and other nationals will shortly be riveted to these pages. Moreover, *A Cup of Tea for Mr. Thorgill* has been the choice of America's Book of the Month Club: hundreds of thousands of our American cousins will have been set agog by it—one can hardly blame them.

Kingsley Amis, *I Like It Here*; Colette, *Claudine in Paris*, January 22, 1958

Kingsley Amis's new novel *I Like It Here* is his third. It comes to us with an austere absence of a blurb, and rightly. The object of blurbs on book jackets is twofold—one, to preserve the reader from mental effort or rude surprise by giving a potted version of the story (if the work be fiction; if it be "thought" one is offered a key to the mental process) and, two, to build up the reputation of the author. In this case, neither is necessary. Even a reviewer cannot grumble at having to read a Kingsley Amis novel from first to last page, instead of having the work done for him, and the simple reader—that one higher form of human life—is not likely, either, to find he requires aid. As for reputation, *Lucky Jim* saw to that.

All the same Mr. Amis is not a reviewer's joy. He's an anti-fine writer, so one cannot quote him. What he means, he says in so many words, so there's no point in dredging his prose for submerged significance. Outwardly, *I Like It Here* is about a Welsh author, Garnet Bowen, resident in South Kensington, who loathes and suspects the idea of "abroad," but is jumped into going there, with his wife and children. And that's what the book *is* about, with no strings to it. The "abroad" is Portugal, where the Bowens, instead of staying in a hotel—cheaper for them, less amusing for us—idiotically land themselves up as p.g.'s[4] in the unspeakable bungalow of an Anglo-Portuguese called Mr. Oates. One of the secondary objects of the journey is for Bowen to check on the identity of Wulfstan Strether (last of the "great writers" in the Conrad-Henry James tradition) whose mysterious going to ground near Lisbon has long been a headache to his publishers.

Is the courteous old gentleman who reacts unsuspiciously to the Bowen probe actually Strether? He seems too good to be true. A high point is the visit to Henry Fielding's tomb. "Bowen thought about Fielding. Perhaps it was worth dying in your forties if two hundred years later you were the only non-contemporary novelist who could be read with unaffected and wholehearted interest." For contrast, study the fearsome passage from the Strether masterpiece which is wickedly quoted.

I Like It Here is funny in every way, including the family-misadventure formula. There is even mother-in-law trouble (offstage). Thought processes are tremendously speeded up. Pathos is absent: one is sorry for Bowen for the same reason one is sorry for oneself—"keeping on the alert for being mature and responsible and so on took it out of him." A deflating book, but all the better for that. I guarantee you'll like Barbara, Bowen's wife; you may not be so keen about his vocabulary.

* * *

The latest Colette novel to appear in English is *Claudine in Paris*. Its author, that great, lately dead Frenchwoman, so entirely French that one might shrink from reading her in any other language—well is it that incorrigible Claudine (fresh from her village schooldays) comes to us via Antonia White, translator of genius. The spirit of the heroine, and the happenings, have been unfailingly caught.

This is not the very best Colette book, but it is enchanting. At large in

Paris, our girl is hardly more trammeled than in the Montigny woods—in spite of a chic, ground-length, tailor-made skirt. She is seventeen; the year is 1901. In those days, adolescence hadn't been invented; in consequence everything was less earnest and a good deal gayer, with no *bonjours* to *tristesse*. Marcel, "the sugar boy," with the cravat and the eyelashes, is no match for his equally shocking aunt. Outrageous, innocent, with more than a touch of magic—who but Colette could have done it?

Stephen Spender, *Engaged in Writing,* February 5, 1958

Stephen Spender's *Engaged in Writing* is, as fiction, a very different kettle of fish.[5] The book consists of two *nouvelles*, or long short stories—of which the first, and more lengthy, provides the title. Of the second, "The Fool and the Princess," one may say what a tribute it is to its strength and worth that it is *not* eclipsed by its stupendous forerunner.

What happens, in "Engaged in Writing," takes place in Venice. Here, in the Doges' Palace, is staged a conference between intellectuals of the East and West, sponsored by a cultural society called Europlume, with, behind that, world-organized Lituno. With one exception (a heavy British scientist) those who attend are authors, each in the avant-garde of his country. Of its kind, this amounts to a summit meeting. The proceedings are seen through the eyes of Olim Asphalt: British, Lituno employee, it is his fate to attend one after another of these conferences.

Olim knows, in advance, what the form is likely to be. So does Mr. Spender: seldom, consequently, can savage comicality have gone further than it does in this uproarious not-quite-farce. Celebrities, French, Italian, or what you like, their mannerisms, egotisms, and idées fixes are (far from ill-naturedly) hit off. It is tempting to quote ad lib from "Engaged in Writing": let me draw your attention, at least, to the opening banquet, at which the three Russian authors "seemed fixed like mountains on which famous public figures have been carved," and to Olim's view of the intellectuals, "the faces like bunions, the limbs like carrots," ascending the magnificent entrance staircase of the palace—"dim procession of mackintoshed moderns with the marble figures towering above them."

The magic of Venice, however, draws out humanity; between platitudinous sessions, real-life flowers. *Engaged in Writing*, be certain, is *not* a sneer at "ideas"; rather it is a giant groan at their exploitation.

May Sarton, *The Birth of a Grandfather,* April 2, 1958

The new May Sarton novel, *The Birth of a Grandfather*, should, in particular, speak to those of us who are hesitating into our middle years. "We start from scratch at each of the different stages of life" is a (*rough!*) translation of the La Rochefoucauld saying the author quotes—in fact, how hard it is to make the transition, onward from one generation into the next, for each of us comes to the borderline unprepared. Here is the tale of a marriage, in which the wife suffers because the husband still, inwardly, shrinks from being an older man. The two love each other: till lately they have been happy. He has great integrity; he is attractive, clever, and well-liked; *outwardly*, he is a fully responsible member of society. Circumstances have, however, combined to preserve in him a protracted boyhood.

Many Englishmen, it is complained, do never grow up. And by Miss Sarton's showing, this is no less true (in fact, it would seem, possibly truer) of gently bred, well-educated New Englanders. John P. Marquand[6] has studied this American type; Miss Sarton does so from the feminine angle—how unstable, though endlessly kind, they may be as husbands, how touchy and unsure of themselves as fathers! Sprig Wyeth, the man in this novel, is made uneasy by the growing-up of his children: Caleb and Betsy, both now in their early twenties, show signs of the fuller maturity *he* has failed to reach.

Frances Wyeth, the delightful wife, has her own problems: though she is forty-five, joie de vivre, impulsiveness, girlhood bubble up in her still. She feels, however, that her and Sprig's marriage is being cheated, somehow, of its fruition. Surely the time has come, now, when hand-in-hand they should fearlessly take the next step forward: not yet *old* age, but "age" of a sort? . . . Young Betsy marries, early on in the story: in the course of a few months comes her announcement—the Wyeths must face up to becoming grandparents.

This scene, and Sprig Wyeth's reactions, is one of the many in which

Miss Sarton has sharply pointed, and brings home, the moral of *The Birth of a Grandfather* . . . The settings (the family holiday house on the island, the comfortable town home in Cambridge, Massachusetts) have the intimacy one associates with May Sarton: poet-novelist with an unfailing eye for all that is eloquent in domestic things.

William Faulkner, *Uncle Willy and Other Stories*, April 23, 1958

The first volume of William Faulkner's collected stories is *Uncle Willy and Other Stories*. As you will understand, the gathering-up of this great southerner's tales is important—the 1949 award, to him, of the Nobel Prize for Literature set a seal on Faulkner's position. He stands right at the top, and may be the most influential of living novelists. Fame does, however, breed an attendant myth. There is a tendency to consider Faulkner as an artist dealing largely in gloom and violence. The short stories correct that one-sided view. In this volume comedy holds sway.

An exuberant raciness predominates, plus rich local color. Often, the narrator is a young boy—the junior Grier tells, in "Shingles for the Lord," how Pap inadvertently burns down the local church; and, in "Two Soldiers," of his own dogged attempt to follow his brother Pete into the army. "Shall Not Perish"—no comedy, but sublimely human—deals, in the youngster's words, with Pete's heroic death, and the reaction to it in the village community. In "Uncle Willy" (one of the Faulkner "classics"), we have a grand old reprobate tearing around the skies in a small plane he cannot learn to control, thereby defeating the do-goods' plans to reform him. We meet yet another sinner in Uncle Rodney, in the family story entitled "That Will Be Fine."

Here or there, the scene of a story shifts. We have New York, Virginia, or California. But mainly the locale is "the Faulkner country"—the state of Mississippi, accounted "backward." The astuteness, nerve, guts of this pack of characters, their majestic background, their well-nigh biblical language make one wonder—*is* there so very much in "progress"?

LAST REVIEWS: 1948 TO 1971

Heart or Soul?

From the Heart of Europe, by F. O. Matthiessen. *Spectator*, December 10, 1948.

Professor Matthiessen, of Harvard, was in Central Europe from July to the end of December, 1947. During the first two months he lectured on American literature to European students of sixteen nations at Schloss Leopoldskron, seat of the Salzburg Seminar in American Studies, initiated and administered by Harvard students. He then, in the autumn, went to Prague, to Charles University; where, as a visiting lecturer for a term, he was the first American to become a regular member of the faculty. The bid for Professor Matthiessen, on the part of Charles University, showed genius; there was thereby secured the author of *American Renaissance*, of *Henry James: The Major Phase* (also, coeditor of the Henry James *Notebooks*), and of *The Achievement of T. S. Eliot*, an essay on the nature of poetry. That the gain was reciprocal need not be said: the distinguished American found himself in the heart of one of the most famous universities of Europe. To be, as was the reviewer, in Czechoslovakia in 1948 was to feel the profound impression left by Professor Matthiessen, and to salute his visit's outstanding success. As for his impressions, they are to hand, set down.

From the Heart of Europe was written during the months abroad, and gives accounts of journeys taken, from Prague, to Brno, Bratislava, and

Budapest. A brief final section notes the return to America. The book is reflective in manner, in journal form; it was concluded on New Year's Day, 1948, just less than two months before the Communist coup in Prague. The author has, honorably, left personal views and predictions which time has falsified to stand; he adds a few footnotes dated March 1948. *From the Heart of Europe* makes, he says in the preface, "no pretence of giving a full report on any of the countries I visited. I am not a trained journalist, and I went to Europe primarily because I had been invited to lecture . . . . This is less a travel book than a journal of opinions, a record of what I thought about during half a year abroad." On the following page the book opens: "I want to write about some of the things it means to be an American today. That is the chief thing I came to Europe to think about."

Here indeed was a subject ripe for reflection. Professor Matthiessen's position in Central Europe was, however, at once complicated and simplified by a further fact: he is not only an American but an American socialist. (It is he who, throughout, abjures the capital letter.) In his official role of cultural representative of his country, he was to find it required some discretion to deliver his own progressive views without reflecting, unpatriotically, upon majority backwardness at home. As against that, he was, from the moment of landing at Prague airport, both personally and ideologically in paradise. This was (apart from a fortnight's visit to an improved England) the first Socialist country he had been in. He is to be felt to draw, throughout the Czechoslovak portion, a series of deep, reassured, and wholly satisfied breaths. His love for the Czechs—which is not to be wondered at: not to respond to the Czech warmth, decency, uprightness, intelligence, and dignity would be a sign of having a soul so dead—is reinforced by thorough moral approval. Czechoslovakia might, indeed, have been found to be the ideal Socialist state—in the sense that the regime made for the full expansion of the most characteristic of the national virtues, and that the disappearance of certain graces was regretted, apparently, by the outsider only.

On the subject of the sturdy, clear-cut Moravians, and of Brno, our author has less to say; his visit was, it is true, brief. In the main Brno would not appear to have left on him—to the extent, at least, that it left on another traveler—any very unique impression visual or moral. And the long-legged, dilatory Slovaks and generally Ruritanian atmosphere of Bratislava would seem to have combined to disconcert him. "It took some time," he remarks, "to find out exactly what the majority party stood for." One likes to know where one is. Yet, across the Hungarian border, the already declared political situation filled Professor Matthiessen with a profound mistrust; he was prone, throughout his visit to Budapest, to a sense of disorientation and nervousness—which the city's surviving graces, the brilliant disabused talk, the good things and good looks only drove in deeper. It is not easy to understand what Professor Matthiessen means when he says he found Prague like Paris; to any other eye Budapest would, surely, appear more so.

The author did not, as may be inferred, bring to Central Europe that particular susceptibility to sensations, that interest in the contradictory for its own sake, which mark the traveler. He did bring the noblest of open sympathies—if, because of his zeal, his bias, his predisposition to see in a certain way, the sympathies circumscribed themselves, he was not aware of it. He truly believed himself eager to meet all sorts. He is a Christian; he is a Socialist for that reason, the most honorable—"to love thy neighbor as thyself seems to me an imperative to social action." He is not a Communist for the same reason—"I find any materialism inadequate." Why, since he is a Christian, does he seem to have remained so curiously out of contact with Czechoslovakia's spiritual life? It was impossible, on at any hour entering any of those churches, to ignore, below the baroque altars, those many figures twisted in an extremity of prayer. True, he met the soul—which is, I believe, the dominating element in Central Europe, so much so that even politics seem to be only one more of its manifestations—in the intense and prodigious response to art. One could have wished, too, that, given his eminence in his own subject, he could have made some effort to account for the fact that Shakespeare is at present sweeping Central Europe: our poet moves forward steadily with the Communist front.

On the other hand, the discussion of the questions brought up by the suppression of Anna Akhmatova's poetry in the U.S.S.R. is honest, admirable. Occasionally, one has the feeling that Professor Matthiessen overshot the mark—as when, asked by a Communist Prague student for names of American texts that should be translated into Czech, "I told him that . . . *In Dubious Battle* was in many ways Steinbeck's best book, and that it gave a picture of labor's struggles in the Depression. He wrote it down, but added that the books didn't have to be about social problems, that he wanted most to know about some of our good works of art." Elsewhere one is surprised by the occasions of Professor Matthiessen's surprise — he was disappointed that the students at the Salzburg Seminar, almost all from still or lately occupied countries, were slow in opening up into free political discussion; and there was the incident of the carpenter and the hand-towel. One has still, surely, to meet a subservient carpenter; and in this case the carpenter was the professor's host . . . *From the Heart of Europe* is a book of the first interest, to be saluted for its own soundness of heart. It may rouse, here and there, impatience, but of the respectful kind.

Salt on the Lips

The Unknown Sea, by François Mauriac, translated by Gerard Hopkins. *Observer*, December 19, 1948.

Les Chemins de la mer appeared in France in 1939. Like other Mauriac novels, it is set back in the years preceding the First World War; its scene is the Bordeaux region. The story opens on crisis: the exposure and suicide of Oscar Revolou, wealthy Bordeaux attorney, ruined by his infatuation for a dancer, and the repercussion of the disgrace upon Mme. Revolou, her two sons, and her daughter. It is Mme. Costadot, mother of Rose's suitor, who, breaking in on the Revolous' Bordeaux house, extracts, in the name of her injured Costadot children, the sum which had been Mme. Revolou's dowry. Balzac might have pictured the ruthlessness; he could not have explored the spiritual corruption of such a scene.

The two younger Costadot boys, in recoil from their mother's act, confer at midnight: Pierre, the poet, rages against the rule of money. "There are only two courses open, either to change the face of the earth . . . the revolution . . . or, there's God." Virtually, it is the revolution which is in force as Rose and Denis Revolou, Robert and Pierre Costadot are thrust, one by one, towards the extremity of each of their natures. God remains silent or, at a remove, acts through the characters, as all of them in turn strip each other of every illusion.

This is a study, and one of the most formidable, of M. Mauriac's studies, of youth. Robert, who makes a lover's attempt to follow Rose into poverty, revolts from her shabbiness and abandons her; Rose's brother Denis, for reasons more complex and less innocent than loyalty, has broken with Robert's brother Pierre. It is Rose Revolou, the imperfect saint, and Pierre Costadot, with his continuous image-poem, who *contain* the story.

All the others retreat—into sensuality, sickness, or the peasant state . . . But for Denis retreat cannot be final: at the end, alone in the country house, he and Rose confront one another: from what is laid bare between them she is the one to flee . . . Saturating all this is the beauty of nature: the autumn evenings, the bird singing in the cold lilac. Without nature, without that involuntary, insidious repose of the senses, such a story of movement "towards an unknown sea" would be unbearable. As it is, M. Mauriac invokes in us, with *The Unknown Sea*, a sort of delectable distress. And Mr. Hopkins's rendering into English has allowed almost no overtone to escape.

Downfall

The Best Days, by Hugh Massingham. *Observer*, April 10, 1949.

Treatment, more than actual subject, makes *The Best Days* an original novel. The demolition of smugness, the downfall of the man who sets himself up, have been a favored study of our fiction and drama. Mr. Massingham takes as his hero a parish clergyman, prosperous, sleek as his own cloth. At the outset, this Reverend Mr. Dewson, "Bobs" to friends, has the simplified outline of a caricature: he acquires his third dimension with the onset of trouble. For Parker, inexpert blackmailer, associate of Dewson's lost detrimental son, is, from the first page, moving in on the rectory. How stave off scandal, how retrieve from the underworld the young man maimed by parental failure? These are to be the rector's problems. We witness disaster in his attempts to solve them—his secretive visits to London, his stomach-turning interview with Ron's wife, his insidiously growing association with Ron's mistress, the vicious child-type May. A picture, one might say, of the suction exercised by positive evil upon negative good. But a picture whose angle and lighting are Mr. Massingham's; and, as such, unique. This author, acting with subtle strength, maintains a peculiar hold on the reader: it is you and I, no less than Mr. Dewson, who are implicated. One is to do more than witness; one is to adjudicate—to adjudicate not coldly but painfully, with a dissolving certainty, with a sort of trembling as though the case were oneself. Bobs Dewson has never been a hypocrite; rather, a man who arrested his own growth.

The resumption of growth, its convulsiveness, and the forms it takes are unseemly: are they preposterous? At the same time, nothing in Mr. Dewson's virtue becomes him, spiritually, like the leaving of it. In his abjection he is for the first time great; through his dereliction he glimpses divine grace. We leave Dewson on the eve of exposure; but—"I want to preach," he says. "I have a longing to be useful."

It may be argued that there are aspects of the inevitable spiritual conflict in this man—who, after all, was throughout continuing his duties as a priest—which Mr. Massingham has ignored. If so, better that than to underrate them. The characters of Wopple, Parker, the two old aunts, and May (the more living for being out of type) are excellent. *The Best Days*, following upon *The Harp and the Oak*, will maintain Mr. Massingham in the prominence, as a novelist, he deserves.

The Young May Moon

The Young May Moon, by P. H. Newby. *Now and Then*, Spring 1950.

This—*The Young May Moon*—is a novel of which the meaning and pattern emerge slowly. Part of the fascination, up to about halfway through, is the effect almost of nonchalance. Mr. Newby has the art of making a scene flower at a touch, and of eliciting, by what might seem a chancy phrase, music from the imagination of the reader. By the hostile or the unwary he might be charged with being the prey of his own gifts, and of strolling through his own earlier pages like a whistling boy—or, indeed, like Rice, hero of *The Young May Moon*.

That is not the case. Mr. Newby, having first assembled his story (and assembled it anything but at random), tautens and welds it into something dynamic. It is the story of a father and son, and of their disjected, puzzling, but powerful relationship. Alec Rice's gaunt wife dies at the beginning of the book; the fifteen-year-old Philip is sent away to an uncle and aunt in Wales to learn to be a baker. A "secret," which Alec has kept from his son out of complex motives, is disclosed to the boy by the aunt in Wales: the disclosure, with the whole emotional legend that lies behind it, has an unsettling effect. At a time when Philip most urgently wishes to reestablish contact with his father, it is found that Alec has disappeared—the great blond, faithless, tranquility-seeking creature has taken to the roads. When he reenters the scene, he is accompanied by the feckless Doll.

The stress, and the potential of tragedy, are in Philip. An inarticulate passionate boy of fifteen, whose passions have still to find direction, has probably seldom been better drawn. The background of the story is haunted by a woman who never appears. It is from the moment when she, Alec, and Philip were last together that the title of the novel has come.

The final scenes, on the Welsh dam and in the engineer's house, are an advance on anything we have had from Mr. Newby yet. He is most forcible, as a poet-novelist, in his use of symbolism. The seeking of affinities between a younger and older novelist is dangerous—were it to be permitted, one might call Mr. Newby a descendant of D. H. Lawrence. Outwardly the resemblance is negligible. Mr. Newby's manner is the reverse of violent—he seems more desultory than Lawrence, and he is more controlled. He does not imitate; he does in some senses continue where Lawrence left off. His climaxes, unlike those of Lawrence, are muffled, muted. In fact, the genius he shows in *The Young May Moon* is that of showing feeling—the feeling of which each of his humans is compact—not as ascending to a peak but as descending to a bottomless depth. The legendary submerged village, below the placid waters of the dam-girt reservoir, becomes more real to Philip (son of a lost love and a vanished mother) than actual streets and houses. Diving, the boy fancies that he hears ringing bells.

For D. H. Lawrence, Life Was Not Peace But a Sword

D. H. Lawrence: Portrait of a Genius But . . . , by Richard Aldington. *New York Times Book Review*, May 21, 1950.

Richard Aldington says that his book is a portrait, not a biography. Call it a narrative portrait, or biography from the angle of an idea. D. H. Lawrence, its subject, could not be expected to offer a static pose; to give account of his life, it is necessary to convey the essence of his dynamism. Mr. Aldington, many readers will find, has done so. The energy which blazed its way across continents, devoured scenes and moments, exhausted friends, now flickers its reflection across this book. Lawrence's existence—alien, inspired, unaccommodating, visionary, desperate—cannot merely be pictured, it must be felt. So far as this can be done from the outside, Mr. Aldington captures and imparts to the reader something of what must have been the sensation of actually being D. H. Lawrence, and a great part of the sensation of being with him.

In an opening note Mr. Aldington, the novelist and biographer, defends his title; that he wholly clarifies it one cannot say. What, he asks, is the reason for the equivocal judgment meted out to Lawrence, both during his lifetime and since his death? He was accorded genius, but in a tone which somehow devalued the attribute. There was a suggestion that genius lost caste by being possessed by Lawrence. Many salutes to him were tinged by a nebulous uneasiness which, apparently, has not been cleared up yet. That row of dots after the "But" has remained more speaking, and ultimately more formidable, than words.

In this book Mr. Aldington has assembled the Lawrence evidence which he aims to set out in an impartial light. The projects and the journeys, the attempts and the experiments, the illusions and the calamities— all are here. The chronicle, supplemented from autobiographical passages in the Lawrence novels, is full and detailed. The experience of vicariously living this Lawrence life is at times fascinating, at times drastic. Having exposed almost the entire picture, Mr. Aldington then calls on us to decide. The more one sees, however, the more complex judgment becomes. We are still too near D. H. Lawrence, who, ironically, in any relationship always desired nearness; indeed, forced it. To assess him anything like justly one would need a long perspective of time. So far, the perspective is not quite long enough.

We stand clear, it is true, of the frenzy Lawrence induced in his contemporaries—though we must react to the frenzy they induced in him. For us, the genius is an accepted fact. We are less aware of the "but" than is Mr. Aldington who, as Lawrence's friend, heard the "but" creep in an undertone round their little circle.

What a little circle Lawrence's London was—intensive, claustrophobic, eclectic, mischievous! The intelligentsia of that epoch do not come out of the story well. To have perceived his virtue (one feels now) should have meant exacting from him restraint. The friends with whom Lawrence found recognition, stimulus, sympathy, and the emotional tension he desired, were, at the same time, fatal to equilibrium.

The young man arrived in this brilliant jungle out of the nonconformist austerity of a mining village. The north-Midland miner's son came, in the human sense, from "a good family": rules, proprieties, and observances had been in the air of his bringing-up. He did not so much react against these as miss them, in his days of so-called expansion when he had come to town. Mr. Aldington stresses Lawrence's puritanism. One should allow also for his innate haughty respectability, his censoriousness, his trend to neatness and order, his wish to repeat the pattern of home. He was no bohemian. It could be arguable that he would have done better in a formal society, and that his attraction toward aristocrats showed a longing for a strong and traditional code.

As it was, he found himself in a disorientating universe of "free" people—creative and critical intellectuals who, having abandoned the middle-class rules of life, lived and acted by personal standards only. Born secure, less detached from their backgrounds than they imagined, these people could afford to experiment. Lawrence could not—but had to. For him the air was heady, the ground treacherous. What could he do but forge a furious faith? The strain of improvisation is to be felt behind his extraordinary behavior.

The extraordinary element in the later novels possibly may be explained by this. Once Lawrence ceased to picture the order and scenes of home he had to work as a novelist without social formulae. Only Dickens can have had to invent so much. The void in Lawrence's knowledge of the ordinary, of the commonplace, of the average, made him have to tax his originality to the last inch. There could be no low gear.

In most fiction, vision and observation blend; Lawrence could work by vision only. His people are isolated phenomena—exceptional, conforming to no known types. If they seem overcharged, it is that they were recipients of the full voltage of Lawrence's pent-up passion, energy, theory. He did not live among types, only individuals.

Should his art, so intensely poetic-visual, have been confined to poetry, painting, and short stories—in which key comes first, of which protracted verisimilitude is not asked? One cannot think so. Without the novels, not only our but his experience would have been incomplete. One cannot ignore his thinking, moral side: his attempt to synthesize was the novel.

England extruded Lawrence. The stages and methods of the process have been savagely, ironically traced by Mr. Aldington. Wherever Lawrence settled on the continent of Europe or in America, the electrical atmosphere set it.

> The absurdity of saying that he "hated America"! [Mr. Aldington writes]. Industrial America, yes, but he hated industrialism everywhere, and no intelligent person can be conditioned to an alien nationalism. But to realize what that mountainside and his ownership of these American acres meant to him, read the last fifteen pages of *St. Mawr*, the last essay of *Mornings in Mexico*, and the essays called "New Mexico," "Pan in America," and "Taos." It was to him an ecstasy, at once fierce and delicious, seductive and appalling. There were times when his active imagination conjured up fears of solitude and of ghosts, fears of Indians and even of the grizzlies, which no longer exist there.[1]

Was there a man, other than Shelley, who needed peace more and yet so consistently murdered it? Friends were invited out, or collected locally; the intimacies, the over-demands, the "hammerings" began again.

Lawrence was martyr not so much to people as to his obstinacy with regard to them. The continuous love-battle with Frieda might have been expected to be enough, but was not. Neither was his art, nor his joy in nature, nor his response to the beauty of each new place. His inordinateness, his demands for submission, his urge to power—were these merely signs in a sick man? One may reply that his was not a sick art.

It is for the happy inverse of this picture that Mr. Aldington will be most truly thanked. The sweetness of Lawrence's nature, his humor, teasingness, tenderness, volatility have been brought out, or, better, allowed to breathe from the pages. He was lovable. A deep down innocence ran through his alternations. His quickness in rounding upon himself, his unself-consciousness, his self-parodies at the unexpected moments were captivating. Above all, his courage soared.

"The artist," said Flaubert, "should so arrange as to make posterity think he has never lived." For Lawrence, as for Shelley, this was impossible. Around these two, since their deaths, there has been an incrustation of personal myth: analysis, anecdote, speculation. Mr. Aldington shows that, as to Lawrence, still more remains to be said.

Life in the Irish Counties

The Fire in the Dust, by Francis MacManus. *New York Herald Tribune Book Week*, February 11, 1951.

Francis MacManus is an important figure in the modern Irish literary scene. Born in Kilkenny in 1909, he had been publishing essays and short and long stories for some years when, in 1940, he received the Irish Academy of Letters's fiction award, the adjudicator being E. M. Forster. *The Fire in the Dust*, this first full-length novel of his to be published in America, is a work of romantic imagination tempered by sober literary skill. In this book, he has been less original in his choice of his subject than he has in its treatment; he, like so many other of his contemporaries, opens fire upon provincial life with its fanatical pruderies and deforming effect on the adolescent. What might be called the provincial malady is by no means limited to Ireland—have we not indeed had drastic novels about it out of America, Britain, Italy, France?—but it does appear with our outstanding Irish writers to be an obsessive theme. We behold genius at once battling against, yet in some odd way stimulated by, claustrophobia.

The Fire in the Dust is a tale of conflicts. The arrival into a small community of a bright-plumaged family, the Goldens, arouses in Larry Hackett, schoolboy narrator, immoral longings. The Goldens—father, daughter, and son, plus a small girl-child of uncertain origin—are "foreigners": i.e., they come from the outside world. Their talk, behavior, and ultimately their morals are found dubious. Young Larry, because of his friendship with Stevie Golden (formed in the course of a series of school battles), begins to frequent the riverside house which the newcomers have rented from Miss Dreelin, ecstatically pious keeper of a religious shop. Mr. Golden senior's trifling with Miss Dreelin's affections, the girl Maria's flamboyance, and Stevie's ironic detachment from local standards and "pagan" regard for art are, together, to kindle fire in the provincial dust. The scene is Kilkenny, which, incorrectly described inside the publisher's jacket as "a small town," is an ancient, nobly reputed Anglo-Norman city, to which, as Frank O'Connor has pointed out, the past somehow adds an extra dimension. Cathedral spires, a castle, and fortification walls loom over the courts and alleys in which this story plays itself out—a fact which makes the thatched cabins pictured upon the jacket particularly misleading and inappropriate. Mr. MacManus's locale is neither bog nor byroad.

Stevie, with his steely gentleness, his complexity, his mental dandyism, is a fine creation; so is his dry, idle father. Maria might seem to be overdrawn—but she is, one must remember, seen through a schoolboy's eye. Miss Dreelin, given her fatal part in the story, may be found underpowered; she lacks, perhaps, some touch which only Balzac, from the passionate angle, or Mauriac, from the religious, could have given her— one might suggest that the final scenes with Miss Dreelin go on for too long. Otherwise, the construction of *The Fire in the Dust* is admirable. So indeed is the dialogue; so much so that the two characters (Katie Costello and Mrs. Hackett) who are in the main evoked by their own speech, rather than by analysis, are the most telling. Katie, so rough, so tender, is a masterpiece—wholly unsentimental. Ultimately, however, there is a paradox: the dominating character in this novel is speechless, being the River Nore. The river, in sunny calm or in angry spate, both reflects and expresses mood and emotion; around it revolves, nay, upon it is strung, the plot. There are many watery passages; each to the full releases all that is most fluid, most luminous, most vital, most elemental in Mr. MacManus's prose.

The Land Behind

Sheridan Le Fanu, by Nelson Browne. *Observer*, July 8, 1951.

Mr. Nelson Browne, in his undertaking to add *Sheridan Le Fanu* to the "English Novelists Series," has been faced by a number of difficulties; some he has overcome, others not. Until *Uncle Silas* reappeared its author was, to more than one generation, hardly more than a name; the greater part of his work is still inaccessible, and, moreover, likely to remain so. With his contemporaries, this Victorian novelist had little but Victorianism in common; and, even so, upon him the time-color slightly alters its dye. Le Fanu was negatively un-English—which is to say that he lacked exuberance, was untouched by confidence in the present day, and did not make good those deficiencies with alternative major qualities of his own. This Anglo-Irishman, French-descended, was the product of an unconsciously tragic world—that of the Irish Unionist after the Union.

To such Protestant families as this novelist's the dislocation, onward from 1800, of a natural relationship with their country did human harm. The future envisaged by Grattan[2] had been wiped out; any hopes of a merger, in work and government, between the "ascendancy" and the old inhabitants of the land were canceled. Lack of function bred queerness; personal peculiarities became marked; there was a retreat into a cloud-land of solitary, astounding fancies. In the Kildare Street Club, a colonel sat drawing a traveler lost on a fearsome heath, at work by the light of a single candle; in mansions and rectories one invented ghost stories, dwelled on the past, told tales, or wrote wistful jingles about the peasants. Such an environment fostered endless potential Le Fanus. Joseph Sheridan, however, had not Sheridan blood for nothing. Intermittent genius went, in him, with energy, staying power, and the ability which was to stamp itself on the *Dublin University Magazine*.[3] In Dublin he was the center of a circle; on and outside Ireland he left his mark. As a novelist, it appears, he wrote too much, and with a sometimes bewildering inequality.

Mr. Browne's research into the Le Fanu writings has been exhaustive; and, it might seem from the tone he takes, often exhausting. One may assume—for few of us are, probably, in the position to contest—that at least a number of those costume romances, touched by the occult, are, after all, rightly oblivion's prey. The fact may be that Le Fanu, as a subject, is not suitable to the categoric method; and that an at once general and more searching analysis of his art and temperament, where both are found at their truest, would be of greater value. As it is, the desiderata of the "British Novelists Series"[4] would appear to weigh heavily upon Mr. Browne, who gives us a conscientious but uninspired study. Dealing with so much that is out of print, he can but state opinion rather than invite judgment; and, with regard to some aspects of Le Fanu, he is stiffened by shyness, if not prudery. The voluptuousness of *Carmilla*, for instance, has not been stressed as honestly as it should be; and the suggestion that *Uncle Silas* suffers from dilution owing to overlength may be found surprising. To delays in production must be charged the now incorrect statement that the most recent edition of *Uncle Silas* is the abridged version issued in 1940. The Cresset Press returned this novel to us, uncut, so lately as 1947.[5]

The biographical chapters and list of the works are useful; this unassuming study deserves its place, for reference; nor should we deny it merits of its own. The outstanding work on Le Fanu is, however, still missing: let us hope it may come.

Books in General

Mr. Beluncle, by V. S. Pritchett. *The New Statesman*, October 20, 1951.

It has been found, in general, that our contemporary novel suffers from some deficiency—there is, somewhere, failure of power, weakness, loss, inability fully to give out heat, light, and conviction, in the mass of serious fiction which comes our way; and in the less serious even the daydream cools. Too often, the preoccupation with art (for never more may the novelist hope to be unself-conscious) makes the aesthetic framework too obvious—not because the aesthetic should not be there but because the human content seems different, thin, and small. There is an effect of internal vacuum. Can this be traced, perhaps, to absence of the necessary obsession? In major novels—is it too much to say?—obsession is to be felt twice over. Its presence provides the theme and its play the plot; at the same time the novelist can be felt to be held by an obsession with his own subject.

The tears shed by Flaubert *as* Emma Bovary are, ultimately, inseparable from the tears and sweat he shed over the work of giving her form in art. Absolute detachment is impossible, and, were it possible, would be fatal—semi-detachment, a sort of shifting, cautious, ambivalent attitude on the part of the novelist to his characters, already serves the novel badly enough. Man matters—no dissolution of ideas round him, threats, pressures, or changes in his condition can dislodge him from his individual fortress of importance. Man is the center of the universe—knowing he is not, he continues to feel he is. He is creator, not creature, of his environment, agent of his own destiny, actor in his own drama. For the novelist who is no longer able to see man as he secretly sees himself, the time has probably come to lay down the pen. The difficulty is, in the present day, to find a man to show as *he* sees himself, without being forced to construct, for his operation, a world almost wholly out of the true. And we have exhausted the merits of the subjective landscape—just as the guise of the character must be realistic, his setting (physical, social, and geographic) must conform to what does now exist and is known. That remains a law of the novel, and we are not to break it. As we now live, and see life, there would seem to be an increasing discrepancy between fact, or circumstance, and feeling, or the romantic will; and the novelist, in his search for a scale to work on, is increasingly worried by the discrepancy. But, looking back, is it not on that very discrepancy that tragedy for its force and comedy for its richness have relied? The thing has never been simple: the novel has never not been at grips with modern society.

It may be that contemporary man, who offers the contemporary novelist his character, begins to be dwarfed by his sense of his own time, to envisage less through the fear of envisaging too much, and to seek anonymity, passivity, uniformity, in some hope of escaping the eye of fate. He may be less apt to tower in his own view, or to assume his own dramatic importance. But this is unlikely—we may conceal but we always generate fantasies: not even the minor character is without them, and the major character not only entertains them but makes them felt. There continue to be giants in possibility—there is something wrong with the novelist who cannot perceive them, who refutes them, says they are obsolete, then complains he does not know where to turn. V. S. Pritchett has never been shy of the outsize character; he triumphs in giving us *Mr. Beluncle*.

This novel could have no other, better name: exactly speaking, the character is the story. There are events, occurrences, but in all cases Philip Beluncle is either directly or indirectly their prime cause. Father-figure, though an uneasy father, Mr. Beluncle also thinks he is God—as his wife Ethel explains, in parenthesis. He has three sons, Henry, George, and Leslie, and a semi-senile mother dwelling under his roof, in an outlying London suburb, Boystone. Ups-and-downs of fortune, switches of occupation, unostentatious changes of residence have been and are likely to be constant: at present (that is, within the time of the story) we have

Beluncle floating on a surface prosperity, partner in a small business, manufacturing furniture. "Bulux" (his inspiration) has become the smiling name of the firm; his co-partner, a widow, is Mrs. Truslove—she has provided the capital, he, he believes, the drive. Religious roving, also, is at a pause; directed by his belief in "Mind," Mr. Beluncle has come to rest in a worship based on the teachings of a Mrs. Parkinson.

> If All is Mind and Mind is All,
> Man cannot sin and did not fall.
> Hold to this thought and we shall be
> At one with Mind in harmony,

sing the Boystone Parkinsonians, on Sunday morning.

> The church of the Parkinsonians was a place of flowers and smiles. The Parkinsonians smiled in the hall as they greeted each other. Out in the town they were proud of the ridicule they suffered and their faces reported to each other the week's tale of quiet triumphs . . . The Parkinsonians—their correct name was the Church of the Last Purification, Toronto—were a healthy-looking collection of clean, smiling people, broad and bummy, whether male or female, and, with the exception of one or two poor people among them, they dressed expensively. Among the summer dresses, the fine hats—some of them from Bond Street—and the scents, there sat living examples of prayer promptly answered; and the satisfaction of it added to the weight of the person. People who were converted to the Purification put on weight at once, as if it had been sent down to them by the Central Committee of the party.

The high social cachet of Parkinsonianism is, in these days of summer, part of the general sunshine in which Beluncle basks. Lady Roads, priestess of the cult, has a well-to-do problem nephew, Mr. Chilly, who has paid a considerable premium into Bulux in order to learn the business: he learns little. Mrs. Truslove, though not a convert to the Purification, has a crippled sister who is among the worshippers; the miraculous curing of Miss Dykes is shortly to be reported to Toronto. Mr. Phibbs, the

Boystone stationmaster, father of Mary, Henry Beluncle's sweetheart, is another adherent of this church. Ethel Beluncle refuses spiritual experience; Henry and George, in this as in other matters, yield, though dividedly, to paternal pressure. The extent and exercise of that pressure, its variations, the attempts of the boys to slither from under it, provide the tormenting comedy of the story—for Beluncle, also, suffers.

> It seemed to Beluncle that he was surrounded by a family who took everything from him and were trying to break him; but what especially he did not like was the physical appearance of his sons. They were growing to be men and he felt this was a sickness that was overtaking them, for their voices were thin, light, and nasal, they were pompous and rash in their opinions, their feelings were evidently in a continuous lightheaded flutter, and their shyness embarrassed them. Every time he saw them he thought them half-grown and he could hardly resist striking them in their weak faces, in which he saw the garbled lineaments of himself. "I'd like," he said apologetically, "to knock their blocks off." He ordered them, he thwarted them abruptly, he shouted at them, his violence growing more troubled as they got older, but not from any conscious policy. They had been in him and now like three callow lunatics they were trying to get out.

Leslie, the precocious last of the trio, has taken up a satiric stand of his own. George, the doglike infatuate, hangs about at home, awaiting the promised job. "'You said when I left school you would see about a job,' said George. 'I left at Christmas.' 'God has the right work waiting for you when you are ready for it,' said Beluncle. 'Hasn't he?' 'I don't know,' said George. 'You said you'd ask Mr. Miller.'" Henry, nineteen, clerk in the firm of Bulux, collapses from resolve after resolve—

> —weak, afraid and secretive before his father. Before that warm, full, decided voice his desires had gone. He had now only one desire, the desire not to burst into tears . . . .

Release for Henry finally is the outcome of a twist at the end of the scene about Mary Phibbs: the love-illusion dissolves, as though under acid, but

Henry makes known his intention of quitting Bulux. Mr. Beluncle for the first time sees in his son a will. Hitherto there has been resistance from women only—from Ethel, the wife, from Mrs. Truslove, the business partner. Mrs. Truslove, pale, abrupt, and collected, has long been waiting to be seduced; her true consummation has been to be seduced financially. Desire, in Beluncle, works upon shifted ground. "He noticed that sex was discussed everywhere, but he preferred to maneuver it out of the way, the sexual instinct interfered with the acquisitive." In him, a burning disturbance is caused by money. Ethel, from whom nothing is to be got, is no longer an object of desire, but she mates with one instinct in Beluncle: she is an inspired, tireless quarreler. Epic showdowns shake the Beluncle home, and are, as unique, a source of family pride—Henry despises the sickly unity of the Phibbses.

What, then, is this operator, this Mr. Beluncle? One has the impression that Mr. Pritchett is not so much his creator as the holder of a secret key to his works. We have a figure heaving forward at us out of the print, a dense, florid, abundant, intolerable, physical personality, collecting detail, fusing extraordinary attributes into itself as the book proceeds. Force gathers, and the Beluncle mind, with its leaps and sidesteps, imposes itself on us by its mad consistency. This is a man in his early fifties, who has juggled with projects and fled from creditors; prosperity now is a crust, with a gulf beneath. Humiliations and flittings have left their scar on his family, but engendered also their haughtiness: they feel themselves set apart. Beluncle has nothing but what he is—he is the indigenous giant of a lower-middle-class jungle of fears and rumors, the manipulator of the success legend, the big boy of the dolls-house suburban and petty business world. Everything he does or touches becomes an affair—with God, with the house Marbella, with the motorcar, with Lady Roads's potential of more money, with the West End offices refurbished, with the lobster so suddenly bought. We quit Beluncle at the lip of yet another abyss: is it real to him? Less real than he has been to us.

Mr. Beluncle, at once acrid and perfect comedy, fulfills requirements: here is our missing novel, without deficiency. Mr. Pritchett has set in motion, it may be found, a revolving rather than a progressing plot: the core is character; events are repercussions. Dialogue illustrates, and the visual setting—July Boystone and Hetley, the built-about city factory—is of a sureness which induces a repeated surprise. The art is deliberate, but what might be for the reader halting or cooling effects of deliberation are dazzlingly swept away; for here is a case of what might be meant by obsession. Mr. Pritchett gives us a preposterous, major man. *Mr. Beluncle* not only reasserts but enriches the English novel tradition.

Exploring Ireland

Wait Now! by Rachel Knappett. *Observer*, May 4, 1952.

Enterprise, in the matter of travel, is not always measured by the length of the journey. Miss Rachel Knappett set out across the Irish Sea in a spirit of high adventure, with open mind, exceedingly little money, and no plans. If she contemplated a book, she does not say: behind her lay a strenuous war, on the land; already she was the author of the well-received *A Pullet on the Midden*. One may be glad she decided to give us *Wait Now!*, an unself-conscious and smiling chronicle of her Irish years. Her writing reflects herself, an engaging person: to say she fell on her feet here would be misleading, for she gives the impression of having never been off them. Dublin met her friendliness with its own; after that she records a drop in morale when a walking tour threatened to peter out in the dusty vacuity of an Irish village. Then one fine morning she strolled into the neighboring castle, where she remained for six months as "spare daughter." That had been the butler's idea, and it worked well.

The exiguities of an Irish household have been described before, but the freshness of their impact upon Miss Knappett gives them freshness for us. The absence of any front door (though there were many others), the drama preceding a bath, the electric wiring—"wires and cables loop and twist about, plunging under carpets and emerging through windows in an exceedingly baffling manner"—and the certainty that any object sought for would be found in the least expected place, all had a formidable charm. How the paying guests reacted, we do not learn. After the castle, Miss Knappett lent a hand to a young English couple, Mr. and Mrs. Brave Pair, expensively fighting for their illusions in a newly purchased, falling-down country house—nobody who has witnessed, from near or far, the attempts of such immigrants to install themselves will query this dire account. Miss Knappett, to her own knowledge, never exaggerates: whether she was not sometimes imposed upon by our Irish tendency to play "stage Irish" for newcomers, one feels less certain. Most original, least to type, is her third adopted home, the big farm of the Ridge of Flat Stones, some miles south of the Border. Family character stands out; the hurried instruction as to the garden door — "Put the key in upside down and turn it the wrong way" — rings true.

A City Growing

Dublin: 1660–1860, by Maurice Craig. *Observer*, May 18, 1952.

Maurice Craig's *Dublin* is by definition an architectural and social history, covering two centuries. As such it is invaluable, and was needed. The book shows, besides its evident claim, close concentration on an internal subject, i.e., the complex evolution and fluid entity of the Irish capital. Architecture is the mold of civilization, an imperfect mold because an expressive one: so much is by nature preset to work against it — to deform the concept, balk the carrying-out, or nullify the idea which lay behind. Nowhere is this more palpable than in Dublin, whose incomparable beauties gain, perhaps, by their air of having never quite been on ordinary terms with life. Were it possible, in writing of any city, to depersonalize its plan and monuments, to abstract façades, colonnades, and perspectives, in their initial purity, from the confused mesh of desires, impulses, thoughts which have made up the being of its inhabitants, it still would be false to do so in the case of Dublin. Of this, Mr. Craig has been well aware. He has cast his net wide as to what is relevant: a surprising variety of material has been integrated into this single, purposeful work.

The survey, or history, is shaped into four parts — "Ormonde's Dublin," "Swift's," "Grattan's," and (on from the Union) "Whose?" "It is difficult," admits the author frankly, "to write with patience of the nineteenth century in Ireland." He has sustained that ordeal up to 1860, at which date, or within the decade following, the classic tradition in building finally ran out. (The lateness of its survival, and consequent pleasing unity of many of Dublin's streets, as compared to progressive London's, he has remarked.) With Restoration Dublin, witty if still inchoate, and with the projects of Ormonde when, as Charles II's viceroy, the inspired duke returned from exile in France, Mr. Craig has been, possibly, happiest—here is an almost unspoiled field for research. Swift's age and the Georgian epoch, not less in themselves congenial, have been, as subjects, more worked over: the author, in this middle part of his book, takes his stand on a bracing accuracy, for a good deal of misinformation has to be cleared away. Ormonde's wish that Dublin should be not only a nominal capital but a visibly civilized and august one was to be realized a century after his own day: by 1760 expansion had well begun—estates were being developed; the Renaissance grid plan succeeded the original tangle; new wide streets struck outward into the country; squares enclosed light; churches, city mansions, and civic buildings multiplied. The architects of this era, as of foregoing ones, are discussed and placed: for detail, region by region, we are given appendixes. The author's picture of Dublin's growth, and effect, conveys a sort of poetic exhilaration:

> Here [he says of the city's longest street] more strikingly perhaps than anywhere else in Dublin, the effects of local fenestrations may be appreciated. The "patent reveal," a thin plaster lining round the windows, which projects about three-quarters of an inch beyond the brickwork and is usually painted white or near-white, whatever the color of the sash- and glazing-bars, is here seen in all the brilliance of its light-catching and reflecting effect. Down the whole length of this street the light ripples in gay vertical streaks, varied within modest limits and disappearing, as cheerful as ever, into the anonymous distance.

Exactitude, a technical edge to style, is a merit in writing about our capital, which too often inspires diffused, subjective prose. Mr. Craig's observation that the lordliest building epoch was not a literary one, and that the literary renaissance of the late nineteenth century coincided with the descent upon Dublin of commercial hideousness, invites thought. Can our literature be due, perhaps, only to the saddening bourgeois habit of introspection? We write, we talk, but our overdue emergence from an aesthetic torpor, from a sort of sensuous negligence or indifference, has barely begun. Mr. Craig's *Dublin* may, like a sunny city, give momentum to living for living's sake.

Ascendancy

The Anglo-Irish, by Brian Fitzgerald. *Observer*, November 16, 1952.

This book traces the rise to power of what has been called "a race within a race." Ascendancy, Mr. Fitzgerald shows, cannot be merely inherited or arrived at; neither birth nor careerist achievement quite accounts for it; only by character is it to be maintained. Continuous action and demonstration, morale and energy are required. Those qualities are exemplified by the three persons here chosen as illustrating the central theme—Richard Boyle, first Earl of Cork; James Butler, twelfth Earl and later first Duke of Ormonde; and Dean Swift. In all other aspects no three could be more unlike. Each overlapping a little upon the other's time, the capitalist adventurer, the martial aristocrat, and the intellectual succeeded to one another upon a stage left empty when, at the Battle of Kinsale, 1601, the Gaelic, feudal aristocracy of Ireland was swept away.

Anglo-Irish dominance lasted for three centuries—dawned with the seventeenth, entered upon its twilight with the close of the nineteenth. Of this period Mr. Fitzgerald's study covers exactly half: that is, from the start to the culmination. We open with Boyle's arrival in Ireland, close with Swift's death, and watch, through 150 years, the first harsh, individual enterprise give place to Protestant nationalism. Grattan is next to come.

The contribution the Anglo-Irish have made to Ireland is now recognized: it is one sign of a happier epoch that the extent, nature, and worth of the contribution should be, by general consent, examined. Mr. Fitzgerald's relation of characters to history, his threading of continuity through three different lives, is therefore not only skillful but apposite. Boyle came to Ireland, frankly, to make his fortune, and, in consolidating himself and his family, founded something more than was swept away when the 1641 rising ravaged Munster. Antipathetic to many as he can but remain (in spite of Mr. Fitzgerald's engaging portraiture), Boyle brought in with him the ideas of the then new world, and imposed one kind of mold of civilization—fruitful land, busy ports, thriving strong little cities, foundries, markets, bridges, and roads.

Boyle *became* Anglo-Irish; Ormonde was born as such. (Of the Butlers, Mr. Fitzgerald says: "Ireland might not be their nation; but it was very definitely their country.") For centuries his Norman-descended family had ruled from Kilkenny, strong and illustrious: it was for him to meet the crisis caused by revolution in England. "Out of the feudal wreckage something indestructible survived, something that was vital to him: the habit of service." From the impact on Ireland of Charles I's breach with his Parliament, total chaos nearly resulted; that it did not was due to Ormonde's temperate leadership. He was to live to see reemergence and, with it, some disillusion: preeminently, he justified his class at a time when its worth to Ireland was put to test, by transforming "faith into honor, morals into manners." Thanks to the Ormonde prototype, his kind were to befriend as well as to ornament their country for two centuries more.

With Swift comes the voice. The dooming, one might almost say, of the English dean to become never quite an Irishman but an Irish patriot provides the third, most telling, part of this book, and gives context for a picture of miseries with which Anglo-Ireland failed, till too late, to grapple. Exploitation of land and labor, repetitive, crippling blows to trade and industries, from the English side, make the dire background of these 150 years. In the Anglo-Irish, those invaders and settlers who came to conquer, stayed to possess and love, national responsibility did come to be born, but social responsibility, alas, not. Where there was benevolence, there should have been reform.

Mr. Fitzgerald, whose increasing importance as a historian and biographer is to be noted, gives us a book to be read on both sides of the Irish Sea. He writes disinterestedly, and his hope that this analysis of the past may throw light on some of Ireland's present-day problems should, the reader will feel, be realized. And *The Anglo-Irish* has a second possible theme: i.e., the effect of Ireland on English history.

A Man and His Legend

Arnold Bennett, by Reginald Pound. *Spectator*, December 5, 1952.

"I have never had a clear or fixed ambition," stated Arnold Bennett, towards the end of his days. The career with its stupendous impetus was, we are to take it, without plan: it was typical that he shrank from autobiography, which implies the wish to stamp a pattern on life. "Everything has gone *wrong*, my girl," he muttered to Dorothy Cheston Bennett as he lay confusedly dying. There had been a succession of ups-and-downs, of eventualities; nothing so singly traceable as an ascent or descent; nothing yet to evaluate as a whole, in the last issue. If he intended to look back, he died too soon. There had been success, a long range of peaks of unequal height, separated by dips of unequal depth, drifted across by some undefined nightmare. There had been the incredible realization of the *vie rêvée* on the part of an original nobody from the Six Towns (he elected to call them Five for the sake of euphony) and the deliberate, prodigal spinning of a legend. There had been accomplishment on a scale wearying even to remember: the unremitting, killing, ambidextrous work—one hand for money, the other for fame in art. There had been "mental efficiency," sustained against a background of insomnia. Almost every day was on record, there in the journals; totals of words per annum were added up. To what it all amounted, others were left to say.

Much too much, accordingly, falls on the biographer. Mr. Reginald Pound has been left to tackle a story which lacks shape—had it had shape, Bennett might well have written it. Mr. Pound's task has been rendered factually easy, psychologically probably more exacting, by the massive existence of the journals; in addition to these he has had recourse to letters till now unpublished, friends' memories, and the talk, albums, and documents of the Bennett relatives. He has followed the track through the Six Towns and back through the scenes of a vanished London. Thoroughness, blended with fascination, has perhaps caused Mr. Pound to mass almost too much material for a single purpose—or too much, at least, for any purpose but his. For he does reflect in a somewhat unwieldy book the high-powered unwieldiness of the life; if his manner is inconsecutive, so were Arnold Bennett's fortunes; if his pages seem overcrowded, so were the years. At least, Mr. Pound has given us a full-sized portrait.

Arnold Bennett desired celebrity, and won it: he reveled in what was won. Only a giant temperament could sustain so much—the glare, the pressure, the tempo. He had been an uncouth adolescent, moody, cramped by a speech defect, an uncertain scholar, a slow developer. It happened that the first story he ever read (read to himself, that was) was

"The Ugly Duckling": it was to fill him with "a sense of the deep sadness which pervades all romance, beauty, and adventure"—nonetheless, it was in search of those that, as a youth, he left the Midlands for London. H. G. Wells, years later, found himself "exposed to the question whether Bennett was an educated type. I would say that in my sense of the word he was absolutely immune to education and that he did not need it." Enough that he learned French, and he read the masters: there set in an association of France with genius, an identification of art with fame. Mr. Pound finds that a desire to emulate, not an intention to excel, was the career's mainspring: a phantasmagoric image of Second Empire afflu-ence, homage, and prestige. Bennett's life conformed, by the end, to his most extreme wish: as a novelist he is probably all the better for having *lived* his fantasies, not written them. Nor, as a man, was he doomed to outlive their spell—the yacht, the dinners, the ballrooms, the palatial hotels, the fine festive houses: nothing gorgeous and concrete came to be Dead Sea fruit. Intangibles, it may be, were less certain: in the major novels, where he allows space, melancholy follows at a slow march be-hind the characters; he traced in fiction what he ignored in life—the inevitability of the route of fate. These are works of fulfillment, not of desire, lacking—it has later been found—in poetry. The great French, it must be recollected, were his masters. The many secondary novels are works of gusto, addiction, dry sense, notation, method. It appears that he sometimes did know, sometimes not, on which of two planes, as a novel-ist, he was writing. He had an almost dehumanized concentration; he had arrived at perfected craft.

"Am I an artist?" The stir, the hope, the premonitory inkling of a sensa-tion began early; the journals registered a suspense between arrogance and uncertainty. Impatience for verdicts, after each book, gave place to impatience with them. Affirmation came with *The Old Wives' Tale*: Wells spoke, Conrad spoke, then Hardy. *Clayhanger* and later *Riceyman Steps* were also to stand up, rocks, over his otherwise tidal reputation. Gener-ally, reception was uncertain, sales only just less so; sales, at home, in America, never completely dropped, but above a point the market stayed unpredictable. Arnold Bennett's intense concern with money, once found faintly repugnant, seems sympathetic now: he was haunted by insecurity, never forgot the pawnshop. Money was an affirmation he had to have; something he had to generate by the brain. Journalism, with which he began and ended, brought in the money rapidly with most sureness; the rate soared, with his authority, to half a crown a word. Power became total in this sphere—Arnold Bennett, book critic, was the kingmaker; the best-seller lists waited upon his pen.

Many of his contemporaries are still living; Mr. Pound must therefore evoke the man both for those who knew him and for those who know but the legend—legend already a little blurred, already worked upon by distortion. The touch on the private life, the domestic chaos, has been, one may say, excellently discreet; the abiding friendships (Bennett broke few contacts) and the dementing relationship with the theater have been accorded the space their importance asks.

About the fact of celebrity there is a touch of miracle. Arnold Bennett's queer body, jutting unfinished face, bounderish hair-crest, puffed eye-lids, and wobbling chin might have been specially molded for their role. There was a sublimation of disability. Bonhomousness, a splendid air of top form, stood guard over the inner tensions; his Midland recalcitrance sprang surprises—you never knew where you had him; that was the best of all. The never-mastered stammer gave further, grand, arresting drama to speech. He had himself charged the stammer, years ago, to the conflict within him of two wills—one anxious to speak and the other not. How much silence stayed in him, we shall never know.

Three Novels by an English Writer with a Keen and Sardonic Eye

Venusberg, Agents and Patients, A Buyer's Market, by Anthony Powell. *New York Herald Tribune Book Week*, December 14, 1952.

The significance of writing—and, it may be, in particular of the novelist's art—is added to by the factor of time. For Anthony Powell, whose position in the English literary scene has been from the first unique, and whose achievement becomes with every book more important, the years, by the pattern of their unfolding, have provided subject, inspiration, and range. In fact, Mr. Powell's attitude to his own epoch is dramatically acute, with a background of philosophic enjoyment. By some paradox, convulsive and drastic change has produced in England a group of artists and novelists, now in their middle years, who write of civilization with authority—an authority which, however satiric, has not in happier ages been excelled. These have seen the conventions falling like autumn leaves; bare, the tree of tradition remains standing. Mr. Powell is of the same generation as Evelyn Waugh, Cyril Connolly, Henry Green, Osbert Lancaster,[6] and, indeed, Graham Greene—though this last has expanded into a different area. All enjoyed the benefits, now so much debated, of the English public school system; all were at Oxford in the years following the First World War, were still young enough to play their parts, militarily or otherwise in the Second, and had fully entered upon creative life in the packed, tense decades lying between the two.

It is misleading—with regard to English, as apart from Continental writing—to speak of "groups," or "schools"; at the most, we have had certain alliances between poets, but there is nothing analogous in the field of prose. Mr. Powell and his contemporaries have in common the quality which at the same time most sets them apart—an almost savage originality. Alike, at the outset, in circumstance, and amicably drawn together by some affinity, they are all the more strongly, as writers, detached from one another. Intellectually, they are fascinated by society—which exercised, one may well recall, that same fascination for Balzac and Stendhal, James, and Proust—but their reactions have been in each case different. They are conscious of looking into a splintered mirror, arresting by its very distortions, in which the central image has been cracked across. No other similarity links together the novels of Evelyn Waugh, Henry Green, and Anthony Powell. An almost uncanny rapport between two visions does, it must be said, constitute Osbert Lancaster the ideal artist for the jacket of *Venusberg* and *Agents and Patients*.

An elegiac streak, a potential of ironic tragedy, runs through the driest, most mannered of his comedy—in the earlier work, this streak is near the surface; in the later, more absorbed, almost submerged. His work as a novelist falls into two distinct parts, which it might not now seem pretentious to call periods—five novels published between 1931 and '39; then, after twelve years, two more. *Venusberg* and *Agents and Patients* belong to the first group, *A Buyer's Market* to the second. Between the London publications of *Venusberg* and *A Buyer's Market*, twenty full, far from negative years extend.

Between the two periods, Mr. Powell's silence, excellent as the reasons for it were—throughout the war he was in the army, then he was editing and writing a study of John Aubrey—caused a sort of hedonistic depression. It is impossible to resign oneself to abstention on the part of a living writer capable of giving acute pleasure, and a nagging gap was felt in the fiction lists till, in 1951, Mr. Powell reentered the field with A *Question of Upbringing*. Reappearance, to which for the reading world so much importance attaches, is perhaps a still greater ordeal than first appearance: the triumph with which Mr. Powell surmounted this could have, alone, been the measure of his powers. He, however, not only fulfilled all expectation: he added an element of surprise—a change of angle, of manner, to an extent a change of subject, though never of temperament, declared itself. The light, apparently brittle, fortuitous-seeming continuity of the novels of the earlier group was gone. There was less impressionism and more reflection. Dialogue, instead of providing the main framework, was now introduced chiefly to add highlight. Characterization went deeper, and was at the same time deliberately more diffused. The aim was texture—almost a painted effect—and the underlying subject was continuity. Mr. Powell, in fact, has transposed himself from the mood of the Thirties to the mood of the Fifties. Instinctively—for such things cannot be calculated—he remains in time with the world.

Because, perhaps, of the very fact of that transposition, the earlier Anthony Powell novels keep their freshness. *Venusberg*, that wry Baltic idyll, and *Agents and Patients*, with its adept London monsters, keep intact their austere, laconic, remorseless funniness. They are classics, comedies of fatality: nothing in them "dates." They fall into the class of books which could not be written now, but which can be read now with, for some reason, redoubled pleasure. The sentimental education of Lushington (all, perhaps, in a moment of picking up flower petals from the floor) and the education through exploitation of Blore-Smith at the hands of Chipchase and Maltravers are themes for all time, in the unspoiled manner of one. Mr. Powell never wore out this manner; he moved onward from it, leaving it at perfection. Nor is Da Costa, for instance, less in Gothic strangeness than those larger-scale figures in the novels to come.

A *Buyer's Market* follows A *Question of Upbringing* in the sequence subtitled A *Dance to the Music of Time*. Jenkins, the "I" of the story, pursues, or is one might say pursued by, the repetitive pattern and recrossing

fate-lines of characters already met at Eton and Oxford or newly encountered during the London summer season of 1928. Uncle Giles reenters,
though too briefly; Stringham and, above all, Widermerpool are operative. The action of the story takes place at a dinner party at the Walpole-
Wilsons', preceding a debutantes' ball; at the ball itself; at a more ambiguous party, that same night; at a certain Mrs. Andriadis's; during a later
weekend at Hinton Hoo with the Walpole-Wilsons, to which is linked a
more taxing luncheon; and in the autumnal mood and bohemian twilight of the ill-fated Mr. Deacon's Soho lair.[7] Association, not passion,
spins the plot—above all, this is a time looked at *down* time: a deliberately narrow, intensified, directed feeling of perspective is never lost. A
peculiar aroma distills itself from that evoked year—the dance tunes, the
topics, the dresses, the little vices, the very light on the streets. There is
something bizarre, something almost hallucinating about the very correctness of this correct scene—this yesterday brought swimming back
into view under the compulsions of our today. Finally, this is a book about
the English, not only then but now—absolute as a comedy of the English
character. Seldom, I fancy, has the almost entire strangeness of that race
been so much beheld from the inside, so equitably rejoiced in, so fully
savored, so mildly analyzed, and so at least nearly completely plumbed.

In Spite of the Words

The Laughing Matter, by William Saroyan. *The New Republic*,
March 9, 1953.[8]

"I do what I please and I am willing to be misunderstood. The thing
which is important is that which comes out in spite of the words." So
speaks William Saroyan, quoted on the back of the jacket of *The Laughing Matter*, his fifth novel. To the newcomer to Mr. Saroyan's work, the
declaration offers a helpful clue. Whether to *be* a newcomer, at this late
date, places one at an advantage or disadvantage, one cannot say: some
claim may be made to a fresh approach; but as against that one cannot
fail to react—can but have reacted well in advance—to the vast, existing,
pervasive reputation. A bulk of feeling, whether for or against, palpably
surrounds the Saroyan name.

Here is what must be called an *affective* writer—one who has, that is to say, worked upon, tinged, and to an extent created a whole mass of persons' conception of life. He supplies what a public is looking for, slant and atmosphere. He has not merely, by some august fortuity, happened, chanced, or blundered upon a public; he may be said to have charmed one into existence and, by his blend of oddity with persuasive strength, bound his readers to him along his way. He is most impressive, apparently, when at his most disarming. "It is good," he has further laid down, "for a writer to act the way that will most effectively give the impression that he is a great writer. I think that I am a potentially great writer. I also think that I am a bum."

So far, short stories and plays have preponderated: since Chekhov, one has perceived, indeed expected, a sort of natural connection between the two forms. It should be added that probably since O. Henry nobody has done more than William Saroyan to endear and stabilize the short story, as it were, to guarantee it, to rescue it from its two extremes of possible disrepute—that of being purely aesthetic, divorced from life, or purely commercial, divorced from virtue. Also, does not this writer tilt against the deadening uniformity of society, constituting himself the spokesman of the odd man out, the champion of the misfit, the chronicler of the bum? Herein may lie some part of his fascination for those who do not dare deviate, but might wish to. Here, one may infer, is a tempting, disturbing, repeated manifestation of innocence, on the part of somebody who has never sold out—the inspired, sometimes flamboyant alien, for whom nothing is yet quite normal in the American scene, and who flutters and dips in Americanism, like a bird in a birdbath, without being in any way processed by it.

This novel, *The Laughing Matter*, is a terrible story. It contains not an iota of consolation, except irony—the last vision of a man trapped in an overturned burning car. A holiday idyll, a man and wife arriving with their children, a boy and girl, to be happy in a house in a vineyard, is soon shot through with misery, rage, remorse. The very first evening, sitting on the porch over drinks in the warm darkness, the wife tells her husband that she is pregnant and that the child is not his. Neighbors arrive into what is already a madhouse scene—slammed doors, someone running away sobbing. Throughout the days in the vineyard, doomed to be few, the duet of agony between Evan and Swan Nazarenus continues: at the same time, an attempt is made to keep a pitch of normality for the children's sake. The neighbors, whose own marriage is precarious, are, with *their* children drawn in as sorts of assistants to the forlorn hope—visits, picnics, river parties go on. A further factor is the Nazarenus family situation; the kind of exacerbated love guilt existing between Evan, his dead father, and his living brother—whose property the house in the vineyard is. Past-haunted, ill-adjusted, hostile, and passionately allied, the Nazarenus menfolk are still unabsorbed aliens. Evan, the brother who has made out, is an instructor at Stanford University; Dade, still vagrant, speculates and gambles—yet it is Dade who carries the key to truth. Three appalling deaths terminate the story—which, like an Elizabethan drama, can be forced to an end in no other way. Violence evades the moral conclusion.

It is in the manner of the telling that Mr. Saroyan is probably most himself. There is, for instance, a constant and it may be saving dilution of stark fact into tenderest whimsicality. Summer lighting of fantasy flickers around the scene, giving the lie to its fixed proportions. The dialogue, particularly that between Evan and his children, makes a succession of adroit, though not always unfailing, escapes from point-blank inanity: the dot-and-carry-one rhythm of the talk has a peculiar effect on the reader's nerves—one may assume the effect to have been designed. At the same time, in some of the encounters between the husband and wife, Mr. Saroyan must be credited with a majestic realism—*why* this realism is not maintained, or whether, and if so why, the author did not wish or choose to maintain it, remains a question. It may be that if *The Laughing Matter* had been written in a wholly adult way, which is to say a wholly responsible way, the situation which is considered would be unbearable—it is not easily bearable as it is. On the other hand, had the novel been written in a wholly adult way, some sort of solution, some sort of elevation above the level of sheer disaster, might have been found. As a tragedy, this contains some flaw, some vein of vacuum or weakness. Symbolism and imagery, much used, intensify and heighten the atmosphere without fortifying the main theme: somehow, the air here is too charged and dense; for tragedy, should not the air be purified? One suspects—the suspicion is fatal, from time to time—that Mr. Saroyan is beholding rather than feeling: if he *felt* more it would, surely, be an instinctive matter for him to exercise more control. Were there more control, there would be greater evenness of the moral tempo, and the "real" scenes, already instanced, would strike with a greater force.

Masterfully economical as to words, Mr. Saroyan is—in this novel at any rate—almost recklessly prodigal as to feeling; or, that is to say, would be if more were *felt*. Too much happens, with too great rapidity and too violently; there is not enough space, nor indeed is there enough time, for anything to resound or echo; and accordingly one loses the sense of magnitude. Perhaps also one suffers from not knowing this family, or from knowing it for only a few minutes, a few pages, *before* it entered its wrecked, abnormal state. Some sense of outrage, some sense of the awesome and shocking impact of the unfamiliar upon the familiar is denied one.

One may, however, be asking of this book something its author never wished to convey—possibly, something foreign to its intention. Alienness, an incapacity for the familiar, a temperamental refusal of the normal— these, together, may be the inner subject. It would have taken less than that dire revelation made on the porch to demoralize the Nazarenus family, for whom there never *was* peace, nothing but dear illusions: the very children were born with hair-trigger nerves, to an inheritance of night-dark apprehensions. Mr. Saroyan has sunk his theme in his plot, his plot in his language, with an extreme cleverness. *The Laughing Matter* cannot, on one level, fail to engage us, fail to shock and distress. If it fails to move us, that may be because we remain at odds with Mr. Saroyan as to what is, in life or art, the important thing. Or, do we? He sketches a search for grace, the last-minute grace: reconciliation. "The thing which is important," let him repeat, "is that which comes out in spite of the words."

Mind and Temperament

Ideas and Places, by Cyril Connolly. *Spectator*, May 22, 1953.

The world of letters is, according to Cyril Connolly, a disappearing one; it might thus seem dubious to say, as one would have said, that his position in it is unique. In fact, if a writer had not a unique position, he would have no position at all, the literary being almost the only world in which it is death not to be dissimilar. Let us rather say that there not only was but is something absolute about the position of Mr. Connolly, not imperiled by the emptying or changing of any scene. He creates reputation for his surroundings. His being not only a writer but much else may be what gives his writing its force and quality. A sort of sardonic passion, a gusto, a trenchant edge to discrimination marked his ten-year editorship of *Horizon*. The high-handed end of the magazine was, as Mr. Connolly anticipated, severely felt. Many will be glad that *Ideas and Places*, this critic-editor's new book of collected pieces, contains the *Horizon* "Comments," in their time-order, onward from 1945.

The "Comments" occupy about two-thirds of *Ideas and Places*. Though they neither overbalance the book nor exclude from it other material of a striking kind, their effect together is dominating; they cannot but set the tone—just as they used singly, from month to month, to decide or at least to direct the mood of each successive number of *Horizon*. They did more; they framed other contributions, they gave to the magazine its peculiar blend of variation with homogeneity, and they linked—sometimes by fantastic contrast—art with event. *Horizon*, it must be generally known, came into being soon after the outbreak of the Second World War: it was a counter-declaration, accompanied by the opening of a front. "A magazine," said the editor in the first number, "should be the reflection of its time and when it ceases to reflect this should come to an end." In 1939, time *had* a reflectable image—history. Ten years later the mirror found itself nothing coherent to reflect—which may have been the trouble with art since. However, for and within those ten years Mr. Connolly had provided an annotation which, always too wayward, sometimes too anarchistic to be journalism, now reemerges as literature. The plucking of these "Comments" from their time context, the running of them together in continuity, was a test they show no reason to fear. For what stands out finally is authority, coupled with a curious staying power. This needs stating, because Mr. Connolly has been so repeatedly called brilliant (which he is) that there comes to be an impression that he is lightweight.

Frivolity, Proust remarked, is an intellectual quality. The "Comments," under analysis, are seldom as frivolous as their tone suggests: they often are, however, shockingly funny, with something of the wit of the executioner—in particular, see "In Jugular Vein," "London Letter," and "Letter from a Civilian." A considerable part of the power goes into diagnosis, though much is also left for attack: we are treating with maladies or enemies. We are also shown that there may be an art of rage; for the effect of the diatribe on the reader is somehow flattering, often exhilarating, never lowering. One only, perhaps, suffers when one feels patronized; one can only be patronized by the dispassionate, and that Mr. Connolly never is. "Inflationary Decadence" and "The Cost of Letters" (a *Horizon* symposium) should be studied as contributory reasons for the literary decline, the artless hush, the apparent triumph of apathy which, in 1949, ended the magazine.

Fascinated by ideas, and exercising the whole of his intellectual fascination in regard to them, Mr. Connolly is happier with places. He shows genius in communicating the pleasure a sight or scene gives; his language, with its sensuous evocation, conveys not only the intimacy of nearness but the dignity of space. Sense of the lyricism of travel, which one dare not remember when one must stay at home, springs almost dangerously from his pages. Fragments occur here of the ideal travel book. Rarely in travel literature is the beholding "I" so completely suspended or lost from view, so sunk into the being of the thing-in-itself. For instance, a showery day over the Dordogne:

> Summer showers pelt down but never create a sensation of darkness: the vast landscape stretches out in its lowering greens broken by the white cliffs along the river, the brown of a castle — and suddenly the sun reappears. The turf is warm and springy, steam rises from the wild quinces along the hedges, the enormous blackberries glisten, the lemon-yellow walnut-trees or dazzling chestnuts shake themselves, the geese go back into single file, the rainbow forms across the Cirque de Montvalent; the deluge is over.

One can but be reminded that what gives body, yes, and a sort of sweetness to Mr. Connolly's writing is love of nature: a love sympathetic, sapient, and informed for plant and creature. With him humanity fares less well, though ultimately perhaps not too badly. He is aware of charity. That education has translated itself in him into a living passion can be felt in his temperament, in his mind. Indeed his mind has a temperament, which is rare.

The Informer

Witness, by Whittaker Chambers. *Observer*, July 19, 1953.

Witness is to be listed as an important book; its author's unhappy prominence, its subject, make such listing practically automatic. How great
is the importance, and what is[9] its nature? Publication in this country
brings the Whittaker Chambers document into a fresh field for reaction
and judgment. Sensation-interest is obviously less; the 1948 Hiss[10] drama,
the confrontation of accused by accuser could not but catch at imagination here, but the surrounding realities had less force. We were not
strangers to an intense concern—in a world contracted by crisis there is
no "elsewhere"—but both the climate and the import of the case were of
a particular foreignness: American.

The effect, in the main, was of moral no less than political dissolution,
and of an insecurity to which there might or might not be any bounds.
Alistair Cooke's day-by-day reporting for the *Manchester Guardian* registered the varying color of the case, though for what was then a specific
public. His subsequent *A Generation on Trial* made a wider, though a
delayed, impression. That book might, fairly enough, be reread as an
impersonal frame for *Witness*.

The unprepossessingness of Whittaker Chambers is photographed in
the Alistair Cooke account. Chambers, victim both by his own showing
and by more or less general later proof of a "smear campaign," engineered by the Hiss defense but also fed by the party Chambers deserted,
played, apart from that, the repellent role of informer. How exactly repellent that role was to him, and why and how he was driven to accept it, are
the internal matter of his book.

Witness—addressed to his children, dedicated to his wife, delivered
(not, one may feel, without some literary confidence) to the waiting
world—is a case history, so shaped as to develop a conscious argument, so
left rough as to show indentation by some not yet perfectly realized force.
The picture is of a man lately choking in the air of his own time, now in
a phase of alleviation. There is a sublimation of crisis, not yet solution.
Intellectually, the intention of the book is to trace thought and analyze
the ensuing action; but the impulse behind the writing is emotional. We
are to be made to know what it feels like to be Whittaker Chambers.

He was born in 1901; his father was a staff artist on a New York paper; his mother, an intellectual, had been on the stage. The restless, dilapidated home was on Long Island; the parents' marriage was unhappy. The horrors attending the elder child's birth were constantly relayed to him by his mother, which seems to have left the boy with some sort of feeling of enormity. He was christened Vivian, a name which he writhed under until he took instead his maternal grandfather's surname, Whittaker. He was an unpopular boy, who craved esteem and affection. To him and his brother, as adolescents, their environment was the sum of bourgeois decay. The brother, insufficiently refuged by alcoholism, killed himself, and Whittaker seems to have carried with him, towards Communism, some notion of the redemption of that dead loss. A hero-figure of his youth was Kalyaev, a pre-Communist revolutionary who as a protest burned himself to death.

Chambers arrived at contacting the Communist Party while he was still at Columbia—a university which (contrary to suggestions made at the Hiss trial) he left, though before his time, of his own accord. Next came a post on the *Daily Worker*; while there employed, he encountered and married Esther Shemitz, an idealist who did not commit herself to the Party. The marriage, exposed to every ordeal, remained the source of his staying power. A misgiving as to the new faith attacked him early: he beheld a purge of the staff of the *Daily Worker*. However, he was back into line again when, in 1932, he was sent for and told to go underground.

He was sent to Washington, to make part of a Soviet espionage apparatus: its structure, its methods, and its activities are described. When, in 1938, he deserted from the Party—"I use," he tells us, "the word 'deserted' in its simple military sense"—he was contact man between the Washington apparatus and his superior in New York City, Colonel Bykov.

Desertion made necessary immediate flight: the silent fate of renegades was well known. Sinister danger—a telephone ringing in an empty house, a prowler in the scrub round a seaside bungalow—isolated the little Chambers family, in mellow Baltimore, in dazzling Florida. In his accounts of tension, sensation, action, as in his own rapid peculiar blend of physical-psychological portrait (Bykov, and others), Whittaker Chambers excels: here appears the ability which brought him up, in the course of "the tranquil years," when he gave up hiding, from third-string book reviewer on the *Time* staff to one of the seven senior editorships of the magazine. But destiny, in the form of its most subtle instrument, decision, had not yet done with him: a day in the autumn of 1939 found him in a plane to Washington, on his way to make disclosures to Adolph Berle, assistant secretary of state. Then it was that Hiss's name in the deadly connection was first spoken.

Anticlimax followed: the information was not acted upon—till, nine years later, Chambers was summoned from his *Time* desk to give evidence before the House Committee on Un-American Activities. The Hiss case started into motion. Uncouth and suspect, Chambers entered the limelight with his appalling charge. Out of a haze of uncheckable memories and changed names, he was at pains, even, to substantiate his identity.

Only he could by the end keep track of himself, of which some part seemed hateful, some unaccountable. He conveys the sense that he *has* kept track, but can offer no proof; for this reason—that it is impossible to write merely ably about the soul. The dignifying irony of *Witness* is that the passages, which should by their content be the most authoritative, singular, and commanding, read as either slipshod or out of focus. By a convulsive process, Whittaker Chambers's soul orientated itself toward its destination, God: he became and has remained a Quaker. Thus he was aided across the bridge he had hoped he would never have to cross. He became an informer: as to the abhorrent act, he does still feel there should be a statement. In the abstract, silence might seem to be better, but not for him. So he has made the attempt to uncover all. It is through its inadequacies, its inadvertences, that the book makes its claim to human importance.

Out of the World of Dickens Comes This Memoir of a Bitter Childhood

A Cornish Waif's Story: An Autobiography, by Emma Smith. *New York Herald Tribune Book World*, May 20, 1956.

Any waif seems, somehow, a child of Dickens. This little Emma who took the Cornish roads, at the age of five, at the time of the Boer War, was in a tradition she did not know of. Unconsciously, she is the real-life image of the dereliction and poetry of childhood—the everlasting longing to be attached, versus the tingle of adventure. Few women now in their sixties, as is this author, could recapture so strange a blend of affright and zest, homesickness for a home that was no more, and resilient, philosophic endurance. Without aid from literary skill, here is the natural genius of the autobiographer: through long years, Mrs. Smith has not lost the gift of naïveté. She doubted, in spite of the promptings of a friend, whether she did right to set down her life story.

Her inhibition, she lets us know, had a dual source—the fact that her mother, whom she today likes better, is still alive, and (which is more interesting) this uncertainty: "I argued with myself that even if the record did no harm, I did not see that it could do good either. It would not help to reform the conditions under which I lived and suffered, seeing that many years have elapsed since then, during which all sorts of reforms have taken place . . . . In the end, however, I decided that I would make the record, having come to the conclusion that though my story might be too late to do any active good, it was after all a bit of history." She was quite right: humanly, this *is* history. Nor, one might well assure Mrs. Smith, has progress yet banished out of existence the inner vices, treacheries, exploitations to which she as a little girl was prey.

Laws for the protection of young children must have existed in England, but failed to operate, when Emma was handed over to the Pratts. She and Harry, her younger brother, were the progeny of a feckless unmarried mother: for long the stigma of bastardy clung to both. In accordance with country custom, the grandmother took the children—wife of a blinded miner, the brave woman had already borne twenty of her own. For small Emma she, not "Maud," was the mother-figure. At Redruth, in the then primitive depths of Cornwall, was the cottage to which lifelong affection clung—the sanded floor, the polished bureau, the picture of Queen Victoria, and the china ornaments. Breakup came when the grandparents moved to Plymouth: sunk in the slums and miseries of the seaport city the children became once more a charge on their mother. Maud cast Emma, forthwith, onto the Pratts.

The Pratts sound worse than Dickens ever conceived. Itinerants, bound to the hurdy-gurdy (then rattling with patriotic tunes), they from time to time nested in a verminous room, rank with continuous frying of cheese and bacon rinds, in whose murk white rats trod round and round in a cage wheel. Emma accompanied this couple on the roads, partly as infant singer, partly as collector of pennies when the hurdy-gurdy played with any success. Her pathos, clearly, was a commercial asset—they saw to it that she was unkempt and ragged. The waif child looked in at windows of homes, and with joy at flowering cottage gardens—today, a Cornish cottage having a garden is the peak of the adult desire of Mrs. Smith. And to ups-and-downs was added a secret horror: the child found herself forced to be passive partner in the indecencies of the elderly hunchback Pratt.

Running away at last, on a dark icebound morning, Emma—still at the age of less than twelve—preferred to entrust herself to the unknown. Ambiguous guilt hung over her; she was come to rest as the extreme junior among a bunch of reclaimed prostitutes (she, technically, was not one) in a convent penitentiary. And here (in spite of the fiction of lost virtue), innocence, home-feeling, and the dear days resumed—the nuns, the cutting of paper lace, the garden, the happy pious routine. Once again her heart was to tear, when she quitted Bagshot to face the world as a domestic servant.

Yet, in the worst of the Pratt days, immortality stirred in her.

> There was something [she says] about those singing excursions that has had a grip on me all my life. The gardens were now no longer attractive, for now it was winter. But those winter sunsets! The roar and splashing of sea waves, the glimpses of cozy interiors as a cottager would come out with a coin, the flicker of firelight, the walk at night in the dark under a clear starlight sky; then moonlight, on a night when full moon and clouds played hide and seek with each other!
>
> Before writing this book, I always felt my young days were just bad and sordid all through; but now, much that was lovely has forced itself upon my memory.

These and other life-loving admissions have led Mr. A. L. Rowse (who introduces A Cornish Waif's Story) to attribute to Mrs. Emma Smith "the right spirit, a good heart, towards such a past." To the full, I imagine, readers will agree with him. No personal past is inglorious, seen sanely: this book, if in places it horrifies, in the main inspires one. One word should be added—"Emma Smith" is not, we learn, this writer's actual name: one cannot but be sorry that her advisers did not suggest to her some other pen name. For Britain has already one Emma Smith, brilliant young author of *Maidens' Voyage* and *The Far Cry*. If confusion were to arise, it would be a pity.

A Haunting, Enchanting Story Set in Budapest

The Mermaids, by Eva Boros. *New York Herald Tribune Book World*, December 9, 1956.

Budapest, and its outlying country, is the scene of *The Mermaids*—the first novel of Eva Boros, a Hungarian lady who writes in English. 1936, August, the rose-tinted dusk of a hot summer; lights are lit, reflected into the Danube water in trembling diadems; there is half-heard music. On the terrace of one of the cafés along the Corso sits Aladar, a young-middle-aged businessman, forsaken by happiness and his wife. He has settled to a sort of regime of loneliness. Yet illusion, with all its perils, has not yet done with him. At the table touching his own, a girl seats herself: she is light-blonde, wears a shockingly green dress, carries a coat. She glances his way, sighs, glances again.

> And then, of course, the inevitable did happen. She started to talk.
> "Look," she said, "look at the Palace!"
> The Palace windows were all aglow, and so was her face. Her eyes were blue. She spoke Hungarian with a melodious, unfamiliar accent.

Thus it is that Aladar makes the acquaintance of "the first and fairest of the mermaids." Where does she come from? What is the mystery behind her rippling confidences and quick withdrawals? She cannot stay; the bus from Vorosmarty Square bears her off to a destination unknown. He retraces his steps and, without purpose, buys the small yellow roses she had admired in a shop window. Her name haunts him; she is Lalla Pirola. Later, a letter comes—will he visit her? And, with Aladar, we are to learn the secret. Lalla is a patient in the sanatorium on a hill in the wooded country some miles from Budapest. From now on, Aladar is to enter, be drawn deeply into, another element, strange as water, whose creatures approach, enchant yet again recede from him. He is spellbound by this universe of consumptives.

Meaningless, more and more, becomes all the rest of existence — mere intermissions between Aladar's visits to the hill. Vivid Franciska, of the inexplicable moods and clever fingers, and Kati, sweet, frivolous, and doomed, are Lalla's familiars and fellow mermaids — their song is rather to the soul than to the senses. The threadbare Count, ill also, is cavalier to the three. The sanatorium and the colony surrounding it, the echoing corridors and white inhuman sickrooms, the merrymaking and tenebrous emotions all have been given, by Miss Boros's art, the super-reality they take on for Aladar. Such magic is more than an accident of prose. *The Mermaids*, austere as it is lovely, is a book wrought out of depths of imagination. The characters, from whom emanates the atmosphere, are three-dimensional. The plot, whose transitions from scene to scene are so skillful that one may be hardly aware of them, has that design which proclaims a masterpiece.

It is right that *The Mermaids* should bring us, at this time, a breath of the genius which speaks in Hungary. That country and its dual capital, old and modern, not even the transient visitor can forget: Miss Boros, who for some time has lived in London, re-evokes air she once breathed, scenes she once knew well, with a certainty too calm to be called — to these the charm, the shimmer, of illusion, the tender-melancholy lightness are all subsidiary. With *The Mermaids*, literature has taken a step forward — it has been granted to Eva Boros to add, through art, to our sense of the immortality of her heroic land.

Welsh, and Quite Explosive

The Rape of the Fair Country, by Alexander Cordell. *New York Herald Tribune Book World*, April 26, 1959.

Here is a novel which may, from the start, intimidate by its violent title. Nor is *The Rape of the Fair Country*, on the whole, pacific in its contents. Wales is the victim in question, and Welsh, throughout, are the atmosphere, happenings, and vocabulary. To me, there is something explosive about Welsh writing: does this come from so dynamic a people's being compressed into what is, territorially, so small a space? Literary self-expression may be a safety valve; certainly it is much resorted to. Mountainousness, a climate prone to depressions, religious urges, political vehemence, and, not least, high-voltage sexual temperament all contribute to the inevitability of Welsh literature, as, also, to that literature's carrying a heavy national stamp. The only other regional art I know which is—in its own and a different way—at once as unmistakable and as pungent is, in this country, that of the Deep South.

How far an individual novel is advanced, or how far hampered, by linking with a region and its tradition, it is hard to decide. In justice to Mr. Cordell's vigorous book, I would wish hastily to point out that it has characteristics all and quite of its own. It is semi-historic, being set in the earlier half of the nineteenth century, stigmatizing abuses peculiar to the early industrial age, and culminating with a splendid march of the Chartists. The Mortymer family, whose fortunes we follow, are Mortymers first, Welsh second: perpetually they amaze their neighbors in the small, poor towns surrounding the iron foundries. And these pleasing beings not only excel in high-spirited bawdy humor; they show, in the face of many disasters, an almost un-Celtic sunniness of disposition, endearing volatility, and a trend to optimism.

Iestyn Mortymer, fourth of the four children, is the narrator of the story, which begins with his going to work, on his eighth birthday, at the Garndyrus furnaces. On his shift, fellow workers are all of around his age; many of the more lively are little girls. Pay amounts to some pence a week; in the children's homes, each penny is sorely needed. Hywel Mortymer, the father, ranks high in skill; he is a forge expert. Morfydd, Iestyn's elder sister, a beauty, is the family revolutionary, outspoken— and a fearless rover, too, when it comes to love. We watch, as the story progresses, the breaking down of the Mortymer parents' creed of fidelity to employers, belief in the good of hard work, abstinence from complaint, by outrageous injustice dealt out by the ironmasters. Alongside, in the Mortymer young, springs up a bitter sense of defilement by the bad system—a sense of what life might be, a longing to live like that. Round them, between the foul smoking foundries, the death-pit coal mines, extend fair fields, or rise up the mountains, free and poetic.

The local battle for human rights occasions a number of wild scenes, and is complicated by faction and counter-faction. "The Cattle," a masked band equivalent to the Ku Klux Klan, beat up the Mortymer father and burn the home; Edwina, the younger sister, is found on the side of a mountain, outraged and dead. A furnace explosion takes fearful toll. Yet life, and the faith to live it, and that faith's rewarding by joyous moments, make for renewals and heal wounds—there is Iestyn's hilarious country wedding, Morfydd's unrepentant joy in the child she christens after its errant father, and the growing, fearless splendor of the resistance which sends Iestyn, singing, to confront an unknown fate.

The Rape of the Fair Country, as an authentic document, makes addition to Welsh industrial history. That the time is "the past" should, I think, be stressed—for the handsome book jacket shows a number of figures in very contemporary garb, topped by tweed caps.

The Long Arm of Chance in Life's Tangle

The Third Choice, by Elizabeth Janeway. New York Herald Tribune Book World, May 17, 1959.

Accidents, whether or not fatal, play an unmistakable part in human fatality. Elizabeth Janeway's new novel, The Third Choice, is an example of good design, yet the plot takes off from an encounter which is a fortuity and turns upon more than one crisis precipitated by chance. This paradox, a boldness on the part of the author, is justified. That much of life is a matter of sheer happening, and that the honest novelist must accept that, we cease to doubt. Conviction is established, onward from the scene in the Connecticut nursing home, when the crippled aunt, the visiting niece, and the unexpectedly-entering young doctor first form their unforeseeable, dangerous triangle.

Mrs. Belchamber, first-rate horsewoman, has had the evil luck to be thrown: a hip has been broken—otherwise, active as she is handsome, at sixty-two, she would not be trapped in this chintzy sickroom. For Lorraine de Koning, this particular visit (there have been others) happens to coincide with a flash of dismaying insight as to herself: on the outward drive from New York she has faced the futility of her marriage—to the world's eye, prosperous and smooth-running. As for Peter Savage, he is not the patient's attendant physician; today he comes deputed to break bad news, the disheartening showing of the last X-ray.

Violent and bitter is the patient's reaction. Lorraine's later, maladroit attempt to placate the insulted doctor (whose name is his nature) leaves the two on the verge of a situation, and their subsequent meeting takes place in the same atmosphere, at once awkward and highly charged. Thus begins a passion, for whose fulfillment chance begins by scattering opportunities—the withdrawal, and the nemesis, is to be all the grimmer.

Does Mrs. Belchamber, whose convalescence keeps the lovers by her side, observe (as she might) what is going on? No: and for the sufficient reason that she is locked in a reliving of her own life. Nor is this absorption in the past, the return to her of the fullness of its emotional content, a thought-stream only. What she relives, *as* she relives it, she is writing down, day after day, secretly, in the book kept hidden beside her bed. And this story, told in the first person, Mrs. Janeway causes to alternate with the other—that of the contemporary fortunes of the niece, told in the third person; that is, by the author.

That is where design, in the good sense, not only enters the structure of the novel but so acts as to give each of the stories a dual emotional force, and, often, extra dramatic irony. For Mrs. Belchamber's experiences have been formidable: temperament, ambition, and passion have made her a character on a large scale, with a natural place on the stage of the great world.

Lorraine, by contrast, is inevitably the lesser woman—which makes the more startling, though also awesome, the struggle for the knife between the married couple, enemies, in the Park Avenue apartment. Chance, again—that of her having been delayed for a few minutes— brought about the unfortunate meeting with her husband: Herbert, a character excellently drawn. In the Mrs. Belchamber story, the accident of a childish wakening in the night to overhear a sinister conversation, accounts, one feels, for the emotional fatalism, plus recklessness, in her, to which a number of dire events are due.

The reader may query whether Mrs. Belchamber would have written as she does—articulately, flowingly, with full command of style. She is by no means a "literary" person; that is, by the outside view of her, seen through Lorraine's and other eyes. She appears, indeed, more effectively in the Lorraine story than she does in her self-told own. But that contrast, or apparent discordancy, may be part of Mrs. Janeway's design, also. I incline to think so—for it is the triumph of *The Third Choice*—the dual selection of the Book of the Month Club for June—that wild elements, while shorn of none of their wildness, are to the end kept within art's control.

Second Home

The Château, by William Maxwell. *Reporter*, May 25, 1961.

A novel need not be a love story, but is the better for being one. William Maxwell's *The Château* is, outwardly, a tale of two people, young Americans, married, spending a time in France; inwardly, there is a passion which spins the plot. From the first page, we are company with a man in a state of love; with his wife, yes, but also there is a focus upon a whole, fresh, other, enormous object. Harold Rhodes is in love with France—the tension, the heightened susceptibility, the joyous disturbance, and the sensation of being weighed upon from time to time are, as symptoms, quite unmistakable. This, his first visit, is the fulfillment of long desire, gathered-up expectation. And more: at the moment he saw the coastline at dawn through his cabin porthole, some anonymous ancestor woke within him; the tears forming a prism over his eyes were those of a homecomer, awaited.

The big ocean-liner is at last at anchor. "The sea was calm, the lens of the sky was set at infinity. The coastline—low green hills and the dim outlines of stone houses lying in pockets of mist—was in three pale French colors, a brocade borrowed from a museum . . . . There it was, across the open water, a fact, in plain sight, a real place, a part of him because he could say he had seen it . . . . He put his head clear out into the beautiful morning and smelled land. His lungs expanding took in the air of creation, of the beginning of everything."

Only a master novelist could be so bold as to open at this high pitch, then so wise as not to attempt to sustain it—though at points in *The Château* it is to be reached again. Harold Rhodes's early vision off Cherbourg is succeeded by the fuss and banalities of disembarkation, followed upon by the dulling fatigues of a daylong train journey, dislocated by changes, no porters, much baggage. The month is July, the year 1948: France is still in disarray after war, scarred physically by the assaults of Allied invasion, psychologically by enemy occupation. Harold and Barbara, spear-head of the returning tourists, find themselves welcome but not prepared for. Ardent travelers are subject to tragicomedies; these two, to whom all things matter acutely, are overhung by a quiver of anxiety, brought to a halt often, sometimes dumbfounded. They turn on street scenes and ruins, on faces, on towns, on the coast of Brittany, and then on the Loire country, their joint, searching, unfaltering gaze.

Love acts twice over in *The Château*. That is to say, the impact of everything felt or beheld, suspected or wondered at, is doubled by the alikeness and nearness to one another, at times almost the identity, of husband and wife. This is most so when they arrive at the Touraine châ-teau which not only names the novel but stages some of its most formi-dable, though muted, scenes. It has been arranged that the Rhodeses stay here for a fortnight, as paying guests of an indigent aristocratic family. From the meeting with Mme. Viénot, their cryptic, wary hostess-to-be, in the château courtyard, the young Americans enter a formal, deeply mysterious social zone—near-arctic, at least at first. Outdoors, a rainy July; indoors, decrepit economy and chill salons. The spellbinding mo-notony of the château, the masks of its inmates, transient or hereditary, portrayed in a mood of ironic comedy, combine to build up a maximum suspense interest exceeding that of the so-called mystery novel. The out-going friendliness of the visitors, linked with a fervent innocent curiosity, is often rebuffed, yet their illusion survives.

Cannot people know each other? *Are* language, custom, and back-ground inevitable dividers? The questions follow the Rhodeses to Paris, needling them most of all during their days encamped in the apartment of Mme. Viénot's nephew. Paris itself is loud with sparrows, dusky with the dusty leafage of summer, emptying as July runs out.

I can think of few novels, of my day certainly, that have such romantic authority as *The Château*, fewer still so adult in vitality, so alight with humor.

Wonders of a Traveler's World

Blue Skies, Brown Studies, by William Sansom. *New York Times Book Review*, June 18, 1961.

"A writer lives, at best, in a state of astonishment. Beneath any feeling he has of the good or evil of the world lies a deeper one of wonder at it all. To transmit that feeling, he writes." So remarks William Sansom, opening *Blue Skies, Brown Studies* with a preliminary essay, "From a Writer's Notebook." The remark remains a key to what is to follow—a collection of travel pieces, all European, each stamped with the unmistakable Sansom touch; or call it, power to transmit wonder. In this, Mr. Sansom, author of *The Cautious Heart, The Loving Eye,* and other books, has been approached by few other living writers that Britain has.

Of his particular faculty, one is most aware when (as so often in the novels and stories) he makes the officially "ordinary" his province. In part, indeed, the hold on us of his fiction lies in that conjury which transmutes the banal—the suburban street, the stale little city park with its asphalt margin, the overlit trite café, the too-glossy living room. This forceful, at times all but hallucinated, imagination kindles at just those scenes from which others shrink. How will such a writer fare when what confronts him is in itself exotic?

The prestige of the Sansom travel books is the answer. I admit to finding *Blue Skies, Brown Studies* less dazzling, as a whole, than its predecessor, the Scandinavian *The Icicle and the Sun,* though as vicarious travel it is as satisfactory, and as a performance no less adroit—in one aspect, even, possibly more so. Mileage is greater (we range from the Mediterranean up to the Baltic); and, with that, the general subject is more comprehensive.

Also, the writer transmits, along with the wonder, impressive and various information: facts weight (though not fatally weigh down) the grace and spontaneity of his prose. We take in Capri, St. Tropez, the Côte d'Azur ("the Old Blue Strip"), Vienna and its wooded or mountain country, Salzburg, Vicenza, London, Minorca, Baden-Baden, Sogne (a Norwegian fjord), Dover. And as a tailpiece, there is Mhailand, "world of my own," fantasy island of all desire: "Here the sun shines—and it shines on most days of the year—at a delicate equinoctial slant, as if it were always spring or autumn, Maypril or Octember sunlight whose long shadows and sideways gilding of all things in a kind of soft limelight quietly burnishes the mystery of our rich pampas marshland and our small greenbaize conical hills."

Here and there, we find just that touch of the scrapbook apt to haunt any volume not conceived as a whole. Here and there, a slight gloss of over-efficiency, instance the fine job done of the Côte d'Azur—at their first appearance, these were magazine pieces: did some editors want reportage, rather than vision? No phrase is flat or mechanical, and no finding obvious. But William Sansom writes best where he is astonished, no doubt of that.

Many outward astonishments awaited him—turning, he found a wolf his neighbor on the next-door stool at a Capri bar; there was the dream-like structure of the Semmering railway. His hard-found, bright-lit little Salzburg hotel vanished while he was out buying cigarettes: "As in so many ghost stories, reality burst the enchanting balloon. Reality here was a main electric fuse blown—which had put out all the hotel's lights." Sogne Fjord's glassiness is Ibsen-haunted; all is not "endless white and gray . . . . The snows shine like stained glass, purple, lilac, rose, golden-red: wrapped in ice, the fjord burns like fire." At St. Tropez the patron saint wore a neat moustache; Mahón, capital of Minorca, was more of a British ghost town than one could credit.

The actual state and sensation of astonishment is constantly, wonderfully rendered—and why not? Mr. Sansom is "a sensation writer"; in that way, though no other, like Henry James (and recall James's travel books!) aesthetically, the two masterpieces of *Blue Skies, Brown Studies* are "The Supreme Table," which is about fine eating, and "Spain . . . the Sixth Hour," about afternoon sleep.

"Siesta," Mr. Sansom explains, "is a Spanish word. It derives from the Latin, *sextus*, the sixth hour after dawn, noon." And he goes on to evoke "the seraglio calm," the silence: "The cicada sounds its resonant chapels, and giant bees extend their tongues to lick the sleeping honey: the mantis, falsely, stands as stiff as all siesta. A fool cock may crow out a single note of strutting nerves—but that is all. The rest is silence; heavy, hot, and huge."

For scope, drama, and pungency, seek the Sansom London: "The mixture and the scale are unique and, overwhelming, can be approximated nowhere else. London is an orderly city, disordered within the apparent order . . . . It is against a strong background of ordered pattern that London produces its eccentricities—just as in that umber brick the wonderful tones of yellow and bistre and olive and lime will hum out of the grime at some sudden illuminative angle of the sun." Vienna, too, he can cause one to taste and smell: "Whiffs of incense, hot plaster, and Egyptian-smelling cigarettes seem to be the prevalent smells. Coffee, whipped cream, hockish white wine, paprika, and, curiously, boiled beef (*Beinfleisch*) are the tastes."

This writer's strength, apart from his way of seeing, is his style — subtle, alert, concrete, racy, poetic. Living style nourished by all five senses, bold in its metaphors — roof tiles of Provençal hill towns likened to "apricot-colored Donegal tweed," the restored Vienna Opera House to "a giant white-and-gold powder compact of exquisite workmanship," distant Italian cypresses to "tomb-green ice-lollies," and so on.

Mr. Sansom, in the remark I quoted, refers to "any feeling he [the writer] has of the good, or evil of the world." As to his own feeling, of such kind, he makes no statement. *Blue Skies, Brown Studies* is, accordingly, something rare in these days, a non-contentious, anti-provocative travel book. It is also a non-egotistical one, which, as the British are apt to say, "makes a change." His attitude to all humans seems festive, amicable, and tinged with sympathy. Whether or not he is fond of animals, he noted at once that the wolf in the Capri bar wore a puzzled frown.

All People Great and Small

The People's War, by Angus Calder. *Spectator*, September 20, 1969.

"The chief aim of this book is to describe, as accurately as possible, the effect of war on civilian life in Britain." So opens Angus Calder's foreword to *The People's War*. And from that aim, be it said at the outset, he has not deviated. The amassing of the facts, social, political, economic, must have entailed a ferocious labor which only a dedicated researcher could carry through: drawn from reports and statistics, they may in general be held to be unassailable. For reasons of morale or security they were withheld from the public during the war; subsequently, they can only not have been brought to daylight because of a lapse in popular interest when war ended: effectively speaking, they were nobody's business. Now Mr. Calder has made them his.

Nonetheless, he expects to run into trouble. "No doubt I shall be accused of willful 'debunking.' But . . . if a mythical version of the war still holds sway in school textbooks and television documentaries, every person who lived through those years knows that those parts of the myth which concern his or her activities are false." *Every* person? This last is a sweeping statement; and Mr. Calder makes it on what authority? It is unfortunate, in that it shakes one's confidence in generalizations which are to follow, and may inspire misgivings that, here or there, opinion is doing duty for knowledge.

Mr. Calder was three when the Second World War ended. He was not, thus, of the generation, any of the generations, that lived through it. To say that this disqualifies him as its historian would be, evidently, most foolish; on the contrary, his relation in time to the time he writes of should make for a greater detachment and objectivity—and does so in the greater part of the book. His coming to consciousness took place during the anticlimactic aftermath. He was, however, sheltered from its contaminating atmosphere—aimlessness, sluggishness, voicelessness, and moroseness—by an enviable if somewhat special environment: child of a distinguished intellectual family with a political bent, he grew up in what would have been an ambiance of discussion, reevaluation, and diagnosis.

His advantages may have carried a certain handicap—he shows signs of not having broken out, or knocked about, much, among persons other than those who formed, or connected with, his family circle and shared its outlook. Personal memories of the war, spoken or written, on which he draws for documentation, are invariably (or such has been my impression) those of a left-wing elite: and this limits his field. Other types he finds difficult to assimilate, which causes an incomprehension of them that is almost total, and as to which he shows a certain complacency. At times, this matters. One may regret, also, outbursts of a youthful censoriousness.

The war on Britain was undergone by all types. Not only The People were people, so were others. For the general run of us, existence during the war had a mythical quality, heightened for dwellers in cities under attack. The majority of us, living through those years, did not attempt to rationalize them, nor have most of us done so since. War is a prolonged passionate act, and we were involved in it. We at least knew that we only half knew what we were doing.

Exuberance during the earlier London blitzes was not a fake: at the same time, nothing deadened the sense of loss, outrage, and horror. There *was* something apocalyptic about the onslaughts. A sort of anarchical pride became the resort as life became more degradingly netted down by restrictions. The drabber years of the war were the real pill—little wonder that, as Mr. Calder points out, they have not until now become a subject. (And even he, I note, condenses 1942–45 into a chapter.) Yet the myth, though bedraggled, somehow persisted. How else should we have gone on?

Going its way once it had served its purpose, the myth dispersed. It left behind it, so far as I know, no feeling that we had been bewitched. I know few who reacted against its memory, none in whom that inspired nostalgia. What, all but twenty-five years later, is there left to "debunk"? Why should what has vanished now be suspect? Mr. Calder desires that there be a non-false picture of civilian reaction to the war, experience in it, behavior during it. That, as a desire, is shared by all. We cannot have enough, now, of the actualities.

But a picture presented in terms of the actualities *only* would be a false one: inseparable from happenings are the mood, temper, and climate of their time. Mr. Calder, one may be sure, would concede that. What alarms him is what he holds to be going on—resuscitation of a bygone glory, and exploitation in the wrong interests, for wrong reasons. But what could those be? With the young of the moment, heroics do not seem likely to "take." "It all seems irrelevant now," pronounced a schoolboy, reported on September 4 last.

As a structure, *The People's War* is quite excellent: so it is in method— alternation of statistics with narrative. Packed with matter, the book is not overweight. Mass Observation, by giving the author access to wartime files, provides not only the most living but the most impartial of the documentation; extracts from memoirs and diaries, if more colorful, seem less so. The prewar suspense (Munich and after), evacuation, the "phoney war," the collapse of allies, Dunkirk, Battle of Britain and the blitz (London and provincial), rationing, the extending call-up, the industrial all-out, industrial tensions—the psychological impacts of all are charted. Cold-bloodedly speaking, the German invasion of Russia could not, for Britain, have come at a better time—unexpected, spectacular, the new drama, the flare-up of pro-Russian enthusiasm, gave the ruin-strewn summer of '41 a saving lift, a needed shot in the arm. The dire monotony of

North African bad results was at least abated. America as a latecomer ally was less popular; the large-scale arrival on our shores of her forces made for an uneasy sense of "invasion."

Sagging or shaken morale, the places and times of its nearness to breaking point, are recorded, *then* for few eyes only; similar secrecy made reports on the devastation of cities as sparing. As bad, often, was the brutalizing slowness of their recovery, for which local inefficiency is indicted. Disaffection, a raw black bitterness in the disarmed army back from Dunkirk, was on a scale not to be measured then—limelight rather fell that "invasion summer," on the optimism and fervor of LDV[11] (later Home Guard). That force, its organization and its performances, have been rewardingly studied by Mr. Calder, as have the different limbs of Civil Defence, their coordination (so far as possible), and the generic temperament each developed: AFS, ARP, the ambulance service, the auxiliary nurses. At off times, harmony did not reign. The indomitable WVS, or green tweed ladies, fell foul, for instance, of us more saturnine wardens: we could not abide the sight of them—why, I wonder? Wardens maintained also a not always tacit warfare with the police. On the whole there was wonderfully little crime.

The war was won on the industrial front. The victory of the factories was the people's; accordingly, it is the epic of this book—as exciting are the decisions behind it, the backroom conflicts, the jockeying for position at top level. Mr. Calder's grip on and treatment of this whole section are admirable, and make for compulsive reading—how controversial it may be, *I* cannot tell. In his chapter "War on the Mind: Science, Religion and the Arts," he may find himself, with regard to some of his readers, on thinner ice. On the whole cautious, he is occasionally provocative—hard not to be. He recalls the predicament of the church—what should be the attitude to belligerence?—and the "mobilization" of arts, painting, and music. There did occur, as we know, a cultural boom which was not without aesthetic reality. But the giant determinants were the mass media: the press, broadcasting. Those two, oracles of the people's war, never had known more power or less freedom: on one hand the dictates of propaganda, on the other the taboos of censorship harried them.

In the main, the voice proved mightier than the pen. Sound made for community of sensation, was emotive (which was required), served entertainment. Genius came to the surface: ITMA[12] began. Most of all, the microphone built up star personalities. The desideratum was not to *address* the masses but speak as one of them; at that, Mr. Calder suggests, J. B. Priestley was better than Churchill. Press and radio combined in keeping the people's collective image constantly in front of the people's eyes, and did well in doing so. It was inspirational; one beheld oneself as one had it in one to be. The image was a winner. It perpetuated itself, alter a little though it might as the Churchillian rhetoric lost hold. Churchill projected it, in the first place.

Mr. Calder's analysis of "Churchillianism" is better than dispassionate; there is affection in it, as in his study of the man. The companion portrait, Bevin, has full dimension; Cripps he has failed to animate — could one? His Beaverbrook is Beaverbrook: enough. No verdict can I pronounce on *The People's War* other than, read it! This is a drastic book, but honorable. There has been room in it, after all, for this: "Sometimes I say if we could stand Monday, we could stand anything. But sometimes I feels I can't stand it any more. But it don't do to say so. If I says anything my girls say to me, 'Stop it, Ma! It's no good saying you can't stand it. You've got to!' My girls is ever so good."

Kindred and Affinity

The Irish Cousins, by Violet Powell. *Spectator*, January 31, 1970.

The book jacket of Violet Powell's *The Irish Cousins* is adorned by a family group: a framed photograph. This perfectly sets the tone of what is within. Kinship, or a close degree of affinity, characterizes the features and general attitude of boater-hatted young women in starched white ankle-length skirts and moustached young men, one in a blazer, at rest at the edge of a tennis court, between games. Backdrop, a twinkling shrubbery. There is, to the Anglo-Irish eye, a palpable give-off of Anglo-Ireland; and in its heyday. Conversation, suspended by the camera, leaves heads turned this way or that, alert and waiting. The personae are the interknit Somerville-Coghill tribes, soon to be further linked by another marriage. On the periphery may be taken to be either accepted neighbors or summer guests. The locale is Castletownshend, West County Cork, the time circa 1886.

In the forefront, vigorously seated, is Edith Œnone Somerville, "Top Dog," by virtue of seniority, and more than that, of a generation consisting largely of brothers. Next to her, beautiful in profile, holding her racquet to her chin as one might a fan, is Edith's second cousin, Violet Martin—the "Ross" of the collaboration to be. *The Irish Cousins* (which takes its title, only a plural added, from the first-fruit novel of that collaboration: *An Irish Cousin*, 1889) introduces itself as a study: "The Books and Background of Somerville and Ross." How inseparable the books and the background are, Lady Violet, Anglo-Irish herself, perceives, and goes on to illustrate.

Greater interest must concentrate on what *was* phenomenal: the collaboration. Interlocking minds, known more to criminal than aesthetic history? No, not that only: this was a rarer case—interlocking creative imaginations. Considering how savagely individual, how overweeningly solitary, as an activity, is inventive writing, how could two practitioners unify into one story?—*and* carry this off not once but again and again? The cousins, we learn, were plagued by what seemed to them fatuous questions on that subject: "Who holds the pen—or pencil, and so on?" Oneself, one retains some sympathy with the questioners. Leave it, that this was a literary miracle, plus something other. Result, a superb degree of accomplishment, a tremendous range.

Lady Violet, too wise to analyze, contents herself with comments—on the joint vision, its extra-powerful focus; on the stylishness of the joint style achieved, likened by her, in its variations, to shot silk. It may be supposed that Somerville, painter already, charged herself with that memorable verbal scene-painting, together with *outer* accounts of action (equine or human), weather, sailing adventures, meets, funerals, fairs, leaving to Ross, more fine-strung, "aware," and tense, the control of dialogue, and, where necessary, penetration into events or persons. Ross's death in 1915 leaves, in the many succeeding novels and stories, a lacuna difficult to locate—bravely though "communication" was carried on, defiantly though the works were, still, double-signed.

The answer may be that when the cousins met—which oddly, given the smallness of Ireland and the high value placed on getting together, failed to happen till both were in their late twenties—there occurred one of those fusions of personality which in one way or another can make history. Their from then on total attachment incurred no censure, and—

still stranger, given the habitual jocularity of their relatives—seems to have drawn down no family mirth. Nor was its nature—as it might be in these days—speculated upon. Absolutely, the upper-class Anglo-Irish were (then) nonphysical—far from keen participants, even, from what one hears of them, in the joys of marriage.

Edith and Violet loved to travel together, but desired no permanent breakaway from parental homes. The Llangollen Ladies, whose Plas Newydd they viewed on a Welsh tour, seemed to them—it is recorded—extremely silly. This couple of gentlewomen from Ireland were encased, armored, in the invincible heartiness of their extroverted tribe and specialized class. Round and upon them blew the prevailing gales of clean fun, anaphrodisiac laughter. Anything "extreme" was comic: that went for passion, that went for art. Dogs, jokes, were the accepted currency. Their initial literary endeavors, daylong disappearances, together, to the neglect of tennis, side-split brothers and sisters, uncles and aunts. Only when books "appeared" did menace begin. The two now ceased to be amateurs: things looked serious. The actual crux, or crunch, was *The Real Charlotte*.

It is owing to *The Real Charlotte* that all this matters: otherwise, who might care? Here, in their third novel, they cut the cable. They made their own a terrain of outrageousness, obliquity, unsavory tragedy, sexual no less than ambitious passion. *What* fired them into full-stature artists? It is on this masterpiece (which long awaited full recognition) that, as almost unwilling, almost unwitting artists, they do in today's eyes take their stand . . . Secondary in literary glory, toweringly "the thing" in terms of success, the *Irish RM* stories are less cut-to-pattern in comicality, turn less undeviatingly on blood sports, than anti-blood-sport generations have been preferred to suppose. In these tales are no meaningless antic caperings: on the contrary, outsize characters, clashes, crises, realistic in their very delirium. These not only *were* Ireland—they still are Ireland, under the skin.

One would like to know more than there seems to be to be known about Violet Martin: "Ross," with her indomitable fragility, her dilated great beautiful hare's eyes—whose nearsightedness had to be aided by pince-nez. The Norman-descended Martins of Ross, County Galway, had it less good than the later coming, Scottish-descended Somervilles, County Cork. Their fortunes foundered under a succession of blows—

those intricate troubles known to landowners. Ghosts were the least of the tribulations of the dying house.

Halfway through Violet's childhood, Ross, the mansion, had to be abandoned: her brother went off to seek a living in England; mother and a bevy of spinster girls (Violet the youngest) for some years camped, on the cheap, in Dublin (from whence sprang the rattling good Dublin passages in *The Real Charlotte*.) After that, the heroic return to Galway; the struggle, headed by Violet, to rekindle life—such as it had been, never could be again—in the shell of the house. The whole of the wisdom of sorrow was this young woman's; she was early acquainted with wailings, dementia, speechless despairs. She is remembered for her delightful gaiety. Yet can one doubt, it was she who introduced into the Somerville and Ross combination that dark streak—which, at the same time, gave it validity?

Lady Violet is to be thanked for *The Irish Cousins*. Her sense of what *is* relevant to her subject, and her use of that, would seem to me faultless. Moreover, she has read, and assimilated, the Somerville-Ross writings in their entirety: no small task. She summarizes each of the many books, in some detail but without an instant of boringness. The effect is to whet a renewed appetite. How many of the lesser-known works are still in print, available, one would like to know? Could not publishing enterprise strike while the iron is hot? There may not yet be a boom; there *is* a "revival" . . . Did these authors impact on their compatriot, James Joyce? Lady Violet holds that they did, and produces evidence—which is daring and interesting. Their place in the Irish literary Valhalla is accorded, their links with the great native tradition traced. I regret only, in this book, a lack of mention of Joseph Sheridan Le Fanu, with whose novels several outlined here would seem to have a marked, if unconscious, affinity.

Gift for the Gaffe

Making Conversation, by Christine Longford. *Spectator*, March 21, 1970.

Christine Longford's *Making Conversation* first came out in 1931. Anyone who was conscious at that time must remember the splash this novel made, and the widening ripples—here came something not only endlessly funny but funny in a manner, and from an angle, not known before. Female purely comical writers were then rare (today, we have rather a "school" of them, of all shapes and sizes) and this one brought fresh air to the literary scene. Moreover, although the antihero was already at large in the novels of Evelyn Waugh, his sister, or counterpart, had been missing. Lady Longford inaugurated the antiheroine. Martha Freke, more than a prototype, was a winner. From the moment she opens her doomed lips, *Making Conversation* is under way.

Was the author accused of iconoclasm with regard to the feminine image? Possibly, in some circles. It had been—and sometimes still is?—expected that women writers fly a flag for their sex, idealize women, anatomize their unmerited sufferings, or at least promote them in the ethical market. Lady Longford, *désabusée* though friendly, could be seen as letting the side down. Herself in the best of spirits, with no chip on her shoulder or score to settle, she is from first to last in a sort of unholy complicity with Martha—whom she does not deplore, defend, or attempt to justify. And Martha is not admirable, to put it mildly.

As a schoolgirl, she is made noticeable by small eyes (it had been hoped they might grow, along with the rest of her person, but they did not) and the unswervingness of a piglike egotism. Lacking in charm, she is still more lacking in moral fiber. Would-be opportunist, she invariably misses the catch. She *is* clever; alas, too clever by half—one cause of her many tangles with destiny. Of her constant vicissitudes, some are due to bad luck, but more to bad management: mortifying! When truth bores her, she embroiders upon it freely:

> That evening Martha went into the drawing-room to say good-night to Miss Pilkington, who asked her how she had enjoyed school.
>
> "Not very much today, thank you."
>
> "Why not, dear?"
>
> "Miss Spencer pulled my hair, and said I had committed adultery."
>
> "Nonsense, dear, you must have misunderstood her."
>
> "I didn't."
>
> "Don't contradict, dear," said her mother.

Downfall, inevitable for such a character, would have held more potential of tragedy had there been any great heights from which to fall down. Sacked from her first school for constructive lying, the child moves on to another and more permissive one. While there, she incurs a round of applause by successfully going up for an Oxford scholarship: Springfield, that illustrious women's college. The triumph gratifies but does not surprise her. "It was taken for granted that Martha would go to Oxford . . . . For Martha it was a place where one finally proved how clever one was. Nothing could be more delightful." But here, too, misunderstandings pursue her: halfway through her second year she is sent down, on account of frivolity (wearing of large tulle hats) and supposed fornication in a Chiltern hotel.

Making Conversation, set back in time by its author (back, that is, from its original publication date) would have had from the first a "period" flavor. Opening in 1911, the story terminates some nine or ten years later, with Martha's disappearance in Czechoslovakia. Thus, for 1931 readers, our antiheroine had the additional fascination of being, in her own way, a period piece—product, maybe victim, of a vanished regime. How far *did* the pre-1914 setup, its taboos, its lore, and its aspirations affect, or perhaps distort, this young person's character?

A formative influence, certainly, was her mother's drawing room, in which, with the loyal assistance of paying guests, impeccable social standards were maintained—the more so because Major Freke, who had come to grief, and indeed worse, had to be lived down. Mrs. Freke, fortified by Miss Pilkington, consistently did so, with flying colors. The child of the house, in consequence, had fine old outgoing Edwardian traditions dinned into her. These, given her opposite propensities, set up conflict.

The primary function of woman is what?—to please. How?—by well-aimed, inexhaustible verbal liveliness. Conversation . . . Self-conscious, with a passion for showing off, Martha reacted fatally to this simple doctrine—which was, in the long run, to ruin her days. (And this gives the book its eloquent title.) She tries hard, too hard, in an inner sweat of anxiety. School playtimes, parties, university life, embryonic friendships, putative love affairs are made tense for her by an unequal struggle—not only to say something, to say something *striking*. Slowly, she recognized the truth: as soon as she opened her mouth, there had been a disaster.

On the whole she gets on better with foreigners, as these only partially understand her.

Though her home, Hillview, is set in a rather sparse Somerset country neighborhood, Martha's life, even prior to Oxford, is not devoid of intellectual contacts, thanks to an overspill from the vicarage. The vicar takes on more young men, of various nationalities, to coach than he is able to house, so inserts them as lodgers with Mrs. Freke.

Hence the American Cecil—by Miss Pilkington designated a "nasty" aesthete—also Harry, who when World War I breaks out goes to jail as an unregistered alien. These two egg Martha on to read Nietzsche. War brings to Hillview a quota of other foreigners: refugees. Martha, non-patriotic, reacts to the war with apathy, some say callousness. Her main desire is that the thing should be over by the time she arrives in Oxford. It just is.

Immediately postwar Oxford is the glorious high point of this novel. Remembering *Making Conversation*, I had thought there was more of this—I regret that there is not. What was to come to be known as the Golden Age excluded, unfortunately, studious young women. Great goings-on either were purely masculine, or were here or there joined by imported beauties. (How things have altered!) Forlorn, the inmates of Springfield and sister colleges made do, sharing some few, dim males, each others' dutiful brothers or loyal cousins. Martha combines with her cronies, Elizabeth and Helen, in at least one effort to crash the barrier: coated in face powder and adorned with millinery they approach the rooms of Mr. Barrington-Ramsbotham, social don, at the infelicitous hour of two P.M. A scout on the landing warns them that there is a lunch party.

> "Oh, but it's very urgent," said Elizabeth. "Will you tell him some students from Springfield want to see him at once."
>
> Through the half-open door, they heard someone saying, "Oh, my God!" and it was Mr. Barrington-Ramsbotham. As he came out, with a few crumbs on his waistcoat, there was a combined smell of incense, cigarette-smoke, coffee, and brandy; and behind him there was a dim, panelled room populated with young men.

"'Please, Mr. Ramsbotham," said Elizabeth in a childish voice, "we do so want to come to your Pindar lectures."

"Really? And what is there to stop you?" he asked in a tone that was sharper and less rich than usual.

"Miss Macdonald won't let us, and she wants us to do Thucydides instead."

"In that case," he said, "far be it from me to interfere with the discipline of your college."

"But we do so want to come to your lectures."

He could not control a smirk . . . .

There is further parley; however, the thing ends badly—Mr. Barrington-Ramsbotham not only goes back but slams the door. "That man is a toad," says Helen, "and I'm not going near his damned lectures." "What a lovely time men have compared with women," laments Elizabeth.

Making Conversation consists largely *of* conversation: dialogue. There are few descriptive and no analytical passages. Lightness of structure, flickering sureness of touch, and an air of nonchalance make this supreme comedy writing, not yet bettered. And the matter is not less well found than the manner. Why, then, had this masterpiece virtually disappeared? The answer may be that Christine Longford suffered the fate of so many innovators—that of being snowed up, till lost to view, under hosts of adherents and imitators. A new genre, having caused a sensation, brings about a change in the literary climate. Its progenitor may come to be overlooked.

Restored to daylight, does *Making Conversation* seem in any way to have suffered from its long burial? In one sense, yes; though in that sense only. During the interim, going on forty years, topics and types which came newly to Lady Longford have turned into the stock-in-trade of accepted comedy. Paying guests, refugees, pukka sahibs, tycoons, young men of peculiar bearing, dotty teachers, mystery monks make their rounds through humorous fiction like a stage army. One is weary of them. They mar, therefore, perceptibly though unfairly, such pages of hers as they take over. But damage confines itself to a small area. By contrast, the core of the book stands out in untarnished, triumphant originality. *Making Conversation* does not, and will never, "date."

The author's marriage to Edward Longford took her to Ireland, where the theater claimed her. But Ireland had time to inspire two further novels: *Country Places*, which I riotously remember, and *Jiggins of Jigginstown*, which I have yet to know. That these be republished in the near future, let us devoutly hope.

Dickens and the Demon Toy Box

The World of Charles Dickens, by Angus Wilson. *Spectator*, May 30, 1970.

At a first glance, the format of *The World of Charles Dickens* could be misleading. The handsomely glossy jacket is slightly whimsical, the shape of the book could mean looking rather than reading, and who knows what the title might not portend—yet another centenary book about Dickens's England, now vanished, alas? You would be wrong. The author is Angus Wilson—who, in a brief preface, forecasts what he is to carry out. The reason for and the aim of his undertaking are made clear. "The world we have inherited," he declares, "is the imaginative world of Charles Dickens . . . . It is as a guide to exploring the Dickens imaginative system— both the various novels which are its planets and the whole marvelous group as it revolves around him—that this account of his life has been written."

Nothing contributory to the life can, by this reckoning, be quite left out, though to include all would be a large order. Extrovert, Dickens was no man for an ivory tower. The Victorian universe, around him, acted upon him at every turn. The action was two-way, reciprocal: if Victorianism to an extent made Dickens, he to no less an extent was to make it—feeding its longings, stoking its deep-down fires, wakening its vision, endowing it with an image of itself. Would he have thriven in another climate, another epoch?—he is unimaginable in any but his own. Those conventions which cramped and taboos which restricted him, may they not by their very repressiveness have accounted for the explosive, maniacal nature of his genius when and where it broke out? He was one with his age in its ghoulish tastes, morgues, maniacs, murderers, as in its sentimental ones. He had a fellow addiction to the grotesque.

All romantic art roots, palpably, in a mythology: individual to the artist, generally infantile. What, Mr. Wilson invites us to ask, was Dickens's, and whence came it? Mr. Wilson's answer, Dickens himself corroborates in a childhood memoir. All began, apparently, when, very early on—how early?—Charles had a dire experience with a Christmas tree, or rather, its denizens. (That year, toy designers seem to have overreached themselves.)

The gifts were as follows: first, the Tumbler, who, hands in his pockets, would not lie down but persisted in rolling about till he twitched still. Next, a purporting snuffbox, out of which sprang a "demoniacal" black-robed counselor with a red cloth mouth. Thirdly, a cardboard man, with jointed limbs, whom, having hung on a wall, one animated by pulling a string—"when he got his legs round his neck (as he often did)," Dickens recalled, he was "ghastly, and not a creature to be alone with." Final abomination, the Mask. "When did that dreadful Mask first look at me? . . . O! I know it's coming! O! The Mask!"

Did those four, in an inexhaustible series of mutations, as the art when on, as each novel bred a new host of characters, reign over the Dickens world of pity and terror? Mr. Wilson thinks, yes, very possibly: "Memory is selective and so it is not surprising that these childhood toys which Dickens recalls when he is nearing forty should have so close a link with some of the adult obsessions in his books."

Other obsessions had a more concrete cause: the collapse of the physical security of childhood. Nothing worse could have happened: Mr. Dickens père went off to prison for debt, his son into a blacking factory to work. There, not so much the dreariness of his task as the degrading company in which he had to perform it (Charles's first contact, and as time was to show a far from unfruitful one, with the underworld) was to set up a long-lasting sense of contamination. He had been brought up to the tightrope-walking genteelism of that most precarious of classes, the lower-middle—the class whose fantasy consolations, heroic feints, and dread of engulfment he was to immortalize. Mammoth success was needed to get him back again into equilibrium: it did. But loathing of chaos, exaltation of "order," and fanatical impatience with fecklessness remained. Ultimately, his charity grew stronger, his heart wiser. After the wretched death of a younger brother, the once bright and delightful Fred, he writes to Forster: "It was a wasted life, but God forbid that one should be hard upon it, or upon anything in this world that is not deliberately and coldly wrong."

Habitually, with the splendid prodigality of genius, Dickens exaggerated everything. Despite being as honest as the day, for a great part of the time he was acting up: many of his letters are hysterical. One may wonder, therefore, whether the proportion he gives some memories may not here or there be out of the true. Did the rebuff he got from Maria Beadnell really maim him (as he asserts) for years? *Something*, as Mr. Wilson points out, arrested his development with regard to women—in his novels they are, as we know, of an insipidity; villainesses being a trifle better.

He never portrays a feminine character in depth; but then, does he portray *any* character in depth, when one comes to think? What matter? His creatures, comic or tragic, are afloat in the rhetoric, staged by the super-humanity of the vision which was to make him the prose Shakespeare. In his life were two women who taught him little: Kate, the wife he left after twenty-two years and a flock of children; Mary, the maiden sister-in-law who died in his arms. From Ellen Ternan, that other eighteen-year-old, an agonizing education came too late. Not too late altogether: in the novels of the Ternan epoch (his last), understanding of passion exists, and deepens.

Mr. Wilson anatomizes the novels splendidly, one by one—relating each, as promised, both to the others in the "imaginative system" and to the being, and growth, of the central man. As a novelist's work on a novelist, *The World of Charles Dickens* could not be bettered. Praise must go, too, to his choice of the illustrations—which do *illustrate*. Gorgeous or curious in themselves, great Victorian conversation pieces (in color) combine with black-and-white portraits and frightening drawings to cover the whole scenic range of the stories: they are pointers, also, to the social extremes on which Dickens dwelt. As a thing of beauty, this is a book to possess. As writing, it is a mine of intelligence.

A. E. Dyson, author of *The Inimitable Dickens*, is senior lecturer in English at the University of East Anglia, and a Dickens expert. His handling of (roughly) the same theme as Angus Wilson's is a shade more didactic, and less suggestive: here or there, he inclines to issue a statement where one would prefer to think, or judge, for oneself. However, he need not scare off the non-student reader, for his manner is friendly, his points are interesting, and his inexhaustible subject cannot but fascinate. There *could* be a book of this kind which is one too many, but Mr. Dyson's, definitely, is not.

The London of Charles Dickens, an engaging sort of a guidebook (compiled by whom?), has a foreword by great-granddaughter Monica Dickens, and is published by London Transport, in association with the Dickens Fellowship—I imagine, to cater for the centenary year. The format is pretty, and pocket-size, and the layout pleasing. Extant buildings, sites of those vanished and public monuments which have a Dickens connection, are listed, alphabetically, with "How to get there" (by public transport) as an invaluable addition.

Ireland Agonistes

Troubles, by J. G. Farrell. *Europa* 1 (1971): 58–59.

Troubles, a novel, is on a scale of its own—a major work made deceptive as to its size by apparent involvement with what is minor. That was inevitable, since the setting is Ireland, where either everything matters or nothing does. A broken cup, a shindy between two characters, can have phantasmagoric significance, not lessened by the fact that the country trembles, shootings and burnings are frequent, violence is rife—a prevailing state of affairs throughout the duration of this story, the time being 1919–20, years of "the Troubles," when the Irish Republican Army heaved up to eject the British.

What could you expect but trouble? And what but trouble was the loss of a cup or a spit in the eye? There's no measuring tape. We are focused, accordingly, on the predicament of the Majestic Hotel, a vast crumbling obsolete pleasure dome on a peninsula off the coast of Wexford. The hotel is a leading protagonist in its own desperate drama. The rest of the cast, guests, owner, and personnel, may be likened to a handful of persons manning a sinking ship. *Their* troubles suffice. *Troubles* has, therefore, a title which bites twice over.

This novel gains force, and demands attention, by being purely a work of imagination. It contains, that is, no shred of personal memory: Farrell was born sixteen years after 1919, in England. Parts of his childhood were spent in Ireland; not, I gather, particularly rewardingly or willingly. Since then he has traveled, and lived, in various other countries more to his choice. This bending of his imagination up Ireland cannot be nostalgic compulsion, or "the return of the native"—yet could there, all the same, be some undertow?

Troubles necessitated the exploration of a time outside his experience and far from it. How was he to enter its psychic atmosphere, even its social one? He could not have selected a time that was more fraught—it was for that reason, clearly, that he selected it. He can have had little to go on but faded hearsay, and the wreathings and writhings, so peculiar to Ireland, of accumulated myth. Most of all, he would have had to combat ambiguous silences: "the Troubles," constantly though they feature in Irish art, have not yet been comfortably assimilated—they are not yet freely or generally spoken of. What is left of their veterans are taciturn.

Yet Farrell has brought it off. How—by inspired guesswork, semi-occult? Possibly a writer (though not all writers) can operate as does a water diviner, holding a twig which twitches when it comes to reality? I knew those days, though scantily, owing to youthful egotism, impatience with the bothers they made, distractions elsewhere: all the same, I can recognize the authentic smell of them, and I do in *Troubles*.

Even while the author studied the national struggle, documenting himself, he must have been aware of how little of it he was, actually, to "use." During most of *Troubles*, "the Shinners" remain off-stage. As said, we identify with the Majestic and its inmates. Tea and tennis parties and outings to the local golf club continue. The grandiose pile, of which portions are peeling off, others caving in, conserves its own obstinate, dotty normality. Isolation has set in; emptiness, largely, fills the three hundred rooms.

It could be easy to make a "symbol" of the Majestic (tottering fortress of the Ascendancy), but I do not feel this to be Farrell's purpose—his clean-cut writing implies no more than it states. The Majestic, brash artifact from the start, in the 1880s, could in no way stand in for moldering feudalism. What the hotel *is*, is symptomatic. Once it was a chic place, in demand annually. Now its world has gone: World War I put the lid on it. A generation has vanished, fashions have switched.

The place meets an end as spectacular as, probably, was its beginning:

it is burned down by a faithful ancient retainer, gone insane. By a bizarre twist, we first see it as it would be today—debris, strewing a deserted peninsula:

> The charred remains of the enormous main building are still to be seen . . . . Here and there among the foundations one might still find evidence of the Majestic's former splendour: the great number of cast-iron bathtubs, for instance, which had fallen from one blazing floor to another until they hit the earth; twisted bedframes also, some of them not rusted away; and a simply pro-digious number of basins and lavatory bowls. At intervals along the outer walls there is testimony to the tremendous heat of the fire: one can disinter small pools of crystal formed in layers like the drips of wax from a candle, which gathered there, of course, from the melting of the windows. Pick them up and they sepa-rate in your hand into the cloudy drops that formed them.

The above having been done with objects so-called inanimate, on an early page, one can see why *Troubles*, moving into its stride as a full-size novel, generates an excitement hard to define—one of its constituents is foreboding. The characters strike one as spelling each others' doom. Caught in the stranglehold of the situation, they have a stranglehold upon one another. Some are Irish (Anglo-Irish or otherwise), some are succumbing to being so.

Major Brendan Archer, an Englishman, recuperating from war shock, is the outstanding innocent, the predestined victim, and yet, at the last, the rallier of the rest of the group. How does *he* come to be one of it? We are told: "In the summer of 1919, not long before the great Victory Pa-rade marched up Whitehall, the Major left hospital and went to Ireland to claim his bride, Angela Spencer. At least he fancied that the claim-ing of her as a bride might come into it. But nothing definite had been settled." It had not: when they meet she appears barely to know him.

Angela being a daughter of the Majestic, the reunion takes place in the Palm Court, where she is entertaining a tea party: she sprays him and it with a burst of ex-debutante chatter, then glides away. She remains on the move, impossible to track down, then, as a final act of evasion, abruptly dies.

By that time, the Major has been latched on to by the entire Majestic — he cannot quit it. Angela's younger sisters, lovely identical twins, semi-enthrall the Major; but it is to be Sarah, local bank manager's daughter, *belle dame sans merci*, who all but wrecks him. Her shady involvement with Edward, Angela's father, is, until she leaves him, tormentingly evident. Edward's loss of interest in the Majestic, which he purports to manage, is progressive. He devotes himself to other experiments, taunts the I.R.A., and gives an enormous ball. The hotel starts splitting in two, like the House of Usher . . .

Summarized, this might sound Chekhovian. But for the soliloquies of the country doctor, it is not—very much is not. The flavor, the mood, the idiom, the way of seeing are unique, Farrell's own. The dialogue, for all its show of inconsequence, is taut, loaded. The comedy, darting through the fabric of the story, here and there bursts out into the quite preposterous: this it carries off. There are shocking episodes, only just not unbearable, such as the massacre of the attic cats. But the weighty base of the book, *and* source of its poetry, is tragedy. It is the tragic characters who tower: semi-monstrous Edward, destructive Sarah, in her own way Angela, the dream-girl, leaving behind her a horde of unworn finery, and the old, old, age-bewildered dog.

"People are insubstantial," muses Dr. Ryan. "A person is only a very temporary and makeshift thing. They really do not ever last . . . . They never last." His verdict—is it also the author's?

But the nature of the framework and theme of *Troubles*, which together give the novel the size I claim for it, has not been touched on yet. The state of the world, the extreme situation of 1919 . . . Unheard by any in the Majestic but the Major, there sounds out a clanging of warning gongs. Chicago riots, uprisings in India, advance of the Bolsheviks, disaffections and fissures within the Empire. Convulsions in Ireland are, only, nearer at hand. Press extracts punctuate these pages—unremarked on, therefore the more telling. *Troubles* is, thereby, not "a period piece"; it is yesterday reflected in today's consciousness. The ironies, the disparities, the dismay, the sense of unavailingness are contemporary.

Advice to a Young Writer

Bowen's counsel to a young writer appeared in *Wales* 31 (October 1949): 2–4. The circumstances of this commentary are not explained, but "Enid Williams" is identified as the young writer in a footnote. The essay is badly edited and typeset. Corrections have been made silently.

1. The word "the" has been added twice to this sentence for coherence.

2. Inner existence of objects: Roy Fuller, in a poem entitled "What Is Terrible," writes of the "furious inner existence of objects." The poem appeared in *A Lost Season* (1944).

English and American Writing

This essay appeared in *The Author* 59, no. 4 (Summer 1949): 73–76. As the official organ of the Society of Authors, this magazine protected the interests of writers, dramatists, and composers. The journal routinely investigated copyright issues, libel, and other legalities of authorship. Bowen was elected to the Society of Authors in 1945. As correspondence in the British Library indicates, the editors of *The Author* approached Bowen about this article on February 18, 1949: "The subject we have in mind is some sort of comparison of English and American writing." They offered to send along three copies of *Partisan Review* with articles by Jean-Paul Sartre, V. S. Pritchett, and American writers involved in a symposium on writers. Translations of Sartre's essays— "What Is Writing?" "For Whom Does One Write?" "Literature in Our Time"—were published in different issues. V. S. Pritchett's essay, "The Future of English Fiction," refers to Bowen as one of the "dispossessed poets" who writes fiction as would a "historian of the crisis in civilization" (1066). In the August 1948 issue of *Partisan Review*, a group of critics and writers addressed seven questions about tendencies, experimentation, middlebrow orientation, academic leanings, poetry, and the influence of Soviet Communism on American writing. Stephen Spender's article, "The Situation of the American Writer," appeared in the March 1949 issue of *Horizon*. With these resources at hand, Bowen agreed to submit an essay on "English and American Writing" by May 1 for a fee of 10 guineas. On May 3, 1949, the editors of *The Author* acknowledged receipt of the article and thanked Bowen for making a "difficult subject" interesting (British Library Manuscripts Add. 63214 ff. 199–222).

1. The original gives "oppresses," but the verb has to agree with a plural subject.

2. The original gives "depth-charge," but the plural "depth-charges" or "as a depth-charge" would be more grammatical.

3. *Terre à terre*: matter-of-fact or down-to-earth.

On Writing *The Heat of the Day*

"On Writing *The Heat of the Day*" was published in *Now and Then* (Autumn 1949): 11. An in-house magazine, *Now and Then*, publicized forthcoming or recent work by authors at Jonathan Cape. This blurb appeared after *The Heat of the Day* was already in print.

Note for *The Broadsheet* on *The Heat of the Day*

This promotional blurb for *The Heat of the Day*, with autobiographical reflections, exists as a three-page manuscript (Elizabeth Bowen Collection, Harry Ransom Center, Box 1, file 5). The published version has not been traced.

Publisher's Blurb for *The Heat of the Day*

This blurb, written and corrected by Bowen, describes the situation of *The Heat of the Day* as she understands it (Elizabeth Bowen Collection, Harry Ransom Center, Box 5, file 5). Emendations are made by hand on the typescript. Some minor errors have been silently corrected.

    1. Bowen crossed out "triangular" in favor of the noun "triangle."

The Technique of the Novel

Recorded on two reels lasting a total of 46 minutes, "The Technique of the Novel" is housed at the Woodberry Poetry Room in Lamont Library at Harvard. The text of this speech is transcribed from those tapes. Some ideas, even phrases, were reused in "Advice" (*Afterthought*, 210–15). By the time she delivered this speech on "The Technique of the Novel" at Harvard University in 1953, Bowen had rehearsed it extensively by giving lectures in Europe and the United States. In some cases, the British Council organized these tours as a means of diffusing British culture on the Continent and around the world. A press release dated February 14, 1950, gives some idea of the intensity of these tours: "Miss Elizabeth Bowen, the well-known novelist, has been invited by the universities of Lausanne and Geneva, and Anglo-Swiss and literary societies to undertake a lecture tour in Switzerland and the British Council has arranged for her to go there from February 19 to 26" (British Library Add. 63214 f. 216). These lectures focused on literary subjects for the most part, although some were broadly cultural. According to the British Council communiqué, Bowen was to "lecture at Lausanne and Geneva universities on 'The technique of the novel' on February 20 and 21 and to the P.E.N. centre at Zurich on the same subject on February 24. She will give a more general lecture on 'English home-life to-day' to the Anglo-Genevese Society, Anglo-Swiss societies in Berne and St. Gullen and the Lyceum club in Zurich" (British Library Add. 63214 f. 216). During a tour that started in Milan and ended in Naples in March 1953, Bowen spoke about "The Contemporary British Novel," "Jane Austen," and, again, "The Technique of the Novel" (British Library Add. 63214 f. 217).

    1. *Grammar*: Aristotle did not write a treatise called *Grammar*. In *On Interpretation*, however, Aristotle discusses grammar at length without reference to the "man of action." In *Nicomachean Ethics*, on the other hand, he considers the nature of human action in terms of morality and individual responsibility.

    2. Small blue lamp: In "Notes on Writing a Novel," Bowen claims that "characters pre-exist. They are *found*. They reveal themselves slowly to the novelist's perception—as might fellow-travellers seated opposite one another in a very dimly-lit railway carriage"

(*Collected Impressions*, 251). In *England's Hour*, Vera Brittain mentions the blue lights in trains during the war: "the railway carriage, if lighted at all, is illumined by a blue pin-point of light not strong enough to enable me to distinguish the features in the pale ovals which are my neighbours' faces" (27).

3. The transcription may be incorrect because the reel changes at this point. The sound, fading out, leaves the words "or maybe a" hard to hear.

4. It is unclear on the tape whether Bowen stutters on "that" or whether she intends to repeat the word as a relative pronoun, then as a demonstrative adjective.

5. Bowen started this sentence with one idea, then changed course. Consequently, the syntax is awkward—spontaneous rather than grammatical.

6. The subject-verb agreement error is Bowen's.

7. It is unclear from the tape whether Bowen says "the language" or just "language," without the definite article.

8. "Method" may be incorrect. Bowen pronounces this word "meta."

We Write Novels: An Interview with Walter Allen

"We Write Novels" was an unscripted discussion recorded on May 4, 1955, and broadcast on June 2, 1955, over the BBC General Overseas Service. The interview, produced by Kay Fuller, lasted 13 minutes 10 seconds. Sellery and Harris refer to this broadcast as "Contemporary British Novelists—We Write Novels" (283), but the first three words of that title do not appear on the typescript itself (BBC Written Archives). Other writers interviewed for this series included Joyce Cary, Philip Toynbee, C. P. Snow, L. P. Hartley, and J. B. Priestley. The interviewer, Walter Allen, wrote novels himself, but he is now remembered for his work as a critic. In *The English Novel* (1954), Allen quotes Bowen's statement from "Notes on Writing a Novel" to the effect that the novel is "the non-poetic statement of a poetic truth" (97). Allen brings up the same phrase again in this interview. Throughout the BBC transcription, square brackets have been inserted by hand around many passages; these passages may have been edited out before broadcast. Some of these passages are short; one, however, extends from Allen's question, "Who are your favourite novelists," all the way to his question about whether women novelists have any advantages or disadvantages. For the sake of inclusiveness, I have not cut any passages. The transcription shows signs of the typist's negligence: punctuation and spelling are erratic. Some errors have been silently amended. Some stops and starts have been edited out altogether. Without the tape of the broadcast, such emendations are guesses rather than verifiable certainties of what was said. I have edited out "I mean" and "I suppose" and similar phrases. Walter Allen begins every one of his responses with "Well, yes," likewise eliminated. Conversation, unlike written text, often links sentences together with coordinate conjunctions. I have deleted many "and's" and replaced them with full stops for the sake of producing a readable text. Where Bowen's text runs afoul of grammar, I try to render it intelligible by altering punctuation, without changing words. Because changes are numerous, I have not noted them all.

1. The transcript reads, "a summer day, a hot summer day." The redundancy has been deleted.

2. The transcription reads "hereditary," but "heredity" makes more sense.

3. The ellipsis appears in the transcription. The typist apparently did not catch a name. Bowen may have said "Richard Sheridan," another Anglo-Irish writer often on her mind. Or she may have mentioned any number of Anglo-Irish "giants."

4. In the typescript, this paragraph was punctuated as a single sentence.

5. The word "go" has been added.

6. The typescript reads "of," not "for."

7. "In" has been added to create a grammatical sentence.

8. The typescript reads "which," but the repetition of the pronoun reads awkwardly.

9. "Day" has been added for sense.

10. The word "although" was removed at the beginning of this sentence to avoid a sentence fragment. Bowen means that Graham Greene's novels are non-poetic statements of poetic truth.

11. The transcription reads "Fielding, Henry Fielding." The first "Fielding" has been deleted.

12. Virginia Woolf committed suicide in 1941, as Bowen well knew. She was not alive at the time of this broadcast.

13. The typescript reads "holding," but "beholding" might be intended.

Reviews: 1935 to 1942

1. *The Immortal Hour*: a 1908 play by Scottish author William Sharp (1855–1905), writing under the pseudonym Fiona MacLeod.

2. *The Passing of the Third Floor Back*: a British film (1935), directed by Berthold Viertel, about a London boarding house. The film is based on a short story and play by Jerome K. Jerome.

3. *Sard Harker*: an adventure novel by John Masefield published in 1924.

4. *Covered Wagon*: a silent, American western (1923) about pioneers traveling from Kansas to Oregon.

5. *Marius* and *Imaginary Portraits*: Walter Pater published *Marius the Epicurean* in two volumes (1885). His *Imaginary Portraits* (1887) are four short stories about men who die young.

6. *âme damnée*: damned soul.

7. *The Green Hat*: Michael Arlen's melodramatic novel (1924) brought him fame and money. The novel was turned into a play (1925), then a Hollywood film with Greta Garbo, renamed *A Woman of Affairs* (1928).

8. James Branch Cabell: American author Cabell (1879–1958) specialized in fantasy and escapist fiction.

9. Powys: John Cooper Powys (1872–1963) was a British author, best known for *A Glastonbury Romance* (1932). He wrote novels and essays on philosophical topics.

10. *Appointment in Samarra*: John O'Hara's first novel, published in 1934.

11. *espagnolisme*: "Spanishism" or a passion for everything Spanish. Bowen borrows this word from Stendhal.

12. Giraldus Cambrensis: Gerald of Wales (c. 1146–c. 1223), a clergyman who chronicled his times, with reference to the history and geography of Wales.

13. The text gives "there two men," but the syntax is muddled. "There are" may be intended.

14. Templeogue: originally a small village in County Dublin, now a suburb of Dublin.

15. *Charles O'Malley* and *Harry Lorrequer*: Charles Lever's novel, *Harry Lorrequer*, was published in 1839; *Charles O'Malley* followed in 1841.

16. Bowen wrote a preface for *The Blaze of Noon*. It was reprinted in *Collected Impressions* (53–55).

17. *original*: in the published text, "original" is spelt "orgional" and "origional." These appear to be typesetters' errors.

18. *Vita Nuova*: Dante's text (1295) about courtly love, with descriptions of his meeting with Beatrice, their remeeting, her death, and its impact on the poet.

19. The original gives "yearn," but that word is not generally used as a noun.

20. The syntax is ambiguous, but it appears to mean either "he paid honors to the play and the players" or, less likely, "he did pay the players the honor."

21. *Cela ne se fait pas*: that is not done, or it's bad form.

Selected *Tatler* Reviews: 1941–1950

1. One must interest: Bowen cites this dictum as Flaubert's, but Flaubert did not say *il faut intéresser* in those exact terms. In a letter dated September 16, 1853, he wrote to Louise Colet: "Je crois, contrairement à ton avis de ce matin, que l'on peut intéresser avec tous les sujets" (*Correspondences* 2:432–33). He had written something similar to Colet on January 15, 1853: "Ce qui me tourmente dans mon livre, c'est l'élément *amusant*, qui y est médiocre. Les faits manquent. Moi, je soutiens que les idées sont des faits. Il est plus difficile d'intéresser avec, je le sais, mais alors c'est la faute du style" (*Correspondences* 2:238). The second statement contradicts the first: apparently not all subjects can generate interest.

2. The word "it" has been added for sense.

3. The word "of" appears after "because" in the text. It has been removed for sense.

4. N.F.S. and W.V.S.: National Fire Service, created in 1941 through an amalgamation of the Auxiliary Fire Service (A.F.S.) and local fire brigades; the Women's Voluntary Service, formed in 1938, was active during the war in distributing clothing, helping with evacuation, and providing food for children, soldiers, and veterans.

5. The word "are" has been added for sense.

6. Mr. Henrey: Bowen is wrong about Henrey's gender. Robert Henrey was a pseudonym for Madeleine Gal (1906–2004), author of numerous books, many of them autobiographical. Bowen reviewed several of Henrey's books without suspecting that "Robert" was a woman. Robert Henrey was the name of Gal's husband.

7. W. W. Jacobs: Jacobs (1863–1943) was the author of novels and short stories. He is best remembered for the story "The Monkey's Paw."

8. The review continues with a synopsis of each of the four novels.

9. First novel: Jean-Paul Sartre's first novel was *Nausea* (1938), not *The Age of Reason* (1945).

10. *Toute vérité n'est pas bonne à dire*: the truth is not always worth telling, or, more colloquially, the truth is sometimes best left unsaid.

11. *Something Terrible, Something Lovely*: Bowen actually called Sansom's book *Something Sweet, Something Terrible*. She mistranscribed or misremembered the real title. The title has been rectified throughout the review.

12. New Look: in 1947 Christian Dior launched the line of clothing that became known as the "New Look." Dresses, falling to mid-calf, used a great deal of material, which caused a scandal in postwar France where people were still living on rations.

Paris Bookshops

This essay appeared in *The Tatler* (August 28, 1946): 279, 284. Like Cyril Connolly and other Francophiles, Bowen longed to return to France as soon as the war ended. Finding this passion for France misplaced, Arthur Koestler referred to the "French flu" among a certain segment of the British literati: "Its symptoms are that the patient, ordinarily a balanced, cautious, sceptical man, is lured into unconditional surrender of his critical faculties when a line of French poetry or prose falls under his eyes. Just as in the case of hay-fever one whiff is sufficient to release the attack, thus a single word like *'bouillabaise,' 'crève-coeur,' 'patrie,'* or *'minette'* is enough to produce the most violent spasms" ("The French 'Flu," 26).

1. *La Vie des morts*: a novel by Agnès Chabrier, published in 1946.

But Once a Year

This essay appeared in *The Tatler* (December 22, 1948): 390. It is of a piece with other essays about Christmas that Bowen published during and after the Second World War.

1. The original reads "buried," in the sense that the toast is buried under wrapping paper. "Burned" may, however, be intended.

Old America

This essay appeared in *Harper's Bazaar* (December 1953): 48–49, 79. Through the offices of Curtis Brown, her literary agents, Bowen had attempted to publish this essay in the American edition of the magazine. On March 9, 1953, Bowen wrote at length to Colin Young at Curtis Brown about her initial concept:

> Do forgive my not having answered, while I was in America, your letter of February 9th, with the suggestion for the further article for *Harper's Bazaar*. I *should* like to write about some social aspects of American life, as it's struck me, but I don't think I know enough about Club Women, etc., to write about them. Also, I should find the proposed article hard to write in a way that would not risk giving some offence—when I'm polite I'm inclined to be dull.
>
> What I'd rather choose, if *Harper's* would accept it, would be "Old America"—that is, the various (and to me pleasing) things, manners, customs, interiors, street-scenes, etc., which give me the impression of having stepped back in time, rather than forward. In fact, America has an old-fashioned streak which fascinates me. The article could even be *called* "The Old-fashioned Streak." I don't think "oldness" is by any means confined to the South, either—as I should like to point out. (Elizabeth Bowen Collection, Harry Ransom Center, Box 10, file 5).

The article was mailed on July 27, 1953, as a penciled note from Marjorie Frost, Bowen's secretary, indicates: "Old America posted 24/7/53" (Elizabeth Bowen Collection, Harry Ransom Center, Box 11, file 1). Editors at *Harper's* in New York turned down the piece on August 20, 1953. It was immediately released to the British edition.

1. The verb "have" appears in the published text, but it does not agree with the subject.

Preface to A Day in the Dark

This preface appeared in *A Day in the Dark* (London: Jonathan Cape, 1965), 7–9. The final question mark, slightly unexpected, is Bowen's.

1. A friend: Cynthia Asquith, who edited *The Second Ghost Book* (1952), in which "Hand in Glove" appeared, as well as *Shudders: A Collection of Nightmare Tales* (1929), to which Bowen contributed "The Cat Jumps." Bowen and Asquith had a long and fruitful collaboration: over the years, she wrote six stories for volumes edited by Asquith.

2. "Are" has been added for grammatical sense.

Biographical Note

This note bears the date "3.6.48," and a single-space version also exists from the same month (Elizabeth Bowen Collection, Harry Ransom Center, Box 1, file 8). The jauntiness of this biographical note is uncharacteristic of Bowen's self-portrayal. Tellingly, she makes no secret of her work for the Ministry of Information.

1. *Castle Anna*: cowritten by John Perry and Elizabeth Bowen, this play was staged in 1948. So far, the script has not been traced.

I Love Driving at Night

"I Love Driving at Night" was published in *The Morris Owner and Nuffield Mail* in summer 1945. On April 12, 1945, Bowen sent a sheet of comments about motoring to Sidney Horniblow at "The Nuffield Organization" in Cowley, Oxfordshire. Horniblow edited *The Morris Owner and Nuffield Mail* from 1942 to 1945; the publication became *The New Outlook on Motoring* from 1946 to 1950. Bowen's original answers to Horniblow's questionnaire are housed at the Huntington Library (Elizabeth Bowen Collection, Box 2, HM 52840). Material was edited from Bowen's responses for publication. Horniblow's questions are not extant, but they can be inferred from Bowen's responses. He asked whether Bowen drove. "Yes," she answered, "Far from brilliantly, but not, I hope, to the public danger." Bowen prefers the front seat: "The only thing that bores me is sitting in the back seat of a closed car and being driven by an entire stranger. This does not seem to me to be 'motoring' in the enjoyable sense." She liked elbow room: "I like one that seems a car and I am afraid that I selfishly dislike being packed in among many other passengers." Horniblow evidently asked what she thought of the sound of motors: "I had not yet analyzed my reaction to different engine notes. I do, of course, prefer an almost silent purr to the 'fussy chattering' motor." Horniblow modified Bowen's comments about talking while motoring: "I think the question of talking or not talking while motoring (if one does so for pleasure) very important. I do as a rule like silence in which to follow the train of my own thoughts; or else the companionship of someone to whom one can say anything that comes into one's head." Bowen often writes about motoring, taxis, and trips in cars, as in *To the North*, *The Death of the Heart*, "The Demon Lover," and *Eva Trout*.

How I Write My Novels

This questionnaire appeared under the title, "Always Welcome Criticism," in *How I Write My Novels* (London: Spearman, 1948), 9–10. The questionnaire was produced for the BBC television program *Kaleidoscope*. Statements by various writers were collected by John Irwin and edited by Ted Jones. In the biographical blurb that accompanies the questionnaire, Bowen's favorite reading is listed as "detective stories" (8). A short extract from the conclusion of *The House in Paris* appears with the interview.

Miss Bowen on Miss Bowen

"Miss Bowen on Miss Bowen," a combination of biographical note and interview, appeared in the *New York Times Book Review* (March 6, 1949): 33. It nearly coincided with the publication of *The Heat of the Day* on February 21, 1949. With customary benevolence, she manages to promote personal friends among her favorite living writers, including Elizabeth Jenkins, Graham Greene, Eudora Welty, Elizabeth Taylor, and Rosamond Lehmann.

Elizabeth Bowen, of Cork and London

"Elizabeth Bowen, of Cork and London" was published in the *New York Herald Tribune Book Review* (October 8, 1950): 9. It resembles the "Biographical Note" and "Autobiographical Note" in its content.

My Best Novel

"My Best Novel" appeared in a pamphlet entitled *My Best Novel* (Islington Public Library, 1950): 3. Twelve authors, alphabetically presented, each contributed one-page statements. Authors included H. E. Bates, Phyllis Bentley, Louis Golding, Eric Linklater, J. B. Priestley, and others. L. M. Harrod, chief librarian and curator at the Islington Public Libraries, explains in the introductory note that library patrons require a "formal guide" to contemporary fiction: "In order to make it of greater value to our readers we have asked the authors to say which they themselves consider their best novel." Bowen hedges about which of her novels she prefers; she invokes several titles, but she does not answer the question.

1. The text gives "possibly" but "possible" makes more sense.

Autobiographical Note

This extensive "Autobiographical Note" exists in two versions with variants (Elizabeth Bowen Collection, Harry Ransom Center, Box 1, file 5). The first version, a carbon-copy typescript on white paper, bears a penciled note: "1 copy sent to Curtis Brown 11/10/48." Although she sent this note to Curtis Brown in 1948, Bowen wrote it earlier, as her references to being in Paris for the Peace Conference in 1946 make clear. In addition to the white carbon copy, two yellow typescript carbon copies exist in the Bowen collection at the Harry Ransom Center. In the yellow copies, certain spelling errors are corrected and a few others are introduced — none of great importance. Yet Bowen changed the tenses of verbs relating to her husband in the paragraph that begins, "In 1935 we left Oxford . . ." She crossed out two paragraphs concerning *The Heat of the Day* and her desire for travel. The final paragraph in the yellow carbon copy, about leaving London and the death of Alan Cameron, makes it clear that she altered this note in late 1952. I have restored the crossed-out paragraphs, even though the temporal markers — "now" and "January of this year," among others — do not align. It should be noted that the final paragraph, despite its first-person pronouns, does not appear to be in Bowen's hand; she may have dictated changes. I use the corrected yellow carbon as the basis for this transcription. For publicity purposes, Bowen frequently crafted short biographies — for *Mademoiselle* and *Everywoman's* (Elizabeth Bowen Collection, Harry

Ransom Center, Box 1, file 5), as well as other magazines and newspapers—that cover the same facts. This note is the longest, most detailed, and most candid of her promotional statements.

1. The yellow carbon reads "spend," whereas the original white carbon gives "spent."

2. Bowen deleted "has," to convert the verb from the present perfect to the simple past.

3. The change of circumstances caused Bowen to alter the sentence, which originally read: "He has now, again, however, returned to work as Educational Adviser to the Gramophone Company (EMI) who are projecting a very interesting scheme of educational gramophone records." When she came to revise this note, Alan Cameron had died.

4. Bowen crossed out the original text: "We still live, in London, in the house into which we moved in 1935–52, Clarence Terrace, Regent's Park."

5. The verb "are" is replaced by "were," a shift in tense that registers both her sense of separation from that house and the rebuilding of that house after its bombing during the war.

6. V1: flying bombs, from the German *Vergeltungswaffen*, meaning "reprisal weapons." These guided missiles, also known as doodle-bugs or buzz bombs because of the sound they made, rained down on London from June to September 1944.

7. Revising, Bowen changed "more than 25 years" to "thirty years."

8. The original white carbon reads, "Since 1941 I have been doing a weekly book page for the *Tatler*." In 1952 Bowen was not writing for *The Tatler*. She resumed her duties as book critic in 1954.

9. These two broadcasts have not been traced.

Selected *Tatler* Reviews: 1954 to 1958

1. Nigger in the woodpile: this offensive phrase means "some important fact that is not disclosed." Bowen does, on occasion, use racially offensive language.

2. V.A.D.: the Voluntary Aid Detachment provided nursing services in the United Kingdom and throughout the British Empire, mostly in hospitals. The volunteer organization was especially active during the two world wars.

3. Steerforth and Rosa Dartle: characters in Charles Dickens's *David Copperfield*.

4. p.g.'s: paying guests.

5. The immediately preceding review concerns Françoise Mallet-Joris's *The House of Lies*.

6. John P. Marquand: American novelist (1893–1960), whose books *Thirty Years*, *Sincerely Willis Wade*, *Stopover: Tokyo*, and *The Late George Apley* Bowen reviewed for *The Tatler* over the years.

Last Reviews: 1948 to 1970

1. "The absurdity of saying": in the published review, this passage bears asterisks. Either through Bowen's inadvertence or through typesetters' error, the passage is inaccurately transcribed. Aldington's text, as it appears in *Portrait of a Genius, But . . .* has been restored.

2. Grattan: Henry Grattan (1746–1820) was an Irish politician who campaigned against the Act of Union (1800). He subsequently sat in the House of Commons in London.

3. *Dublin University Magazine*: this Irish magazine ran from 1833 to 1882 and was devoted to literary and political issues. Sheridan Le Fanu published several stories in the magazine, then purchased it in 1861, at which time he took over as editor.

4. British Novelists Series: earlier in the review, Bowen correctly refers to the "English Novelists Series." English rather than British, the series included short books on distinguished novelists: Julian Symon on Charles Dickens, Anthony West on D. H. Lawrence, Beatrice Curtis Brown on Anthony Trollope, P. H. Newby on Maria Edgeworth, and so forth. Published by Barker, the series ran in the early 1950s.

5. Cresset Press: although she neglects to say so, Bowen wrote an introduction to the Cresset Press edition of *Uncle Silas*.

6. Osbert Lancaster: Lancaster (1908–1986) was an artist, book designer, and cartoonist, best known for his cartoons in the *Daily Express*.

7. The punctuation in the published text is ambiguous. Semicolons have been added to create regularity.

8. *The Laughing Matter*: Bowen also reviewed this book in the *Tatler* (March 17, 1954).

9. The word "is" has been added for sense.

10. Hiss: Alger Hiss (1904–1996), trained as a lawyer, worked for the U.S. State Department. Whittaker Chambers initially accused Hiss of being a Communist Party member, then accused him of being a Communist spy. Hiss was convicted of perjury and sentenced to two concurrent, five-year jail terms.

11. LDV: Local Defence Volunteers, comprised during the Second World War of local volunteers who were otherwise not eligible for military service because of age or health.

12. ITMA: *It's That Man Again*, a BBC radio comedy, ran from 1939 to 1949. "That Man" is Adolf Hitler.

WORKS CITED IN INTRODUCTION AND NOTES

Archival Sources

Elizabeth Bowen Collection. Harry Ransom Humanities Research Center. University of Texas, Austin. Thirteen boxes.

Bowen, Elizabeth. Letter to Phyllis Bottome. Dated October 2, 1944. British Library 78835 f. 231.

——. Letter to L. P. Hartley. Dated September 19, 1954. University of Manchester. John Rylands University Library. Papers of L.P. Hartley Box 1/2 (1945–1961).

——. Letter to John Lehmann. Dated October 8, 1947. John Lehmann Collection. Harry Ransom Humanities Research Center. University of Austin, Texas.

——. Letter to William Plomer. Dated July 2, 1946. Castle Green Library, Durham University, William Plomer Archive, MSS 19/7.

Jameson, Storm. Letter to Elizabeth Bowen, dated January 18, 1939. Harry Ransom Humanities Research Center, University of Texas, Elizabeth Bowen Collection, Box 11, file 5.

"Novelist to Lecture in Italy." Communiqué from the British Council dated March 5, 1953. British Library Add. 63214 f. 217. Manuscript.

"Novelist to Lecture in Switzerland." Communiqué from the British Council dated February 14, 1950. British Library Add. 63214 f. 216. Manuscript.

Society of Authors. Correspondence with Elizabeth Bowen. Various dates. British Library Manuscripts Add. 63214 ff. 199–222.

Published Sources

Allen, Walter. *The English Novel.* London: Penguin, 1954.

Aristotle. *The Categories: On Interpretation and Prior Analytics.* Trans. and ed. Harold P. Cooke and Hugh Tredennick. Cambridge, Mass.: Harvard University Press, 2002.

——. *Nicomachean Ethics.* Trans. and ed. Robert C. Bartlett and Susan D. Collins. Chicago: University of Chicago Press, 2011.

Bentley, Phyllis. "Reviewing Reviewed," *Author, Playwright and Composer* 53, no. 4 (1943): 65–66.

Bowen, Elizabeth. *Afterthought.* London: Longmans Green, 1962.

——. "Book Reviews." Rev. of Walter Allen, *Rogue Elephant. Tatler* (September 18, 1946): 374–75.

——. "Book Reviews." Rev. of Vercors, *Guiding Star. Tatler* (January 29, 1947): 168–69.

——. "Book Reviews." Rev. of Elizabeth Jenkins, *Young Enthusiasts. Tatler* (March 19, 1947): 346–47.

——. "Book Reviews." Rev. of Francis Steegmuller, *Flaubert and Madame Bovary.* *Tatler* (September 10, 1947): 343–44.

——. "Book Reviews." Rev. of Elizabeth Taylor, *A View of the Harbour.* *Tatler* (September 24, 1947): 406–7.

——. "Book Reviews." Rev. of Edward Lustgarten, *A Case to Answer*; Percy Lubbock, *Portrait of Edith Wharton*; Peter Cheyney, *Dance without Music*; and Arthur Gardner, *Western Highlands.* *Tatler* (October 8, 1947): 54–55.

——. "The Civilised Lord M." Rev. of David Cecil, *Lord M., or the Later Life of Lord Melbourne.* *Tatler* (November 3, 1954): 294, 310.

——. *Collected Impressions.* London: Longmans Green, 1950.

——. "Fiction." Rev. of James Joyce, *Finnegans Wake*; John O'Hara, *Hope of Heaven*; and Flann O'Brien, *At Swim-Two-Birds.* *Purpose* (July–September 1939): 177–80.

——. "Fiction." Rev. of John Steinbeck, *The Grapes of Wrath*; Randal Swingler, *To Town*; Rayner Heppenstall, *The Blaze of Noon*; and Jan Struther, *Mrs. Miniver.* *Purpose* (January–March 1940): 37–41.

——. "Fiction." Rev. of Henry de Montherlant, *The Lepers*, translated by John Rodker; Desmond Hawkins, *Lighter Than Day*; Stephen Spender, *The Backward Son*; Frank O'Connor, *Dutch Interior*; and H. E. Bates, *Country Tales.* *Purpose* (July–December 1940): 145–49.

——. *Listening In: Broadcasts, Speeches, and Interviews.* Ed. and intro. Allan Hepburn. Edinburgh: University of Edinburgh Press, 2010.

——. "A Man and His Legend." Rev. of Reginald Pound, *Arnold Bennett.* *Spectator* (December 5, 1952): 778.

——. "New Novels." Rev. of Eleanor Carroll Chilton, *Follow the Furies*; Mark Van Doren, *The Transients*; and George Albee, *Not in a Day or Seven.* *New Statesman* (August 17, 1935): 225–26.

——. "New Novels." Rev. of Hugh Walpole, *The Inquisitor*; H. L. Davis, *Honey in the Horn*; Helen Beauclerk, *The Mountain and the Tree*; and Rosalind Wade, *A Fawn in a Field.* *New Statesman* (August 31, 1935): 282, 284.

——. *People, Places, Things: Essays by Elizabeth Bowen.* Ed. and intro. Allan Hepburn. Edinburgh: University of Edinburgh Press, 2008.

——. "The Perfect Theatergoer." Rev. of Desmond MacCarthy, *Drama.* *Spectator* (January 3, 1941): 18, 20.

——. "With Silent Friends." Rev. of Garrett Mattingly, *Catherine of Aragon*; Sir William Rothenstein and Lord David Cecil, *Men of the R.A.F.*; and T. M. Bousfield, *Vinegar and Cream.* *Tatler* (April 29, 1942): 150, 152.

——. "With Silent Friends." Rev. of Inez Holden, *There's No Story There.* *Tatler* (January 31, 1945): 150–51.

Brittain, Vera. *England's Hour.* London: Macmillan, 1941.

Flaubert, Gustave. *Correspondences.* Vol. 2. Ed. Jean Bruneau. Paris: Pléiade, 2008.

Glendinning, Victoria. *Elizabeth Bowen: A Biography.* 1977. New York: Anchor, 2005.

Heppenstall, Rayner. "Rates for Reviewing," *Author, Playwright and Composer* 57, no. 4 (1947): 65.

Koestler, Arthur, "The French 'Flu." In *The Yogi and the Commissar*, 26–32. London: Hutchinson, 1965.

MacGillivray, James. "Legal Cases." *Author, Playwright and Composer* 51, no. 3 (Spring 1941): 42–45.

Nicolson, Harold. "Reviewing Reviewed." *Author, Playwright and Composer* 53, no. 4 (1943): 71.

Plomer, William. "Rates for Reviewing," *Author, Playwright and Composer* 57, no. 4 (1947): 66.

Powell, Anthony. *The Kindly Ones.* 1962. London: Fontana, 1984.

Pritchett, V. S. "The Future of English Fiction." *Partisan Review* 15, no. 10 (1948): 1063–70.

"Rates for Reviewing." *Author, Playwright and Composer* 57, no. 4 (1947): 64–68.

"Reviewing Reviewed." *Author, Playwright and Composer* 53, no. 4 (1943): 65–74.

Sellery, J'nan M., and William O. Harris. *Elizabeth Bowen: A Bibliography.* Austin, Tex.: Humanities Research Center, 1984.

Wedgwood, C. V. "Rates for Reviewing," *Author, Playwright and Composer* 57, no. 4 (1947): 68.

Wells, H. G. "Reviewing Reviewed," *Author, Playwright and Composer* 53, no. 4 (1943): 73–74.

Woolf, Virginia. *The Second Common Reader.* 1932. New York: Harcourt, 1960.

INDEX

fantasy, 4, 60, 65, 72, 110, 120, 171, 221, 234, 316, 366, 386

farms, 43, 47–49, 63–64, 68–69, 94, 156, 171, 196, 205, 240–41, 295, 344

Farrell, J. G., 388–91

Farrow, John: *The Blaze of Noon*, 397n16

fascists, 289

Faulkner, William, 9, 45, 50, 62, 87, 162, 263, 281; *Uncle Willy and Other Stories*, 324

feeling, xvii–vxiii, 12, 19, 23, 36, 40, 41, 43, 44, 45, 51, 58, 60, 61, 74, 76, 90 91, 93, 97, 117, 123, 128, 135, 137, 138, 144, 153, 154, 175, 183, 186, 190, 194, 198, 200, 202, 203, 210, 213, 217, 226, 228, 246–47, 292, 304, 315, 331, 339, 341, 353, 355–56, 360, 363, 371, 373, 375; art, 116; character, 128; family, 53, 122, 316; frozen, 237; immediacy, 18; judgment, 92; mutual, 50; personal, 19, 111, 289; war, 120, 140, 245

Fielding, Henry, 27, 125–26, 204, 225, 263, 284, 321, 396n11

Firbank, Ronald, 50, 263

Fitzgerald, Brian, 346–47

Fitzgerald, F. Scott, 8–9

flatness, 61, 80, 81, 86, 92, 101, 110, 128, 162, 372

Flaubert, Gustave, xxvi, xxx, 4, 9, 22, 27, 86, 97, 225, 232, 263, 308, 334, 338, 397; *Correspondences*, 397n1; *Madame Bovary*, xxx, 27, 225, 284; *Salammbô*, 232; *Sentimental Education*, 116–17

Fleming, Ian, xv

Forster, E. M., xvii, xxix, 8–9, 27, 147, 263, 274, 335; *Alexandria*, xxix

Fortune, G., and W. Fortune, 162–64

France, 96, 109, 118, 129, 145, 154, 162–64, 183, 188–89, 202, 208, 210, 212–13, 215–17, 243, 245–47, 253, 257, 264, 267, 269, 281, 296, 303, 308–9, 317, 328, 335, 345, 349, 369, 397n12, 398

French Indo-China, 298

French North Africa, 226

French Restoration, 209

Freud, Sigmund, 42, 288

frivolity, 71, 98, 198, 200, 226, 227, 303, 357, 365, 382

Frost, Marjorie, 398

Fuller, Kay, 395

Fuller, Roy, 393n2

furniture, 29, 39, 179, 283, 305, 340

future, 14, 21, 44, 59, 70, 71, 92, 94, 98, 118, 140, 141, 144, 168, 185, 192, 194, 223, 231, 233, 240, 245, 295, 305, 309, 337, 385, 393

Gabain, Marjorie, 215

Gaelic League, 123

Galsworthy, John, 108

Galway, 380

Garbo, Greta, 396n7

Garnett, Constance, 150

General Strike (1926), 289, 310

genius, 3, 74, 91, 114, 128, 136, 152, 155, 177, 179, 195, 229, 237, 276, 279, 281, 286, 289, 296, 299, 301, 308, 316, 320, 325, 331–35, 337, 349, 358, 362, 365, 376, 385, 387

genre, xvii, xix, xxix, 81, 94, 384

Germany, 130–31, 170, 213, 222, 271, 273

Gestapo, 213

Gide, André, 200, 308

Gilbert, Stuart, 43–46

Giono, Jean, 109

glamor, 51, 56, 93

God, 32, 68, 85, 98, 110, 208, 221, 223, 249, 279, 297, 300, 328, 339, 341, 342, 361, 383, 386

Godden, Rumer, xv, 263; *Black Narcissus*, 192; *Breakfast with the Nikolides*, 192; *A Fugue in Time*, 189–192

Gogol, xxix, 125, 225; *The Government Inspector*, xxix

Golding, Louis, 400

Goldsmith, Anthony, 116–17

Goolden, Barbara, 40–43

Gorman, Herbert, 111–14

Gozzoli, Benozzo, 167

Gramophone Company (EMI), 264, 268, 270, 401n3

Granville-Barker, Harley, 108

Grattan, Henry, 337, 344, 346, 401n2

Gray, Thomas, 276

Great Rebellion, 285

Green, G. F., 61

Green, Henry, 263, 351

Greene, Graham, 27, 111, 154, 263, 269, 351, 396n10, 400; *The Heart of the Matter*, 222–24; *Night and Day*, 269; *The Power and the Glory*, 97–101; *The Quiet American*, 298–99

Spender, Stephen, 6–7, 110, 393; *The Back-
ward Son*, 101–5; *Citizens in War—and Af-
ter*, 189–92; *Engaged in Writing*, 322–23;
"The Situation of the American Writer," 6;
Trial of a Judge, 110
Spring, Howard: *Rachel Rosing*, 46–51
Springfield, 382
Stanislaus, John, 114
Stebbing, L. Susan, 114–16
Steegmuller, Francis, xxx
Steele, James, 43–46
Steinbeck, John, 327; *In Dubious Battle*, 327;
The Grapes of Wrath, 94–97; *Of Mice and
Men*, 87; *The Long Valley*, 84–87; *Tortilla
Flat*, 87
Stendhal (Marie-Henri Beyle), 113, 210, 225,
263, 308, 351; *De l'amour*, 210; *Le Rouge
et le noir*, 284
Sterne, Laurence, 200
Stevenson, Lionel, 82–84
St. Loe Strachey, Cecelia, 46–51
Stopes, Marie, 311
Strachey, Ray, 57–59
Strindberg, August, 108
Struther, Jan, 94–97
Stuart, Francis, 37–40
Stuart, Warren, 144–45
style, xv, xxiii, xxiv, xxvi–xxvii, xxxi, 10, 20–
23, 28, 31, 35, 37, 39, 43, 50, 56, 61, 64,
68, 74, 81, 86–87, 95–97, 108, 114, 116,
133, 149, 155, 164, 168, 206, 214, 231,
239, 251, 260, 280, 287, 301, 308, 343,
368, 373, 378, 397n1
supernatural, 64, 120, 255–56
superstition, 69, 101, 233
Sutton, Eric, 216, 225
Svevo, Italo, 125
Swift, Jonathan, 200, 225, 344–45, 346–47
Swingler, Randal, 94–97
Switzerland, 264, 267
Symon, Julian, 402n4
Synge, John Millington, 125

Tatler, xv, xix–xxi, xxiii, xxv–xxvi, xxix–xxx,
xxxii, 87, 203, 233, 269, 398, 401n8,
402n8; reviews in, 127–242, 271–324
Taylor, Elizabeth, xx, xxiii, 10, 263, 400; *At
Mrs. Lippincote's*, 236; *Palladian*, 236;
A View of the Harbour, 217–19, 236; *A
Wreath of Roses*, 236–39
Tchaikovsky, Pyotr Ilyich, 139

technique, xxiv, xxvii, 14–24, 32, 56, 128,
134, 190, 232, 254–55, 262, 269, 308
Templeogue, 83–84
tempo, xxv, 61, 292, 348, 356
Tennyson, Alfred Lord, 54
Terry, Ellen, 280
Thackeray, William Makepeace, 35, 125
theater, xxxi, 4, 14, 65–66, 79, 97–98, 106–
8, 110, 123, 125, 130, 138, 165, 243, 269,
307, 308, 310, 350, 385
Third Programme (BBC), 315
Thomas, Dylan, 97–101
thriller, xix–xx, xxix, 15, 35, 40, 43, 84, 99,
144, 153–55, 223, 224, 277
Time, 360–61
Times, The, 97, 181
Times Literary Supplement, The, xvii, 181
Tolstoy, Leo, 5, 183, 263; *War and Peace*, xix,
149–53, 284
Toynbee, Philip, 10, 395
tragedy, 9, 31, 66, 68, 72, 84, 94, 106, 120,
135, 153, 155, 176, 195, 203, 208, 223,
238, 282, 286, 288, 300–301, 307, 331,
339, 351, 355, 379, 382, 391
translation, 102, 116, 150, 160, 206, 209,
211, 212, 215, 229, 231, 246–47, 276, 318,
323, 393
travel, 17, 63, 70–73, 75, 78–90, 95, 99, 129,
166, 170, 186, 191, 243, 251–52, 257,
293–95, 301–3, 315, 325–38, 343–44, 358,
370–73, 379, 389, 396n4; and Elizabeth
Bowen, xv, 257, 263, 264, 267, 269
Trevelyan, G. M., 274–76
Trinity College, 274
Trollope, Anthony, 35, 246, 269, 402n4
Turgenev, Ivan, 5, 125, 183, 225, 263; *Liza*,
156–61; *Month in the Country*, 161

Ulster, 84, 119
United States, 7–8, 44, 79, 94, 281, 309, 312–
13, 394. *See also* America
Upward, Edward, 110
U.S.S.R., 49, 110, 156, 327, 360, 393

V1s, 12, 202, 222, 268 401n6
V2s, 202
Van Doren, Mark, xxiii, 31–34
Vance, Ethel: *Escape*, 154; *Reprisal*, 153–55
Veiller, Bayard, 108
Venice, 195, 322
Vichy, 154–55, 164